Women Waging War and Peace

WOMEN WAGING WAR AND PEACE

International Perspectives of Women's Roles in Conflict and Post-Conflict Reconstruction

Edited by

Sandra I. Cheldelin
and
Maneshka Eliatamby

continuum

2011

Continuum International Publishing Group
80 Maiden Lane, New York, NY 10038
The Tower Building, 11 York Road, London SE1 7NX

www.continuumbooks.com

© 2011 by Sandra I. Cheldelin & Maneshka Eliatamby

Library of Congress Cataloging-in-Publication Data
Women waging war and peace: international perspectives of women's roles in conflict and post-conflict reconstruction / edited by Sandra I. Cheldelin, Maneshka Eliatamby.
  p. cm.
 Includes bibliographical references and index.
 ISBN 978–1-4411–0306–2 (hardback : alk. paper)
 ISBN 978–1-4411–4493–5 (pbk. : alk. paper)
 1. Women and war. 2. Women and peace.
 I. Cheldelin, Sandra. II. Eliatamby, Maneshka. III. Title.

JZ6405.W66W65 2011
303.6'6082—dc22

                                                    2011012182

ISBN: HB: 978-1-4411–4493–5 (PB)
       PB: 978-1-4411–0306–2 (HB)

Typeset by Newgen Imaging Systems Pvt Ltd, Chennai, India
Printed and bound in the United States of America

This book is dedicated to the extraordinary women working to make ours a more peaceful world.

Contents

Foreword

Every book is both a product of labor and a gift; created from a labor of intensive dedication, it provides a gift of great understanding. Books emerge out of conversations and commitment. This book can be understood at multiple levels. It is the product of its authors, women writing about women, academics writing to academics, researchers writing to researchers. It is also a gift from the authors to a larger community of scholars and practitioners, especially those in the conflict resolution field, who are trying to make sense of the questions related to women waging war and peace. It is a gift of understanding that gathers and questions, engages and challenges. Conflict resolution is an emerging field of inquiry at the crossroads of many disciplines: Social psychology, political science and anthropology, as well as history, mathematics, and computer modeling. Many more impact and are being influenced by it. This volume is intended to contribute to our collective understanding of women waging war and peace, focusing on both their agency and the environments in which they operate. It is embedded with conflict resolution methods, theories, and practices as they are defined, employed, and developed by women. It does so by focusing on the women's capacity for change. It is a line of research that must be pursued further. Far too often we hear parties to a conflict expressing the constraints of the system by saying: "There is no choice" or "I have no other choice." This is never completely true, and the expression of human freedom that emerges from the courageous attempts to voice choice, to produce change, to dream and actualize change is very relevant.

Today, no serious, relevant, and sustained negotiation process may be achieved without the input, influence, and debate generated by women. The era of critical decisions made only behind closed doors is over. Today, major negotiations include the growing presence and activism of women. They are engaged in conflict resolution activities in many forms and are now present in all phases of that work: prevention, peacemaking, peacekeeping, and peace building. In each phase, women contribute in a different way but consistently offer innovation and adaptability, while also drawing attention to frequently ignored challenges surrounding effectiveness, coordination, and accountability. In several cases, we have seen powerful actors use the gender platform to advance important political and ideological agendas. On every continent, the number of leaders moving away from white-male-dominated "Track One," (such as the official negotiations between heads of state and their representatives), to the "Track Two" arena (contacts, dialogues, and explorations in which citizens' groups at all levels of society operate), is remarkable.

These trends demonstrate the relevance and permanence of the contribution of women to conflict resolution activities. Women cannot be confined to the role of victims. They are powerful actors able to shape history and its contours. This influence will remain a significant and expanding feature for decades to come. Still, what is lacking in this area is a careful examination of women's activities through the gathering of empirical data. Local and international actors should not accept any action by women (or that of any actor, for that matter) without an evaluation of the results of those actions. This book is a wonderful step in this direction. Women's leadership realizes that to equate positive motivation with positive outcome is a fallacy. Women's contributions must be factual and measurable, tangible and actual. The cases presented in this book make a convincing argument in this direction. These contributions have been challenged by observers who have argued that women's participation is not truly meaningful but rather an expression of manipulation by more masculine actors. It is important not to be overly optimistic about women's roles but rather consistently committed to results.

This course of action leads us to an appreciation of a community of learning. Women waging war and peace are understood better when researchers are engaged systematically in a conversation that has learning as its center. I am writing this foreword at the time in which the Institute for Conflict Analysis and Resolution founded at George Mason University more than a quarter century ago is becoming the School for Conflict Analysis and Resolution. This is not just a building (and actually it was a very small institutional presence a few years ago) or a curriculum or a set of courses. It is a community of scholars and practitioners that together have dedicated themselves to the understanding and practice of conflict resolution. It is a point of pride and hope that this volume is published as one of the first tangible results of the new Center on Gender and Conflict Resolution that Professor Sandra I. Cheldelin envisioned at the beginning of my tenure as director. Her team of researchers and colleagues has assembled an impressive series of contributions and particular recognition must be given, thankfully and joyfully, to Maneshka Eliatamby, the coeditor of this volume, who has been consistently leading change at our School and beyond.

This volume offers, analyzes, and enriches frames of reference that are emerging from the field of conflict resolution as they pertain to women and their contributions. The opportunity to present in one narrative an overview of the "problematique" together with illustrative cases is intended to promote further understanding. I see this volume as a contribution to future endeavors in the field, especially in the area of research. It is my hope that this effort will continue to enrich the new school and the field as a whole. Conflict resolution is a field of inquiry, a community of practitioners and scholars, and a body of knowledge and procedures aimed at addressing conflict constructively. I believe that this volume contributes significantly to an inclusive community of practice and learning and calls for the re-engagement of the field of conflict resolution through the practice to theory movement. Scholars should and must develop the interpretive frameworks, research tools, and empirical research projects needed to uncover and understand further the many aspects of women waging war and peace. This book uses the analysis of the contribution of women as an opportunity to reflect more widely on the work of the field of conflict resolution itself. Practice is not only an occasion to implement theories developed elsewhere, it is the starting point of a shared understanding that may be accurately and correctly interpreted through proper models. To contribute something to this process of collective, shared, verified knowledge is the wonderful contribution of this text, which I am confident, will be welcome with gratitude in the field of conflict resolution at large.

Andrea Bartoli
Dean, School for Conflict Analysis and Resolution
George Mason University

Preface

Nearly a decade ago as a professor at the School for Conflict Analysis and Resolution—formerly the Institute for Conflict Analysis and Resolution (ICAR)—Sandra Cheldelin led an initiative to explore the gendered dimensions of deep-rooted conflicts by offering a graduate-level course on the topic of gender and conflict. Over time, the initiative grew to include a number of components and an ever-expanding scope of activities. Today, graduate and undergraduate courses on the topic are offered regularly, and faculty, staff, and students have organized the Gender and Conflict Working Group, which sponsors lectures, brown-bag luncheons and conducts consultations and research projects on gendered issues of conflict, violence, and intervention. Currently the group is launching a Gender and Conflict Research Portal on the school's Web site as a place where scholars, practitioners, academics, and donors can find the most current events, research and intervention projects, scholarly papers, and national and international conference opportunities on the topic of gender, conflict, and violence.

Over the decade, our research on gendered issues of conflict and violence has evolved, developing and drawing to it scholars (including many of the authors in this volume) from war-torn regions who have firsthand knowledge of the painful realities it attempts to address. During the same period, The Institute for Inclusive Security established the Hunt Inclusive Security Fellowship program to support graduate students conducting research on women, peace, and security. It was difficult for the ICAR selection team to choose among its applicants because there were several compelling projects. Maneshka Eliatamby, native to Sri Lanka, was the recipient of the first fellowship.

The combined influence of the course and the working group, research funding, the development of a research portal, and the remarkable gathering of scholars interested in women's roles in war and peace became the impetus for pulling together this collection. A new reality began to emerge from our collaboration—that in conflict zones around the world women have demonstrated their agency and are making a difference in war and in peace. This directly challenges the dominant narrative about women in conflict, which would have us believe that women are, for the most part, victims. In case after case, our research provides evidence that women mobilize to stop war and find ways to secure and sustain peace.

Realizing we are unusually positioned to tell the stories of these women, we contacted the contributors to this volume and invited them to join us in its creation. All of the authors have a direct relationship with our school—as faculty, alumni, students, practitioners, and, in the case of Ambassador Swanee Hunt, as significant friend. They have contributed to the Gender and Conflict course, the Conflict and Gender Working Group and the gender research portal and have conducted ongoing study on specific gendered issues of violence.

It is our intention that this book will become part of a larger work in progress for the field. As the discipline of conflict analysis and resolution evolves, we expect new theories and conceptual frameworks to emerge that take into account the nuances of gender. We expect that the work of practitioners will inform our research questions and in turn add to the body of theory. With the publication of this work, our hope is that more people—men and women, students, faculty, practitioners, and researchers—will contribute to an ever-expanding understanding of the gendered role of conflict and violence and will find ways in which to effectively intervene.

Acknowledgments

Endeavors such as these are never the work of a single individual. Much like peace, a book, too, is the product of an entire community. This was our experience. To our colleagues at the School for Conflict Analysis and Resolution at George Mason University, we offer our sincere appreciation. We especially thank Dr. Andrea Bartoli, dean of the school, who has enthusiastically supported our passion for furthering the discourse on gender and conflict. He has stayed positive about this project over the past two years, providing encouragement, guidance, and feedback.

We offer a special thank you to Lori-Ann Stephensen and Johnny J. Mack who graciously lent us their time in providing advice, edits, guidance, and wisdom, especially during the final stages of the book. In addition, Johnny provided us photos for the front cover taken of women in the field—their agency evident in their faces—while doing our work.

We acknowledge with affection Ambassador Swanee Hunt, president of the Hunt Alternatives Fund. We appreciate the efforts of Miki Jacevic, deputy director for training and consultations at The Institute for Inclusive Security. With Ambassador Hunt, his commitment to gender and peace building led to the establishment of the Hunt Fellowship at our school.

Our gratitude is extended to the women and men at the school who embraced the need for gender-focused discourse in our fields of conflict analysis and resolution and peace building and provided the support to create the Gender and Conflict Working Group in 2006. Many of its founding members are authors of chapters in this edited volume.

To our authors who have worked tirelessly from various parts of the world, including in conflict and post-conflict zones, you have been patient with us throughout the conceptualization, birth, writing, and editing stages of this book. Thank you for your dedication to our field and the work that we strive to do. Your own life experiences contribute to the uniqueness of the stories told.

We deeply appreciate the enthusiasm and support provided us by Marie-Claire Antoine at Continuum Publishing, who from the beginning believed this project was worthwhile. It continues to be a pleasure to work with you.

This volume would not be possible without the efforts of the many women and men around the globe who entrusted us with their stories and have dedicated their lives to building peace and human security in their local communities and internationally. You are the true change agents of the world and are an inspiration to those of us striving to build and sustain peace.

Our heartfelt gratitude to our families: Gene Rice; Mary and Ben Eliatamby and Deepal and Meg Eliatamby.

All errors and omissions are the editors' own.

List of Abbreviations

AGOA	African Growth and Opportunity Act
AIDS	acquired immune deficiency syndrome
AWAW	Association of War Affected Women
AWID	Association for Women's Rights in Development
BP	British Petroleum
CCC	community conferencing center
CPA	comprehensive peace agreement
CPN	Communist Party of Nepal
CSM	Committee of Soldiers' Mothers
DOCS	Doctors on Call Service
DDR	disarmament, demobilization, and reintegration
DDRR	disarmament, demobilization, rehabilitation, and reintegration
DRC	Democratic Republic of the Congo
ELF	Eritrean Liberation Front
EPLF	Eritrean People's Liberation Front
FFRP	Forum of Rwandan Women Parliamentarians
FGM	female genital mutilation
GBV	gender-based violence
GPA	Global Political Agreement
GSBV	gender- and sexual-based violence
GoSL	Government of Sri Lanka
HIV	human immune deficiency virus
HRW	Human Rights Watch
IBA	International Bar Association
ICC	interim care centers
ICC	International Criminal Court
ICTR	International Criminal Tribunal for Rwanda
ICTY	International Criminal Tribunal for the Former Yugoslavia
IDP	internally displaced persons
IPKF	Indian Peace Keeping Force

IRC	International Rescue Committee
JAMA	*Journal of American Medical Association*
LAMA	Legal Age of Majority Act
LSZ	Law Society of Zimbabwe
LTTE	Liberation Tigers of Tamil Eelam
LURD	Liberians United for Reconciliation and Democracy
MARWOPNET	Mano River Women's Peace Network
MDC	Movement for Democratic Change
MIA	missing in action
MUDHA	*Movement of Dominican-Haitian Women*
NATO	North Atlantic Treaty Organization
NCA	National Constitutional Assembly
NGO	nongovernmental organization
NPLA	Nepali People's Liberation Army
NSAG	non-state armed group
PLA	People's Liberation Army
POSA	Public Order and Security Act
PSMIA	Parents of Servicemen Missing In Action
RPF	Rwandese Patriotic Front
RPG	rocket-propelled grenade
SADC	Southern African Development Community
SLA	Sri Lankan Army
UML	Unified Marxist Leninists
UNIFEM	United Nations Entity for Gender Equality and the Empowerment of Women
UNOCHA	United Nations Office for the Coordination of Humanitarian Affairs
UNSCR	United Nations Security Council Resolution
US	United States
USIP	United States Institute of Peace
WAC	Women's Auxiliary Corps
WCGJ	Women's Caucus for Gender Justice
WCoZ	Women's Coalition in Zimbabwe
WHRD	Women Human Rights Defenders
WOZA	Women of Zimbabwe Arise
ZANU PF	Zimbabwe African National Union-Patriotic Front
ZEF	Zimbabwean Exiles Forum
ZESA	Zimbabwe Electricity Supply Authority
ZHRF	Zimbabwe Human Rights NGO forum
ZLHR	Zimbabwe Lawyers for Human Rights
ZoP	Zone of peace

Notes on Contributors

The Editors

Sandra I. Cheldelin is the Vernon M. and Minnie I. Lynch Professor of Conflict Resolution at the School for Conflict Analysis and Resolution at George Mason University. Cheldelin was the former director of the institute and is currently the director of the doctoral program. Over her four decades in the academy, she has held faculty and administrative appointments at several colleges and universities including provost at the McGregor School of Antioch University (Yellow Springs, Ohio) and academic dean at the California School of Professional Psychology (Berkeley). She is an active scholar-practitioner, psychologist, and expert in organizational conflict. She has worked with more than 150 organizations and is often a keynote speaker and invited lecturer on workplace issues of violence, change, race, gender, and conflict. She has facilitated large-scale interethnic and interfaith community dialogues on topics of fear, terrorism, violence, and suspicion and has convened large and small groups to build community resilience. She has conducted conflict resolution trainings, interventions, and research projects in Italy, Malta, Bosnia, Tajikistan, Ukraine, Georgia, the Middle East, Turkey, Liberia, and China. She has written extensively on intervention and practice and is coauthor (with Ann Lucas) of *Conflict Resolution* (Jossey Bass, 2004) and coeditor (with Daniel Druckman and Larissa Fast) of *Conflict* (Continuum, 2003; 2nd edn., 2008). She has served on a variety of conflict resolution related boards.

Maneshka Eliatamby is vice president of programs at Communities Without Boundaries International, Inc. She has more than twelve years of experience working as a scholar-practitioner in the fields of peace building and development, focusing on nonviolence and peace-building education, conflict and post-conflict development, and youth and women. Eliatamby is author of

"Religious Zones of Peace" in *Zones of Peace II* (Continuum Press, 2011) and co-author (with Johnny L. Mack) of "Peacemaking and the Legacy of Martin Luther King, Jr. in *Peacemaking: A Comprehensive Theory and Practice Reference* (ABAC-Clio, 2001). She teaches at the School for Conflict Analysis and Resolution and has conducted extensive nonviolence and peace-building education and training activities in South Asia and the Balkans. She is a founding director of Reconcile and Rebuild Sri Lanka and director of the Center for Peacebuilding International in Washington, DC. During her work with the United States Holocaust Memorial Museum, she was involved in post-conflict and genocide prevention work related to Rwanda, Darfur, the Democratic Republic of the Congo, and Srebenica. Eliatamby began her career at KPMG, where she conducted consultancies with the United Nations Development Program (UNDP) and the United Nations Fund for Population Activity (UNFPA). She is the recipient of numerous fellowships, including the Hunt Inclusive Security Fellowship, the Mahbub al Haq Fellowship, and the Drucie French Cumbie Fellowship.

Contributors

Vanessa Noël Brown conducts research on gender issues in post-conflict stabilization contexts and on conflict prevention approaches for vulnerable youth. A David L. Boren fellowship recipient and graduate of the School for Conflict Analysis and Resolution, Brown has worked throughout Africa and the Middle East in a variety of capacities including as a refugee officer with the US government and as a visiting scholar at Search for Common Ground in Morocco. Her published works include *Reconciliation in Rwanda: Building Peace through Dialogue* (2008) and *Foundations for Repatriation and Peace in DRC* (2010). Brown has managed a broad array of human rights initiatives and has served as editor and program specialist at the Center for Global Studies at George Mason University. She is also a conflict management trainer with experience designing and leading courses for incarcerated adults and juvenile offenders.

Susan F. Hirsch is professor of conflict analysis and resolution at George Mason University. Her training in legal anthropology (Yale 1982; Duke 1990) led to extensive ethnographic research on Islamic law, gender relations, law reform, and conflict in Kenya and Tanzania, supported by the Fulbright Foundation, the National Science Foundation, the American Bar Foundation, and other institutions. Her academic publications include *Contested States: Law, Hegemony, and Resistance* (coedited with Mindie

Lazarus-Black, Routledge, 1994), *Pronouncing and Persevering: Gender and the Discourses of Disputing in an African Islamic Court* (Chicago Series in Law and Society, 1998) and numerous articles and book chapters on law reform, gender and conflict, participatory research, and language in the disputing process. She is a past editor of *PoLAR: Political and Legal Anthropology Review* and currently serves on the editorial board of the *Law and Society Review*. Hirsch's latest book, *In the Moment of Greatest Calamity: Terrorism, Grief, and a Victim's Quest for Justice* (Princeton University Press, 2007) received the 2007 Herbert Jacob Book Prize awarded by the Law and Society Association. Her research interests and public speaking topics include the politics of capital punishment and victims' rights, new forms of global justice, and the contested role of law as a response to mass atrocity and environmental disaster.

Ambassador Swanee Hunt is the Eleanor Roosevelt Lecturer in Public Policy at Harvard University's Kennedy School of Government, where she teaches the course *Inclusive Security*, exploring why women are systematically excluded from peace processes. She founded the Kennedy School's Women and Public Policy Program and has lectured at universities worldwide, including MIT, Peking University, and Moscow State University. She is founder and president of Hunt Alternatives Fund, supporting local, national, and global initiatives. She chairs The Institute for Inclusive Security based in Washington, D.C., which has conducted research, training, and advocacy to integrate women into peace processes in more than 40 countries. Hunt served as President Clinton's ambassador to Austria (1993–97), where she hosted negotiations and international symposia focused on stabilizing the neighboring Balkan states. She became a specialist in the role of women in post-communist Europe, leading to the July 1997 "Vital Voices: Women in Democracy" conference of 320 women leaders in business, law, and politics, and the documentary film *Voices*. Hunt is a member of the Council on Foreign Relations and serves on the board of Crisis Group. She holds two master's degrees, a doctorate in theology, and six honorary degrees. She has provided news commentary on international and domestic television networks and is a widely published researcher and columnist. Her three books (Duke University Press) include the award-winning *This Was Not Our War: Bosnian Women Reclaiming the Peace*; a memoir, *Half-Life of a Zealot*, and the forthcoming *Worlds Apart: Bosnian Lessons for Global Security*.

Yves-Renée Jennings is a conflict resolution professional and scholar-practitioner with deep understanding of the societal and structural issues that contribute to social conflicts. She is interested in human development and empowerment within the context of the transformation of social and structural barriers that hinder groups from fully realizing their potential as social agents. Jennings founded and serves as chief executive officer of Partners for Sustainable Peace (PSP), a nonprofit organization. She worked in the private sector in Haiti for more than ten years and retired from the World Bank after a career of more than twenty years. She has extensive risk management, facilitation, mediation, and training experience and has led numerous group processes for the World Bank in Madagascar, Mali, Mauritania, Kenya, Ghana, Senegal, Niger, Togo, and many other African countries. She has conducted training and facilitation sessions for the Northern Virginia Mediation Services, the US Institute of Peace Haiti program, the University of Liberia trauma training program (with Sandra I. Cheldelin), the Fairfax Country Public Schools system, and the Arlington Community Immigration Dialogue in Virginia.

Jennifer Langdon is a feminist scholar-practitioner of conflict resolution, specializing in restorative justice and applications of mediation in the US criminal justice system. She earned a Ph.D. in conflict analysis and resolution from George Mason University—a recipient of the Provost's High Potential Graduate Scholarship—and is an assistant professor of criminal justice at Towson University in Baltimore. Her research focuses on making the connection between theory and practice, specifically the application of narrative analysis to the practice of community conferencing. Langdon's commitment to connecting theory to practice also is evidenced by her work as cofounder and board president of the Conflict Resolution Center of Baltimore County and a cofounder of the Circle for Restorative Initiatives for Maryland (CRI). She is a trained mediator and community conference facilitator and has published on practice in the *Journal of Radio Studies* and in an edited collection, *Zones of Peace*.

Patricia A. Maulden is assistant professor of conflict resolution and director of the Dialogue and Difference Project at George Mason University. Her research interests include generational and gendered dynamics of conflict and peace, social militarization/demilitarization processes, urbanization, post-conflict peace economies, and peace-building practices. She has written about child soldiers as well as the roles of girls and women in conflict—whether as soldiers, combatants, or associates of fighting forces. She is currently investigating the dynamics of NGOs as private peace-building contractors and their roles in the post-conflict peace economy, the post-conflict paradox—engaging war while creating peace, and exploring peace building over time, more specifically the trajectories of post-conflict knowledge. As part of an ongoing research project she is exploring community-based peace education in Sierra Leone and Burundi and, building on a recent field assessment in Liberia, has organized a palaver management project bringing students to Liberia to work with local youth-focused organizations. Domestically, Maulden researches and teaches about youth gangs as well as gang-related community peacemaking programs. As a practitioner, she conducts seminars on interpersonal conflict resolution, facilitates intergenerational and interethnic dialogues, and has served as a restorative justice caseworker.

Martha Mutisi is an academic-practitioner specializing in conflict resolution research, intervention design, assessment and training. A Fulbright scholarship recipient and a PhD graduate from the School for Conflict Analysis and Resolution, Mutisi currently works as senior researcher at the African Centre for the Constructive Resolution of Disputes (ACCORD), in Durban, South Africa. In this role, Mutisi identifies and implements practice-oriented research for ACCORD's intervention programs. In addition, she provides technical and substantive expertise to strengthen ACCORD's knowledge production and management. She has experience in teaching, training, and research, having served as lecturer and trainer at Africa University's Faculty of Humanities and Social Sciences (FHSS) and at the Institute for Peace, Leadership and Governance in Mutare, Zimbabwe, and serving as adjunct professor at the School for Conflict Analysis and Resolution. Mutisi has conducted trainings in gender analysis and mainstreaming and has worked on a reproductive health project evaluating the impact of HIV/AIDS intervention programs in Zimbabwe. She works with many organizations on critical issues at the intersections of peace, conflict, and development including the University for Peace, Africa Program, University of Zimbabwe Center for Defense Studies, the Open Society Initiative of Southern Africa (OSISA), the Common Market for East and Southern Africa (COMESA), the Department of Peace and Conflict Research (DPCR) at Uppsala University, and the Institute for Multi-Track Diplomacy (IMTD), among others. Her research interests include building and peacemaking, gender and development, regional institutions, democratization, governance and transitional justice. She has authored book chapters and journal articles covering these areas.

Ekaterina Romanova is assistant professor in the International Peace and Conflict Resolution Program at the School of International Service, American

University, where she teaches courses on the theory and practice of conflict analysis and resolution. Romanova conducted extensive research on the role of women in the conflicts in Chechnya, focusing on women's peace activism as well as women's engagement in terrorist activities. She worked with women's organizations both in the United States and Russia and was a member of Gender and Conflict Working Group at the School for Conflict Analysis and Resolution at George Mason University. Her research interests include migration, nationalism, identity politics, gender, youth, and interactive conflict resolution. Romanova has been actively involved in the conflict resolution work and trainings in the Caucasus and Asia, contributing to a series of problem-solving workshops between South Ossetian-Georgian civil society leaders and trainings for youth leaders from that region.

Erica K. Sewell holds a B.S. with honors in political science from the University of the Ozarks and an M.S. in conflict analysis and resolution from George Mason University. She is the former Youth and Education Program manager at Sister Cities International and former executive director at the Institute for Multi-Track Diplomacy. She has worked with the International Rescue Committee and taught high school students alternatives to violence. Sewell has been published in InterAction's *Monday Developments* and Women for Women International's journal, *Critical Half.* She conducted original fieldwork in Liberia resulting in *Women Building Peace: The Liberian Women's Peace Movement.* Her research interests include conflict and gender and African affairs.

Terra Tolley is an instructor for New Century College at George Mason University. She is an avid environmentalist, field anthropologist, and HIV/AIDS activist. She has worked in the areas of antihuman trafficking, refugee rights, health education, outdoor experiential learning, and environmental peace building and is currently the business development coordinator at OZ Systems International. She has conducted damage evaluations in the Gulf of Mexico and spent much of 2005–2010 assessing the social and economic impacts associated with Hurricane Katrina, Hurricane Rita, and the BP oil spill. She is a cofounder of the Balkans Peace Park Photography Project. Her regions and areas of expertise include Central and Eastern Europe, East Africa, Latin America, Southeast Asia, and natural resource conflict in the United States.

Peace Uwineza is a researcher at the Institute of Research and Dialogue for Peace (IRDP) based in Rwanda. A Fulbright recipient and graduate of

Conflict Analysis and Resolution, Uwineza has worked with different organizations and in different capacities as a peace-building researcher and practitioner, including the Women in Transition Initiative (1997–1999), Rwanda's National Unity and Reconciliation Commission (1999–2001), the Women Waging Peace Project in Rwanda; and presently with IRDP (2002–2011). She also served as a member of a national working group charged to formulate new teaching methods and materials for the controversial *History of Rwanda*, 2004. Uwineza has authored *The Role of Women in Rwanda's Peace Building Process* (Yaoundé, Cameroon, 2010) and coauthored *Sustaining Women's Gains in Rwanda: The Influence of Indigenous Culture and Post-Genocide Politics* (Hunt Alternatives Fund, 2009), with Elizabeth Pearson. She has conducted extensive research on the role of dialogue in resolving protracted conflicts and history as a major factor in the creation and perpetuation of conflict. Through her work as a peace-building practitioner, Uwineza has widely traveled in Asia, Europe, North America, and East, West, and southern Africa.

Saira Yamin has worked extensively in the development sector in Pakistan advocating human rights for women and children. Currently she teaches at the Department of Defense and Strategic Studies, Quaid-e-Azam University, Islamabad, Pakistan and at the School for Conflict Analysis and Resolution, George Mason University. She has frequently lectured at the University of Peshawar, University of Karachi, and at the American University, Washington D.C. Yamin has been involved with Women In Security Conflict Management and Peace (WISCOMP), New Delhi, as a resource person at its annual Conflict Transformation workshops working with Pakistani and Indian youth and professionals. Her publications include a book, *Stability Through Economic Cooperation in a Nuclear Environment* (Manohar Publishers, 2005, New Delhi). Her work has been published in *The Oxford International Encyclopedia of Peace*, *The New York Times*, *The International Herald Tribune*, *The Christian Science Monitor*, *The Nation*, *The Politico*, *The Friday Times*, *The Daily Times*, *The News International*, *Journal for the Institute of Peace and Conflict Studies*, *Peace Prints* and *The Foreign Policy in Focus*. Yamin has made appearances as a security analyst on Al-Jazeera, BBC, Canada TV, Pakistan Television and Voice of America. She was a French and English News Reader for Radio Pakistan and a DJ on FM 100, a popular radio station in Islamabad.

CHAPTER ONE

Overview and Introduction

Sandra I. Cheldelin and Maneshka Eliatamby

Introduction

Women Waging War and Peace provides a number of stories that beg a reconsideration of the current, dominant narrative about the ways that violence and protracted conflict are gendered. Traditionally, women have one paramount role in the war story—that of victim. Women are essentially and overwhelmingly portrayed as the *victims* of war, whether as mothers grieving for sons dead and missing, or raising fatherless children; as widows struggling to survive in male-dominated societies; as refugees displaced from their home, community, and country; or as those raped, tortured, and left physically impaired, psychologically distressed, shamed, humiliated, or dead. While the reality of such scenarios is widespread and without doubt women and children are adversely affected during war and its aftermath, the dominant version of the narrative has several limitations and misconceptions—chief among them the idea that men are spared victimhood and women are limited to it.

Men—especially civilians—are prodigiously the casualties of mass genocides. Gendercide Watch has studied more than 20 cases against men (and women) in political, military, and ethnic conflicts over the past 125 years and found that "state-directed gender-selective mass killings have overwhelmingly targeted men through history, and that this phenomenon is pervasive in the modern world as well.... [M]en are, indeed, generally the victims of the most severe gender-selective atrocities in such situations" (Gender Watch: What Is Gendercide?). For example, men were overwhelmingly victims in the Bangladesh genocide as the Pakistani Army responded to the Bengali bid for independence. The army's intention was to rid the country of boys and men who could, one day, become freedom fighters. The soldiers targeted five groups specifically: Bengali military men, Hindus,

Awami Leaguers (the party in Bangladesh who significantly won the national elections), students—especially boys, and Bengali intellectuals.

The prevailing narrative also ignores how women's lives change as a result of war and traumatic experiences and how women are able to forge creative strategies to survive those situations. Rarely do we read or hear about women demonstrating their capacities of agency—accessing their voice and engaging in action—adopting new roles that transform gender dynamics in the societies from which them come. *Women Waging War and Peace* presents such evidence as it identifies a multitude of ways in which women are agents of change. Several cases focus on women serving as combatants. Suicide terrorism presents one of the deadliest and unconventional forms of warfare and the Chechen Black Widows and the Black Tigresses of Death in Sri Lanka are cases of such acts. These lethal tactics beg understanding of the motivation for its use. Some women employ them out of retaliation, having witnessed family members being tortured and killed and their homes set ablaze. Others believed they had limited alternatives, because they had already been shunned by their communities.

As an outcome of war and its aftermath, there are many women who have assumed the roles of peace builders and leaders of social movements—transforming and rebuilding economic and social structures, organizing the disenfranchised, challenging systemic injustices, and promoting social justice. A common postwar story is reflected in the research by Physicians for Human Rights in Sierra Leone conducted in 2000, documenting the extent of sexual violence in their decade-long war. Of 991 households of internally displaced persons (IDPs), the organization found that 94 percent reported being the victim of such abuses as abduction, sexual assault, torture, or forced labor, yet an overwhelming majority (90 percent) also believed that women and girls should have the same access to education as men and boys and should have the right to express themselves freely with legal protection (55 percent)—a dramatic cultural attitudinal shift from prewar days.

This book pushes the boundaries of popular scholarship and rhetoric surrounding women's roles in conflict situations, reclaiming and illuminating the richness of women's experiences during wartime and disasters and exploring the wide repertoire of activities within which women engage. Using cases set across the globe, we present a collection of stories about women's authorship of change. As in our previous examples, in some cases the authors write scenes of violence, with women choosing to be suicide bombers or active combatants in armed movements. In other cases, the authors narrate the cessation of conflict or active engagement in peace-building initiatives. In all of the chapters, the evidence of women's capacity to act as change agents is extraordinary. The Black Widows of Chechnya and the Black Tigresses of Death of Sri Lanka, along with girl soldiers in Sierra Leone and Liberia, stand in stark contrast to the work of the Hmong women in the Gulf of Mexico and the WOZA women of Zimbabwe, but in each case the women stand. Each chapter makes the case that women not only can be but are significant players in conflicts—natural or manmade—as well as in intervention efforts. The examples are intentionally drawn from around the globe—sub–Saharan, North, and West Africa to South Asia, Europe, and the Americas. If human agency is "the capacity for human beings to make choices and to impose those choices on the world" (*The Free Dictionary*), then women's agency is the capacity for women to make choices—good and evil—and to impose their choices on the world. What follows are examples of such choices and action.

Cases of Agency

The book begins with the only chapter focusing on the traditional victim role, Chapter 2, "Rape and Genderside." Sexual violence during wartime is well documented, and women (as well as men) continue to be victims of the most unimaginable and inhumane behavior. Cases of atrocities offer insights into the trauma and challenges faced by victims and members of their families and communities. As rape is now a war system, it is essential that we understand and acknowledge the horrors of such torture that often lead to psychological damage or death. Sandra Cheldelin tells this story of all wars, offering evidence of war's underbelly and the ways it underscores our moral imperative to intervene. She demonstrates how the victim narrative is incomplete: describing women who have emerged as agents of their own healing processes, have testified in court against perpetrators of heinous crimes, have worked with health care and news service organizations to bring this issue to the public, and have engaged the international community in a call for change through gender mainstreaming—bringing gender-specific activities into the public to promote gender equality.

Following Cheldelin's chapter are four sections that explore the ways in which women wage and intervene in war and the ways in which they wage and sustain peace. The cases demonstrate women's agency in contributing to violence and conflict intervention. Most of the cases focus on war or postwar efforts. Some, however, are examples of women-based interventions during disasters or in crime-ridden inner cities. The cases are only limited to the number we can put in this volume, and we hope the choices we made will encourage the reader to engage in further study.

Section I presents the uncommon story of women as perpetrators in Nepal, Chechnya, Sri Lanka, Eritrea, Sierra Leone, and Liberia. In Chapter 3, "Searching for Emancipation," Maneshka Eliatamby presents women's involvement in war in three of these countries as constituting more than 30 percent of the fighting forces and showing how the patriarchal cultures that prevail in these countries contributed to the adoption of violence by women. Many women saw few alternatives—they viewed their violent actions as holding the keys to their emancipation. The three cases reflect ways in which women seek to reposition themselves in society and change the social and political structures within which they live.

Eliatamby and Ekaterina Romanova present stories of the Black Widows and the Black Tigresses of Death in chapter 4, "Dying for Identity," where they document the emergence of women in the role of suicide bombers. While suicide attacks are often attributed to the irrationality, fanaticism, extremism, and madness of the perpetrators, this chapter explores the agency of women voluntarily (though sometimes involuntarily) engaged in suicide terrorism and argues that female suicide bombers can be both perpetrators and victims of terror tactics. Despite the low numbers of female suicide bombers in Chechnya, their extreme and lethal tactics in the Beslan school massacre and the Moscow theater bombing drew worldwide attention (earning them the designation Black Widows). In Sri Lanka, women contributed to nearly 40 percent of all suicide missions carried out between 1980 and 2008. One of the most prominent suicide bombers was involved in the death of the former Indian prime minister Rajiv Gandhi. She was a victim of violence herself and joined the ranks of the Liberation Tigers of Tamil Eelam (LTTE) to avenge the death of her parents and brother.

The final chapter in the section on ways women wage war is Chapter 5, "Fighting Young," and is based on Patricia Maulden's research on child soldiers in West Africa where the recruitment of girls, while systematic and widespread, was primarily accomplished through abduction. The gendered domains of war present fundamental challenges to girls' social navigation skills. The ways in which girls align themselves with fighting factions can mean life or death. The conflicts in these two countries demonstrate the nuanced roles of girls during intrastate war. By using their unusual circumstances of having to navigate wartime challenges, girls shifted between the various support roles of temporary wife, girlfriend, cook, looter, porter, sex slave, and fighter. As girls are not considered dangerous, they are often invisible, a status requiring them to rely on themselves and their own agency for survival

Section II—Women Intervening in War—begins with a country-based case, followed by an international story of extraordinary success. In Chapter 6, "Challenging Warfare," Eliatamby speaks to a group of women building peace out of the ashes of the deeply protracted Eelam War in Sri Lanka. The war consumed a quarter of a century (1983–2009) until the Sri Lankan military defeated the Liberation Tigers of Tamil Eelam (LTTE) who were seeking to create an independent state. In response to the devastation, Visaka Dharmadasa and 12,000 other mothers who lost their sons in the war formed a sustainable grassroots peace movement. More than anyone else, these women understood the value of life and that it was critical to stop the killing. Their intervention brokered dialogue between the Sri Lankan government and the Liberation Tigers, earning them the status and privileges awarded to other prestigious organizations such as Médecins Sans Frontières (Doctors Without Borders). The chapter explores the relationship between gender and peaceful agency, using the example of Dharmadasa and the women of Parents of Servicemen Missing in Action (PSMIA) and the Association of War Affected Women (AWAW). It examines women's agency during times of extreme protracted conflict and highlights the milestones achieved by these women and the ways in which their actions shaped grass-roots activism in Sri Lanka.

The extraordinary international women's social network developed by Ambassador Swanee Hunt is chronicled in Chapter 7, "Building a Peace Network," and is the source of the title of this book, drawn from the original name of the network, Women Waging Peace. Her full understanding of the importance of women in peace building began in the Balkans while she served as the US ambassador to Austria. As her story unfolds, she makes a case that sustainable peace requires the full participation of women at all stages of the peace process. Women had been largely excluded from formal efforts to develop and implement fresh, workable solutions to seemingly intractable struggles, yet she knew their involvement in these mechanisms—which prevent conflict, stop war, and stabilize regions damaged by warfare—was essential. This chapter is about women community leaders with formal and informal authority bridging ethnic, religious, political, and cultural divides. It identifies ways women have navigated the treacherous waters of war and violence, as well as ways they invest in preventing, stopping, and recovering from conflict. She concludes the chapter with an explanation of the development of her global network of women peace builders and the ways these women impact and sustain local conflict interventions. She quotes Haris

Silajdzic, president of Bosnia-Herzegovina, in their conversation: "If we'd had women around the table, there would have been no war, because women think long and hard before they send their children out to kill other people's children."

The third section of the book presents four cases of women waging peace—especially where peace is used as a metaphor of stopping violence. Cases presented here are from Africa and the United States. It begins with Chapter 8, "Countering the Currents," in Zimbabwe. Martha Mutisi writes about a women-led movement called the Women of Zimbabwe Arise (WOZA), which came into being as a protest movement against the deteriorating socioeconomic and political situation in Zimbabwe during the past decades. Enormous problems, including the crash of the country's economy, forced women to find alternate ways to support their families. Informed by women's work in other African countries where women moved beyond "victimhood"—Burundi, Liberia, Congo, Namibia, Tanzania, Sudan, and Uganda, to name a few—women in Zimbabwe confronted these protracted and deteriorating conditions, their stories chronicled as early as the 1990s by Ranger (1992) and Schmidt (1997). WOZA is now 35,000 strong and welcomes the membership of men who support its mission to empower Zimbabwean women. It takes on even the largest structural issues in its country, claiming a place in peace building and addressing the economic and political challenges that conflict brings to women and their families.

Peace Uwineza and Vanessa Noël Brown bring us a story of "Engendering Recovery" in Rwanda in Chapter 9. Women in Rwanda have successfully demonstrated that radical change is possible even after years of what they experienced as the greatest individual and community calamity of wartime fallout. Following the 1994 genocide, women who survived were left alone with no husbands or family and with broken social networks. Many organized friends and community members and collectively took on responsibilities traditionally held by men, including the reconstruction of homes, roads, and schools. They educated themselves and started women-led businesses. Though not without its problems, this is quite a success story. There was a significant shift from Rwandan women's former place as the secondary gender—in large part due to both grassroots initiatives and large-scale structural and political reforms—when large numbers of both rural and urban women took on new responsibilities and leadership roles. Today Rwandan women make up 48 percent of the parliament and 38 percent of the cabinet and participate in decision making at all levels, forcing the society to address gendered issues. Rwanda's genocide was a tragedy, yet the operational narrative is this: Rwandan women have transformed this tragedy to increase their participation in public life and decision making. It is remarkable and inspiring.

The next two chapters are based in the United States. Chapter 10, "Rebuilding the Gulf," is told by Terra Tolley, summarizing her five-year field research in more than 100 coastal communities throughout Florida, Alabama, Mississippi, Louisiana, and Texas (2005–2010). Two large and disastrous situations over the past decade occurred in the Gulf of Mexico region—Hurricane Katrina and the Deep Water Horizon oil spill (commonly referred to as the BP oil spill). The chapter begins with an especially engaging story of Vietnamese American women's ability to transcend religious and cultural differences following Hurricane Katrina in order to rebuild their economic and social capital. Katrina drastically disrupted everything in the gulf region including its environment, economy, social networks, and culture. In this time of tragedy, people revisited their historical grievances as well as former strategies for survival both in the United States and Vietnam. After Katrina, the fishing industry was sorely weakened, but the women came together to anchor one another emotionally and financially. They partnered with biologists, local and federal government representatives, educators, seasonal workers, and artists to rebuild the Gulf. These resilient, hardworking southern women survived in a region filled with challenges. On April 20, 2010, the largest manmade environmental disaster occurred in the region—the BP oil spill in the Gulf of Mexico. Oil flowed underwater and uncapped for three months. Extensive damage, once again, occurred to the marine and wildlife habitats and tourism industries. This was particularly painful for the fishing industry families and social networks that were finally beginning to recover from Katrina. Once again, women stepped in to maintain the foundations of industry, home, and culture. The interview data tell stories of the previously unheard voices of women working in the bayous and of their efforts to maintain peace, livelihood, and security in an unstable environment, economy, and culture.

Another pervasive problem in the United States is serious crime, especially in the inner cities and poor neighborhoods. Baltimore, Maryland, is ranked among the most violent cities in the United States (Johnson 2010), and while the traditional approach to confronting crime and violence is to declare "war" on the perpetrators—drug dealers, prostitutes, misbehaving teenagers, and gang members—an extraordinary new strategy is unfolding and getting high marks for success. The story is told by Jennifer Langdon in Chapter 11, "Conferencing Serious Crime." Many conflict resolution scholars believe systemic crime problems in communities are indicators of underlying structural conflicts or violence. Restorative justice, a subfield of conflict resolution, is founded on the reconceptualization of crime as conflict. Following this premise, people who advocate for and implement collaborative responses to crime are peace makers. The case of Lauren Abramson and her powerful activism in the crime-ridden urban environment of Baltimore serves as one such example of a woman waging peace. In 1995, Abramson, a psychologist and faculty member at Johns Hopkins University, brought the practice of community conferencing to the city. Using conferencing as an intervention in communities plagued by juvenile offenders and other urban problems, Abramson works as an agent of positive change, mobilizing existing untapped human assets in marginalized communities. Abramson's work is especially important for the field of conflict resolution, inside and outside the United States. If we reframe crime as one of many forms of conflict, then we can imagine conferencing as one of many forms of intervention. Her work is an interesting segue from waging peace (stopping crime) to the next section, sustaining peace (building resilient and peaceful inner-city communities).

Section IV involves cases around the world where women are engaged in peace-sustaining processes, working for peace and justice. Susan Hirsch, in "Promises of Justice," considers Rwanda, Uganda and the Democratic Republic of the Congo as the backdrop of Chapter 12. The expansion of international law to address war crimes, crimes against humanity, and genocide has meant that law is increasingly an available form of intervention in conflict and post-conflict situations. Some of the new legal instruments, such as the International Criminal Court, offer special recognition to women as victims of the world's most serious crimes, including crimes of sexual abuse and torture. The increased use of these legal mechanisms prompts an important question: Does identifying women as a special category of victim increase or decrease their agency? This chapter addresses the question by interrogating the routine link made in regard to agency—having a voice and receiving justice—and by examining the interests and experiences of women in relation to episodes of conflict in sub-Saharan Africa where international law figured as a central response. The cases suggest that recent attention to gender in international criminal law has expanded women's options for agency and that many women involved in international prosecutions gained new perspectives on themselves and their social positions, including their rights and entitlements.

In Chapter 13, "Engaging Legislation," Romanova and Erica Sewell identify specific ways legal systems can work for women. In October 2000, the United Nations Security Council unanimously passed Resolution 1325 on women, peace, and security, recognizing the challenges faced by women and children caught in armed conflicts. This resolution reaffirmed the significance of women's equal participation in prevention, decision making, and peace-building processes. It calls for parties in conflict "to take special measures to protect women and girls from gender-based violence, particularly rape and other forms of sexual abuse, in situations of armed conflict" (OSAGI 2000). Women's wartime mobilization in Liberia and Chechnya serve as examples of differing strategies employed to advance peace and reconciliation. While the sociopolitical and cultural contexts of the wars in these countries make seemingly different cases, the similarities are the women working for peace. Women in Liberia used more visible tactics—publically demanding a place at the negotiation table through international news networks. While Chechnyan women did not have broad-based political mobilization, they were the first to address the ethnic differences and needs of the various communities following the devastation of their country's two wars. Through the lens of Resolution 1325, the ways women succeeded in challenging the structural barriers of patriarchal societies is discussed.

In Chapter 14, "Challenging Patriarchy," Saira Yamin tells of various forms of cultural and systemic injustices toward women—female genital mutilation (FGM), rape, and honor killings—and examines ways that women cope and contribute to social change in Egypt, Pakistan, and Turkey. She points to manifestations of culturally induced sexual violence as well as the ways in which culture, religion, state institutions, development, and social class contribute to violence. As a result, notions of shame and honor in these societies are brought into sharp focus as three women's movements are compared historically and located within this international context the local dynamics of women's agency. The conflation of Islamic and patriarchal values and parallel legal systems complicate access to and provision of justice for women, yet despite these obstacles, secular and religious actors have developed their own feminist constituencies. Though they are in various evolutionary stages of development, feminist campaigns and movements in these three countries draw inspiration from one another as well as from the arts, literature, women's networks, and international conferences.

Section IV concludes with Chapter 15, "Organizing the Disenfranchised" by Yves-Renée Jennings. Most stories of agency in this book involve the work of groups of women, though nearly all imply, at least, the need for some kind of leadership if changes are to occur. This chapter presents the stories of two Caribbean women—Colette Lespinasse and Sonia Pierre—from Haiti and the Dominican Republic, respectively, whose individual agency transcended and transformed the dominant patriarchal social and cultural history of the region. Their involvement in their communities and in state and regional affairs during the last decades have changed the patriarchal discourse about women's ability to be full social agents and contributors and to positively influence policy decisions that promote societal transformation. The story of these two women leaders' determination to serve and inspire others through their contribution to constructive social change offers a firsthand view of the ways in which individual efforts at the grassroots level affect greater social and political change. They shared a common goal—to help disenfranchised Haitian migrants—and designed interventions to advocate for migrants' basic human needs. In the face of the most recent disaster, the Haiti earthquake in January 2010, the Dominican Republic's demonstration of solidarity and support toward the victims and its Haitian neighbors holds promise they may ultimately find ways to address their historical antagonisms to live in harmony and cooperation.

Section V concludes with Chapter 16, "Challenging the Dominant Narrative". It is our attempt to integrate the series of stories presented in *Women Waging War and Peace.* In it, we provide an expanded conception of conflict and intervention from a different voice. Reflecting on the lessons learned from cases around the world—more than 16 countries—we offer several insights. Unfortunately, the story of all wars continues—women are overwhelmingly victims of rape, torture, and physical abuse. Many are killed. Women and their children make up the majority in refugee and internally displaced persons (IDP) camps. Yet the cases highlighted in this volume identify instances where women have been changed because of their experiences in these conflicts and their trauma, and as an outcome have initiated strategies for survival and sustainable peace for their communities and for their countries. In some cases such as the Black Widows and the Black Tigresses of Death, their behavior has exacerbated conflict. In most cases, though, women demonstrate their agency through organizing non-violent movements and initiating peace-building efforts, seeking ways to heal personal and societal traumas. They consistently embrace family and societal challenges by addressing the needs of their broken societies and by learning to work together without violence. They do so by accessing and mobilizing multiple layers of society including the grassroots organizations, NGOs, religious institutions, parliaments, regional actors, and international actors such as the United Nations.

We believe we have provided enough evidence that the practical recommendations we offer in the final section for academics, peace builders, practitioners, and donor communities will seem plausible. We call for structural changes around the world, and some of the recommendations are not new. Pulitzer Prize winners for journalism Nicholas Kristof and Sheryl

WuDunn (2009) offered concrete ways to stop oppression of women in their passionate best-seller, *Half the Sky: Turning Oppression into Opportunity for Women Worldwide*. They document oppression stories—slavery, prostitution, rape, maternal mortality, and the like—while also capturing evidence of successes—education and microfinancing—where women are included and empowered. Rwanda, as an example, now has one of the fastest-growing economies of Africa. Kristof and WuDunn call it the China of Africa (211). Their stories are evidence that when women are empowered, their family changes. So do their communities, regions, and entire countries.

When it comes to war and peace, conflict and violence—gender matters. Women play active roles in all aspects of war and peacemaking: as perpetrators, combatants, and sustainers of peace. The compilation of actual stories of women's movements from around the world demonstrates their ability to become agents of change despite, even because of, their unique and sometimes dire circumstances. The growing fields of conflict analysis and resolution, peace building and development must acknowledge that women's roles are not monolithic. Their engagement in making war and building peace is a complex phenomenon whose nuances must be understood through a gendered lens.

References

Free Dictionary. Definition of "agency." Retrieved from http://encyclopedia.the-freedictionary.com/Human+Agency.

Genderwatch. "What is Gendercide?" Retrieved from http://www.gendercide.org/what_is_gendercide.html.

Office of the Special Adviser on Gender Issues and the Advancement of Women (OSAGI). 2000. Retrieved from http://www.un.org/womenwatch/osagi/wps/.

Physicians for Human Rights (2000). War-Related Sexual Violence in Sierra Leone: A Population-based Assessment. Retrieved from http://physiciansforhuman-rights.org/library/report-sierraleone-2000.html.

Ranger, T. 1992. "Afterworld: War, Violence and Healing in Zimbabwe." *Journal of Southern African Studies*, 18(3), 301–10.

Schmidt, H. 1997. "Healing the Wounds of War: Memories of Violence and Making of History in Zimbabwe's Most Recent Past." *Journal of Southern African Studies*, 21(2), 301–10.

CHAPTER TWO

Victims of Rape and Gendercide: All Wars

Sandra I. Cheldelin

Introduction

Sexual violence during wartime is well documented. The primary story that emerges is that women are victims of the most unimaginable and inhumane behavior. This type of gendered wartime violence is nothing new. Rape and torture have been integral parts of wars from the beginning. As Swiss and Giller (1993) note, there are written records of wartime rape from ancient Greece. They go on to describe that "the induction of Helen of Troy and the rape of the Sabine women are archetypal in Western culture, so much so that their human tragedy is obscured" (612). Whether the victors take conquered women home as sexual slaves, sexually assault them as punishment for their opponents' resistance, use them to satisfy their sexual desires, or hold them hostage until impregnation, rape has and continues to threaten women and girls in every conflict across the globe throughout the millennia. The many cases of atrocities offer insights into the trauma and challenges faced by victims and members of their families and communities.

As rape has become more and more tactical and strategic during wartime, the horrors of such torture lead to prolonged psychological damage or death and can no longer be dismissed. In this chapter we witness the underbelly of all wars and are challenged as a moral imperative to intervene. It concludes by demonstrating that the victim narrative, as real as it is, is incomplete—women have emerged as agents of their own healing processes—and offers recommendations to stop the hideous and predictable situation women find themselves in when violence begins.

Several personal accounts set the context. The first is presented by Nat Hentoff in the *Village Voice* (February 2001) in response to a *New York Times* editorial on the government of Sudan's terrorism against black Christians and animists in the southern part of the country. The *Times* focused on the national Muslim military regime that had targeted black Africans and, as a result, more than four million southern Sudanese were displaced—the most displaced in the world. Clearly this was an atrocity but so, too, was what was known to the editor but not reported: the extraordinary personal horrors experienced by women like then 20-year-old Aluel Mangong Deng. In her own words, she tells of her abduction story in southern Sudan:

> I was enslaved five years ago [1996] during a raid on my village, Agok. I tried to run away from the soldiers, but they caught me and threw me to the ground. I struggled to get away, so they held down my hands and feet and cut my throat and chest with a knife. As I grew faint, one of them named Mohammed raped me then and there. That night, I was again raped by different men. They came one after another. This also happened to other women, and even to young girls. It took about 30 days before we reached Poulla, north of Babanusa. This kind of rape happened just about every day along the way. (Hentoff 2001)

When Deng desperately tried to escape from her captors she was brutally gang-raped while simultaneously having her throat slit. As she endured this violence, she was told of her inferiority based on her ethnicity. Spending years as a slave—where she also suffered repeated gang rapes—Deng finally escaped and was discovered in a displaced persons camp in southern Sudan (Hentoff 2001). Why was this left out of the *New York Times* account of Sudan's terrorism? Are the horrors of women such as Deng not newsworthy?

A second story is told by Jasmine Tesanovic (2003a, 84) about a 19-year-old woman who lived with her family in Bosnia. As the war began her brothers fought for the Serbs while she hid in basements in the army-occupied part of her country. One day her luck ran out, and she was found and raped by soldiers. When it was discovered that she was pregnant, her father banned her from their home but later stated that he would allow her to return if she had a boy. Again a misfortune; the baby was a girl. Desperate, she gave her baby for adoption and went home. Soon, though, she was overwhelmed with guilt, returned to her village to find her child, reclaimed her, and relocated to another town. Not long after, a friend found her standing on the ledge of a window. The friend successfully coaxed her down, and in the ensuing conversation she explained that when she looked at her baby's face—whom she loved more than anyone—she saw her rapist's face—whom she despised more than anyone. Her options seemed limited to either killing herself or killing her baby.

Tesanovic's story was not uncommon in 2003 and again in 2005 when I interviewed women of the Association of Concentration Camp Torture Survivors of Canton Sarajevo, though at that point their situations were slightly more complicated. The children that resulted from their rapes were now preadolescents. Many of the women and their children were not welcome in their former communities, banned from their families, medically impaired, dealing with long-term psychological illnesses and depression, and economically desperate.

Another account of wartime rape comes from the Congo. Chris McGreal (2006) tells the poignant story of a then-23-year-old woman from Walikali, a territory within the Congolese province in the eastern regions of the Democratic Republic of the Congo (DRC), who was among the thousands attacked in her country. She travelled 90 miles to a hospital for surgery in Goma after the Rwandan Hutu militia gang-raped her. In her words:

> Where I lived they were in the forest … we had to go there to find food. There were four of us and we were stopped by seven Interahamwe. [We] tried to run away. One was shot dead. The other got a bullet in the leg. They still raped her. I fainted because there were seven of them. I really got damaged. I couldn't hold in my urine. I heard these people came back and killed my father. (McGreal 2006)

Also a victim of the Hutu militia was a 54-year-old woman from Kindu, the capital of Maniema province in the DRC, who was repeatedly raped by a group of Mai Mai, an ethnic militia in her area. She states:

> They came in the morning and raped me, two of them. That didn't disturb me so much after what happened later. In the afternoon five men came into the house. They told my husband to put three kinds of money on the table: dollars, shillings, francs. But we didn't have any of that kind of money. We are poor. We don't even know what dollars look like. So they shot him. My children were screaming and so they shot them. After that they raped me, all of them. (McGreal 2006)

McGreal reports that as the woman lay bleeding the attackers thrust the barrels of their guns into her vagina. The Doctors on Call Service (DOCS) hospital in Goma have treated thousands of rape victims such as the woman from Kindu. One in four requires surgery, and more than one-third are under 18.

Rape and War

Brownmiller (1975b) provides insight as to how difficult it is to make the war/rape story public in her introductory paragraphs on the *Women of 1971* website documenting the rape in Bangladesh. In 1971, Brownmiller read in the *New York Post* that the government of Bangladesh was declaring all of the women raped by Pakistani military "heroines" of the war for seeking independence. The concluding sentence read, "In the traditional Bengali village society, where women lead cloistered lives, rape victims often are ostracized." This story launched her research. She asked a friend who worked on the foreign desk of the *New York Times* about a story on the "Rape of Bengali Women" and reports that he merely laughed: "I don't think so. It doesn't sound like a *Times* story." Similarly, a friend at *Newsweek* was "skeptical." She states, "I got the distinct impression that both men, good journalists, thought I was barking up an odd tree. NBC's Liz Trotta was one of the few American reporters to investigate the Bangladesh rape story at this time. She filed a TV report for the weekend news" (Brownmiller 1975b). Is this just weekend news? Was Hentoff right—that rape is not *New York Times* (or *Newsweek*) worthy?

Individual stories of horrific crimes demand an empathic response, but when we consider the collective stories—all of the women raped and tortured in all of the wars—it is clear that rape is a gendered crime and requires comprehensive and persistent interventions. The data that follow, provided by the United Nations Office for the Coordination of Humanitarian Affairs (OCHA), seem almost unimaginable. While the number raped in Vietnam is unknown, in the 1980s in South Africa, 25,000 women were raped. During the Bosnia-Herzegovina war, 1992–1993, there were 20,000 to 70,000 raped. In 1994, 250,000 women were raped in Rwanda, which resulted in 2,500 to 10,000 pregnancies. In just the first six months of 2006, more than 12,000 rapes of women and girls occurred in eastern Congo (OCHA/IRIN 2007, 37). It will be years before a complete account of the numbers will be available as rape continues there.

Rape has no boundaries of age. As Goodwin reports (2004), Maria, age 70, was victim to the Hutu militia that led Rwanda's 1994 genocide and who are now part of the 140,000 rebels in the DRC. They came to Maria's home and in her words:

> They grabbed me, tied my legs apart like a goat before slaughter, then raped me, one after the other. Then they stuck sticks inside me until I think.... War came. I just saw smoke and fire. Then my life and my health were taken away.

Maria's entire family—five sons, three daughters, and her husband—were murdered. "She was left with a massive fistula where her bladder was torn, causing permanent incontinence. She hid in the Bush for three years out of fear that the rebels might return, and out of shame over her constantly soiled clothes" (Goodwin 2004).

The greatest threat to civilian women during conflict is rape and sexual violence by armed, uniformed, state and nonstate forces and civilians (OCHA/IRIN 2007, 37). That means that in the 35 countries currently in conflict, being a civilian woman in these countries will likely result in being violated. It is and has been commonplace for centuries for rape and sexual violence against women to go unchallenged. Only in the past quarter century, when human rights organizations began to document testimony from women, have the doors opened to provide a voice for these victims. Prior to documentation, though, no one will ever know the extent of damage women and girls experienced from assaults (37).

Unfortunately even now, with laws in place to convict perpetrators, women must testify, sign indictments, and deal with the family and community fallout. "If they admit rape, women cannot protect their children from rape, from suffering social stigmas" (Tesanovic 2003a, 84). So there remains the shame, the humiliation, and ultimately silence for the majority of women victims. Anneke Van Woudenberg, a Congo specialist for Human Rights Watch (HRW), tells of a 30-year-old in North Kivu who was brutalized to make sure she would not identify or testify against her attackers:

> [She] had her lips and ears cut off and eyes gouged out after she was raped.... Now, we are seeing more and more such cases ... as the rebels constantly seek new ways to terrorize, their barbarity becomes more frenzied.... Gang-raped victims [have] their labia pierced and then padlocked. 'They usually die of massive infection,' I was told." (Goodwin 2004)

A medical team of researchers (Johnson et al. 2010) reported in the *Journal of American Medical Association* (*JAMA*) their survey results on the prevalence of rape and sexual violence in eastern Congo and their assessment of basic health care needs and available access. From their door-to-door interviews of more than 1,000 villagers in north and south Kivu and Ituri, they confirmed widespread incidence of rape: Nearly 40 percent of women (and 23 percent of men) had suffered sexual assault, and sexual violence victims had mental health disorders at twice the population rate.

A controversial finding, too, was the number of women reported as perpetrators of sexual assault—41 percent of the assaulted women and 10 percent of the men reported they were victim to women (Johnson et al. 2010). Caution was advised from the head of the US-based NGO International

Rescue Committee (IRC) in the DRC, Ciarán Donnelly. He confirmed the findings of Johnson's team in regard to the high level of sexual violence and its impact but suggests further investigation needs to be conducted on the gender-based perpetrator data. It is not clear, for example, "whether women kidnapped by armed groups [were] forced to perform sexual acts on others [and therefore became] the perpetrators of conflict-related sexual violence" (IRIN, Africa 2010). Clearly the rape/war problem is complicated when women, too, resort to rape and violence, regardless of whether or not they were under duress.

War Booty

In the West, images of rape typically reflect a masked male stranger suddenly emerging from the dark to attack a vulnerable lone female. As terrifying an image as this is, Katz (2006) points out that it is "also oddly reassuring—to both women and men" (149) because women believe "that if they are smart and take the necessary precautions, they will drastically reduce their chances of being assaulted. For men, the image of the crazed rapist diverts the critical spotlight away from them" (149). This is not the image or story, however, for the millions of women (or men) in war and conflict zones. They are not reassured at all; rather, they are fearful of assault on a daily basis.

A longstanding excuse for the persistence of rape during and after war is the "war booty" thesis (Pankhurst 2008) wherein the rape of "enemy women" is accepted as fair game or as a just reward for victory. This poem by Imani Woomera (OCHA/IRIN 2007, i) makes the story of booty vivid and insidious:

The Soldiers
They come from a land where soldiers control each spot and not
One woman's body is free
Woman once sacred flower blossom to dawn
Slowly devoured until life inside of her is gone
Exterior wasted
Been tasted by too many men
Slapped pinned down again and again and
There is no exit from this trip
Pools of blood in the center of her lap
Dripping into cracked spaces
Covering once beautiful faces
Embraces

Have no place here
The land where sex breeds fear and
Babies are born out of torn wombs
Woman they pray cry out to the moon
For there can be no god
Who watches their pain and remains
Still
Like they are
Still
Being beaten with whips
Still
Being torn apart each night by a different poet stick
And they
Still
Watch their mothers dip their hands below Earth tears
This is the land where soldiers control each spot and not
One woman's body is free

The "war booty" thesis is remarkably chronicled in *A Woman in Berlin: Eight Weeks in the Conquered City* (Anonymous 2000) written by a female German journalist who details two months surrounding the arrival of Soviet troops at the end of the war. After the first time that Soviet soldiers raped her—the first of many men to rape her many times—she writes:

> One of them grabs my wrists and jerks me along the corridor. Then the other is pulling as well, his hands on my throat, so I can no longer scream. I no longer want to scream, for fear of being strangled. They're both tearing away at me; instantly I'm on the floor. ... I end up with my head on the bottom step of the basement stairs. I can feel the damp coolness of the floor tiles. The door above is ajar and lets in a little light. One man stands there keeping watch, while the other tears my underclothes, forcing his way—... grope around the floor with my left hand until I find my key ring. I hold it tight. I use my right hand to defend myself. It's no use. He's simply torn off my garter, ripping it in two. When I struggle to come up, the second one throws himself on me as well, forcing me back on the ground with his fists and knees. Now the other keeps lookout, whispering, "Hurry up, hurry." (Anonymous 53)

Following the fall of the Nazi regime in 1945, it is estimated that more than 100,000 German women were raped in Berlin by their Russian conquerors (Anonymous xi). For the average Russian soldier, the conquest of Berlin meant an entitlement to the German women of the city after a long and difficult war. The mass rapes in Berlin were not used as a strategy of war; rather they symbolized revenge, sexual gratification, and just reward. Anonymous's diary supports this assertion. She overhears a conversation between Russian soldiers about "Stalin's decree" that seems to suggest that Stalin had "declared that 'this kind of thing' [rape] is not to happen" (52). Stalin may not have endorsed the mass rape, but neither did he act to stop it.

The rapes usually occurred at night after the Russian soldiers had consumed a great deal of alcohol; the alcohol presumably helped to lower inhibitions against sexual violence. The German men were by and large unable to protect their women, and the author writes of the men's misery and powerlessness. "The weaker sex. Deep down we women are experiencing a kind of collective disappointment" (42–43). Anonymous also tacitly writes about the shameful experience of the German men: "I think our men must feel even dirtier than we do, sullied as we women are" (75). It was expected that the German women of Berlin would be forced to acquiesce to the Russian soldiers, and by doing so, they were the ones who were able to protect their men against the wrath of the Russian soldiers.

In the early phases of war, women speak with one another about their suffering. However, as months and years follow, an implicit oath of silence takes hold. Thus, the collective experience becomes private as each victim is isolated in silence. What is a collectively shared experience becomes a private one. A nurse tells Anonymous, for example, that "it's better not to speak of such things [mass rape]," (246) and her friend Ilse confides that her husband cannot bear to hear about the rapes. Even their language insures silence: the euphemism *forced intercourse* was adopted to describe the mass rape (215). Knowing they had become "spoiled" and would be rejected by their men because they would be seen as "damaged," the vow of secrecy prevailed (Cheldelin 2006).

The notion of war booty was evident during World War II when the Japanese armed forces had access to the hundreds of thousands of Koreans and Chinese women kidnapped and enslaved as "comfort women." These women were forced to provide sexual services to the Japanese, and following the war, the Japanese set up sexual service stations for American GIs "with the tacit approval from the US occupation authorities who had full knowledge that women were being coerced into prostitution" (Talmadge 2007).

A day before the Japanese began their negotiation for the country's surrender and occupation—September 19, 1945—the Ibaraki police were told to set up sexual comfort stations for the occupation troops. They converted a police officer dormitory into a brothel, "stocking" it with 20 women. The next day it was operating. For the cost of one dollar—the price of a half pack of cigarettes—paid up front, GIs received a ticket and a condom. When the first brothel opened, a line of more than 500 occupying GIs immediately formed. Each woman served 15 to 60 clients per day. Seven months later, General MacArthur declared all places of prostitution off limits—his decision likely was informed by medical necessity as nearly a quarter of the 35,000 troops had contracted sexually transmitted diseases (Talmadge 2007).

Gendered War

Though the war booty thesis is documented and persistent over the centuries, the latter part of the twentieth century, especially, is witness to an even more horrifying and sinister use of war rape. It is mass rape as a deliberate, state-sanctioned strategy of war to exterminate a race of people, also known as genocide. Mary Anne Warren (1985) makes a further distinction, the deliberate extermination of a particular sex (or gender), known as gendercide. Illustrations of female infanticide, maternal mortality, and the witch-hunts in early modern Europe (and the United States) are explored by Warren. *Gendercide Watch* summarizes 22 current and historical gendercide cases including atrocities in Armenia (1915–1917), the Jewish Holocaust (1933–1945), Nanjing (1937–1938), the many Stalin's Purges, Bangladesh (1971), the Kashmir/Punjab/Delhi massacre (1984), Bosnia-Herzegovina (1992–1995), Rwanda (1994), Srebrenica (1995), Kosovo (1998–1999), East Timor (1999), and Colombia (since 1948) (Gendercide Watch, case studies). The state-sanctioned gender-selective mass killings over the years have overwhelmingly targeted "battle-age" men, and Gendercide Watch is concerned that ignoring the massive male killings "is one of the great taboos of the contemporary age, and must be ignored no longer" (Gendercide Watch: What Is Gendercide?). Their collective case analyses offer data about the ways in which men and women are targeted; rape continues to be the dominant tool against women.

The compelling documentation of this "shame of war" is found in the UN IRIN's second book—of the same title—on gender-based violence (OCHA/IRIN 2007). Each of the six chapters highlights a woman's story—Francoise's, Marni's, Kibakuli's, Elizabeth's, Helena's, and Pewa's. Many of the women and girls featured in the book agreed to be photographed and have their lives chronicled during and after their violations in wartime, as this type of documentation allows us to understand the depth of organized rape and ethnic cleansing. While war booty was a dominant story of World War II—Chinese or Korean "comfort women" in Japan or German women raped by Soviet soldiers in Berlin—it was not specifically a war tactic. What follows are three cases of tactical gendercide as occurred in Nanjing, Bangladesh (East Pakistan), and Bosnia. These are discussed in historical chronological order and reflect changes over time in tactics and international responses.

Nanjing Massacre

During the Japanese invasion of Nanjing, China, in 1937, 20,000 to 80,000 women were raped by the Imperial Japanese Army; 300,000 men, women, and children were killed. The Nanjing Massacre, also known as the Rape of Nanking (Nanjing), is a case of gendercide against both women and men. While the invading Japanese gang-raped women—then killed them or left them tortured and traumatized—they rounded up 250,000 Chinese civilian men as prisoners of war and "murdered them *en masse*, used for bayonet practice, or burned and buried [them] alive" (Gendercide Watch: Nanjing). Chang (1998) writes that "surviving Japanese veterans claim that the army had officially outlawed the rape of enemy women, but the military policy forbidding rape only encouraged soldiers to kill their victims afterwards" (49–50). The callous nature of the rape and killings is reflected in a soldier's recollection that

> It would be all right if we only raped them. I shouldn't say all right. But we always stabbed and killed them. Because dead bodies don't talk. . . . Perhaps when we were raping her, we looked at her as a woman, but when we killed her, we just thought of her as something like a pig. (Chang 49–50)

Other Japanese soldiers report that they "were hungry for women" and were told to use bayonets or rifles to kill the women after they were raped so that no one would be able to trace the killers (Yin & Young 1996).

Many who witnessed the massacre have captured its gruesome qualities. Li Ke-hen is quoted in Yin and Young:

> There are so many bodies on the street, victims of group rape and murder. They were all stripped naked, their breasts cut off, leaving a terrible dark brown hole; some of them were bayoneted in the abdomen, with their intestines spilling out alongside them; some had a roll of paper or a piece of wood stuffed in their vaginas (195).

Another account, from the diary of a German Nazi businessman, is quoted in Chang (1998):

> Groups of 3 to 10 marauding soldiers would begin by traveling through the city and robbing whatever there was to steal. They would continue by raping the women and girls and killing anything and anyone that offered any resistance, attempted to run away from them or simply happened to be in the wrong place at the wrong time. There were girls under the age of 8 and women over the age of 70 who were raped and then, in the most brutal way possible, knocked down and beat up (119).

The war memorial of the Nanjing Massacre introduces visitors at its entrance to dramatic and moving larger-than-life sculptures depicting the horror and sorrow of this six-week catastrophe. The first has a man dragging his wife, and the caption on the sculpture of *The Helpless Struggle of a Dying Intellectual* reads: "My dear poor wife! The devil raped you, killed you. ... I'm right after you!" The second sculpture shows an old man leading two children away and looking toward the sky: "The devils have sent the bombers again. ... The poor orphans, Frightened by the vicious laughter of the brutal devils, Terrified by the corps[es] piling up in the alley, Have lapsed into numbness." There is also a statue of an elder son guiding his mother: "My dear mother in the eighties, Hurry up! Run away from the bloody hands." One sculpture of a woman partially clothed and in despair bears these words: "Never will a holy soul bear the humiliation of the devils! Only to die! Only to die! Only death can wash the filth away!" Finally, a sorrowful child is sitting looking at his dead mother: "Frigidity and horror have frozen this crying baby! Poor thing. Not knowing mum has been killed, Blood, milk and tears, Have frozen, never melting."

On a wall inside the memorial are captions of verdicts from the International Military Tribunal of the Far East and the Nanjing Military Tribunal for the Trial of War Criminals. One poignant statement reads: "After the seizure of the city the Japanese army went raping everywhere to satisfy their sexual lust. ... On December 16–17, Chinese women raped by Japanese soldiers exceeded one thousand. The ways they performed such atrocities are appalling and cruel, unprecedented in the world history. ... Every woman left in Nanjing found themselves jeopardized."

One of the heroines of the war was Minnie Vautrin, a missionary from Illinois, working as a teacher of women at the Ginling College in Nanjing. Nearly singlehandedly she turned the college into a sanctuary for 10,000 girls and women. Her careful chronicles of daily life are recorded in an edited book (Vautrin with Suping Lu 2008). The war memorial has a gravestone honoring her: "Minnie Vautrin, 'Goodness of Mercy,' Missionary to China 28 years, 1886–1941."

Bangladesh Massacre

Nearly 35 years later (1971) in East Pakistan (now Bangladesh), 200,000 women were raped by the Pakistan Army with local political and religious militia support. The rapes were part of the massive genocide of the East Pakistani Bengalis, as a military response to their seeking independence from Pakistan. The Bangladesh Genocide Archive Website provides the women's historical account. Following the national elections in December 1970, the Awami League—the oldest and largest party in Bangladesh—won overwhelmingly. Two months later, February 22, 1971, the generals in West Pakistan initiated a genocide campaign against the Bengali, especially against the Awami League and its supporters, with the declaration from Pakistani president Yahya Khan at the February conference: "Kill three million of them and the rest will eat out of our hands" (Payne 1972, 50).

On March 25 the genocide was launched. The university in Dacca (Dhaka) was attacked and students exterminated in the hundreds. Death squads roamed the streets, killing approximately 7,000 people in a single night. It was only the beginning. "Within a week, half the population of Dacca had fled, and at least 30,000 people had been killed. Chittagong, too, had lost half its population. All over East Pakistan people were taking flight, and it was estimated that in April some thirty million people were wandering helplessly across East Pakistan to escape the grasp of the military." (Payne 48)

As a result, ten million refugees fled to India. This likely launched the eventual Indian military intervention. According to the Bangladesh Genocide Archive Website, the number killed by the genocide was estimated at 1 to 3 million.

Men were overwhelmingly targeted in the genocide primarily to rid the country of boys and men who could become freedom fighters. According to Mascarenhas (1972), they intentionally targeted five groups: Bengali military men (the East Pakistan Rifles, the police, and paramilitary Ansars and Mujahids), Hindus, Awami Leaguers, students—especially boys, and Bengali intellectuals (116–17). The stunning omnipotence is reflected by a Punjab captain reported to have said to journalist Don Coggin, "We can kill anyone for anything. We are accountable to no one" (Rummel 1994, 335).

While men were murdered during the genocide, women were raped. More than 20,000 women were raped, with some accounts reporting up to 400,000. Lieutenant General Amir Abdullah Khan Niazi did not deny rapes were being carried out and even excused them, as a booty reward, by his comment, "You cannot expect a man to live, fight, and die in East Pakistan and go to Jhelum for sex, would you?" (Bangladesh Genocide Archive). Brownmiller (1975a), however, tells the female gendercide aspect of the conflict. Eighty percent of the women were Muslim (the remaining were Hindu and Christian) (81). Reporter Aubrey Menen told Brownmiller of a common assault story:

> Two [Pakistani soldiers] went into the room that had been built for a bridal couple [married one month previously]. The others stayed behind with the family, one of them covering them with his gun. They heard a barked order, and the bridegroom's voice protesting. Then there was silence until the bride screamed. Then there was silence again, except for some muffled cries that soon subsided. In a few minutes one of the soldiers came out, his uniform in disarray. He grinned to his companions. Another soldier took his place in the extra room. And so on, until all six had raped the belle of the village. Then all six left, hurriedly. The father found his daughter lying on the string cot unconscious and bleeding. Her husband was crouched on the floor, kneeling over his vomit. (Brownmiller 1975a, 82)

Tragically, the victim was banned from her home, shamed, and later found living in a shelter.

Rape had no boundaries—young girls and old women alike were sexually used and abused. "Pakistani soldiers had not only violated Bengali women on the spot; they abducted tens of hundreds and held them by force in the military barracks for nightly use. Some women may have been raped as many as 80 times tonight" (Brownmiller 83). Young Hindu women were either killed or captured as sex slaves in the military bases. Men kept the women naked so they could not use clothing to hang themselves and shaved the women's heads so they could not strangle themselves with their long hair.

Bosnia

Twenty years later, the war in Bosnia-Herzegovina erupted. The mass rape of Bosnian Muslim women from 1992 to 1995 was systematic, deliberate, and sanctioned by the Serbian military. There is no greater evidence of this than the "rape camps" that sprang up during that war—the mass rape of Muslim women was a critical element of the Serbian "ethnic cleansing" campaign (Cheldelin and Wiskin 2010). A report by the UN Commission of Experts (1994) on the atrocities committed in Bosnia defined ethnic cleansing as "a purposeful policy designed by one ethnic or religious group to remove by violent and terror-inspiring means the civilian population of another ethnic or religious group from certain geographic areas" (Allen 1996, 44). The rapes in Bosnia were the most organized and systematic attempt to "cleanse" the Muslim population, in particular, from territories that the Serbs wanted in order to create what was called a Greater Serbia. Certainly Croatian women were also targeted for sexual violence by Serbian forces. However, Bosnian Muslim women accounted for the largest number of reported victims (47).

The ethnic cleansing in Bosnia was an explicitly gendered phenomenon. At its most basic level, the rape against Bosnian women was a demonstration of male power. The war was specifically aimed at forcing the permanent expulsion of civilians—predominantly women and children—during wartime (Cockburn 2003). The Bosnia women's plight was a common story. Due to patriarchal gender roles, women are vulnerable during conflict: They are usually unarmed, and because they are their children's primary caregivers, they are less mobile then men. Unfortunately, traditional female gender roles leave women with few options during war (Cheldelin and Wiskin 2010).

The 1991 Ram Plan, written during the Croatia civil war, was found to be an official document ordering ethnic cleansing and genocidal rape as military policy. During a military strategy meeting, Serb army officers expanded the Ram Plan to specifically target noncombatant women. Their decision was influenced by the belief that targeting women and children, the most vulnerable civilian population, was the surest way to ensure Muslim flight. Allen (1996) explains it this way:

> Our analysis of the behavior of the Muslim communities demonstrates that the morale, will, and bellicose nature of their groups can be undermined only if we aim our action at the point where the religious and social structure is most fragile. We refer to the women, especially adolescents, and to the children. Decisive intervention on these social figures would spread confusion among the communities, thus causing first of all fear and then panic, leading to the probable [Muslim] retreat from the territories involved in war activity (57).

The best way to target women and instill fear in the civilian population was to sanction rape as a weapon of war. Serb paramilitary units entered villages and raped women in public to create the climate of fear and humiliation. Yugoslav Popular Army officers would arrive at the village later to expel civilians (Allen 74). Homes were destroyed, men were murdered or forcibly deported, and women became refugees. As Bloom (2001) points out, the reason rape is a powerful weapon is because its use humiliates its victims and thereby lowers their attachment to a place and/or geographic community. Women who have been raped and dislocated during war are therefore much less likely to return home. Similarly, Askin (1997) notes that Bosnian Muslim women were targeted because of their patrilineal culture. Babies born from rape would then become Serbs—ultimately the death of Bosnian Muslim culture if all babies had Serbian fathers. As a result of humiliating or demoralizing the Muslim population—women lost their virginity or fidelity, and men were unable to intervene—they would likely flee. This is an extreme case of cultural violence (Gultung 1990): By completely negating the value of Bosnian Muslim culture and life, the Serbs were able to legitimize their ethnic cleansing campaign (Cheldelin and Wiskin 2010).

Rape as a War Crime

The recent determination of rape to be a crime of war is an important legal decision. However, it is not that rape has not been considered a war crime for centuries. An international military tribunal in 1474 convicted Sir Peter von Hagenbach of rape during a military occupation of the Austrian town of Breisach. (His conviction and ordered execution was the first recorded international criminal tribunal.) Murray (2002) describes von Hagenbach's situation:

> He had been sent as governor of the occupied town by the Duke of Burgundy (known as Charles the Bold to his friends and as Charles the Terrible to his detractors). Von Hagenbach's instructions were to keep order and these he executed with savage zealousness. Murder, rape, illegal taxation and the wanton confiscation of private property were carried out by his soldiers and officials to terrify the local population into submission.

Shanker has chronicled many documented crimes of rape in his *Crimes of War Project* (1999–2003), including the American Civil War whereby there was an order signed by President Abraham Lincoln in 1863 making rape a capital offense. Rape was explicitly included in such treaties as Article 46, annexed to the Hague Convention of 1907 regarding regulations respecting the laws and customs of war on land. In Section III, it states that "military authority of the territory of the hostile state, insuring family, honor and rights, the lives of persons, and private property, as well as religious convictions and practice, must be respected" (International Committee of the Red Cross, Article 46). This article was the basis for bringing charges of war crimes against the Japanese soldiers before the Tokyo tribunal for the rape of women in Nanjing, China. Article 27 of the Fourth Geneva Convention of 1949 states that "women shall be especially protected against any attack on their honour, in particular against rape, enforced prostitution, or any form of indecent assault" (International Committee of the Red Cross, Article 27). Nevertheless, it seems Swiss and Giller (1993) got it right, in their reflections on the newly created international tribunal, that "only recently, with the media focus on allegations of widespread rape in the former Yugoslavia, there has been a significant increase in public awareness and support for measures that respond to the trauma and crime of rape in war" (612).

On May 25, 1993, the United Nations approved the creation of the first International Criminal Tribunal for the Former Yugoslavia (ICTY). The only precedents for this court were the post–World War II international war crimes tribunals at Nuremberg and in the Far East. International laws of war, for the most part, did not include rape. In March 2000, the ICTY convened, and in July, the Foca trial began—named after the town in southeastern Bosnia, victim to the Serb mission to rid the district of its Muslims—focusing on rape as a war crime against humanity. The Foca traial was established by the United Nations in The Hague, Netherlands. Jerome Socolovsky (2000), the Associated Press journalist covering the Yugoslav war crimes tribunal in The Hague, reported 16 Bosnian Muslim women from the Foca district "confronted their alleged rapists, speaking out about the systematic assaults for a war crimes tribunal—and for history books." Each of the 16 was assigned a code (e.g. FWS-87 or FWS-105), and each testified to their horrific experience in the "rape factories." For the first time prosecutors in The Hague were trying to make rape punishable as an international crime. Three Bosnian Serb paramilitary fighters, Dragoljub Kunarac, Radomir Kovac, and Zoran Vukovic, were accused of raping Muslim girls and women in a sports hall, a high school, and at a construction site in Foca:

> Almost every night in the summer and fall of 1992, Serb soldiers would enter the detention centers and select their victims from among the female prisoners lying on gym mats, the witnesses testified. The women were taken to classrooms and private apartments where they were

sexually assaulted, forced to dance nude and then compelled to perform degrading domestic chores. Some were kept as personal sex slaves by former neighbors—much older men whose wives and families they knew. (Socolovsky 2000)

The Foca trial was critical for a number of reasons beyond determining the innocence or guilt of the three men. The International Criminal Court needed a precedent to be able to prosecute such atrocities in all other wars. Socolovsky speaks to other aspects of its significance:

One of the more important precedents established at the Yugoslav tribunal is that witnesses who have suffered traumatic experiences are not necessarily considered unreliable, as has been the case elsewhere. The court's statute is considered progressive on gender crimes, requiring no corroboration for the testimony of sexual assault victims.... Now the tribunal must weigh the testimony of Kunarac, the key defendant, against that of his alleged victims, including FWS-50, who was raped at knifepoint.

More than one year after the tribunal in Bosnia was formed—in November 1994—the International Criminal Tribunal for Rwanda (ICTR), established by the United Nations Security Council Resolution 955, was convened. Its purpose was to bring to justice the people responsible for the Rwandan genocide in 1994. As a result of the two trials presided over by the ICTY and the ICTR, rape as war booty, genocide, or gendercide can no longer be deemed a "natural" part of war. Rape is an international crime against humanity.

In his speech at Fordham University in 1999, James Scheffer, US ambassador-at-large for war crimes issues, made the following remarks:

... [T]oday we find ourselves in an enormously stronger position to investigate, document, and prosecute rape and other forms of sexual violence. Rape and sexual violence now have a firm foothold as specifically enumerated offenses under international humanitarian law. This cementing began in 1993 and 1994 after rape, and sexual violence, was specifically codified for the first time as a recognizable and independent crime within the statutes of the International Criminal Tribunals for the Former Yugoslavia (ICTY) and for Rwanda (ICTR). These two historic international instruments are now the foundation upon which crimes of rape and sexual violence are punished.

As a result, the two ad hoc criminal tribunals have changed the course of history—and war: Rape and sexual violence are tactics of genocide and are individual crimes against humanity. In the Rwanda tribunal, rape and sexual violence "were put on equal footing with all other offenses. ... [L]ike torture, rape is used for such purposes as intimidation, degradation, humiliation, discrimination, punishment, control or destruction of the person. Like torture, rape is a violation of personal dignity..." (Scheffer 1999). The Bosnia tribunal recognized rape "as a violation of the Laws and Customs of War and as a basis of torture under the Geneva Conventions. ... [I]t considered rape of any person to be a despicable act which strikes at the core of human dignity and physical integrity" (Scheffer 1999).

A Moral Imperative to Change

When it is the woman's primary responsibility to protect her virginity for the sake of not being perceived as contaminated or impure, rape has extraordinary social consequences for its female victims. In Bosnia, for example, unmarried victims could no longer be married within the community, and husbands were free to reject their wives (Kennedy-Pipe and Stanley 2001). Without marriage, the woman could not fulfill her family identity as a mother and wife or her gender identity as caretaker—the valued "private sphere" expectations of the culture. These consequences were in place due to a patriarchal system that valued women most for their reproductive identity and virginity. Brownmiller (1993) notes, "And if she survives the assaults, what does the victim of wartime rape become to her people? Evidence of the enemy's bestiality. Symbol of her nation's defeat. A pariah. Damaged property."

Just as in 1945 Berlin, the aftermath of the mass rape in Bosnia included the women's silence. Women were reluctant to speak about their rape experiences for a myriad of reasons including their feelings of shame, lack of trust, severe traumatization, and fear of reprisals against them and their families (Allen 1996). It was widely believed that women who had been raped brought shame and dishonor to their families. The stigma and the attitudes of Muslim men toward rape therefore discouraged women from seeking psychosocial counseling. Women also felt silenced because they feared being judged and blamed for the assault. It was common for rape victims to be abandoned by their families (Falice and Vincent 1995).

Ironically, even after war's end, women continue to be raped by soldiers, former combatants, and even by the peacekeepers who are meant to protect them (Pankhurst 2008). Women who have been raped need to receive proper health care and psychosocial trauma healing (Cheldelin and Wiskin 2010). (The work of antiviolence NGOs such as Medica Zenica was crucial in providing such services to Bosnia rape victims.) War violence also leads to an increase in domestic violence at war's end. It is evident that male former combatants also need access to the programs and resources to learn how to function in a post-conflict society (Tsjeard et al. 2005). Entire communities are in need of psychosocial healing and rehabilitation (Cheldelin and Wiskin 2010).

In January 1993, the UN Commission on Human Rights passed the resolution categorizing rape as a war crime. Since then, a worrisome trend has emerged in which rape continues to be used as a strategic weapon of war (i.e. Rwanda, Democratic Republic of the Congo). The sociopolitical motivation of organized rape as a strategic military objective uses tactics at two levels. The individual woman is humiliated, intimidated, terrorized, and punished. The community/society tactics result in destabilization, demoralization, and forced submission with the goal of getting people to leave the country (OCHA.IRIN 2007, 34). The ethnic cleansing in Rwanda is an extraordinary example of this strategy. "Women were raped by men from a rival ethnic group and thus, in a culture where ethnicity determined by paternity, bore children of that opposing ethnic community" (38). Two thirds of the Tutsi women who were gang raped in Rwanda are now HIV positive. Ethnic cleansing in the Sudan is reflected in the reports of Arab rapists telling African women, "We will make you a lighter baby" (38). The cultural motivation of gendercide suggests that sexual violence marked by the systematic breaking of taboos undermines cultural values. The danger becomes a shift from cultural violence to a new and dominant culture of violence.

Today, peace remains gendered. Djuric-Kuzmanovic, Drezgic, and Zarkov (2008) note that women in Bosnia have responded faster and with greater numbers than men in engaging in peace and humanitarian initiatives, but women are not yet central to peace-building processes. This disparity needs to be remedied. Mainstreaming efforts allow men and women to have equal power and influence in addressing gendered issues in their post-conflict societies. Building sustainable peace requires a societal shift from an enmity—of hostility and disregard toward half of its population (women)—to one of partnership and respect. It is ultimately about transforming relationships, not only between social groups (ethnic or religious, for example) but also between men and women. We must find ways to prevent women's bodies from being used as battlegrounds. Acts of rape and genocide impact the formation and deconstruction of identity (Cheldelin and Wiskin 2010). Because this is the case, female gender identity needs to be broadened so that women are valued for more than just their sexual and reproductive identity. Qualities that have been gendered as "feminine" need to be given higher status. Rape and its consequences need to be reframed and recontextualized so that women are not stigmatized and blamed for the sexual violence. This would go a long way toward helping women restore their sense of dignity and rebuild their identities. The moral narrative needs to shift so that rape is seen as unacceptable under any circumstances and never the fault of the victim.

The legal system has set the stage to demand equal rights through international law It is time for leaders around the world to be institutionally accountable in regard to gender crimes and provide gender equality in such social structures as education and health care, and insisting on gender equality in setting social and political agendas. We must work toward the recognition of victims as people and not stigmatized cultural symbols and establish programs wherein women are valued beyond their reproductive capabilities. However, as Susan Hirsch (Chapter 12, "Promises of Justice") elegantly speaks to the ways international law has expanded women's options, she also notes that there are limits to the use of law as a response to conflict.

It is important that women continue to speak out and push forward to obtain positions through which they can help to make a difference. The women for whom this is most important are those who are victimized by war and institutions that promote it. The incidence of violence against women is not a women's issue, a feminist issue, or an international development issue. It is a human issue. So says President Nelson Mandela, demonstrated in this statement:

> As long as we take the view that these are problems for women alone to solve, we cannot expect to reverse the high incidence of rape and child abuse ... and domestic violence. We do know that many men do not abuse women and children; and that they strive always to live with respect and dignity. But until today the collective voice of these men has never been heard, because the issue has not been regarded as one for the whole nation. From today those who inflict violence on others will know they are being isolated and cannot count on other men to protect them. From now on all men will hear the call to assume the responsibility for solving this problem. (President Nelson Mandela 1997; National Men's March, Pretoria, South Africa, quoted from Katz 2006, 253)

May the wisdom of President Mandela prevail.

Key words

rape, genocide, gendercide, mainstreaming, international criminal tribunals, war booty thesis.

Discussion Questions

1. Why is rape so persistent across all wars on all continents over the millennia?
2. What differentiates rape as war booty from a tactic of war?
3. How would you advise leaders to change the course of rape incidence during wartime?
4. Why is considering rape a war crime under international law only a partial solution to the problem of wartime rape?

References

Allen, Beverly. 1996. *Rape Warfare: The Hidden Genocide in Bosnia-Herzegovina and Croatia*. Minneapolis: University of Minnesota Press.

Anonymous. 2000. *a Woman in Berlin: Eight Weeks in the Conquered City*. New York: Metropolitan, Henry Holt & Company.

Askin, Kelly Dawn. 1997. *War Crimes against Women: Prosecution in International War Crimes Tribunal*. Cambridge, Mass.: Kluwer Law International, Martinus Nijhoff Publishers.

Bangladesh Genocide Archive. Retrieved from http://www.genocidebangladesh.org/.

Brownmiller, Susan. 1993, January 4. "Making female bodies the battlefield." *Newsweek*. Retrieved from http://www.newsweek.com/id/115895.

Brownmiller, Susan. 1975a. *Against Our Will: Men, Women and Rape*. New York: Simon and Schuster.

Brownmiller, Susan. 1975b. "Against Our Will: Women, Men and Rape," in *Women of 1971*. Retrieved from http://www.drishtipat.org/1971/war-susan.html.

Chang, Iris. 1998. *The Rape of Nanking*. Retrieved from http://en.wikipedia.org/wiki/The_Rape_of_Nanking_(book)#The_book.

Cheldelin, Sandra I. 2006. "Gender and Violence: Redefining the Moral Ground," in Daniel Rothbart and Karina Korostelina (ed.), *Identity, Morality and Threat*, Chapter 11 (p. 299). Lanham, Md.: Lexington Books.

Cheldelin, Sandra I. and Wiskin, Alisa. 2010. "Rape and Gendercide: The Story of All Wars." Paper presented at the annual meeting of the Theory vs. Policy? Connecting Scholars and Practitioners, New Orleans, La., February 17, 2010.

Cockburn, Cynthia. 2003, Spring. "Bosnia: The Postwar Moment: Lessons from Bosnia-Herzegovina." *Women & Environments Magazine*, 58–9.

Djuric-Kuzmanovic, Tanja, Drezgic, Rada, and Zarkov, Dubrava. 2008. "Gendered War, Gendered Peace: Violent Conflicts in the Balkans and Their Consequences," in Donna Pankhurst (ed.), *Gendered Peace: Women's Struggles for Post-War Justice And Reconciliation*. New York: Routledge.

Djuric-Kuzmanovic, Tanja, Drezgic, Rada, and Zarkov, Dubrava. Case Studies. Retrieved from http://www.gendercide.org/case.html.

Djuric-Kuzmanovic, Tanja, Drezgic, Rada, and Zarkov, Dubrava. Case Study: The Montreal Massacre, December 6, 1989. Retrieved from http://www.gendercide. org/case_montreal.html.

Djuric-Kuzmanovic, Tanja, Drezgic, Rada, and Zarkov, Dubrava. Case Study: The Nanjing Massacre, 1937–38. Retrieved from http://www.gendercide.org/case_ nanking.html.

Djuric-Kuzmanovic, Tanja, Drezgic, Rada, and Zarkov, Dubrava. Gendercide Watch. What Is Gendercide? Retrieved from http://www.gendercide.org/what_is_gendercide.html.

Goodwin, Jan. 2004. Silence = Rape, *The Nation*. Retrieved from http://www.thenation.com/article/silencerape.

Hentoff, Nat. 2001. *Gang Rape in Sudan: They Came One after Another,"* February 6, 2001. Retrieved from http://www.villagevoice.com/2001–02–06/news/gangrape-in-sudan/.

Hirsch, Susan F. 2011. "Promises of Justice: Northern Uganda, Democratic Republic of Congo and Darfur, Sudan," in Sandra Cheldelin and Maneshka Eliatamby (eds), *Women Waging War and Peace*. New York: Continuum Publishing.

Integrated Regional Information Networks (IRIN)-Africa, United Nations Office for the Coordination of Humanitarian Affairs (OCHA) (2010). Retrieved from http://www.irinnews.org/Report.aspx?ReportID=90081.

Integrated Regional Information Networks (IRIN)-United Nations Office for the Coordination of Humanitarian Affairs (OCHA) (March 16, 2007). *The Shame of War: Sexual Violence Against Women and Girls in Conflict.*

International Committee of the Red Cross (ICRC), International Humanitarian Law—Treaties and Documents. Article 27. Retrieved from http://www.icrc. org/ihl.nsf/385ec082b509e76c41256739003e636d/6756482d86146898c125641e 004aa3c5.

—. Article 46, Retrieved from http://www.icrc.org/ihl.nsf/4e473c7bc8854f2ec12563 f60039c738/e719fbf0283e98e3c12563cd005168bd!OpenDocument.

Johnson, K, Scott, J. Rughita, B., Kisielewski, M., Asher, J., Ong, R. and Lawry, L. 2010. "Association of Sexual Violence and Human Rights Violations with Physical and Mental Health in Territories of the Eastern Democratic Republic of the Congo." *Journal of American Medical Association*, 304(5), 553–62.

Katz, J. 2006. *The Macho Paradox: Why Some Men Hurt Women and How Men Can Help*. Naperville, Ill.: Sourcebooks, Inc.

Kennedy-Pipe, Caroline and Penny Stanley. 2001. "Rape in War: Lessons of the Balkan Conflicts in the 1990s," in Ken Booth (ed.), *The Kosovo Tragedy: The Human Rights Dimensions* (pp. 67–84). Portland, Ore.: Frank Cass Publishers.

Mascarenhas, Anthony. 1972. *The Rape of Bangla Desh*, Delhi, India: Vikas Publications.

McGreal, Chris. 2006. "Hundreds of Thousands Raped in Congo Wars." Retrieved from http://www.guardian.co.uk/world/2006/nov/14/congo.chrismcgreal.

Murray, Don. 2002. "Judge and Master." CBC News. Retrieved from http://www. cbc.ca/news/reportsfromabroad/murray/20020718.html.

Pankhurst, Donna. 2008. "Post-war Backlash Violence Against Women," in Donna Pankhurst (ed.), *Gendered Peace: Women's Struggles for Post-War Justice and Reconciliation.* New York: Routledge.

Payne, Robert. 1972. *Massacre.* Retrieved from http://www.genocidebangladesh. org/.

Rummel, Rudolph. J. 1994. *Death by Government.* New Jersey, New Brunswick: Transaction Publishers.

Scheffer, David J. 1999. " 'Rape as a War Crime.' Ambassador-at-Large for War Crimes Issues Remarks at Fordham University, New York." Retrieved from http://www.converge.org.nz/pma/arape.htm.

Shanker, Thom. 1999–2003. *Crimes of War: A to Z Guide.* Retrieved from http:// www.crimesofwar.org/thebook/sexual-violence.html.

Socolovsky, Jerome. 2000. "Bosnian 'Rape Camp' Survivors Testify in The Hague," Special to WEnews. Retrieved from http://www.womensenews.org/story/ rape/000719/bosnian-rape-camp-survivors-testify-the-hague.

Swiss, Shana, and Giller, Joan E. 1993. "Rape as a Crime of War." *Journal of the American Medical Association,* 270(5), 612–15.

Talmadge, Eric. 2007. "GIs Frequented Japan's 'Comfort Women.' " *Washington Post.* Retrieved from http://www.washingtonpost.com/wp-dyn/content/ article/2007/04/25/AR2007042501801.html.

Tesanovic, Jasmine. 2003a. "Women and Conflict: A Serbian Perspective." In Daniela Gioseffi (ed.), *Women on War: An International Anthology of Writings from Antiquity to the Present.* New York: The Feminist Press at the City University of New York.

Tsjeard, Bouta, Frerks, Georg and Banno, Ian. 2005. "Gender-based Violence and Sexual Violence: A Multidimensional Approach," in *Gender, Conflict and Development.* World Bank., available at http://www-wds.worldbank.org/servlet/ WDSContentServer/WDSP/IB/2004/11/15/000090341_20041115142901/ Rendered/PDF/30494.pdf

United Nations Commission of Experts. 1994. Final Report of the Commission of Experts. Retrieved from http://www.his.com/~twarrick/commxyu1.htm.

United Nations Office for the Coordination of Humanitarian Affairs/Integrated Regional Information Networks (UN OCHA/IRIN). 2007. *The Shame of War: Sexual Violence Against Women and Girls in Conflict.*[AU: Please provide complete details]

Vautrin, Minnie with Suping Lu (eds). 2008. *Terror in Minnie Vautrin's Nanjing, Diaries and Correspondence,* 1937–38. Urbana: University of Illinois Press.

Warren, Mary Anne. 1985. *Gendercide: The Implications of Sex Selection.* Lanham, Md.: Rowan and Littlefield Publishers.

Yin, James and Young, Shi. 1996. *The Rape of Nanking: An Undeniable History in Photographs. Japanese Carnage in China During World War II.* New York: Triumph Publishers.

SECTION I

Women Waging War

CHAPTER THREE

Searching for Emancipation: Eritrea, Nepal, and Sri Lanka

Maneshka Eliatamby

Introduction[1]

Many experts in the field of conflict analysis and resolution have a tendency to view women as peacemakers and men as being inclined toward war. Francis Fukuyama even goes as far as stating that, "males are genetically predisposed to violence" (Bouta et al. 2005, 11). Despite popular discourse of women being naturally inclined toward the task of peacemaking, there are a number of cases where women have defied such stereotypes and assumed active roles in war. Bouta et al. (2005, 11) found that females are actively participants in fighting forces in 55 different conflicts.

This chapter explores the case of the National Union of Eritrean Women in the Horn of Africa, the Nepali People's Liberation Army, and the Liberation Tigers of Tamil Eelam in Sri Lanka. It assesses cultural issues (or sources) and dynamics that contribute to these women's involvement in nonstate armed groups (NSAG). The chapter explores women's involvement in combat and asks the questions, Did culture and power or the lack of power play a role in the violentization (Richardson 2001, 111) of women in Eritrea, Nepal, and Sri Lanka? Was there something deep seeded in the cultures from which these women come that contributed as sources of their violence? In this analysis, I utilize positioning theory as a tool by which to analyze the phenomenon of the female combatant in these NSAGs. We will discuss how woman have sought emancipation from suppression and oppression through violent means as combatants in NSAGs as well we introduce the concept of repositioning as a phenomenon of this process.

Repositioning Through Combat

James Luberda in his analysis of George Elliot's *Middlemarch* describes positioning theory as "… the name given to recent attempts to articulate an alternate way of reading and understanding the dynamic of human relationships
within a social constructivist paradigm" (Luberda 2000, 1). As humans we
are constantly in the process of consciously or subconsciously positioning
ourselves—our actions and words indicate the position we either wish to
impress or the position that has been imposed on us. Luberda goes on to
explain the difference between *role* and *position* and refers to the former as
being somewhat static, while the latter has a greater sense of dynamism about
it. Luk van Langenhove refers to our concept of repositioning as "fluid positions," (Van Langanhove and Harre 1999, 17) and says "positions can and do
change. Fluid positions, not fixed roles, are used by people to cope with the
situation they usually find themselves in" (Van Langanhove and Harre 1999,
17). We use this theory to help illuminate the changes that have occurred in
gender relations of Eritrean, Nepali, and Tamil culture as a result of women's
entry into violence.

"Men and women may be involved in actively supporting conflict for
similar reasons including forced recruitment, agreement with the war goals,
patriotism, religious or ideological motives, a lack of education opportunities, and economic necessity" (Bouta et al. 2005, 12). I would suggest that
while Eritrean, Nepali, and Tamil men and women shared certain common
motivations for joining in their respective battle, women also had their own
agendas for enlisting in the EPLF, NPLA, and LTTE's female fighting units.

The question at this point is, Did these women have a natural propensity
to kill, or did their circumstances in traditional patriarchal Eritrean, Nepali,
and Tamil society force them to prove their worth on the battlefield and
achieve some semblance of equality?

Some experts suggest that many women in these three case studies
joined the fighting forces hoping that their actions on the battlefield will
change their social status in day-to-day life. Many state that joining these
forces is their only chance of survival. Women have joined in expectation
of achieving emancipation, as well as to fight oppression. A main feature of
positioning theory is its positioning triad (Figure 3.1). The three corners of
this triad represent the position, act-action and storyline, and these three
elements are intrinsically connected. In placing the second triangle directly
above yet connecting with the first, I suggest that Eritrean, Nepali, and
Tamil females, through their involvement in combat activity, have changed
their positioning within society, while at the same time maintaining some

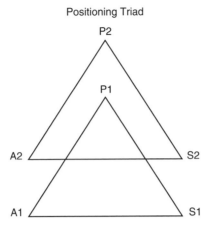

Positioning Triad

A1 = Initial Act S1 = Initial Storyline P1 = Initial Positioning

A2 = New Act S2 = New Storyline P2 = New Positioning

Figure 3.1 Positioning Triad

of the fabric of their former culture. For instance, despite the women entering the ranks of the LTTE, it never became a fully integrated force. Though in combat together, the two groups maintain separate training camps, thereby consciously maintaining a division between males and females. While Nepali and Eritrean women fighters may have integrated with their male counterparts at the front lines, this integration does not appear to have translated to their civilian lives—the men and women that once fought on the front lines together returning to their separate lives in post-conflict times.

In reference to the positioning triad above, it appears that some combatant women, especially those that were a part of the EPLF, NPLA, and LTTE, have achieved relative degrees of emancipation and thereby repositioned themselves and their storylines within their cultures. At this point, I hypothesize that their supposed emancipation and repositioning may have become what is referred to as their chosen glory. Vamik Volken refers to chosen glory as being "[t]he mental representation of a historical event that induces feelings of success and triumph. Usually such triumphs are deserved victories over another group" (Volkan 1997, 81). He goes on to say that new life is often breathed into chosen glories in order to augment the group's self-worth, and like chosen traumas, they too "become heavily mythologized over time" (Volkan 1997, 81).

Women's Involvement in Eritrea's Struggle

> Reactions of surprise, or even incredulity, were not so uncommon in the beginning, because it was taken for granted that we were fragile and unsuited for certain kinds of work. However, when they saw how actively we participated in the struggle, they came to realize how wrong they had been. Fighters in the frontline have had to take the guns out of the hands of their dead women comrades before burying them. They realize that women too are making Eritrean history.
>
> Nuria, 23-year-old female (Gil 1981, 14)

In 1961, the Eritrean Liberation Front (ELF) was formed with a 13-member army (Gil 1981, 76). The Horn of Africa entered into what has now become Africa's longest standing war, a conflict that has taken the lives of more than one million people (Medhanie 1986). Araya Tsegai claims that Eritreans have been fighting their colonial oppressors since 1941, "at first through peaceful political means and later ...through armed struggle" (Tsegai 1988, 67). A majority of the ELF members were young people with aspirations for an independent state. However, the leadership and actions of the ELF began to be viewed by the younger generation as being neocolonialist (Tsegai 1988, 76). This caused friction within the ELF, as the younger recruits began to agitate. The ELF's leadership responded by killing about 500 of the fighters who were demanding change within the group. The Eritrean People's Liberation Front (EPLF) splintered from the ELF in 1971. This split led to a civil war in Eritrea, at the end of which the EPLF emerged as that country's primary liberation movement. The manifesto of the EPLF explicitly stated that they would "not only fight the enemy and set up an independent Eritrean Government, but would also go beyond this in order to bring about fundamental changes in the life of the Eritrean people" (Tesgai 1988, 76).

An area that saw immediate change was that of women's involvement in the liberation struggle. Unlike previous liberation struggles around the world, such as the Troubles in Ireland where women played support roles, one of the distinct dynamics of the Eritrean struggle against Ethiopian occupation was the involvement of women in armed conflict. Susan Leisure notes, "An outstanding feature of the Eritrean struggle for independence was the heavy participation of women in the fighting force" (Leisure 1999). The National Union of Eritrean women was first launched by the men in the Eritrean People's Liberation Front, an action that implied they were in fact committed to the concept of women's empowerment, or they were in dire need of the (wo)manpower necessary to forge ahead with the national liberation struggle (Leisure 1999, 95). Both of these concepts will be revisited in the analysis section of this paper. Whatever their reasoning might have been, at the end of the 30-year war, women made up approximately one-third of the EPLF, occupying leadership roles and serving at the front lines along with the men (Bernal 2000).

> Just as there is no donkey without horns, so there is no woman with brains.—Eritrean proverb (National Union of Eritrean Women 1980a, 12)

As in many traditional societies, women in Eritrea occupied a lower station in life compared to men, merely by virtue of birth. In rural parts of the country, both men and women were involved in agricultural production. Most often the men tilled the land and threshed grain, and women were tasked with weeding the farms and harvesting produce. Despite their involvement in production, these women were denied ownership and control of the land. They were "excluded from any direct land ownership, the father has the full rights of users (ownership) and in the privately owned lands, the right to bequeath it to his heirs, who are almost invariably his sons or male relatives" (National Union of Eritrean Women 1980a, 11). This condition was not restricted to women in poor rural areas of Eritrea. Women in urban Eritrea suffered a fate similar to their peasant sisters (National Union of Eritrean Women 1980a, 11). Even illness and the birth of a child were not reason enough to lay women off from their jobs.

While the Eritrean masses were subject to oppression at the hands of the Ethiopian government and its officials, the patriarchal system that existed in Eritrea further suppressed women in their homes as well as in workplaces and society in general. This has led to many experts speculating that the power asymmetry that existed in Eritrean society may have been a contributing factor in women's involvement in armed conflict.

> Yes, in Eritrea, women are emerging from their feudal heritage, destroying the old order, posing a challenge to the new society. For them, the struggle for their country's liberation in no way distracts from their own. Pilar Gil (Gil 1981, 16)

Prior to their official entry into the EPLF, women in Eritrea supported the nationalist troops in a number of ways by providing them food and shelter, acting as informants, and signaling enemy movements. Women were also known to have taken it upon themselves to grind hot peppers and throw them into the eyes of Ethiopian troops (National Union of Eritrean Women 1980a, 14). Despite the fact that few Eritrean women were allowed to attend school, this did not stop them from taking to the streets and participating in student protests against Ethiopian suppression. Many women faced imprisonment for their actions (National Union of Eritrean Women 1980a, 14). In 1967, out of their own initiative, female factory workers decided to begin contributing 10 percent of their monthly earnings to the EPLF (National Union of Eritrean Women 1980a, 15).

Beginning in the early 1970s, after decades of having played support roles in the liberation struggle, women were finally able to mobilize and participate in the armed struggle as members of the EPLF. Tens of thousands of women (workers, peasants, and members of the urban bourgeoisie)abandoned their roles as daughters and sister, and sometimes even as wives and mothers, and took to the battlefield, joining the EPLF alongside men and taking on a number of different roles, including that of the combat fighter.

Thus, Eritrean women did not limit themselves to playing mere support roles and are said to have been ruthless on the battlefield. If female emancipation factored into women's enlistment in the armed struggle in Eritrea, could it be possible that these women employed extreme levels of violence as a means of proving their worth? Do women who have suffered repression at the hands of patriarchal structures feel the need to establish themselves as capable actors in what was previously strictly a man's world? "As Members of the Eritrean People's Liberation Army, Eritrean women are resolutely fighting as combat leaders or regulars and have shown unsurpassed heroism in hand to hand combat, blowing up tanks with hand-grenades and capturing their occupants" (National Union of Eritrean Women 1980a, 19).

An EPLF fighter, Sara Ogbagergis-Dubarwa, states that the challenge is to demonstrate her bravery and ability as a soldier in order to win respect from the men both at the front and in her village near Asmara. She believed that success on the battlefield would create changes in Eritrea's traditional patriarchal society. "We are showing by our power that we can do the same things as men," she said. "We can go back into society and society will understand, 'Okay, women should not just do house work'. In this way we will be able to participate in every aspect of life" (Gilmore 1999).

"All these feats of heroism which Eritrean women are demonstrating in practice is tearing apart the reactionary feudal myth that women are weaklings" (National Union of Eritrean Women 1980b). Not unlike women in other resistance movements such as the Sri Lankan LTTE, Eritrean women, too, appear to have adopted heightened levels of violence in order to prove their equality on the battlefield. "Female soldiers are also recruited because of their desire to prove themselves, which encourages male soldiers to do their best" (Bouta et al. 2005, 13). This analysis of women in combat by Bouta et al. may in fact ring true in the case of Eritrea.

> In the past, when I discovered that any of my female relatives, let alone my wife, or even neighbors, had left the house without my consent, I used to beat them. I find it hard to believe the transformation which I've undergone. Look … my sister is discussing with me here and we work alongside each other in the people's assembly. It took a long time, but I have come not only to accept that the emancipation of women is necessary for the revolution, but to actively work for it. El Amin (Gil 1981, 22)

Social reforms were achieved as a result of efforts by not only the men in the EPLF but also due to the hard work of the women's and peasants' associations that had formed during the war. Nineteen seventy-seven appears to have been a watershed year in the history of the restructuring of gender relations in Eritrea. The EPLF adopted and administered a land reform policy during this period. With the redistribution of land, women became the legal owners of property for the first time in the nation's history. "[L]arge tracts of land were redistributed to the landless and poor peasant. For the first time, women were given lands in equal share to that of the men. The customs and conditions of centuries were broken down as women were encouraged to put their hands to a plow" (Gil 1981, 20).

Land reform was not the only change achieved during this period. The second regular meeting of the central committee of the EPLF took place in November 1977. The practice of polygamy was abolished and banned at this meeting, and a new law was passed against the institution of compulsory marriage—from 1977 on, marriage would be based on "free consent, and the equality of rights between husband and wife" (Gil 1981, 15). The law would also protect women and children in the instance of divorce.

Female Involvement in the Peoples War of Nepal

> *Today, the image of tired malnourished women carrying children at one end and rearing cattle at the other end has been transformed into the image of dignified fighting women with guns.*
>
> Hsila Yami (Manchanda 2010, 9)

Rita Manchanda (2010) notes that during the ten-year "Peoples War" in Nepal, women were integral to the economic and political life of the country. She notes with half of male householders caught up in seasonal migration, and women being the mainstay of subsistence agriculture, it was essential to mobilize women for the agrarian-based revolution in revolutionary struggle. Property rights for women were a key demand in the Maoist 1995 Mann charter. Moreover, overriding traditional constraints, the Maoists opened up the fighting ranks to women. The result was the mass visibility of illiterate women, the majority from indigenous communities, in the movement—as propagandists and mobilizers, party cadres and district secretaries and above all as soldiers in the people's militia and People's Liberation Army (9).

Gautam et al. (2001, 215) state that, in the case of Nepal's Maoist People's Liberation Army (NMPLA), every third guerilla was a woman. National Public Radio (NPR) estimates female participation in the NMPLA was as high as 50 percent. Many females participated at the front lines of combat and carried out activities such as seizing banks, conducting strategic bombings, and performing assassinations. In an interview with National Public Radio (NPR), Comrade Parvati, one of the most senior women in the Maoist insurgency, stated that "[Women] participation has been phenomenal, sometimes even surpassing that of men" (National Public Radio 2008). Sources state that, although the NMPLA required that at least two women be a part of each squad, by 2005 the number of women recruits had skyrocketed, and one in every three soldiers was a woman. Their ranks varied from that of commanders to vice commanders and political commissars.

In an article titled "Women's Participation in People's War in Nepal," Comrade Parvati discusses what she believes are the key sources of women's oppression in Nepalese society and thus those factors responsible for increasing participation in the insurgency (Parvati 2009) In her article, Comrade Parvati talks about the oppression faced by women in three key aspects of life, economy, society, and politics. It was commonly believed by the Maoist women that existing "feudal" systems of production and economics left women marginalized. The "patrilinear and patrifocal" nature of land ownership and agriculture was the main reason for the economic oppression of women. The fact that women cannot inherit tenancy or paternal property only made it more difficult for them to get equal access to loans and the banking system in general and grossly limited their opportunity for economic growth. This was especially evident in the Terai region of Nepal where remnants of ancient social "etiquettes" of serfdom and debt slavery made women highly vulnerable at the hands of their landlords and often subjected to "voluntary" labor and sex services to the landlord's families (von Furer-Haimendorf 1956, 15–38). High levels of human trafficking and the sexual exploitation of rural women reported in the urban centers of Nepal also contributed to the social stratification of Nepalese men and women.

Nepalese women have long been considered victims of other forms of social oppression as a result of the ethnic, political, and cultural framework of their society. Economic participation, lineal inheritance, and political involvement were reserved for the men in the family. This often led to high female feticide and infant-girl mortality rates. These gross inequalities subjugated women and rendered them politically mute for centuries. The lack of laws to support paternal inheritance for women, educational empowerment, and economic sustenance thoroughly dented the status of women in Nepal. Given the economic and educational disadvantage, there were no open avenues for women to express their political will and exercise their rights in society.

The Maoists capitalized on these conditions to create an agenda addressing the emancipation of women in Nepalese society. They started a women's wing under the central committee of the party to mobilize women across Nepal to participate in the "New Democratic Revolution." There have been reports that the Maoist Communist Party of Nepal (CPN) had joined with the All Nepalese Women's Association supported by the Unified Marxist Leninists (UML) in creating a special task force for addressing women's issues (www.dawn.com 1998). The Maoist women's revolutionary wing cited the complete elimination of women's economic, social, and political oppression as their primary agenda. The main theme of this agenda was to address the inequality of paternal land inheritance in society. The Maoists claimed that the People's War would instill an agrarian society with women sharing equal access to land and property with men, in both rural and urban areas. They also claimed that by creating an antifeudal "New Democratic System," the religionization of Nepal would be prevented, and, instead, a secular state would be established. This would, in their opinion, eliminate the patrifocal culture in Nepal and, hence, remove bias against women.

Despite well-known atrocities against women and children, the Maoists have been fairly successful in recruiting female guerillas. The representation of women in the People's Liberation Army (PLA) had grown threefold in 2004 as compared to when it started, and a few women were active members in the central committee and the politburo (www.dawn.com 1998). The reason for their success is not hard to comprehend given their claims of emancipating the women in their society. The CPN (Maoist) had devoted a separate section to women and family in its policy manifesto, promising that under Maoist rule, "all forms of patriarchal exploitation of women shall be ended, and women shall be given all rights equal to men. Like son, daughter shall enjoy equal rights to parental property" (http://www.ucpnm.org/english/doc11.php).

Women would be provided with special rights for participating in all organs of the state (http://www.cpnm.org/worker/issue8/urpc.htm). They also vowed to eradicate commercial sex work, take harsh action against traffickers, permit only marriage by mutual consent, permit abortion, and give special consideration to women in divorce proceedings (http://www.cpnm.org/worker/issue8/urpc.htm). Cultural indoctrination programs held at rural centers had a powerful impact on the villagers who have seldom been exposed to political and motivational speeches. By addressing and listening to their grievances, the villagers felt that the Maoists were empathizing with and sharing their concerns (Schneiderman et al. 2004). The villagers became appreciative of the efforts of the Maoists to speak to them, ask the villagers' opinion on important national topics, and treat them with respect. Men and women were informed of their individual responsibility in changing the economic and political landscape of Nepal. They were encouraged to become active agents of political change and empower themselves out of a deep history of marginalization (Schneiderman et al. 2004).

Violence and the Repositioning of the Tamil Woman

A boy will grow to be a man. This is why he should get food early. A girl grows up to serve the man. She cannot reach further than womanhood.

(Skjonsberg 1982)

In pre-1983[2] Tamil society, the actions of females were restricted by the position that they occupied. The civil war in Sri Lanka officially erupted in the late summer of 1983 after the bloody riots of July that in a matter of five days took the lives of thousands of Tamils in the country's capital, Colombo. This event is known as Black July and is considered by some Tamils to be their own "genocide".

In a speech Velupillai Prabhakaran, the former LTTE's leader, stated

The women's wing of our liberation movement has contributed substantially to advance the legitimate struggle of our oppressed people. The courage, determination and commitments of our women fighters have awakened the patriotic spirit of the female masses and has mobilized them toward the cause of national liberation.

Thus post-1983 Sri Lanka has seen a major shift in the actions of Tamil women in the Northern and Eastern provinces, especially those that became involved in armed combat. This signifies a shift in their position, and caused a change in their storyline.

> After being born the next social event in the life of a child is the day of the first rice meal. If the child is a boy this takes place after 6 months, if it is a girl after 7 months. A saying guides this traditional practice: 'A boy will grow to be a man. This is why he should get food early. A girl grows up to serve the man. She cannot reach further than womanhood. (Skjonsberg 1982, 45)

This passage is from Else Skjonsberg's ethnography of Thoppikudu, a predominantly Tamil village in the north of Sri Lanka, in which she paints a vivid and relatively accurate picture of the role of the woman in that society. The research for this ethnography was carried out in the late 1970s and the book published merely a year prior to women official entering into combat activity with the LTTE. Was this group of Tamil women so blinded by their grief, by their loss, that they were willing to turn themselves into perpetrators of even greater violence than had been bestowed on them? Or is there more to this brutality? Could it be that the dual nature of their oppression created a more than usual sense of group identity, which thereby led to stronger feelings of chosen trauma and chosen glory (Volkan 1997, 81)?

> In a statement made on March 8, 1993, the leader of the LTTE, Velupillai Pirabaharan, asserted: "… The ideology of women liberation is a child born out of the womb of our liberation struggle.… The Tamil Eelam revolutionary woman has transformed herself as a Tiger for the liberation of our land and liberation of women (http://www.tamilnation.org/ltte/vp/women/vp9303.htm) and "In the field, Tiger fighters, especially the women cadres, display a fantastic degree of ferocity and motivation—so much so that they have won the respect of their foes" (http://www.tamilnation.org/ltte/vp/women/vp9303.htm).

The statement made by Prabhakaran indicates a heroic vision of a group that commands a great deal of respect in society and maintains a position that is, at the very least, equal to that enjoyed by men within the same culture. Adele Ann Balasingham (1993) in her book *Women Fighters of Tamil* states that female Tigers have taken up a life "outside a normal woman's life"

(2). She goes on to say, "Training and carrying weapons, confronting battle conditions, enduring the constant emotional strain of losing close associates, facing death almost every day, are situations that most women not only wish to avoid, but feel ill at ease with" (2).

The LTTE, in what it claimed was its efforts to create equality among its male and female cadres, put women through the same rigorous training routines. Balasingham states that there is evidence suggesting that females were given the same roles and responsibilities as their male counterparts: "... [T]hey conduct suicide bombings, they are trained and prepared like men, they are given arms and taught how to use them, and they must carry a cyanide capsule with them which they are to take in the event of capture" (Beyler 2004, 7). The question remains, Did these women join men in the role of combat solely due to the basic secessionist goals of the LTTE, or was there another gender-intrinsic factor propelling their violence? Might it be that through their actions they were making a statement to their own patriarchal society? Might it be that these women were attempting to prove that they were equal to men by fighting on the front lines alongside their male counterparts?

When the Sri Lankan Army launched a major offensive in 1995 to regain the Jaffna Peninsula (location of the capital of the Northern Province, Jaffna), some male cadres felt that female cadres would not be able to withstand the heavy fighting. Tamilachi, a former cadre, said "... many LTTE men felt female members would not be able to cope and wanted them to flee with civilians" (Alison in http://www2.warwick.ac.uk/fac/soc/pais/staff/alison/research/women_as_agents_/womenasagents.pdf). However, the female units insisted on remaining on the battlefield and, at the end of the encounter, had been viewed as heroes by even those that had requested them to leave the battleground previously (Alison in http://www2.warwick.ac.uk/fac/soc/pais/staff/alison/research/women_as_agents_/womenasagents.pdf). If their objective was to be viewed as equals to men, they had certainly achieved their goal in this particular instance. But the question remains, Is violence these women's only ticket to equality?

Conclusion

Bouta et al. (2005, 9) state that "*[k]ey development challenges* are to acknowledge women's and men's participation in armies, and to target *all* women that joined the armies—with or without weapons—with assistance." Instead of viewing women solely as innocent bystanders of conflict, one must acknowledge that thousands of women join armed groups as combatants to achieve social emancipation. Only once we have acknowledged this fact and found the root causes of these women's violence will we be successful at countering this trend.

Various liberation and revolutionary movements have included women's rights and equality for men and women in their programs for political change" (Bouta et al. 2005, 12–13). Unfortunately such liberation achieved in battle does not always transfer to postwar society, and women are required to return to prewar social norms. However, this concept is difficult to comprehend at the point when the AK-47 one is holding has begun to earn the respect of males on the battlefield and women begin to experience more freedom and emancipation than they ever had prior to taking up arms.

In conclusion, it is clear from these case studies of women who became collectively violent in Eritrea, Nepal, and Sri Lanka that isolated sources and triggers do not by themselves create violent conflict. They operate in a system. This further indicates that the structures that create sources should be transformed in order to prevent such high levels of violence from breaking out. John Paul Lederach states that peace building is more than merely returning to the previous status quo. He says that peace building is about transforming structures. How do you really address the issue of structural violence? You can only do this by changing the structure. Altering structures might demand some sort of conflict—constructive conflict in the form of social change brought about by nonviolent actions or movements.

Keywords

culture, Eritrea, EPLF, female combatants, Nepal, NMPLA, LTTE, patriarchy, repositioning, Sri Lanka

Questions

1. Does culture play a role in women's decisions to adopt violence and join armed groups, especially nonstate armed groups? Explain.
2. What other nonstate armed groups have recruited women, citing their emancipation as a recruiting tool?
3. How are their experiences similar to the female combatants in Eritrea, Nepal, and Sri Lanka?
4. If extreme patriarchal structures are a contributing factor in women's decisions to take up arms, what steps can be taken to prevent women's adoption of violence?

5. What role if any does education, specifically gender-mainstreaming education, play in preventing women's adoption of violence?

References

Bernal, Victoria. 2000. "Equality to Die For? Women Guerilla Fighters and Eritrea's Cultural Revolution." *Politcal and Legal Anthropology Review*, 23(2), 61–76.

Beyler, Clara. 2003. "Messengers of Death: Female Suicide Bombers." International Policy Institute for Counter-Terrorism (ICT) (accessed March 7, 2004).

Bouta, Tsjeard, George Frerks, and Ian Bannon. 2005. *Gender, Conflict, and Development*. Washington: The International Bank for Reconstruction and Development/The World Bank.

DeVotta, Neil. 2002. "South Asia Faces the Future: Illiberalism and Ethnic Conflict in Sri Lanka." *Journal of Democracy*, 13(1), 84–98.

Gautam, Shobha, Amrita Banskota, and Rita Manchanda. 2001. "Where There Are No Men: Women in the Maoist Insurgency in Nepal," in Rita Manchanda (ed.), *Women, War and Peace in South Asia: Beyond Victimhood to Agency* (pp. 214–51). New Delhi, India: Sage Publications India Pvt Ltd.

Gil, Pilar. 1981. "Eye Witness Reports and Testimonies on the Role of Women in the Eritrean Revolution." In *Women in the Eritrean Revolution*, edited by National Union of Eritrean Women: National Union of Eritrean Women.

Gilmore, Inigo. 1999. "Women Hold the Line in Africa's Forgotten War." Dehai News Mailig List Archive.

Haile, Semere. 1988. "Historical Background to the Ethiopia-Eritrea Conflict," in Lionel Cliffe and Basil Davidson (eds), *The Long Struggle of Eritrea for Independence and Constructive Peace* (pp. 13–20). Nottingham, England: Russell Press Ltd.

Leisure, Susan. 1999. "Exchanging Participation for Promises: Mobilization of Women in Eritrea," in Jill M. Bystydzienski and Joti Sekhon (eds), *Democratization and Women's Grassroots Movements* (pp. 95–110). Bloomington: Indiana University Press.

Manchanda, Rita. 2010. "Nepali Women Seize the New Political Dawn: Resisting Marginalisation after Ten Years of War." Center for Humanitarian Dialogue.

Medhanie, Tesfatsion. 1986. *Eritrea: Dynamics of a National Question*. Amsterdam: B.R. Gruner.

National Union of Eritrean Women. 1980a. *Women and Revolution in Eritrea*. Rome, Italy: National Union of Eritrean Women.

National Union of Eritrean Women. 1980b. "Women in the Eritrean Revolution: Eye Witness Reports and Testimonies." National Union of Eritrean Women.

Pateman, Roy. 1990. *Eritrea: Even the Stones Are Burning*. Trenton, N.J.: The Red Sea Press, Inc.

Pruitt, Dean G., and Sung Hee Kim. 2004. *Social Conflicts: Escalation, Stalemate, and Settlement*, 3rd edn. New York: McGraw Hill.

Rhodes, Richard. 2000. *Why They Kill*, 1st edn. New York: Vintage Books.

Skjonsberg, Else. 1982. *A Special Caste? Tamil Women of Sri Lanka*, 1st edn. London: Zed Pres Ltd.

Trevaskis, Gerald Kennedy Nicholas. 1960. *Eritrea: A Colony in Transition*, 1941–52. London: Oxford University Press.

Tseggai, Araya. 1988. "The History of the Eritrean Struggle," in Lionel Cliffe and Basil Davidson (eds), *The Long Struggle of Eritrea for Independence and Constructive Peace*. Nottingham, England: Russell Press Ltd.

Volkan, Vamik. 1997. *Blood Lines: From Ethnic Pride to Ethnic Terrorism*, 2nd edn. Boulder, Colo.: Westview Press.

CHAPTER FOUR

Dying for Identity: Chechnya and Sri Lanka

Maneshka Eliatamby and Ekaterina Romanova

Introduction

The past three decades have seen a surge in suicide terrorism, beginning with the first attack in Beirut[1] in December 1981 (Foreign Policy Association). Less than two years later, in October 1983 once again in Beirut, two suicide bombers killed almost 300 American and French peacekeepers by driving explosive-laden trucks into military barracks. The first official record of a female suicide bomber is that of Sana'a Mehaidli who drove a vehicle laden with explosives into an Israeli Defense Force installation in Lebanon in 1985[2] (Zedalis 2004). Within just a few years, suicide terrorism as a tactic spread to a number of countries across the globe, ranging from Israel to Sri Lanka, from the Russian Federation to Kenya, Tanzania, Great Britain, Iraq, and Afghanistan. In the span of just a few decades, women became increasingly involved in terrorist activities in more than a dozen countries worldwide.

Willingness to die in order to inflict pain and cause massive destruction on one's enemy defies the common belief of self-preservation. The mere idea of women participating in such acts seems even more repugnant to some, and others deny even the existence of female suicide bombers. It strongly contradicts the common belief of the woman as the "giver of life". Suicide attacks are often attributed to irrationality, fanaticism, extremism, and the "pure" craziness of perpetrators (Hoffman 2006). This chapter explores women's agency by analyzing their engagement in suicide terrorism, acknowledging that, while women are often victims of war and terrorism, they are also perpetrators in the form of suicide bombers. Assessing women's involvement in terrorist activities in Chechnya and Sri Lanka, this chapter clarifies some of the widespread misunderstandings about female suicide terrorism and addresses the following four questions:

1. What causes women to engage in suicide terrorism?
2. Does participation of women allow terrorist organizations to reap greater benefits?
3. Is there a difference in the effects of male and female suicide terrorism?
4. What role do women play in warfare that involves the use of terror as a tactic?

Background

Suicide terrorism presents one of the deadliest and "unconventional" forms of warfare, with its destructive potential, profound fear, insecurity, and apprehension of imminent threat that continuously looms over the public. Unfortunately, this act of terrorism raises more questions than there are satisfactory answers: What motivates terrorist organizations to choose suicide attacks as a strategy of war? Why are some organizations more likely to employ suicide terrorism than others? What motivates group members to pursue these horrific tactics? What are the countermeasures to suicide terrorism?

Analysts and scholars offer ranging explanations and accounts of suicide terrorism. Some describe suicide attackers as "deranged" fanatics and apply psychoanalysis to the study of these individuals. Others offer psychological explanations that range from claiming the vulnerable mental state of an individual to abuse and manipulation that drives individuals to engage in acts of suicide terrorism. While these psychological arguments provide some insight into the driving forces of suicide terrorism, they fail to recognize the agency of people carrying out those acts. There is also evidence that many suicide cadres are enticed by witnessing the elite status and privileges afforded to the families of suicide cadres who have carried out their missions—this is especially true in the case of the LTTE. While this is an important factor, this is not specific to the female suicide bombers.

Religious extremism, particularly radical Islamic beliefs, is often weaved into the discussion surrounding the rise of suicide terrorism in the modern world (Rapoport 1990; Harris 2005; Iannaccone 2006; Europol 2007). Ideas of extremism, indoctrination, and martyrdom persist in many analyses (Rapoport 1990; Hoffman 2006). Such beliefs of religious fervor are often deceptive and are based on the popular idea of cultural differences causing a "clash of civilizations" (Huntington 1996). The theory of religious extremism, however, fails to explain high numbers of suicide terrorist attacks carried out by the Liberation Tigers of Tamil Eelam (LTTE) in Sri Lanka or by Chechen rebels in the Russian Federation, as well as in other parts of the world. Neither of these groups is particularly religious in nature, with the LTTE having claimed to be a group that espoused Marxist beliefs.

Robert Pape (2005) argues that the perception or presence of foreign forces is one of the major reasons behind suicide terrorism. Alan Krueger and Jitka Maleckova (2003) cite such socioeconomic reasons as extreme poverty, lack of education, and the denial of basic human needs as circumstances and preconditions leading to suicide terrorism. At the same time, there are numerous examples where people live in profound poverty, endure protracted and violent conflicts, and suffer tremendous deprivation without turning into violent perpetrators willing to take the lives of others as well as their own. The deprived basic human needs argument[3] finds little support in the accounts of personal stories of many suicide bombers. Large numbers of those participating in terrorist activities do not conform to the widely held image of a young, poor, desperate, and radical male but rather tend to be educated, of middle-class backgrounds, and promising opportunities in life (Iannacone 2006).

This chapter recognizes that no single theory or hypothesis can explain the phenomenon of suicide terrorism. Profiling these perpetrators presents a practical challenge, where the complexity of the situation, socioeconomic context, type of conflict, as well as the psychological predisposition of the individuals are among the multiple small pieces that make up a much larger puzzle of suicide terrorism. This puzzle is further complicated when gender is added to the picture. Increasingly women's names are added to the growing list of suicide terrorists. One cannot help but wonder what this "innovation" in the form of female participation contributes to suicide terrorism. The tactical advantages, the fear factor, and its continuous spread make suicide terrorism an already "successful" warfare technique. Robert Pape (2005) convincingly argues that suicide terrorism works because it pays off well.

The Chechen Black Widows

The Russian Federation is a country where female suicide terrorism has become a gruesome reality. In Russia, women who carry out terrorist attacks are known as Black Widows[4]—their black dresses and the dark attire that covers their bodies from head to toe becoming a trademark, symbolizing their personal loss/es resulting from the Chechen wars. Black Widows are believed to be responsible for a number of fatal attacks in multiple Russian cities over the past decade, some of the deadliest being the Moscow metro bombings in the early 2000s and as recent as in April 2010, the rock concert attack in 2003, two simultaneous plane explosions in 2004, and the hostage sieges in a Moscow theater in 2002 and in a Beslan school in 2004.[5]

Terrorist tactics and particularly the use of women in such attacks are associated with the two subsequent military campaigns in Chechnya (1994–1996; 1999–2005), but it was the second war that produced and frequented the use of this form of terrorism. To provide some background, the conflict between the Russian Federation and Chechen rebels evolved over time beginning as a secessionist movement that turned into a full-blown war between 1994 and 1996. In 1999, the second war in Chechnya started as a counterterrorist operation and, following the September 11, 2001, attacks in the United States, was folded into the broader global fight against terrorism (Hill 2002; Baev 2006).

Russia's policies in Chechnya, profound lawlessness, the ruthlessness of both Russian and Chechen military personnel, the pervasive disregard for human lives, a somewhat questionable human rights record, and habitual violence are some of the causes attributed to radicalization of the second Chechen war and the increase in the use of terrorist tactics (Kramer 2004; Ware 2005). Others argue that suicide tactics are weapons of the weak, aimed at creating mass spectacles, instilling fear in the minds of the public, and manipulating the government of a more powerful adversary (Madsen 2004). There is no justification for such horrendous acts that aim to inflict pain and cause as much destruction and human loss as possible, but it is important to understand what drives people (and women in the case of female suicide terrorism) to pull the trigger of the bomb strapped to their bodies and inflict pain and destruction on their fellow citizens.

Women are responsible for more than 68 percent of all suicide attacks committed in the Russian Federation (Reuter 2004). Since the first attack by a female, Hawa Baraeva and her female accomplice killed two and injured five Russian special forces officers in June 2000 at the military posts in Alkhan-Yurt (Zedalis 2004), female suicide attackers became a reality in the country. A large number of attempts to draw a profile of a female suicide bomber in Chechnya produced varying descriptions. A majority of these profiles yield an image of emotionally unstable women who are forced to join terrorist groups out of unbearable grief, despair, misery, and poverty produced by the wars. They are believed to have lost loved ones to military campaigns, counterterrorist or cleansings operations carried out by the Russian military and law enforcement personnel. The grief and psychological trauma sustained during the war motivates these women to seek revenge for the death of their loved ones—husbands, brothers, fathers, and sons who died or disappeared during the military campaigns. The accounts of the mental and emotional conditions of female terrorists are often secondhand and sketchy. The nature of the attacks encompasses elimination of the perpetrator and possible links to the organizers of the assault. There are only a few surviving suicide terrorists from Chechnya, captured because they failed to carry out the attacks. Their testimonies, as well as statements by the survivors, are often conflicting, depicting very different images of the female terrorist.

Victims of the Dubrovka theater siege, for example, say that women terrorists told them horrific stories about their lives and hardships in Chechnya (Groskop 2004; Murphy 2004). Some accounts cite sexual violence used against women to force them into terrorist groups (Groskop 2004; PeaceWomen 2004). Rebel groups use various methodologies to recruit women, such as drugging, blackmailing, and showing videotaped rapes to the Chechen women's families in order to brainwash women and force them into terrorist activities. Regardless of the recruitment techniques, women are selected based on the assumption that they have experienced personal "life drama" and, consequently, can be easily manipulated (PeaceWomen 2004).

The image of an emotionally unstable Chechen female terrorist, who is highly traumatized, coerced, or drugged (Baker 2004) may provide some explanation as to why women commit those acts of terror, but in many ways, it takes the "agency" away from them, leaving the power in the hands of those who recruit and manipulate the women. Such an image tries to justify a behavior that is believed to be uncharacteristic for women and suggest that they are forced to commit acts of terror by their life circumstances, by people around them, or because they are simply emotionally unstable. The extent of violence, the persistency of terrorist activities over time, their elaborate nature, and the constantly rising number of victims of terrorist attacks in Russia initiated by women forces one to question the nature of women's involvement. Also, the women's role in the two hostage-taking incidences in Moscow and Beslan, where children were among the casualties, challenges the stereotypical image of women as caretakers. Moreover, the personal characteristics of those women, such as their degree of religiosity, education level, and marital status, may also challenge the psychological argument of why women engage in terrorism. It is recognized that the Black Widows differ in their profile from female suicide bombers in other countries. They tend to be educated, older, married, and have children (Speckhard and Akhmedova 2005). It is the combination of the factors such as personal trauma, religious fervor, terrorist support, and networking that create conditions where women are likely to join the rank of suicide bombers (ibid.). It is often also the response of the population that encourages the use of women in terrorist activities (Pape 2005). In Russia, there is a growing recognition of the role and extent of women's participation in the terrorist activities, which leads to a significant shift in public opinion about women terrorists and government's tactics to tackle this problem (Speckhard and Akhmedova 2005). No longer are women perceived as unwilling participants. They became active agents of terrorism, inhuman perpetrators who are seen as having "lost" their feminine or womanly nature. They created a new image of themselves of agendered or malelike individuals in their readiness and willingness to kill other civilians, particularly children.

A logical question about the role and reason of women's participation in terrorist missions in the Russian Federation intrigues many analysts (Groskop 2004; Zedalis 2004; Speckhard and Akhmedova 2005). Were women used for suicide terrorism in Chechen conflict because of its shock effect? Or was it because the rebel groups ran out of other terror tactics to achieve their desirable goal to establish independence in Chechnya? With little doubt, the effect of these heinous acts stunned the country as well as the global community. However, there are strong doubts about their accomplishments. In the Chechnya case, suicide terrorism targeted predominantly civilians, as well as military personnel. In Sri Lanka, on the other hand, many targets were government and military officials. The enemy is clearly identified there as representatives of the power structure, rather than civil society. The attacks in Sri Lanka proved to be "successful" by killing key government and military leadership. In Chechnya, targeting civilians only further disenfranchised the rebels and led to harsher military action and retaliation. The terrorist acts did not seem to pay off in Chechnya as Robert Pape argued (2005). Heavy military and government tactics suppressed rebel movements and actions. Such a response is a temporal solution, though, which leaves the potential to break into severe violence.

The Black Tigress of Death

She walks through the security gate and joins a line of people waiting to be handed a pass to meet with the Minister. It is "public day"—every week the minister sets aside a day to meet with his constituents. There are already quite a few people ahead of her, but she is not in a hurry—after all, it is only the rest of her life that she has to wait. Her demeanor is calm, and she is impeccably dressed in a simple off-white saree—almost like the one she

should have worn at her own wedding. Her turn comes, and after being asked
a few questions she is escorted to a sitting area. There is a problem with her
documentation, and she is told that she needs to first speak with the secretary
to the minister. She walks up to the desk and sits in the chair across from him.
It appears as though she is explaining something to the secretary. He says
something. She nods. She has either received what she wanted already, or she
is being asked to come back another day with more documentation—we will
never know the answer. She nods and stands to leave. She fiddles with her
saree blouse. All we see is a flash of light …

(YouTube 2007)

This describes the events that took place at Minister Douglas Devananda's
office in Colombo, Sri Lanka, on December 3, 2007, just moments before
a suicide bomber took her own life and the lives of several others. For
the first time in the history of terrorism, the entire event was captured by
close circuit surveillance cameras at the government building in Colombo.
The footage was posted on Youtube.com by Sri Lanka's Ministry of Defense
less than a day after the attack. She was not the first female suicide bomber,
and it is doubtful that she will be the last.

In its war with the Government of Sri Lanka (GoSL), the LTTE had
become one of the forerunners of suicide attacks carried out worldwide. The
nonstate armed group's first suicide attack was on July 5, 1987, at a Sri Lankan
Army camp in the town of Nelliady in the Jaffna Peninsula. This attack was
masterminded by Captain Miller, whose act was viewed by the LTTE as one
of heroism and bravery. By 2007, the LTTE had successfully carried out 227
suicide attacks (this number does not include attacks carried out during the
latter part of 2007 or attacks in 2008) (Pape 2005). Seventy-five of the two
hundred and twenty-seven missions were orchestrated and carried out by
women, amounting to more than 33 percent of all suicide attacks committed
by the group (Pape 2005). This elite group of suicide cadres, who called themselves the Black Tigers, was believed to have reshaped terrorism—and suicide
terrorism, in particular—being the architects of the suicide vest, which was
built to fit the form of a woman. This vest designed by the LTTE is used by
many suicide bombers around the world today, including in Israel-Palestine,
Pakistan, Iraq, Afghanistan, Kenya, and Tanzania.

Given the high numbers of females involved in suicide missions in Sri
Lanka, there is a great deal of speculation among scholars and authors as
to the roots and motivations of females who resort to this tactic. Rosemary
Skaine (2006) argues that in Sri Lanka "history has allowed women to
participate in the act … ," while experts such as Robert Pape (2005) cite

occupation or the perception of occupation as one of the main factors motivating women's participation in suicide terrorism.

One of the most prominent suicide bombers in the history of the use of the practice was a 25-year-old Tamil woman, Gayatri, alias Dhanu, who was responsible for the assassination of former Indian Prime Minister Rajiv Gandhi on May 21, 1991 (Bloom 2005). This is the first of only three instances in which a head of state (or former head of state) was the target of such an attack. The late Sri Lankan president Ranasinghe Premadasa's assassination, also carried out by the LTTE, and the assassination of former Pakistani president Benazhir Bhutto are the only other instance. Evidence unearthed after the attack suggests that Dhanu did not act alone but was part of a team that masterminded Gandhi's killing. A woman by the name of Nalini, another member of this team, is currently serving a life sentence in prison in the south Indian state of Tamil Nadu for her active role in Gandhi's death.

It is clear that Gandhi's assassination was a targeted killing, planned to its most minute detail, and carried out like clockwork. There were no mishaps or mistakes. Why, then, did the LTTE target Rajiv Gandhi, and further, why was Dhanu assigned to this particular suicide mission? Such an inquiry requires reviewing a brief history of the few years preceding the attack and the presence of the Indian Peace Keeping Forces (IPKF) in Sri Lanka. On July 29, 1987, India, under the leadership of the late Prime Minister Rajiv Gandhi, signed the historic Indo-Sri Lanka Accord (which many believe the GoSL signed under much duress from the Indian government), a move that was welcomed at the time by LTTE's leadership. The Indo-Lanka Accords gave the IPKF complete freedom to take control of security operations in the Northern and Eastern provinces of the island. Approximately 100,000 members of the Indian armed forces were stationed in Sri Lanka at this time. Despite their initial enthusiasm over India's entrance into Sri Lanka's affairs, the relationship between India and the LTTE soon soured. News of incidences of the mass rapes of Tamil women, the killing of entire families, looting, pillaging, and massacring of villages in the North and East soon began to reach Sri Lanka's capital, Colombo. Before long, the IPKF became known as the "Innocent People Killing Force." This reflects a significant shift in relations between India and the LTTE. It is also symbolic of the trauma experienced by the Tamil people at the hands of the IPKF.

In addition to group trauma felt by those living in the Northern and Eastern provinces of the island, there is also evidence that Dhanu experienced her own individual trauma. Reports suggest that she witnessed her family members being tortured and killed by the IPKF and their home set ablaze by the troops. This not only sheds light on this particular suicide attack but illuminates some of the events that may have factored into Dhanu's decision to become a human bomb. Rajiv Gandhi was participating in a political rally in the south Indian state of Tamil Nadu, in preparation for elections that were scheduled to take place shortly. Gandhi was tipped to achieve a landslide victory at the elections. The LTTE, which did not favor such an outcome, made a successful strike against Gandhi.

Unfortunately Gandhi's assassination was just one among many attacks that were carried out by LTTE and the group's female members. On April 25, 2006, in a suicide mission undertaken by the group, a female assassin disguised herself as being" pregnant in order to gain tactical advantage when carrying out the attack. Sri Lanka's army commander, Lieutenant General Sarath Fonseka, was the intended target of this failed attack. Previously the woman made claims the unborn child's father was a Sri Lanka Army serviceman, a guise by which she was able to gain access to the campus of the Sri Lanka Army headquarters where the medical corps was located.

The LTTE's Black Tigers—the world's first nonstate armed group to boast air power—had a standing resource, the Tamil Eelam Air Force. In one of the best-orchestrated suicide missions by the LTTE, a 21-member Black Tiger suicide team attacked a Sri Lanka Air Force base in Anuradhapura in September 2007. This was one of the group's most recent suicide missions, taking place on September 22, 2007. Writing about the attack, the *Daily Mirror* journalist Sunil Jayasiri claims that this was "a devastating attack on the highly fortified air base" (Jayasiri 2007). According to Jayasiri, the base was the headquarters of forward operations for military activity in the north. All members of the LTTE team carrying out the attack lost their lives, including three high-ranking females. Less than a year later, in September 2008, a group of ten Black Tigers raided the Sri Lanka Air Force base in Vavuniya. The Tiger team consisted of ten members; five were females (*Sri Lanka Daily News* 2008).

These incidents clearly indicate the tactical nature of suicide attacks carried out by the LTTE. Despite analysts' and the mainstream media's depictions of female suicide bombers as deranged and religious extremists, the actions of the Black Tigresses indicate otherwise. What is apparent in the Sri Lankan terrorist case—the Chechen case too—is that one factor alone cannot explain the phenomenon of the female suicide bomber. It is clear that the LTTE understands the advantages of including women in suicide missions and has been successful at harnessing this advantage. In times of war, women are often used as messengers and support staff. In the case of the LTTE, these women are "messengers of death." Women are less prone to security checks and hazards experienced by men. A saree-clad female is capable of camouflaging more than a male can, thereby creating a tactical advantage to use women in their missions.

Further discounting the "deranged" and "religious" arguments is the fact that this group does not carry out random acts of violence. Rather, the violence is tactical in the choice of targets. Even the bus and train bombings that have occurred on the island appear to have had an ulterior motive. They are specifically meant to evoke a sense of fear among the people of Sri Lanka.

In addition to being specific about their targets, the LTTE members are tactical in their choice of attackers. Many of the female assassins are women previously victimized at the hands of the state or by the IPKF, and many perceive themselves as victims. Even those who have not been directly victimized adopt a victim identity and empathize with their sisters. The continued victimization of Tamil women by Sri Lankan and India's IPKF has created what is known as a victim identity among such Tamil women as Dhanu, the one who carried out the assassination of Rajiv Gandhi. During an interview with journalist Jane Goodwin, a failed female suicide cadre stated that she had witnessed the brutal murders of some of her family members by Sri Lankan security forces. It is clear that the LTTE capitalizes on violence experienced by these women to their own advantage. The LTTE also propagandizes the brutality that is experienced by those caught and arrested by security forces, creating a further hatred and fear of the Sri Lankan state apparatus from these women.

Another set of factors that contribute to the surging numbers of female suicide cadres comes from within Tamil culture. Tamil society is traditionally a patriarchal culture where women have lower status and therefore see the adoption of extreme violence as a form of agency. Judging from the narratives of women who have joined the LTTE's Black Tiger Suicide Squad, many claim their goals of achieving equality as one of the reasons to join this group. As Clara Beyler states in *Messengers of Death*, women take on the role of the human bomb not only in the name of their country and religion but also as a way of redefining their gender role in the society from which they come (Beyler 2003). Here we see clear similarities between the Black Widows of Chechnya and the Black Tigresses of Sri Lanka.

Violence experienced as a result of actions by the state, trauma experienced by or identified with women, and LTTE propaganda play a major role in creating the Black Tigress. According to author Cynthia Keppley Mahmood, in her book *Fighting for Faith and Nation* (Mahmood, 1996), female militants in other nonstate armed groups (NSAG), including the

Sikh militants, view women in the LTTE as heroines. She quotes a female Sikh militant as saying "Today people hail that Tamil who killed Rajiv Gandhi..." (Mahmood 1996, x). This sheds light on the implications that female LTTE suicide bombers may have on a more global perspective and calls for more research to be carried out on this phenomenon. This has become ever more clear, as suicide bombings, especially by women, have become a common occurrence in Iraq and Afghanistan during the past several years.

Discussion and Conclusion

Female suicide bombers defy a belief that cuts across time and cultures and portrays women as being nurturing and life giving. Though some women's bodies are a source of life, nurture, care, and love, some also cause death and destruction. In the growing body of literature on female suicide terrorism (Zedalis 2004; Pape 2005; Eager 2008; Ness 2008), there is a slow, yet observable shift from treating women terrorists as victims to understanding that they are willing perpetrators. Arguments about the psychological vulnerability of women as well as the use of force and coercion to lure women into terrorist groups continue to dominate the discussion of suicide terrorism (Speckhard and Akhmedova 2007). Ironically, some such statements follow traditional gender stereotypes and deny the idea of women's active role in terrorist activity. The current popular descriptions of female terrorists reinforce gender stereotypes of women being weak, vulnerable, emotionally unstable, or drugged, and as such easy to manipulate.

The cases of Chechnya and Sri Lanka provide sufficient evidence that it is paramount to understand that female suicide terrorists are simultaneously victims and perpetrators trapped in the calculated logic of men's wars. The growing numbers and persistency of suicide terrorism that employ women more than hint that this horrifying trend is relentless and shows signs of continuity. Analysts and scholars concur (Bloom 2005; Pape 2005) that as long as conflicts, violence, and instances of occupation last, there will be more cases of suicide terrorism and the role and numbers of women intimately involved will grow.

The shock effect of suicide terrorism is a major reason for the persistent nature of this gruesome warfare tactic. Female suicide terrorism is even more distressful and draws more attention. This effect seems grounded in the manner that gender stereotypes, cultural assumptions, or societal barriers are being challenged. There is a profound contradiction in the actions of female terrorists and the ways of portraying them. On the one hand, women's bodies become the source of destruction and death. On the other hand, these women are portrayed within a traditional gender framework, which views them as weak and vulnerable, and only capable of violence, murder and destruction through force, coercion, and manipulation.

The nature of suicide attacks carried out by women demands the reformulation of the rationale behind female suicide missions. The case of female engagement in suicide terrorism in Sri Lanka as well as in Israel, Lebanon, or Algeria, for example, demonstrates that many women eagerly join terrorist organizations and voluntarily become members of suicide groups. Attempts to find explanations of suicide terrorism in religion or extremism are another way to strip away the role of personal choice, individual power, and agency from the actors. In both cases described in this chapter, arguments of religious extremism as a motivating factor find little or no support. Religion is only a lens through which people try to find meaning for one's action but not the source of those actions.

In Chechnya and in Sri Lanka, women consistently act on behalf of a group. Indeed, there are examples of manipulation and coercion in terrorist groups. However, the accent should be placed not on the psychological differences between men and women but on the structure of these organizations. The structural violence embedded in the structure of terrorist groups, as well as society in general positions women in subordinate roles. The structures of a society, in the form of strict traditions and cultural practices that subordinate women and ascribe them their particular roles, often ostracizes women who do not fit into these roles or who are marginalized by life misfortunes. Once women are excluded and are left with few options constructed by the societal structures for them, some become members in terrorist groups, where the organization structure steers them toward suicide missions. In order to find ways to stop suicide terrorism, particularly female terrorism, it is important to find ways to provide for women's basic human needs, to attend to women with acute histories of physical or emotional violence in times of war, and to intentionally integrate them into society. The realization that women are capable of violence challenges gender stereotypes but also strips away the shock effect from the suicide mission, which is one of the reasons for the successful persistency of this tactic.

Keywords

Black Widows, Black Tigresses, Chechnya, female suicide bombers, identity, Indian Peace Keeping Force, Liberation Tigers of Tamil Eelam, nonstate armed group, Russian Federation, Sri Lanka

Discussion Questions

1. What is the role of women in terrorist activities?
2. Why do terrorist organization employ women for their suicide missions?
3. How do you see the role and participation of women in terrorist organization change over time?
4. What measures can be taken to overcome the growing trend of females becoming involved in suicide terrorism?
5. At the conclusion of a war, such as is the case in Sri Lanka, what becomes of women who had been trained to become suicide terrorists? Do they return to society or remain incarcerated for life?

References

Baev, Pavel. 2006. "Has Russia Achieved a Victory in Its War against Terror?" PONARS Policy Memo #415.

Baker, Peter. 2004. "New Stage of Fear for Chechen Women: Russian Forces Suspected in Abductions." *Washington Post.*

BBC. 1991. "Bomb Kills India's Former Leader Rajiv Gandhi.".

BBC. 2010. "Moscow Metro Hit by Deadly Suicide Bombings."

Beyler, Clara. "Messengers of Death: Female Suicide Bombers." International Policy Institute for Counter-Terrorism (ICT), 7 March 2004.

Dolnik, Adam and Richard Pilch. 2003. "The Moscow Theater Hostage Crisis: The Perpetrators, Their Tactics, and the Russian Response." *International Negotiation,* 8(3), 577–611(35).

Eager, Paige Whaley. 2008. *From Freedom Fighters to Terrorists: Women and Political Violence.* Ashgate.

European Police Office. 2007. EU Terrorism Situation and Trend Report. The Hague, The Netherlands: Europol Corporate Communications.

Foreign Policy Association. 2005. http://www.fpa.org/newsletter_info2478/newsletter_info_sub_list.htm?section=Aero-Terrorismerrorism."

Giduck, John. 2005. *Terror at Beslan: a Russian Tragedy with Lessons for America's Schools.* Archangel Group.

Groskop, Viv. 2004. "Women at the Heart of the Terror Cells." *Guardian,* September 5, 2004.

Hagen, Ryan. 2000. *What Makes a Terrorist: Economics and the Roots of Modern Terrorism.* Princeton, N.J.: Princeton University Press.

Harris, Sam. 2005. *The End of Faith: Religion, Terror and the Future of Reason.* New York: W.W. Norton.

Hoffman, Bruce. 2006. *Inside Terrorism.* New York: Columbia University Press.

Iannacone, Laurence. 2006. "The Market for Martyrs." *Interdisciplinary Journal of Research on Religion,* 2.

Jayasiri, Sunil. October 25, 2007. "Anuradhapura Air Base Attack: The Full Story." *Daily Mirror Newspaper.*

Karon, Tony. 2002. "Behind the Moscow Theater Siege." *Time,* October 25, 2002.

Knight, W. Andy, and Tanya Narozhna. 2005. "Social Contagion and the Female Face of Terror: New Trends in the Culture of Political Violence." *Canadian Foreign Policy*, 12(1), 141–66.

Kramer, Mark. 2004/2005. "The Perils of Counterinsurgency: Russia's War in Chechnya." *International Security*, 29(3), 5–63.

Lynch, Dov. 2005. "The enemy is at the gate': Russia after Beslan," *International Affairs*, 81(1), 141–61.

Mahmood, Cynthia Keppley. 1996. *Fight for Faith and Nation: Dialogues with Sikh Militants*. Philadelphia: University of Pennsylvania Press.

Murphy, Kim. 2004. "Black Widows' Caught up in Web of Chechan War." *The Los Angeles Times*. February 7, 2004.

Ness, Cindy. (ed.). 2008. *Female Terrorism and Militancy: Agency, Utility, and Organization*. Routledge.

Pape, Robert A. 2005. *Dying to Win: The Strategic Logic of Suicide Terrorism*. New York: Randon House.

Paper, Robert. 2003. "The Strategic Logic of Suicide Terrorism." *The American Political Science Review*, p. 97.

PeaceWomen. "Women at Heart of the Terror Cells." http://www.peacewomen.org/ news/Chechnya/news.html.

Pedahzur, Ami. 2005. *Suicide Terrorism*, 1st edn. Cambridge, England: Polity Press.

Peuch, Jean-Christophe. 2003. "Suicide Bombers Kill 13 In Moscow; Russia Blames Chechen Separatists." Radio Free Europe/ Radio Liberty. http://www.rferl.org/ content/article/1103732.html.

Radio Free Europe/ Radio Liberty (RFERL). 2004. "Factbox: Major Terrorist Incidents Tied To Russian-Chechen War."

Rapoport, D.C. 1990. "Sacred terror: A case from contemporary Islam," in W. Reich (ed.), *Origins of terrorism* (pp. 103–30). Cambridge, England: Cambridge University Press.

Reuter, John. 2004. "Chechnya's Suicide Bombers: Desparate, Devout, or Deceived?" *The American Committee for Peace in Chechnya*, http://www.peaceinthecaucasus.org/reports/SuicideReport/SuicideReport.pdf

Speckhard, Anne and Akhmedova, Khapta. 2007. "Black Widows: the Chechen Female Suicide Terrorists," in Yoram Schweitzer (ed.) *Female Suicide Terrorists*. Tel Aviv, Israel: Jaffe Center Publications.

Ware, Robert Bruce. 2005. "A Multitude of Evils: Mythology and Political Failure in Chechnya," in Richard Sakwa (ed.), *Chechnya: From Past to Future*, London: Anthem Press.

Zedalis, Debra D. 2004. "Female Suicide Bombers." Strategic Studies Institute www.strategicstudiesinstitute.army.mil/pdffiles/pub408.pdf

CHAPTER FIVE

Fighting Young: Liberia and Sierra Leone

Patricia A. Maulden

Introduction

I had a boyfriend who was a soldier, and I followed him from Freetown to Daru. I was attracted by the uniform. Full combat looks smart. I sent my mother a picture of me in full combat. ... That was the first she knew I had joined. ... Lots of young women followed the rebels because they offered them items, and their regular men did nothing for them.

The quotation, taken from an interview with a female ex-combatant aligned with an irregular unit of the Republic of Sierra Leone Military Force (RSLMF), illustrates part of the story of girl soldiers (Peters and Richards 1998). When asked if she felt it was wrong to fight, this young woman (16 years old when she became a combatant, 20 years old at the time of the interview) stated that she was defending her country. The interviewer inquired if she ever felt sorry for the dead rebels, and she replied:

At first, when we advanced and saw their dead bodies, I would feel sorry for them. ... They would kill us if they had the chance. Rebels kill and split open the bellies of pregnant women. Rebels rape any soldiers they catch ... [Government] soldiers raped us sometimes in the forest, but they are more careful ... The rebels, they all joined in.

She eventually decided to leave the army because of the rank smell of blood and the sight of dead comrades, their arms and legs smashed by RPGs (rocket-propelled grenades). She hoped to become an air hostess but raised doubts about her ability to accomplish this. She had a large tumor on her leg that appeared before she joined the army and had grown progressively and painfully worse.

This poignant interview excerpt highlights some of the realities faced by girl soldiers as they navigate violent environments, confront scarce and questionable opportunities, and exercise agency or control over their circumstances to the greatest extent possible. While this chapter focuses on Sierra Leone and Liberia, girls fill the ranks of most irregular military forces fighting around the world. For these individuals, such experiences can be a fact of everyday life. International and nongovernmental organizations estimate that approximately 300,000 children serve today as child soldiers or persons under 18 years of age associated with fighting forces, the average age just over 12 years. Soldier, as used in this context, includes both combat and support activities. Overall, girls comprise approximately 40 percent or 120,000 of the total number of child soldiers (Brett and McCallin 1998; Save the Children 2005; Global Report 2008; Singer 2010).

Studies exploring causal variables leading to the continued and expanding use of child soldiers worldwide vary widely in their focus, from primordialist views of cultural practices or ethnic divisions to the effects of socioeconomic dislocation, political marginalization or exclusion, the logic or utility of resource appropriation from the child's point of view, or a breakdown of warrior honor (Sesay 2003; Singer 2010). More specifically, the recruitment of girl soldiers, given these additional causal variables, is not an anomaly or incidental occurrence but a widespread and systematic strategy as part of intrastate wars in particular. This chapter narrows the scope of exploration to the experiences of girl soldiers within the contexts of gender and agency, conflict and peace. The discussion begins with an overview of girl soldiers, followed by an exploration of the conceptual frameworks concerning gender and agency. Both of these sections also bring in conflict related dynamics as they impact girl soldiers in the countries profiled. The next section begins the discussion of gender and peace processes that affected girl soldiers in Sierra Leone and Liberia followed by a section that critiques post-conflict gender constructions. The chapter concludes with observations and suggestions.

Girl Soldiers

To begin, gender refers not to the biologically determined but to the socially constructed identities of males and females. Gender roles are assigned early in the socialization process and cut across public and private spheres, shaping definitions of acceptable responsibilities and functions for men and women (and boys and girls) in social and economic activities, in access to resources, and in decision-making authority (Mazurana and Carlson 2004).

Experiences of child soldiering in general can be linked to serious disadvantages, for example, physical injury, sexual abuse, illness, infection, loss of education, trauma, feelings of guilt, fear of retribution, shame, stigmatization, and ostracism by family and community. On the other hand, soldiering can bring situational benefits, in part through individual agency and reappraisal processes to make the most out of very difficult circumstances. Benefits could include finding a sense of purpose, mission, or importance, gaining protection, inclusion, validation, respect, identity, skills, and access to resources (Maulden 2007).

Girls as soldiers balance the two ends of the experiential spectrum, struggling to "play" their environment to ensure their own and their children's survival. That anyone so young must do so seems unthinkable; that tens of thousands of the young do so on a regular basis remains a deplorable fact of modern war fighting. In order to explore more deeply the situational and personal dynamics of girl soldiering, this section will examine gender in recruitment methods, conflict-related roles, and domain constructions.

Recruitment and Conflict Roles

Although most reports of child soldiers interviewed after demobilization note that they had voluntarily joined their fighting faction, the majority of girl soldiers across cases were abducted, taken by force while working in fields, walking down roads, or sitting in classrooms (Save the Children 2005). Most of these girls, and indeed the vast majority of girl soldiers overall, did not go through demobilization or reintegration processes and did not participate in research conducted immediately following war's end, for reasons that will be discussed further below. Although some girls did volunteer as the introductory quote evidences, agency and scholarly reports often qualify that choice by citing the coercive factors existing in the circumstances of the vulnerable girl child. The idea of coercion can be extrapolated from the reasons given for joining, as will be discussed below, and will be explored again in the section discussing agency and gender.

Children in areas of civil war witness fighting, see bloodshed, lack basic necessities, and face disrupted family relationships and increasing patterns of family violence (Singer 2010). Against this backdrop, communities fracture, social structures weaken, and adults increasingly prove unable to protect children or keep them out of war. It becomes almost a matter of semantics to use the word *coercion* in cases where violence enters into the normal experience of country residents. Individuals must interact with the violence in one way or another by virtue of its omnipresence. The girls (and boys) that claim they chose to join declare that they did so to defend their country, to avenge family members, to escape conflict or abuse at home, or because their families were too poor to provide for them. In conditions of uncertainty, such as existed in Sierra Leone and Liberia during their civil wars, alignment with an armed group often seemed the best chance for any access to resources (Cohn and Goodwin-Gill 1994; Brett and Specht 2004; Save the Children 2005).

Girls associated with fighting forces, whether through abduction or volunteering, fill a multiplicity of roles, such as porter, cook, cleaner, medic, spy, temporary wife, minesweeper, messenger, child care provider, food producer, or fighter, depending on the needs dictated by male commanders. Most of these roles correlate to traditionally gendered tasks, replicating sociocultural constructions and expectations of females in the larger social context (Denov 2010). Participating in combat as a fighter, however, remains far outside the traditional expectations of girls, as will be discussed in detail below. Levels of abuse—sexual, physical, and emotional—suffered by girl soldiers, however, seems to correspond with recruitment type and armed group philosophy or lack thereof (Fox 2004). For example, abduction coincides with extreme abuse (Sierra Leone and Liberia) while recruitment via propaganda or persuasion can be accompanied by a policy of limited male/female contact or even a practice of gender equality such as occurred in Mozambique and Ethiopia (Veale 2003; West 2004).

To build on the preceding discussion, it can be said that roles within the armed group varied between combatant and support services in the case of both boys and girls. Girls, however, dealt with the implicit or explicit expectation of sex (Boyden and de Berry 2004; Coulter 2009; Denov 2010). Boys, on the other hand, responded to the implicit or explicit expectation to perpetrate violence, including sexual violence (Honwana 2006). Boys also became recipients of sexual violence, however the sociocultural stigma of homosexuality, the perception that the boys themselves must be homosexual, and the feminization of rape victims limited male willingness to talk about what happened. Sociocultural pressure eventually curtailed further research into the scope of the problem (HRW 2003).

The widespread sexual violence perpetrated against girls and women (whether associated with fighting forces or not) during wartime in Sierra Leone and Liberia has been studied in some detail. Rape during the course of war was used strategically, for example to control the population through fear, to cause further breakdown of traditional and family structures and limit potential resistance, as an initiation ritual to gain entrance into armed factions, and by certain males to demonstrate wealth and status accumulation to subordinates. War rapes also, however, reflect the low sociocultural status given to women and girls and the lack of legal protections accorded to victims of sexual assault. That said, the extent and brutality of sexual violence exploited during the war were unprecedented in type and scope.

Gendered Domains

For the most part, adult males manage the recruitment of child soldiers. Whatever the form of recruitment, either volunteering or abduction boys and girls both confront a significant power imbalance. A girl or a boy, as the socially and politically powerless child, cannot overcome a socially and politically powerful adult—unless the child has a weapon and the adult is unarmed. In both Sierra Leone and Liberia, the possession of an AK-47 or, in some cases, a machete produced an instant realignment of the traditional power structure. This fact, played out within a context of grievance against adults in general, accounts for a large number of the atrocities perpetrated in both civil wars by children and youth.

Within the less powerful child category, however, girls are placed below the boys in terms of gendered social value. For example, historically boys more often receive an education than do girls. Boys are expected to go out into the world and provide for extended families, generally following the development trajectory of child, youth, adult (upon marriage and economic self-sufficiency), and elder. Traditionally, girls leave the natal home only to join the family group of their husbands, following the sociocultural path of child, wife, and mother (Argenti 2002; Honwana 2006). Sierra Leone, Liberia, and other African countries often verbalize this hierarchy by referring to a female as a girl child. Associating with fighting forces, while perhaps mitigating immediate problems can, over the long term, block a girl's road to adulthood via marriage in ways that do not apply to boys. Tradition expects girls to be virgins upon marriage and soldiering or association with soldiers implies sexual relations that can categorize the girl as damaged goods, leading to social stigma and potential separation from the natal community. Unmarried young women who have children as a result of their soldiering experiences, referred to as girl mothers, can be further stigmatized by their communities.

When girl soldiers were given a gun and told to fight, they did so because to refuse would mean death but also because through the possession and use of a gun they gained feelings of empowerment. Girls judged being a fighter significantly better than being the wife of a common soldier. The gun allowed them to protect themselves, gain access to food and looted goods, and perhaps facilitate a chance to escape; fighters were not guarded as carefully as were captive wives (Coulter 2009). As girl war fighters occupied a social space outside the gendered female tradition, they became in consequence all the more frightening. That a girl child could kill and maim without apparent difficulty somehow called the nature of reality into question. Throughout the course of civil war in both country cases, girl members/captives of fighting forces became girl perpetrators until they surrendered their weapon, at which time they shifted back to the member/captive category.

Most girls, while occasionally allowed to fight, were continuously expected to perform sexual services for commanders and frequently raped not only by opposition forces but also by their compatriots. Girl soldiers may well operate in the male domain of war fighting, but they do not usually benefit socially from the experience. For example, in Sierra Leone it was easier for a boy who had amputated hands of villagers to be accepted back into the community than it was for a girl who had suffered rape (Brett and Specht 2004). In essence, the presence of girl soldiers does not significantly challenge or change the primacy of sociocultural masculine domination.

Gender and Agency

This section examines the presence of girl soldiers within the complex and militarized sociocultural space of relations (Bourdieu 1999) in Sierra Leone and Liberia during and after their civil wars. The space of relations includes interactions within the individual, between individuals, and within and between groups under conditions of time, place, violence, and sociocultural norms. Within this frame, individual, social, economic, and political continuity or change can happen. As such, it becomes the locus for the confrontation of individual agency, gendered norms and expectations, and protracted social conflict.

Agency refers to the human capacity for making meaning out of existing circumstances, accepting or rejecting norms, values, and practices, and making decisions for action in ways that matter to the individual. In general, the decisions an individual makes relate to individual capacity to mobilize internal defense mechanisms, external resources, and conceptualizations of the individual's place in the world (Cairns 1996). Social identity theory (Tajfel 1978) enters into the dynamic as individuals shift attitudes and behaviors to align themselves with a larger cohort in order to maximize individual capacity, external resources, and to enhance conceptualizations of one's place or role, particularly under conditions of uncertainty. To expand the discussion of agency somewhat, girls can strategically demarcate a space within the armed groups through volunteering. The reasons given for volunteering as indicated above certainly reflect a significant level of uncertainty, threat, and prior mistreatment. If we determine that, as a result, these girls joined through coercion then individual agency can be seen as null and void. The individual then shifts from the category of making the best of a bad situation (agency) to the category of helpless victim of overwhelming events. Abducted girls, on the other hand, who were coerced in the most blatant fashion, have to pick up the threads of agency under significantly more trying conditions.

Irrespective of recruitment type, once aligned with an armed group, gendered interactions come into play. If strategic agency pushed the girl to join the group, once she did so tactical agency or social navigation (Utas 2005) takes over, the individual struggling to find a place and a value within the larger, often male-dominated, militarized unit. If abducted, the girl focuses immediately on effective social navigation as she struggles to find and hold a place where she will suffer the least and gain the most. Within these environments, young women and girls often find it necessary (using their agency to make decisions in ways that matter to them) to forge links with more powerful and resource-rich males. As males hold social capital, girls that align themselves with these individuals extend their own access to a social network and associated resources, a process termed *girlfriending* (Utas 2005). Girls also create social networks with fellow girl soldiers in order to share scarce resources, help with feelings of isolation, and exchange child care duties when possible. In other words, these social ties facilitate girls' life chances under very difficult conditions (Vigil 2007).

In conclusion, impoverished living conditions, relative deprivation (the difference between the actual and the potential), protracted social conflict, and violence of all types—present in both recruitment methods discussed above—exist in all environments where the practice of using child soldiers flourishes. These extreme forms of human insecurity created situational vulnerability that eventually drew girls in Liberia and Sierra Leone into the violent dynamic of war.

Generational Domains

Intrastate or civil wars can be considered as physically violent forms of protracted social conflict. Throughout the trajectory of social conflict, structural and cultural violence threads through interactions from the national to the village levels. Over time the tendency toward direct violence increases in response, as in the cases of Sierra Leone and Liberia. In terms of violent conflict, behaviors in that particular field have historically been determined and acted out by adult men, although historically young boys acted in support capacities, doing so under adult male guidance and scrutiny (Bennett 2002). The historical record also notes legendary females such as Boadicea, Joan of Arc, or Colombia's Amazon women who bridged the gendered military divide but such examples remain the rare exceptions. Moving from male/female domains specifically to domains of the adult/child, it should be noted that similarities exist between the two constructions. The adult (like the masculine) domain comprises political and economic power, sex, and violence. The child (like the feminine) domain consists of any appropriate socioculturally dictated activity such as learning, child care, play, farming, or other economic support for the family.

Protracted social conflict and violence, however, blur the boundaries between adult and child. As violence intervenes, it filters through perception, attribution, and appraisal processes. Over time, an alteration of attitudes and behaviors can result, which, again over time, can become normalized. Changes in sociocultural norms and values can reflect and rationalize the effects of the intervention of violence. One consequence of this process can be the loosening of the boundaries between domain-associated tasks. In time, tasks become less and less age or domain specific, and the expectations and responsibilities of either domain can become inverted. Under these conditions of social militarization (Maulden 2007), children move into the formerly adult realm of sex and violence. As children perpetrate violence against their own family or community during their "initiation" into the armed group, the link between child, family, and community breaks down. The child then, by default, forms a stronger connection with the armed faction. The factional alignment, reinforced and rationalized through personal meaning, also offers the rewards of providing an opportunity to exercise power or agency and to reduce feelings of victimization (Straker et al. 1992).

When the violence stops, however, the social and political tendency is to return the domain structure to its original configuration, with power, sex, and violence reverting to the hands of adults. Former child soldiers are ascribed back into the disempowered child domain, either as a child in crisis, a traumatized victim, or someone who needs reintegration (Scheper-Hughes 2000). Without violence, the political and economic power of the adult is withheld from these former fighters. They are left with underfunded, post-conflict programs that often replicate and rationalize the adult/child domain structure young former soldiers feel no longer applies to them (Peters 2005). This reconfiguration results in thousands of disaffected young men hanging around the streets, waiting for *something*. Thousands of young women, seen as damaged and therefore unmarriageable, are left with children to care for in an environment of uncertainty similar to, if not worse than, what they faced before their soldiering experiences. These young women frequently find it difficult to return to their families and villages and are often left with no means of support other than girlfriending-type strategies that repeat the pattern of alignment of the less powerful female with the more powerful male.

Post-Conflict Programming

Intrastate wars and cross-border movements of fighters from one civil war to another have wracked the West African region. Within this violent dynamic, girl soldiers attempt to build social networks, attach themselves to male leaders and their social capital, and to basically survive the best they can. This section examines the realities of disarmament, demobilization and reintegration programming that relate specifically to girl soldiers after the conflicts in Sierra Leone and Liberia officially ended

The small West African country of Sierra Leone suffered through a civil war that began when Foday Sankoh brought his rebel forces across the border from Liberia in 1991 and lasted until 2002. Although estimates placed the number of Sierra Leonean child soldiers at 30,000, only 6,774 children (22.5 percent) entered disarmament, demobilization, and reintegration (DDR) programs. Further estimates claimed that girls made up about 30 percent (9,000) of the total number of child soldiers, yet only 513 girls (5.7 percent) went through the DDR process (Global Report 2008). After the DDR program finished in 2003 and international agency personnel took notice of the lack of girls' participation in the formal process, an additional 714 girls participated in the Girls Left Behind Project. In addition, NGOs recategorized girl soldiers into "girls associated with fighting forces" and later to "girls affected by fighting forces," technically in order to provide another range of services for those who were "the last in the DDR line" (Save the Children 2005).

The neighboring country of Liberia experienced two recent wars—from 1989 to 1996 and from 1999 to 2003. By October 2004, more than 10,000 children, including about 3,000 girls, had been disarmed and demobilized. (In Liberia, the program was referred to as Disarmament Demobilization

Reintegration Rehabilitation or DDRR.) Another 8,000 girls, however, were either excluded or did not register for benefits. Some reasons for the girls' low levels of participation in both Sierra Leonean and Liberian DDR/DDRR programs include being held back by their commander husband, self-exclusion through fear of community rejection, lack of trust in the program structure, illness, lack of information, misinformation about risks of participation, and the focus on weapon turnover as part of program entry (Amnesty International 2008; Coalition 2008). As part of the demobilization process for those girls who did register, agencies provided skills training and basic education. Resources, however, proved inadequate to accomplish the goals of either skills training or education (Maulden 2007), and few girl participants gained skills sufficient to support themselves. On the other hand, girls reported some unintended consequences of their placement in these programs—increased self-confidence and greater social coping skills. Coulter (2009) posits that these programs served marginalized and stigmatized girls as a form of trauma healing, providing a safe environment where girls could begin to deal with emotions and experiences from the war as well as to realize that they were not alone in their difficulties. While these are positive benefits, girls required livelihood skills that would allow them to earn their own living, which due to policy and resource limitations did not meet expectations or needs.

Reintegration programs, which follow after disarmament and demobilization, are designed to return ex-combatants to a place or circumstance that existed previously. In the case of former girl soldiers, that usually means returning to their natal home and community. Such a return, however, could be fraught with problems, for example the girls being ostracized without resources or sufficient skills to support themselves. As part of the post-conflict reintegration programming trajectory in Sierra Leone and Liberia, recategorizations of former girl soldiers occurred, classifying them as girls associated with or affected by fighting forces. The new terms in part reflected role variation as experienced by girl soldiers. On the other hand, they further removed girls from the male-dominated soldier/combatant organizational structure around which the vast majority of post-conflict DDR resources flowed. In the postwar period, organizations and influential community members working with girls frequently encouraged or reinforced the girls' return to traditional structures and patriarchal practices. This tendency created conflict within the girls and among the girls and their community. These young female former soldiers had changed as a result of their soldiering experiences and often came to challenge traditional roles that no longer seemed acceptable. As a result, they were often cast as troublesome, adding to the potential that they may be further ostracized by their communities (McKay and Mazurana 2004).

For girl soldiers everywhere, DDR or DDRR package benefits can act as a signpost pointing to their involvement with armed groups. These girls get further caught in a gender double bind as they are forced to maneuver between recriminations from the armed group if they leave and from community members if they return. As such, girl soldiers must maneuver within the broader contexts of gender inequity or discrimination that exists as part of the sociocultural normative framework of their societies. In consequence, their situational vulnerability does not lessen after they separate from armed groups—in many cases it increases. Studies gauging community reaction to returning child soldiers indicate that, while the reaction to boys is mixed, the reaction to girls is overwhelmingly negative (Save the Children 2005).

This negativity reflects the notions that their association with armed forces means that they have either been sexually abused or had multiple sexual partners. They can, therefore, be considered as having lost their value and in some cases having dishonored their families. Fear also plays a large part in family and community reluctance to welcome the girls home: fear of HIV and other diseases, of retribution or revenge by former military husbands, and that the girls have acquired a "military mentality" causing them to be brutal, impolite, aggressive, and criminal. Finally, families and communities are well aware that children committed most of the community atrocities. As such, former girl soldiers have transgressed the gendered and generational norms (children should be submissive, obedient, incapable of violence) and are twice held to account.

Adding to the discussion of family and community fears of returning girls in general, pregnant girls or those with a child face additional stigma. If the father of their child is unknown, the girls have heaped further dishonor on the family in addition to becoming an extra charge that either the family or the community can ill afford. The child can also be considered a potential enemy because of the father's ethnicity or nationality. Finally, communities also fear that the former girl soldier will contaminate or corrupt the other girls, encouraging sexual relations without family consent, dowry, or official sanction.

Girl soldiers pay an exceptionally high price for both their age and their gender. In many ways, these girls personify political, economic, and societal level failures. On the other hand, as they face these daunting challenges, they also personify creativity and determination in their desire either to reunite with their communities or to move to urban centers and build a new life for themselves.

Post-Conflict Assumptions

The previous sections outlined girl soldiers' experiences as they navigated the war and postwar environments of Sierra Leone and Liberia. This section examines more closely some assumptions that fuel the continuation of gender neutral or gender exclusionary post-conflict programs. The first assumption links boys, danger, and the necessity to act quickly to mitigate the potential negative consequences of that gendered linkage. The youth bulge and superpredator theories (Sommers 2006; Urdal 2006) lend the connection of boys and danger theoretical grounding. The crux of the youth bulge theory posits that large numbers of male youth increase the probability of political violence. The superpredator theory equates the proportion of young men of color in a given population with a rise in the number of criminal young men. Both of these theories propose causal links that are not supported across world cases and that are, in any case, limited primarily to urban young men.

That wars in both Sierra Leone and Liberia started and continued primarily in the countryside, involving both men and women and boys and girls, would seem to dilute the efficacy of these theories. The fear of dangerous and potentially violent young men, however, continues to drive the gendered DDR program focus. Taking the dangerous boy framework into account as well as the fact that the word *solider* implies a male actor, the DDR programs are gendered, de facto, as male (Zuckerman and Greenberg 2004). Girls and women can fit into these gender-blind offerings as best they can. However, significant gender-specific realities do exist and require programmatic responses. While former girl soldiers do not constitute a dangerous category in the international view, they can be considered dangerous by their families and communities. As such, ostracism and further marginalization frequently result with few offsetting programs or options on which these young women can depend. In many ways, these girls become invisible as the international and community gaze turns toward the more dangerous or socioculturally valued male.

Adolescent girls, however, in response to unacceptable conditions and lack of program resources, organized and led riots and attacks at interim care centers (ICC) where underage soldiers were processed during DDR. These individuals recognized that the post-conflict stakes are higher for them than they might be for young men. Without support or care from their former military husbands, their own families, or the state, these girls can and do engage in civil unrest to call attention to their plight. The weight of civil unrest as compared to the larger category of political violence, however, limits the impact of the girls' actions (Mazurana and Carlson 2004). Perhaps the real answer lies in making the connection between gender inequality and the likelihood of violence.

Making the case linking gender inequality and security threats requires that gender equality be considered beyond just a matter of social justice. In reality, the negative repercussions of gender inequality go beyond the negative impact on women to negative repercussions at the societal level. Recent studies link gender inequity and levels of structural and/or cultural violence with an increased probability of internal conflict (Caprioli 2005; Hudson et al. 2008). That alignment makes gendered inequality a matter of danger and security—human security and state security. If taken from that point of view, the international and community gaze might return to reevaluate gendered realities in terms of reducing the potential for violence.

Global development personnel recently determined that if young women receive the same schooling as young men, their families would have a path out of poverty (Rucker 2008). As poverty, the inequitable distribution of available resources, and the lack of educational opportunities fueled the wars in both Sierra Leone and Liberia, the linkage between security and inequality (resource and gender based) can be considered valid. In partial recognition of these dynamics, the World Bank–driven program Adolescent Girls Initiative will bring job skill instruction to young women in post-conflict countries. Perhaps this model could become part of the post-conflict training options available for former girl soldiers.

Conclusion

In a comparative case study of girl soldier experiences, Wessells (2010) determined recruitment of girls to be systematic, widespread, and primarily accomplished through abduction. Armed groups did so to exploit the girls sexually as well as to use them as domestic servants, porters, and general laborers. The girls, upon removal from the armed groups, faced stigmatization, health problems, and a range of adjustment and livelihood challenges as they tried to piece together their lives and to take care of any children born while they were with the military faction.

This chapter examined realities and tensions experienced by girl soldiers during their association with armed groups as well as after that association ended. The case examples of Sierra Leone and Liberia provided a context for what might otherwise be an easily dismissed set of generalities. The conditions of uncertainty and vulnerability encountered by girls in these countries on a daily basis provided a set of options for agentic choice. With that in mind, the girls created meaning through a new social/military role, accessed resources, and exercised power and agency to reduce feelings of victimization. As they did so, they evidenced determination and courage. These girls have much to offer their families, communities, and their countries as a result of their experiences. It can only be hoped that with time the international as well as the sociocultural gaze will refocus on not only the needs of these young women but also on their strengths.

Keywords

girl soldiers, intrastate war, situational vulnerability, recruitment, demobilization, reintegration, domains, social navigation, experiential spectrum, sexual violence, gender double-bind, security

Discussion Questions

1. What theories could inform the conceptualization of gendered domains?
2. How might policies be formulated to better address gendered post-conflict dynamics?
3. What is the responsibility of the community in girl soldier reintegration?
4. How could security be reframed to include gendered dynamics?
5. When agentic choice is limited, does that diminish the value of those choices? Why or why not?
6. How did violence come to be the marker for what is most important in war transition and the post-conflict programming?
7. How can policy makers think differently about war to peace transitions?

References

Amnesty International 2008. *Liberia: a Flawed Process Discriminates against Women and Girls.* www.amnesty.org.

Argenti, Nicolas. 2002. "Youth in Africa: A Major Resource for Change,"In Alex de Waal and Nicolas Argenti (eds), *Young Africa: Realising the Rights of Children and Youth.* Eritrea: Africa World Press, Inc.

Bennett, Tom. 2002. *Using Children in Armed Conflict: A Legitimate African Tradition?* Essex, UK: Institute for Security Studies. http://www.essex.ac.uk/armedcon/Issues/Texts/Soldiers002.htm.

Bourdieu, Pierre. 1999. *Language and Symbolic Power.* Cambridge, Mass.: Harvard University Press.

Boyden, Jo and Joanna de Berry (eds) 2004. *Children and Youth on the Front Line: Ethnography, Armed Conflict, and Displacement.* New York: Berghahn Books.

Brett, Rachel and Irma Specht. 2004. *Young Soldiers: Why They Choose to Fight.* Boulder, Colo.: Lynne Rienner Publishers.

Brett, Rachel and Margaret McCallin. 1998. *Children, the Invisible Soldiers,* 2nd edn. Växjö, Sweden: Rädda Barnen.

Cohn, Ilene and Guy S. Goodwin-Gill. 1994. *Child Soldiers: The Role of Children in Armed Conflict.* Oxford: Clarendon Press.

Cairns, Ed. 1996. *Children and Political Violence.* Oxford: Blackwell Publishers, Ltd.

Caprioli, M. 2005. "Primed for Violence: The Role of Gender Inequality in Predicting Internal Conflict." *International Studies Quarterly,* 49(2), 161–79.

Coulter, Chris. 2009. *Bush Wives and Girl Soldiers: Women's Lives through War and Peace in Sierra Leone.* Ithaca, N.Y.: Cornell University Press.

Denov, Myriam. 2010. *The Making and Unmaking of Child Soldiers in Sierra Leone.* Cambridge, U.K.: Cambridge University Press.

Fox, Mary. 2004. "Girl Soldiers: Human Security and Gendered Insecurity." *Security Dialogue,* 35(4), 465–79..

Global Report. 2008. *Child Soldiers.* Coalition to Stop the Use of Child Soldiers.

Honwana, Alcinda Manuel. 2006. *Child Soldiers in Africa.* Philadelphia: University of Pennsylvania Press.

Hudson, Valerie M., et al. 2008. "The Heart of the Matter: The Security of Women and the Security of States." *International Security,* 33(3), 7–45.

Human Rights Watch. 2003. "We'll Kill You If You Cry: Sexual Violence in the Sierra Leone Conflict. 15(1A), 1–74. http://www.hrw.org.

Maulden, Patricia A. 2007. *Former Child Soldiers and Sustainable Peace Processes: Demilitarizing the Body, Heart, and Mind.* Unpublished doctoral dissertation. Fairfax, Va.: George Mason University.

Mazurana, Dyan and Khristopher Carlson. 2004. *From Combat to Community: Women and Girls of Sierra Leone.* The Policy Commission, Women Waging Peace, http://www.huntalternativesfund.org.

McKay, Susan and Dyan Mazurana. 2004. *Where are the Girls? Girls in Fighting Forces in Northern Uganda, Sierra Leone and Mozambique: Their Lives During and After the War.* Québec, Canada: International Centre for Human Rights and Democratic Development.

Peters, Krijn and Paul Richards. 1998. "'Why We Fight': Voices of Youth Combatants in Sierra Leone." *Africa,* 68(2), 183–210.

Peters, Lilian. 2005. *War Is no Child's Play: Child Soldiers from Battlefield to Playground.* Occasional Paper No. 8, Geneva Center for the Democratic Control of Armed Forces.

Rucker, Phillip. 2008. "$20 Million Job-Skills Ladder Created for Girls in Poor Nations." *The Washington Post,* October 11, A18.

Save the Children. 2005. *Forgotten Casualties of War.* http://www.safethechildren.org.uk.

Scheper-Hughes, Nancy. 2000. "After the War is Over." *Peace Review,* 12(3), 423–29.

Sesay, Amadu (ed.) 2003. *Civil Wars, Child Soldiers, and Post Conflict Peace Building in West Africa.* Breinigsville, Pa.: College Press and Publishers Ltd.

Singer, P. W. 2010. "The Enablers of War: Causal Factors behind the Child Soldier Phenomenon." In Scott Gates and Simon Reich (eds), *Child Soldiers in the Age of Fractured States*. Pittsburgh: University of Pittsburgh Press.

Singer, P. W. 2005. *Children at War*. New York: Pantheon Books.

Sommers, Marc. 2006. *Fearing Africa's Young Men: The Case of Rwanda*. Social Development Paper No. 32, Conflict Prevention & Reconstruction. The World Bank.

Straker, Gill, Fatima Moosa, Risé Becker, and Madiyoyo Nkwale. 1992. *Faces in the Revolution: The Psychological Effects of Violence on Township Youth in South Africa*. Cape Town, South Africa: David Philip.

Tajfel, Henri, ed. 1978. *Differentiation Between Social Groups: Studies in the Social Psychology of Intergroup Relations*. London: Academic Press.

Urdal, Henrik. 2006. "A Clash of Generations? Youth Bulges and Political Violence." *International Studies Quarterly*, 50, 607–29.

Utas, Mats. 2005. "Victimcy, Girlfriending, Soldiering: Tactic Agency in a Young Woman's Social Navigation of the Liberian War Zone." *Anthropological Quarterly*, 78(2), 403–30.

Veale, Angela. 2003. *From Child Soldier to Ex-Fighter: Female Fighters, Demobilisation, and Reintegration in Ethiopia*. Monograph 85, Institute for Security Studies.

Vigil, James Diego. 2007. *The Projects: Gang and Non-Gang Families in East Los Angeles*. Austin: University of Texas Press.

Wessells, Michael G. 2010. "Girls in Armed Forces and Groups in Angola: Implications for Ethical Research and Reintegration," In Scott Gates and Simon Reich (eds), *Child Soldiers in the Age of Fractured States*. Pittsburgh: University of Pittsburgh Press.

Zuckerman, Elaine and Marcia E. Greenberg. 2004. *The Gender Dimensions of Post-Conflict Reconstruction*. A Gender Action Publication. www.genderaction.org.

SECTION II

Women Intervening in War

CHAPTER SIX

Challenging Warfare: Sri Lanka

Maneshka Eliatamby

I want to see my country get out of this mess. I want to see women make decisions in the peace process. I want women sitting at the negotiating table. I am trying to change things for the betterment of all of us in Sri Lanka.
—*Visaka Dharmadasa*

Introduction

The quarter-century-old war waged on the Indian Ocean island of Sri Lanka since 1983 has taken the lives of more than 80,000 people. Men, women, and children belonging to both sides of the divide—the Sri Lankan government and the Liberation Tigers of Tamil Eelam (LTTE)—have lost their lives. But out of the ashes of this brutal and bloody war arose an amazing story of resilience and hope. Despite her immense personal loss, Visaka Dharmadasa, the mother of a Sri Lankan soldier missing in action (MIA) since September 1998, created the Association of Parents of Servicemen Missing in Action (PSMIA) and the Association for War-Affected Women (AWAW).[1] By 2007, the initiative of one single woman was translated into a membership of 12,000 women, both Sinhalese and Tamil, all of whom were directly affected by the loss of a child or loved one as a direct result of the war. More than anyone else, these women understand the value of life and that it is critical to stop the killing. The purpose of this chapter is to explore the relationship between gender and peaceful agency, using the example of Visaka Dharmadasa and the women of PSMIA and AWAW. It examines women's agency during times of extreme protracted conflict, the milestones achieved by these women, and the ways in which their actions shaped grassroots activism in Sri Lanka.

My Son, His Name Is Achintha

If you know your son is dead, you can at least mourn him. But now, for me, the issue is eternally pending ...

Visaka Dharmadasa

On September 27, 1998, the LTTE attacked the Sri Lankan Army (SLA) base at Kilonochchi, in the island's Northern Province, overrunning the camp. To this day this is one of the largest and most brutal single attacks in the history of the conflict between the Government of Sri Lanka (GoSL) and the LTTE. As a result of this attack, the GoSL reported 609 SLA personnel missing in action. Visaka Dharmadasa's 21-year-old son, Achintha, was among the Sri Lankan government soldiers that went missing that fateful day.

According to Dharmadasa, Achintha had only been in the field for three months when Kilinochchi was attacked, stating that "[h]e had not even got his first paycheck." She states that matters were made worse since the army had not yet issued Achintha a dog tag—"[t]he army didn't think it was important! If he had been wearing it, I would have known what really happened to him. If you know your son is dead, you can at least mourn him. But now, for me, the issue is eternally pending." She is not alone. Many other mothers, wives, and sisters cling to the hope that their loved ones will walk back into their lives someday. This is the fate suffered by those whose relatives are MIA and who lack the opportunity for closure.

Despite their grief, out of their moment of greatest despair arose an amazing story of resilience and hope. Visaka Dharmadasa joined hands with other mothers who found themselves in a similar predicament and converted an immense personal tragedy into a glimmer of hope. Unable to obtain any information as to the whereabouts of their sons, this group of parents of servicemen came together, setting the stage for the birth of a women-led grassroots peace movement in Sri Lanka. These mothers' initial goal was to bring to the forefront the issue of finding out details on the whereabouts and the condition of their sons who had been identified as missing in action. The group called itself the Association of Parents of Servicemen Missing in Action. The members decided that three major issues needed to be urgently addressed:

1. Take all necessary steps to find out the fate of those MIA;
2. Secure the release of all detainees; and
3. Prevent such problems by bringing peace to the country.

PSMIA's formal creation was marked by a flower offering at the Gatambe Buddhist Temple in Kandy, the capital of the Central Province on March

27, 1999. Among the estimated 800 people in attendance were parents and families of servicemen missing in action and Buddhist, Catholic, and Hindu clergy. During the ceremony, mothers of missing soldiers read poetry about their sons and spoke of their intense pain. The end of the ceremony was marked by floating flower offerings down the Mahaweli River. This in itself has great symbolism attached to it, since the Mahaweli, which is the island's longest river, runs from the center of the country to the northeastern port of Trincomalee, serving farmers and citizens on both sides of the conflict divide.

One of the organization's first missions was to find out the where-abouts of the members' sons. They went about their search by lobbying the International Committee of the Red Cross (ICRC) to register all missing individuals and initiate tracing their whereabouts. However, at this point they were faced with a major structural challenge, as the ICRC did not have the mandate to open tracing requests without official recognition of the miss-ing by their commanding force. This was further complicated by regulations that required such a request to be made within six months of the individ-ual's disappearance. The situation was compounded by the fact that the Sri Lankan Army had established an official court of inquiry on the attack on Kilinochchi and were not able to collaborate with the ICRC until the official inquiry was closed. Unfortunately the SLA inquiry process would take more than six months, surpassing the ICRC's time limit for inquiry.

Realizing that they may never find out the fate of their sons if they worked within the constraints of ICRC and GoSL's formal structures, PSMIA, led by Visaka Dharmadasa, set the wheels in motion to ensure that this issue was addressed. They lobbied the ICRC's delegation in Colombo, and the direc-tor of personnel administration at the Sri Lanka Army Headquarters in Colombo for assistance, requesting that they take necessary steps to expedite the process. At the end of December 1998, the Ministry of Defense provided the ICRC with a list of names of those missing as a result of the attack on Kilinochchi. This was the first among many victories achieved as a result of the agency of this group of women. These structural changes would not only alter the way in which the missing are treated in Sri Lanka but also change the way the ICRC and the international community treat the missing and their fates.

The mothers did not stop there. The group persevered, requesting that the ICRC take still and video photographs of the bodies of military person-nel found during wartime, comparing them with photographs on file with their respective militaries so as to verify the identity of the dead. They also requested that the ICRC collect all items that could be used for identification and, most importantly, to advise all combatants to wear and respect identification discs (dog tags). They lobbied the Sri Lankan Army, requesting that service members wear identification discs at all times, irrespective of their station. Further, PSMIA lobbied for the creation and maintenance of computerized dental records of personnel in order to secure identification. They stressed the Sri Lankan Army's need to promptly accept bodies of servicemen before they begin to decompose and requested that the ICRC, Sri Lankan military, and the LTTE agree on a mode of transfer for bodies. They also stressed the importance of the need to follow the Geneva Conventions and International Humanitarian Law concerning the treatment of wounded and captured soldiers from both sides.

PSMIA stressed their point by preparing a booklet featuring photographs of soldiers wearing identification discs with a request in English, Sinhala, and Tamil. This booklet was released in Anuradhapura, the capital of the North Central Province and the last major city en route to the contested lands of the Northern Province on October 22, 1999, among a crowd of more than 3,000 family members of those reported MIA. A copy of the booklet together with a request letter was sent to the LTTE leader, Velupillai Prabhakaran. The launch of this booklet was accompanied by the release of 900 gas balloons with messages of peace attached to them and sent across the border to LTTE-controlled areas.

They Don't Have Claws!

According to Visaka Dharmadasa, this was the first time parents of servicemen came out and made a public call for peace, addressing both the GoSL and the LTTE. It set the stage for the extremely risky endeavor of meeting face to face with the LTTE—during most of the war, there were restrictions on the movement of people from the conflict zones in the north to the southern part of the country. In September 2001, exactly three years after the disappearance of Lieutenant Achitha Parua and 608 other servicemen, Dharmadasa, along with six other members of PSMIA who were also bereaved mothers, made the journey into the LTTE's heartland.

The GoSL and LTTE were in an all-out war against each other during this period, and understanding the extreme risk involved with this endeavor, this group of women was compelled to carry out the visit in complete secrecy. The mothers obtained clearance from the government to visit the Madu Church on the pretext of making a pilgrimage to the Catholic shrine. Madu is home to a Catholic church located in the formerly LTTE-controlled Vanni District. Situated in the heart of the conflict zone, this shrine enjoyed the status of a zone of peace (ZoP) during most of the conflict. Despite open warfare between the Sri Lankan Government forces and the LTTE, there was an unwritten understanding between the two groups about the sanctity of this religious shrine. Dharmadasa states that "[t]he church was always out of bounds for the fighting."

Visaka and the six other mothers put their own lives at risk by making this trip. They made the journey to Madu, passing through the last government checkpoint, and crossing into LTTE-controlled territory. Once in Tiger territory, their vehicle was surrounded by young boys carrying machine guns and belonging to the LTTE, who provided them an escort on their bicycles. Visaka speaks of her experience, stating that once they made it safely to the shrine, "the seven of us went and lit candles at the Church." The clergy at the Madu Shrine were previously aware of this visit by Dharmadasa and her colleagues and had arranged for a clandestine meeting between the group of mothers and the LTTE. Dharmadasa states that "[t]hrough the Catholic Church we were able to meet with the LTTE." The clergy had informed the LTTE about Visaka and her colleagues' visit and requested a meeting between the two groups.

Dharmadasa recalls that, although there was an initial sense of mistrust between the groups, they were able to break the ice by sitting on the floor across from the members of the LTTE and offering them food they had carried with them. Visaka jokingly states that she realized at this point that they did not have claws! The mothers' initial visit lasted five days, with each group getting to know the other. During her interactions with the LTTE, Dharmadasa states that she often brought the conversation to a deeply personal level, asking them about their own children and breaking the ice. However, she was clear with the LTTE about her organization's mission and goals. According to Shyam Selvaduari, Dharmadasa states that "I told him, '[a]s much as you are proud about your striped uniform, we are proud of our uniform, too" (Selvadurai 2008, 2). Here she clearly attempted to establish a parallel positioning, ensuring that a hierarchical relationship was not established. Dharmadasa and the other mothers that made this journey were not going to allow the LTTE to draw an exclusive picture of their trauma alone. By speaking of the atrocities committed by both sides, these mothers were ensuring their narrative's acceptance on a parallel level.

Dharmadasa acknowledges the pain that mothers from each side feel and states that perhaps the Tamil mother's pain is more acute. However, while they talked about the sufferings on both sides, Dharmadasa was determined to conduct the conversation on an equal footing. While she accepted the stories the LTTE told of the atrocities committed by Sri Lankan armed forces, she gave them stories of atrocities committed by the LTTE against Sinhalese and Tamil villages. For every story that was told by the LTTE, Dharmadasa and her colleagues told one of their own. At the end of the day, she told them that the atrocities need to cease and the war must stop.

Building Trust Through Dialogue

Generally speaking, the first nonviolent act is not fasting, but dialogue. The other side, the adversary, is recognized as a person, he is taken out of his anonymity and exists in his own right, for what he really is, a person. To engage someone in dialogue is to recognize him, have faith in him. At every step in the nonviolent struggle, at every level we try tirelessly to establish a dialogue, or reestablish it if it has broken down. When I say 'the other side,' that could be a group of persons or a government.

—*Hildegard Goos-Mayr*

Their first visit to the Madu Church and the Vanni region turned out to be the first among many meetings between the LTTE and PSMIA and the beginning of a relationship based on mutual respect that eventually evolved into mutual trust over the years. More importantly, Dharmadasa states that this was the beginning of the nurturing of a relationship that included mutual trust. The significance of this trust building cannot be underplayed, especially in the context of the Sri Lankan conflict, where trust between the people of the north and south is extremely lacking due to a number of reasons. Over the course of the more than quarter century of war on the island, there has been restricted movement of civilian populations from the northern and eastern territories to the southern regions and vice versa. Traveling from the north to the south (the incidences of individuals from the south traveling to the north are slim to none) required that an individual obtain the permission of the GoSL and often the permission of the LTTE as well. There were many occasions when such permission to travel was denied. This lack of interaction between the people has led to a great deal of mistrust between the groups and in many instances has also led to the dehumanization of the other.

The trust-building process began when Dharmadasa and her colleagues crossed into LTTE territory, and young Tiger cadres risked their own lives to assist the group of mothers on their journey. PSMIA's gesture of goodwill by visiting Tiger territory was reciprocated by the LTTE, thereby opening the door to the opportunity to build trust between the two groups. Dharmadasa and her colleagues were surprised to learn that, despite the protracted nature of the conflict between the SL government troops and the LTTE, many Tigers attribute legitimacy to members of the Sri Lanka armed forces Many members of the

LTTE have great respect for the government soldier's uniform and the role they play as protectors of their motherland. Similarly, however, the LTTE expected Visaka Dharmadasa and the mothers from the south to respect that their men are no different from her son and his colleagues. It appears that Dharmadasa and her colleagues, as well as members of the LTTE, make distinctions between the structures that caused the distrust and the soldiers who fight the battle.

James Gibson in his analysis of the Truth and Reconciliation Commissions in South Africa argues that "an elemental component of reconciliation is mutual respect, and a fundamental ingredient in mutual respect is the willingness to judge people as individuals rather than brand them with group stereotypes. A more reconciled society is one in which people understand, accept, and even appreciate differences in groups other than their own" (Gibson 2004, 118). He goes on to say that "[w]ithout understanding, it is perhaps not surprising that levels of interracial trust are not particularly high" (Gibson 2004, 124). Dharmadasa emphasizes the need to treat humans with dignity and states that it is the key to conflict resolution. During our conversations, Dharmadasa drew attention to the importance of listening, mutual respect, and the need to heal minds. James Gibson states that "… people are reconciled when they come to interact with each other more (barriers across races break down) and communicate more, perhaps ultimately gaining understanding and perhaps even acceptance, which result in their appreciation and exaltation of the value of racial diversity" (Gibson 2004, 118).

From PSMIA to AWAW

PSMIA's first visit in September 2001 to Tiger-controlled territories set the stage for further interactions between the two groups. The conversations that took place were not restricted to the leadership of PSMIA and the LTTE. PSMIA made it a point to speak with the rank and file of the LTTE, Buddhist, Hindu, Christian, and Muslims religious leaders, as well as the parents and families of LTTE cadres. Through PSMIA, mothers of Sri Lankan government servicemen met with the mothers of LTTE soldiers, many of who had lost a son or a daughter in the conflict. Such meetings strengthened cross-national partnerships between the groups and created a sense of solidarity among the mothers from the north and the south. These types of cross-national partnerships are extremely few and far between and are considered radical in the Sri Lanka context.

During their conversations with mothers of LTTE soldiers missing in action, PSMIA's membership (made up exclusively of southern mothers whose sons were MIA) recognized the unfortunate reality that many of the soldiers reported missing may no longer be alive. Recognizing the need for mothers and loved ones on both sides to have a space to mourn their loss/ es after receiving news of the death of their sons, PSMIA decided to create a spaceor forum in which to mourn. Thus, the Association of War Affected Women or AWAW was created.

Visaka Dharmadasa and the other mothers saw the AWAW as yet another opportunity to establish a connection between mothers in the north and south who had lost their sons. They acted under the premise of creating contact between mothers and bringing women together across the divide. Speaking of the symbol of motherhood and mobilizing for reconciliation, Visaka Dharmadasa stresses the need for reconciliation to come from within. She recognizes the importance of the ability of motherhood to evoke a spe- cial quality of generosity and its ability to pursue a common goal of ensuring the safety of children on both sides of the conflict.

According to Dharmadasa, AWAW's primary objective is to achieve peace through socioeconomic development with active participation of the affected women. As part of this program, AWAW was able to meet with mothers of LTTE cadres, and in 2002, 200 women from the north and east joined mothers from the south in protesting the war, calling for an end to the death and destruction that has plagued the island since the war began in 1983. The first event took place outside the Fort Railway Station in the heart of Colombo. This was not only a historic moment for PSMIA and AWAW but was one of the first openly direct challenges to the GoSL and the LTTE for carrying on a merciless war. This challenge carried a sense of gravity that was out of the ordinary, having been put forth by the mothers of soldiers either missing or killed in action while serving in the military of the GOSL or the LTTE. These women had a platform of moral legitimacy, having paid the ultimate price of losing a child to the war.

This meeting of mothers continued when AWAW took 300 mothers from the south to Jaffna, the capital of the Northern Province, and carried out a similar protest. AWAW is currently made up of a group of more than 2,000 women from across Sri Lanka who are directly affected by the war. Their sons, husbands killed/missing in action or disabled due to the war is the common thread that binds these women. In his book *The Moral Imagination*, John Paul Lederach asks the question, "[h]ow do we transcend the cycles of violence that bewitch our human community while still living in them?" (Lederach 2005, 5). Lederach goes on to write that

> [t]ranscending violence is forged by the capacity to generate, mobilize, and build the moral imagination.... Stated simply, the moral imagination

required the capacity to imagine ourselves in a web of relationships that includes our enemies; the ability to sustain a paradoxical curiosity that embraces complexity without reliance on dualistic polarity; the fundamental belief in and pursuit of the creative act; and the acceptance of the inherent risk of stepping into the mystery of the unknown that lies beyond the far too familiar landscape of violence" (Lederach 2005, 5).

It is clear that the members of AWAW have been successful at building this moral community—a community that has begun to transcend the barriers caused by more than a quarter century of open warfare.

The Power of Contact

We are all in the same boat—we simply need to understand each other better and be more respectful of each other's culture
—*Truth and Reconciliation Commission(1998, vol. 9, ch. 5, p. 425)*

Visaka Dharmadasa stresses the need for contact and communication as a tool of peace building. She claims that "[a]ny culture respects the dead, and if they could transfer dead bodies with some respect, this would require some kind of communication even with ICRC playing a role." Here she stresses the importance of communication and dialogue as being key. According to Camilla Orjuela, "[t]hese organizations of victims from the government forces, and relatives of victims, aimed simultaneously to cater to the needs of their members—the needs to find out what happened to their loved-ones, ... and to work for an end to the war and build trust over ethnic boundaries" (Orjuela 2004). Mohammed Abu-Nimer states that "[a]ttempts to establish dialogue and communication between conflicting parties are usually welcomed regardless of their content, structure, motivation, or outcome" (Abu-Nimer 1999, xvii). This is especially important in the case of Sri Lanka, where the populations of the Northern and Eastern provinces have little to no chance of journeying into other areas without receiving prior consent from both the LTTE and the Sri Lankan government. This leads to a situation where the people of what Dharmadasa terms *the North* and *the South* rarely if ever meet. Unfortunately, this lack of contact between the people has created a great deal of distrust and also dehumanization of the other. Hence, any form of contact between these two populations is seen by PSMIA and AWAW as an improvement over the current prevailing situation and a chance for peace through dialogue.

According to Abu-Nimer, "initiatives of encountering adversarial parties are usually considered to be an integral part of the forces that act for change in the relations between the conflicting parties or the different ethnic groups in the divided societies" (Abu-Nimer 1999, xvii). According to Sanam Anderlini, "it is this trust that has sustained their contact, even when formal peace talks stalled" (Anderlini 2007, 106). It appears that it was this trust earned during the many encounters that took place between PSMIA, AWAW and the LTTE that created confidence in the minds of the rebels—a confidence that became evident when, in 2003, they shunned even the Norwegians who were the official mediators of the peace process and relied on Visaka Dharmadasa to deliver their messages to the government. According to Camilla Orjuela, "[t]hese organizations of victims from the government forces, and relatives of victims, aimed simultaneously to cater to the needs of their members—the needs to find out what happened to their loved-ones, ...and to work for an end to the war and build trust over ethnic boundaries" (Orjuela 2004).

For the first time in the history of the conflict, the status quo of enmity and hatred that has existed between the warring parties in Sri Lanka for almost three decades was challenged by the mothers of Sri Lanka's heroes. Dharmadasa states that this visit to Madu and the conversation with the local LTTE leader "was the first time that a civil society group had a meeting with the LTTE, and this paved the way for the ceasefire and the peace talks." According to Roy J. Lewicki, "[m]ost people think of trust as the 'glue' that holds a relationship together. If individuals or groups trust each other, they can work through conflict relatively easily" (Lewicki 2006, 92). He goes on to describe identification-based trust (IBT), which "exists because the parties can effectively understand and appreciate one another's wants..." and "develops as one both knows and predicts the other's needs, choices, and preferences, and as one also shares *some* of those same needs, choices, and preferences as one's own" (Lewicki 2006, 96). It is clear that these mothers from the two sides were afforded a level of acceptance that had previously not been awarded to other grassroots peace groups.

According to Sanam Anderlini, "[i]n Sri Lanka, Visaka Dharmadasa's work on missing soldiers has led her into the world of the military and a deeper understanding of the motivations and fears driving fighters" (Anderlini 2007, 106). She quotes Dharmadasa's reflections on disarmament, demobilization, and reintegration (DDR) and how the very concept can be unnerving for nonstate fighters. Her interactions with this nonstate armed group has led to the realization that the very terms *disarmament and demobilization* denote a sense of disempowerment in the minds of these men and women. According to Dharmadasa this term induces a fear among the actors—the fear of being stripped of their only known means of protecting themselves, their identity, and their livelihood. Anderlini quotes Dharmadasa as stating that "[i]t would be more effective to first demobilize and support their reintegration and, once they have a sense of security about life and their livelihood as civilians, address the question of disarmament" (Anderlini 2007, 106). This is an especially important concept in the context of conflicts such as the one in Sri Lanka, which has continued for over a quarter century and has in some ways become a way of life and an integral part of the group identity of those involved with the LTTE. Her understanding of the identity needs of the LTTE and the people in the north and east of Sri Lanka is indication of the success of contact—it is through the group's interactions with the LTTE that Dharmadasa and the other women in the group are able to understand the fears of the other.

Coping With Grief and Shifting Identities

It is unfortunate that this happened to me. But I want to open the eyes of many others to issues that are not taken seriously," she said. "I have met mothers from Chile, Russia and Kosovo. I am just a mother with no agenda. Frankly, I am a victim, but I have also learned how to assume leadership.

—*Visaka Dharmadasa*

As is depicted in Figure 6.1, it is the individual's nationalist social identity that leads to the individual joining an armed group—whether it be a state or a nonstate armed group—in this case, the Sri Lankan military and the LTTE. When a family looses a loved one to war, the family usually does one of three things; (1) takes on a hyperviolent nationalist individual identity, (2) takes on a productive peace-builder-type individual identity, or (3) takes on an ultrapassive individual identity.

In the case of the first scenario, the individual copes with his/her loss of a loved one by becoming a greater proponent of the war that the loved one or relative fought in and gave his or her life to. In this instance, the hyperviolent nationalist individual identity feeds back into the nationalist social identity, further empowering the nationalist social identity. Believing that their loved ones died for a cause is a coping mechanism for their grief.

Those that take on the second individual identity of being productive peace builders are those who, while recognizing their own social identity, decide that no other mother, parent, or loved one should feel the grief and pain that they are suffering. It is this individual identity group that feeds into the peace builder group identity and works toward making contact with the other, understanding the other, and building a mutually respectful and

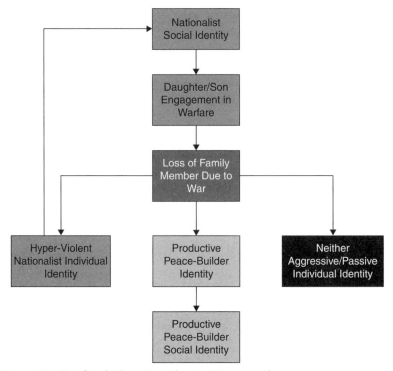

Figure 6.1 Grief and Changing Identity Framework

trusting relationship with the other. Visaka Dharmadasa and the mothers that make up AWAW would fall into this category. Peace building has become their social identity, surpassing their national identities.

The third group is made up of those who take on a neither aggressive nor passive individual identity. These individuals do not become hyperviolent nor do they become peace builders—the families of soldiers missing in action tend to fall into this group.

Conclusion

I would suggest that organizations such as PSMIA and AWAW in Sri Lanka initially began with the missions and goals of catering to the needs of their own membership (grieving parents of servicemen missing in action). However, their work took them to the heart of the LTTE and the people of the Northern and Eastern provinces in Sri Lanka. It was this contact that eventually led to a rehumanization of the other and an understanding and respect for those people. This contact laid a foundation for both the LTTE and the members of PSMIA to understand some of each other's grievances and actions and created an opportunity and a platform on which they were able to build a trusting relationship.

I would also suggest at this point that these women have begun a journey similar to the religious pilgrimage analyzed by Benedict Anderson in his book *Imagined Communities* (Anderson 1983, 13). Giving the example of the pilgrimage to Mecca undertaken by many devout Muslims, the author claims that, despite the relative heterogeneity of the thousands of pilgrims that arrive from places such as Indonesia and sub-Saharan Africa, there is a common thread that binds these worshipers as a result of having completed the *hajj* or *umrah* (Anderson 1983, 13). Anderson goes on to state that "[t]hough the religious pilgrimages are probably the most touching and grandiose journeys of the imagination, they had, and have, more modest and limited secular counterparts" (Anderson 1983, 55). He refers to journeys to places such as England, undertaken by colonized youth in search of an education. There is a common thread that binds these women who make up AWAW—the fact that they have all suffered a personal loss as a result of the war. It is this thread that brought them together and provided them a legitimate platform from which to call for an end to the war.

While PSMIA and AWAW do not constitute a geographic zone of peace as is referred to by Mitchell et al. (2007) in *Zones of Peace*, these women formed a metaphoric/virtual zone of peace—one that traveled with them as they crossed into LTTE-controlled territory numerous times and which afforded them security in the face of open warfare. PSMIA earned the rights and privileges that have been awarded to organizations such as Médecins Sans Frontières. These women give all of us in the field of peace building hope—hope that there is room for forgiveness and positive transformation even in the most protracted of conflicts.

These women who have lost family members in the war in Sri Lanka, and especially those whose family members have been declared MIA, are taking action in their own way and calling for an end to the war. PSMIA and AWAW are not alone in their women-led grassroots approaches to peace-building work in the context of highly protracted conflicts and polarized populations. Other women's groups such as Madres de la Plaza de Mayo (Mothers of the Plaza de Mayo) in Argentina, and the Northern Ireland Peace Movement were also involved in similar work. These examples clearly indicate the ability to replicate and succeed in such grassroots peace-building movements and the necessity for community-driven endeavors of peace.

Keywords

AWAW, contact (hypothesis), identity, imagined community, Madres de la Plaza de Mayo, PSMIA, Sri Lanka, trauma, zones of peace.

Discussion Questions

1. How do women contribute to peace movements?
2. What roles does women's identity play in peacemaking, peacekeeping, and peace building?
3. Are women-led grassroots movements successful at building and sustaining peace at the local and structural levels?

References

Abu-Nimer, Mohammed. 1999. *Dialogue, Conflict Resolution, and Change.* Albany: State University of New York Press.

Anderlini, Sanam Naraghi. 2007. *Women Building Peace: What They Do, Why It Matters.* Boulder, Colo.: Lynne Reinner Publishers, Inc.

Anderson, Benedict. 1983. *Imagined Communities: Reflections on the Origins and Spread of Nationalism.* London: Verso Books.

Gibson, James L. 2004. *Overcoming Apartheid: Can Truth Reconcile a Divided Nation?* N.Y.: Russell Sage Foundation.

Lederach, John Paul. 2005. *The Moral Imagination* (p. 5). Oxford: Oxford University Press.

Lewicki, Roy J. 2006. "Trust, Trust Development, and Trust Repair," in Peter T. Coleman Morton Deutsch, and Eric C. Marcus (eds), *The Handbook of Conflict Resolution: Theory and Practice* (pp. 92–96). San Francisco: Jossey-Bass.

Orjuela, Camilla. 2004. "Civil Society in Civil War: Peace Work and Identity Politics in Sri Lanka." Gothenborg, Sweden: Gothenborg University.

CHAPTER SEVEN

Building a Peace Network

Ambassador Swanee Hunt

Introduction

Stability requires full participation of women in all stages of any peace process. Yet sadly, women are routinely excluded from official efforts to develop fresh, workable solutions to seemingly intractable struggles. For lasting peace, women must help restore regions damaged by war. With the Balkans as a backdrop, this chapter shows how women with formal and informal authority bridge ethnic, religious, political, and cultural divides. It also traces how The Institute for Inclusive Security—a global research, advocacy, and training organization—is spearheading the international movement to elevate women leaders who are helping countries prevent, stop, and recover from conflict.

Inclusive Security: Ten Years and Counting

On January 20, 2009, I stood before 450 policy makers packed into a hotel ballroom in Washington, D.C. This was a watershed moment, as we announced the creation of The Institute for Inclusive Security at our tenth annual colloquium, which featured 19 women leaders from various conflict zones. Those powerful activists, journalists, and officials told stories of courage and leadership in places where fear and violence reign. They spoke about bridging cultural divides that men could not or would not. And they discussed their different strategies of forming coalitions across the conflict lines.

Over the several days of the conference, as I listened to these women leaders, I recalled the lessons that inspired the creation of the Institute in 1999. Today it is intuitive that real stability requires the participation of all stakeholders, but the real benefits of inclusive security took time for our team to recognize and appreciate. Over the past decade, it has required many more people and a great deal more time to translate that message into a global movement. With the announcement of the Institute, we were signaling that the movement was on its way.

Broken Region: Inadequate Solutions

My first recognition of the importance of women in peace building began in the Balkans. When I first began speaking with women in that region, they were being systematically excluded from all conflict resolution efforts. If women were mentioned at all, it was as helpless victims, not agents for change. I, too, was part of the problem.

In late 1993, I had just arrived in Vienna as US ambassador to Austria. Nearby Yugoslavia had broken apart in a series of bloody wars. Serbian president Slobodan Milosevic was "ethnically cleansing" the region (a horrible euphemism for a purge that is anything but "clean"). More than 70,000 Bosnian and Croatian refugees had fled the atrocities for refuge in Austria. Since it was unsafe for our diplomats to be based in besieged Sarajevo, our embassy in Vienna housed the US embassy to Bosnia. I had the opportunity, and felt the responsibility, to try to push through the quagmire of international arguments that kept us from intervening in order to stop the genocide.

As Yugoslavia broke into pieces throughout the 1990s—with widespread atrocities in Croatia, Bosnia, and eventually Kosovo—the most respected policymakers in the West searched for solutions. They spent thousands of hours negotiating and determining the fate of the local people. As I met with the stream of government officials and military officers, I did not notice that they were all men. Even though I had been a feminist activist in the States, I did not see the absence of women, because I was not looking for them. Yet women were virtually absent, even though throughout the region they had the same professional credentials as men, they had tried to prevent the war, and they now were working arduously to save the lives of those around them.

Because of war deaths, women were overrepresented in the population. In Bosnia alone, they led more than 40 cross-ethnic civil society organizations providing relief and pushing for an end to the war. They were intimately connected to their neighbors. Had they been integrated into the peace process, I am convinced that they would have bridged the divides deepened by the war. In addition, women would have provided the critical link between policymakers and civil society, strengthening and cultivating local ownership of the peace process.

Despite a clear potential value in a peace process, women's opinions were never sought. Policymakers, from inside and outside the region, never consulted them. So what would have been the smartest strategy to end the war? Women's connections in local communities should have been leveraged. In the few instances when women were invited to participate, their agendas were ignored. In not involving women, policymakers were losing a critical opportunity to ensure that local communities felt ownership of the rebuilding process. The decision makers were forgoing an opportunity to promote reconciliation as they promoted conflict resolution.

Agent of Transformation—Vjosa Dobruna

Even as I was trying to stop the carnage in Bosnia, I received a visit from a different part of Yugoslavia that eventually transformed my fundamental political analysis of war and peace. In 1994, Vjosa Dobruna spent three difficult days traveling from Kosovo to our embassy. She told me later that she had heard there was an American woman in Vienna who cared (I probably gave her less than an hour). She said she lived in Kosovo the majority of her life as a middle-class pediatrician. Although the region had a strong civil society with a history of pacifism, Dr. Dobruna sensed violence was about to erupt. Milosevic was flexing his political muscle, using ethnic Albanians (90 percent of the population of that semiautonomous sector) as scapegoats, much as he was doing with Catholics in Croatia and Muslims in Bosnia.

Despite her warning of the danger she saw unfolding around her, I had other responsibilities in Vienna competing for my attention: personnel problems, visiting American artists, a sick child, speeches on European Union expansion, and conversion to the euro. Nevertheless, following the meeting I cabled the State Department with a brief summary of her message, went on to my next meeting, and hoped (although doubted) that someone back in the United States would heed her warning.

Had I stopped to listen, perhaps I could have helped prevent hundreds of deaths and tens of thousands of displacements. And what would I have learned had I kept up with her? Soon after Dr. Dobruna travelled home from her visit to me in Vienna, life as she had known it crumbled. As was the fate of professionals throughout Kosovo, she was locked out of the hospital where she worked only because she was Albanian. When more ferocious violence started in 1998, she joined the civil society opposition movement to help displaced persons who had fled their villages and were living in the hills, under trees. She began to report human rights abuses to the United Nations and documented firsthand reports as she treated wounded civilians and refugees. She also created "she-mail," an e-mail warning and emergency aid system.

Because of her activities, the Serbian special police targeted her for capture. When they broke into her house just before the NATO bombing began, she jumped from a second story window into her garden and ran for her life. The Serb forces ransacked her home and destroyed the evidence she had collected. This time, at last, NATO fulfilled its promise as Supreme Allied Commander Wesley Clark led the bombing of Serbia. Watching on television refugees streaming out of Kosovo, I realized the enormity of my mistake. Had I kept in contact with Vjosa I would have understood what was happening to her community. She could have brought life on the ground to the policymaking tables in Vienna and Washington.

In 1999, Dr. Dobruna was one small speck in the massive exodus that I watched on television. Crossing the border into Macedonia, she found a warehouse and set up a field clinic for women who had been raped or otherwise traumatized. After air strikes stopped Milosevic's tanks, the UN formed the Joint Interim Administrative Structure of Kosovo to create democratic governance. Under the new configuration, one Kosovar and one UN representative co-led each ministry. Dr. Dobruna accepted the position of Kosovar minister in charge of democratization, good governance, and media. Her portfolio included everything from establishing new protocols for free elections to instituting a system of independent and impartial news reporting.

Minister Dobruna understood the new political structure to be a model of cooperation between internationals and nationals, government and grassroots organizations. She advocated for the ministry to take into account traditionally marginalized stakeholders. With this strong advocate of the people serving as the critical link, the focus shifted to rebuilding people's homes and having genocide and apartheid recognized by the international community. She set up her office in a café, using her cell phone and car, so she would be accessible to the people and have, as she said, her "hand on the pulse."

As the months, then years, passed, Vjosa's—and the people's—ideals were largely disregarded. Decision making followed a familiar top-down model, with an emphasis on creating rigid governance structures rather than reweaving and revitalizing communities in crisis.

Throughout this time, Minister Dobruna emphasized the importance of uniting Kosovar women across ethnic lines; preparing for the elections, she held meetings with civil society organizations. The women agreed that they needed a platform for action, and they talked about a quota for women in the new government. However, when it was time to draft a new constitution and new laws, civil society and the interim governing structures that were already in place were not integrally involved. The UN mission in Kosovo made the final decisions as to the path back to stability and prosperity for the country.

In 2000, the United States Institute of Peace (USIP) convened Kosovar Albanian leaders to develop a framework for the transition to democracy. Dr. Dobruna—one of the few women to participate—emphasized the importance of women's involvement in the democracy-building effort. She reported later that, despite her urging, the prevailing view of conferees was that women could work on social issues but not "higher politics," such as national governance, which also directly affected them. How could power be transferred from the UN to the local people with half of the population left out of the process? She objected.

Through her work during the war and after, Vjosa had won the confidence of not only Albanian but also minority Serbian Kosovars. She stepped forward to create a multiethnic women's caucus in the new parliament. In July 2002, Hashim Thaci, president of the assembly, noted, "This women's caucus is the only structure bringing together people from all sides. It will be a model, giving us hope that we can live together" (Durham and Gurd 2005, 254). Once again, national and international policymakers failed to take advantage of Vjosa's capacity to bring together former enemies, connect and involve local communities in reconstruction, and ensure Kosovar leadership of the rebuilding process. Citing the lack of partnership between the international community and civil society, Dr. Dobruna decided that her strongest statement would be to resign from the ministry.

Bridging Divides—Kada Hotic

Vjosa Dobruna's experience in Kosovo was typical of the stories I heard across the former Yugoslavia as I spent several years gathering interviews with 26 widely diverse Bosnian women for my book *This Was Not Our War: Bosnian Women Reclaiming the Peace*. I began having these conversations before the Bosnia peace agreement was signed in December 1995. Michael Steiner, a German diplomat who served as principal deputy in the Office of the High Representative of the International Community, was one of the few policymakers with an interest in Bosnian women as a potential force for stabilization. He called me in Vienna to encourage me to meet with the multiethnic Mothers of the Missing, who had emerged from the devastation, connect them with potential supporters, and do everything

I could to elevate their voices as they called for reconciliation after the war. I contacted these women who had crossed conflict lines to find their missing sons, fathers, and husbands, and I was continuously impressed by their ability to transcend personal tragedy and focus on restoring their homeland.

The women in Bosnia who had the most significant impact on me were those whose leadership was borne of their trauma. One of my great privileges was to assist the women survivors from Srebrenica on the anniversary of the massacre of more than 7,000 of their boys and men in July 1995. After almost a year receiving scant aid and virtually no information about their missing family members, they started to protest. During a demonstration in Tuzla, they threw stones at the windows of the International Red Cross office, which they said had been unresponsive to their desperation. Describing the women as "armed," a State Department official insisted that we should stay away from the women because they were dangerous. I said ignoring them was more dangerous; they were expressing rage and pain within their community that needed to be addressed if peace was to take hold.

Kada Hotic was one of the protestors. She later told me how, before the war, she worked in a textile factory, and her husband used his degree in sociology to hold various white-collar jobs. In April 1993, the UN had declared several of the remaining pockets of Muslims in eastern Bosnia "safe areas," to be protected by UN monitors and sustained by international humanitarian organizations. The reality was that these remained some of the most dangerous places in the world.

As Serb soldiers overran the surrounding countryside, the spa town of Srebrenica became bloated. The prewar hamlet of 12,000 became refuge to around 40,000. Two years later, on July 6, Serb soldiers overwhelmed the UN forward observers.

In the following days, Serb paramilitary—some disguised in UN uniforms—started taking men behind houses, murdering them, and leaving their bodies in plain view. During the night, the screaming began. Women were raped. Mothers and children were killed. Kada told her husband that she would rather be slaughtered than live through another such night.

Eventually, Serb general Mladic gave the order to separate the men and teenaged boys from the women, elderly, and children. Kada watched her husband led away, no chance for good-bye. Samir, her best friend and son, was also taken. For days she held out hope that they would send the men and boys back later. She walked up and down the streets asking everyone if they seen her son, husband, two brothers, and brother-in-law. None escaped.

For Kada and the other survivors, the tragedy was not political. It was poignantly personal. Still, in the same conversation in which she described to me her longing to just have a cup of coffee together, to watch her son blow smoke rings, she explained to me that "the soldiers were awarded medals for committing the worst crime, killing the most people in the fiercest way, or raping the most women." They must be having terrible flashbacks now, she said, worriedly, as if speaking of her own. Hearing her concern drove home for me the pull toward reconciliation many women bring to crisis. "Those boys who killed my boy, I'm sure they didn't understand what they were doing. They were just following orders ," she told me (Hunt, 2004).

Yet Mrs. Hotic is in no sense wishy washy. After the war she cofounded the grassroots organization Mothers of Srebrenica. Over the past 15 years they have been a thorn in the side of the national government and a prod in the conscience of the internationals. As they continue to push for justice, investigate murders, search for the missing, and assist survivors who have miraculously returned to their destroyed homes, Kada Hotic and this association have become international symbols of the need for justice and postwar closure.

International Community: Initial Support

Organizing a group for action—whether a town or the international community—is an acquired skill with a required network. The platform of an ambassadorship provided me both, and as I organized one meeting after another, I collected bits of understanding that would be eventually woven together in The Institute for Inclusive Security.

For example, before leaving Austria I approached President Clinton to suggest that we elevate the voices of Bosnian women. He responded immediately, setting aside $10 million to launch a Bosnian Women's Initiative to enhance the skills of women and ensure their participation in Bosnian reconstruction. The president's public announcement at the 1996 Group of Seven Industrialized Nations in Lyons made public the place of Bosnian women in restoring a peaceful society.[1]

Then in August 1997, General Clark recognized the potential of the Bosnian women and contacted me from NATO headquarters as he prepared to bring US Senator Kay Bailey Hutchison to Bosnia. The Texas senator had been repeatedly calling for the pullout of American troops, and Clark asked if I might put together a group of women who could impress on her the importance of the troops' role in maintaining stability. We organized a multiethnic meeting of 13 activists from all over the country to meet with the senator. Though she did not agree with their assessment of the fragility of the situation, we had also used the two-day occasion to create the League of Women Voters of Bosnia and Herzegovina.

As one more among many examples, around the same time, I co-organized and chaired a three-day conference in Sarajevo to which Bosnian political parties sent several of their most active women. The women represented 40 different parties yet had not been to their capital in more than four years. Although they had conflicting viewpoints on the war, they were able to create a common platform for increasing women's participation in politics. As a result, the Organization for Security and Cooperation in Europe mandated that three of the top ten candidates on upcoming election party lists had to be women. The number of women in parliament jumped tenfold, to nearly 30 percent.

Beyond the Balkans: Fundamental Change Requires Women

Now, with an improved perspective and some initial support, I understood the lessons of Vjosa Dobruna and Kada Hotic and the need to involve women to redress the brutality of war and its aftermath on the ground. Leaders such as President Clinton, General Clark, and Ambassador Steiner had instilled in me the confidence that a paradigm shift was possible. The multinationals should no longer dictate to civil society what was best for locals. A bottom-up process for planning and decision making would need to be used and women would be the key to the altered framework, with new institutions and foreign policy ideals.

In the 15 years since arriving in Vienna, I have learned firsthand in more than 40 war zones that thousands of women leaders are doing strong work to bring peace to conflict-ridden societies. Simply put, social change from the ground up is required to prevent renewed hostilities, and women are often uniquely positioned to create that change. Women are often most prevalent and active outside government, in civil society organizations and at the grassroots level. Because women are not wielding the weapons and are not in positions of formal leadership, those in power consider them less threatening, allowing them to work unimpeded. They hold up families, not rifles. They can reach across conflict lines. They are also more accepted by women on the other side, because it is assumed that they did not do the actual killing. Women use their identity as mothers to cut across international borders and ethnic enclaves; they often regard the hardened soldier as someone's son. Because of their roles, they have a huge investment in the stability of their communities. And since women know their communities, they can sense tensions preconflict, articulate a peace process during violence, and figure out how to shape a postwar peace agreement that will be accepted by the community.

As very brief examples, while the women of Bosnia toiled for peace, women were bridging divides elsewhere, even where the leaders deemed conflict resolution futile in the face of intractable hatred. In Sudan, after the 20-year civil war from 1983 to 2005, women worked together in the New Sudan Council of Churches and conducted their own version of shuttle diplomacy. They successfully organized the 1999 Wunlit tribal summit to bring an end to hostilities. As a result, the Wunlit Covenant guaranteed peace between the Dinka and the Nuer peoples, who agreed to share rights to water, fishing, and grazing land, which had been key points of disagreement. The covenant also returned prisoners and permitted freedom of movement for members of both tribes. Such compromise might not have been possible if only the aggressive and violent male members were at the peace table.

On another continent, women overcame seemingly insurmountable differences between India and Pakistan by organizing huge rallies to unite citizens from both countries. Beginning in 1994, the Pakistan-India People's Forum for Peace and Democracy overcame the hysterical fear mongering of the nationalist media and governing elites by holding annual conventions where Indians and Pakistanis affirmed their shared histories, forged networks, and acted together on specific initiatives. In 1995, women activists joined forces on behalf of fishers and their children who were languishing in each other's jails because they had strayed across maritime boundaries. As a result of their advocacy, the governments released the prisoners and their boats.

Observing these various developments in the 1990s, I came to believe that if women could bring about change in these hostile environments, inclusive peace processes could be effective everywhere. But to move this agenda forward globally, to transform peace-building processes everywhere, women leaders needed a way to share their experiences. Through a network, the global community of women leaders could learn collectively from successes and challenges, becoming a global movement for change.

The Birth of Women Waging Peace

Having completed my tenure as ambassador in 1997, I relocated to Cambridge, Massachusetts, to accept a position at Harvard University's Kennedy School teaching and creating the Women and Public Policy Program. In tandem, what is now The Institute for Inclusive Security was launched by Harvard and our family's private foundation, Hunt Alternatives Fund, which had worked to promote social justice since its founding in 1991 by my sister Helen LaKelly Hunt and me. Two seminal meetings in 1999 led to the program that was initially known as Women Waging Peace. The first was at our kitchen table and included several women peace builders I had invited to speak at Harvard. The second took place in Sarajevo with women peacemakers from different countries in conflict. In both meetings, the energy was palpable as the women leaders insisted that they needed a global network to encourage one another's participation in preventing conflict, stopping war, and restoring peace.

Each also said that she was not in a position to try to create a global network herself. And so, with the strength of the Harvard platform and the flexibility of the foundation's support, we moved forward. Against advice from many who thought we should start small and build on success, we decided to spread a wide net from the beginning in order to illustrate that the phenomenon of women leaning forward into leadership to stop wars is endemic to conflict. Initially, we invited local partner organizations from ten conflict zones to help us design our first conference and select the original 110 members of the Women Waging Peace Network. The large group met for the first time in December 1999 for two weeks of meetings at Harvard. Joseph Nye, at the time dean of the Kennedy School, and Senator Ted Kennedy opened our first "Policy Day," which brought some 100 policymakers from New York and Washington, D.C., to Boston to hear from the women leaders how women improve peace processes. A subsequent two-day research seminar involved more than 70 academics who wished to meet with the women and with one another. Subsequently labeled the colloquium, the gathering would be repeated annually, with an average of about 26 women, some new and some returning. We organized those subsequent groups around themes like negotiations, training, government, the security sector, or youth leadership.

Colloquia were, and continue to be, indescribably powerful. Leaders from the most diverse circumstances find common cause and built lasting bonds. Northern Irish women connect with South Africans. Rwandese share experiences with Israelis and Palestinians. Guatemalans and Sri Lankans talk strategy. A decade later, many remain in contact with one another.

We have helped nurture the career of leaders such as Awut Deng, an original Women Waging Peace Network member who was one of the Sudanese leaders involved in brokering peace among tribal leaders as a member of the Council of Churches; today she is the Government of Southern Sudan's minister of public works, having participated in negotiation of the Comprehensive Peace Agreement that ushered in peace between north and south Sudan in 2005. Nearby, Rwandan senator Aloisea Inyumba is among those most responsible for that country being the first and only in the world to break past 50 percent women's participation in parliament. We began working extensively with Inyumba and hundreds of other Rwandan leaders in 2000.

More Than a Network: The Institute for Inclusive Security

By 2001, the Network had grown rapidly to include some 400 women, outgrowing the annual research symposia that were part of the original Harvard-based colloquia. Research was still, however, an important part of the equation; policymakers like Leon Fuerth, national security advisor to Vice President Gore, were asking for concrete evidence demonstrating that women add value to peace-building processes. In truth, there was almost no documentation. We were at the leading edge of a movement, and the library shelves were bare when it came to studies showing how women add value to peace processes.

In addition to beginning a video collection of hundreds of lengthy first-hand interviews, we responded in 2002 by creating the Women Waging Peace Policy Commission to close the research gap. The commission hired international and local researchers to produce 11 case studies documenting how women enhance peace building. At the suggestion of the US Department of State, the commission then published *Inclusive Security, Sustainable Peace: A Toolkit for Advocacy and Action*, which provided a discussion of women's contributions in each stage of peace processes.

We also realized that the key to driving forward this new paradigm of inclusive security was strengthened advocacy. In 2002, we opened an office in Washington, D.C., and began advocating for women's inclusion generally, as well as within specific conflict regions. As soon as the US bombing of Afghanistan stopped in late 2001, we convened women to design a track to stability, called Transition Within Tradition. After the United States invaded Iraq in 2003, we held meetings with groups of female leaders, giving them a setting in which to create an agenda for stabilization and post-conflict reconstruction. Civil society leaders such as Hanaa Edwar collaborated with leaders in government such as Minister of Public Works Nesreen Barwari, mobilizing across ethnic divides to protect women's rights in the new constitution and forming an organization connecting women in Iraq with members of the diaspora community. That organization, Women for a Democratic Iraq, continues to promote economic and political progress today.

As the years progressed, we built up our staff and led more and more consultations with women in the field. For example, in Colombia, we encouraged policy makers to include women in efforts to reintegrate former fighters, provide justice to victims of violence, and reunite frayed communities. Network members such as Senator Gina Parody returned home from our colloquium to help institutionalize a cross-party women's caucus in the Colombian senate, staffed by Network member Isabel Londoño. Other Network members such as Ana Teresa Bernal were appointed to the National Commission for Reparations and Reconciliation and promoted an agenda that included increased attention to gender and victims' rights.

As we generated country-specific stories of success promoting women's inclusion, those stories were used to support the broader global case for women's inclusion. Simultaneously, our colloquium and Policy Day evolved as well. It still showcased the women leaders, who were the primary speakers at a 400-person luncheon; but advocacy in conjunction with colloquia was used to provide policy makers evidence of how women could help them in their work. Recommendations developed during colloquium have been widely implemented, and the Institute has become one of the world's leading specialty clinics in this area.

Despite such a sophisticated strategy, we have recognized that a much broader movement is required to achieve a global paradigmatic shift. An infiltration into the current mainstream is essential. In 2005, we began developing partnerships with prestigious organizations not traditionally focused on promoting women's involvement in peace processes, such as the Council on Foreign Relations and Crisis Group. Through them, we could reach a wider policy audience.

We also began collaborating more extensively with Network members on advocacy for inclusion. Women leaders were most likely to gain influence if they asked for it themselves as opposed to our trying to be their voice. Additionally, we wanted to make sure that as policy makers became prepared to include women, female leaders were ready to contribute. So, we increased our emphasis on training to arm women with the proper terminology, a concrete case for inclusion, ideas for peace building from around the world, and the ability to deliver a persuasive message to varied audiences.

Women Waging Peace was also renamed The Initiative for Inclusive Security. (At the request of the members, the network remained the Women Waging Peace Network.) We wanted policymakers to understand better that we were about the efficacy of peace processes, not simply "women's issues." Inclusive peace building was about achieving security, not about advancing women's rights. We also wanted to recognize that women are one among many stakeholder groups marginalized in peace processes. *Inclusive security* needed to become a term of art signaling the need to approach conflict resolution differently, a seminal concept on par with human security, civil society, social movement, or soft power.

An Enduring Presence and Role

While The Institute for Inclusive Security was originally created as a program of Hunt Alternatives Fund that would at some date certainly complete its work, we now realize that there will be an enduring need to advocate for the inclusion of all stakeholders in peace processes around the world. The current generation of women will need to be followed by a next generation equally ready to lead peace building. New policy makers will need to understand why women must be involved and how to involve them meaningfully in peace processes. For that reason, the initiative has grown into The Institute for Inclusive Security.

In a little more than a year, we have broadened our reach substantially. After extensive consultations with experts, including women in the field, we released *Inclusive Security: A Curriculum for Women Waging Peace*—a flexible training program that can be customized to enhance the skills of women in all stages of the peace-building process. The curriculum also can be used to help policy makers envision ways to realize inclusive security. With support from the Norwegian and Dutch governments as well as the Open Society Institute and private individual supporters, our work is expanding in the Middle East, Afghanistan, Liberia, Sudan, and Rwanda. The Organization for Security and Cooperation in Europe, the UN Development Fund for Women, and the UN Development Program's Bureau for Crisis Prevention and Recovery are exploring how to transform multilateral institutions. Our Network has grown to include more than 1,000 women leaders around the globe, and we have engaged more than 5,000 policy makers in our efforts to drive change.

What the Future Holds

Since 1999, there has been progress. Policymakers speak regularly about the need for women's involvement; our Network members have access to the most powerful government officials in the world. Some of them, like Liberian president Ellen Johnson Sirleaf, have joined the ranks of the most influential. Women leaders are more frequently speaking before the UN Security Council and the US Congress; I am regularly asked to address the need for inclusive security. Women's accomplishments and priorities are more often referenced and discussed in reports and in assessments of priorities for peace building. A multitude of women's groups promote women's inclusion locally, regionally, and globally.

Over the last decade, the Club of Madrid (an organization of former democratic presidents and prime ministers), the Elders (an association of eminent leaders such as Desmond Tutu and Graca Machel), the Centre for Humanitarian Dialogue, US Institute of Peace, and International Alert are among organizations dedicated generally to conflict resolution and good governance that have adopted women's leadership as a priority. These associations and organizations work independently and with Inclusive Security to highlight women's leadership and help women move forward their agenda on the ground. In every case, the key to success is collaboration with insightful and inspiring spokespeople—women with character and understanding like Vjosa Dobruna and Kada Hotic.

Today, the Institute helps strengthen and facilitate all-women cross-party parliamentary caucuses and civil society coalitions among Afghans, Israelis, Liberians, Palestinians, Sudanese, and Ugandans. In our eleventh colloquium, January 2010, 25 women focused on countering extremism. As we are called upon now by documentary filmmakers and news wire services, we believe we need to stay our course, adding more and more partners and building momentum for this movement over decades.

Returning wartorn societies to peace and prosperity requires more than bombs and bullets. It necessitates the involvement of all stakeholders, especially the women who are most vested in stability and most able to reweave communities. Haris Silajdzic, president of Bosnia and Herzegovina, said, "If we'd had women around the table, there would have been no war, because women think long and hard before they send their children out to kill other people's children" (Durham and Gurd 2005, 256). Indeed, it is precisely because women are not a primary source of war that they should be called on to shape the peace.

Keywords

Balkans, Bosnia and Herzegovina, The Institute for Inclusive Security, diplomacy, civil society, Kada Hotic, Kosovo, Serbia, Swanee Hunt, Vjosa Dobruna, Women Waging Peace Network, "women, peace, and security," Yugoslavia.

Questions for Discussion

1. Why were there so few women among the military officers and government officials Ambassador Hunt met?
2. Which conflicts best demonstrate the capacity women have to bring about peace?
3. How did the Women Waging Peace Network begin?
4. What multilateral organizations have supported the work of women peace builders?
5. Why does negotiation to resolve conflict so often involve only armed factions?

References

Durham, Helen and Gurd, Tracy (eds). 2005. Listening to the Silences: Women and War. Boston: Martinus Nijhoff Publishers.

Hunt, Swanee. 2004. This Was Not Our War: Bosnian Women Reclaiming the Peace. Durham, N.C.: Duke University Press.

SECTION III

Women Waging Peace

CHAPTER EIGHT

Countering the Currents: Zimbabwe

Martha Mutisi

Introduction

Conflict between political parties, Zimbabwe National African Union, Patriotic Front (ZANU PF) and the two formations of the Movement for Democratic Change (MDC) has had economic and social ramifications for the entire Zimbabwean citizenry but has had particularly devastating effects on women. Osirim (2001, 2003) contends that Zimbabwe's crisis has seriously eroded the status of women in the country as they have increasingly been exposed to violence perpetrated by both individuals and the state. Established in 2003 amid a worsening socioeconomic and political environment in Zimbabwe, WOZA has a membership of more than 60,000. WOZA is an acronym, but serendipitously, the word *woza* means "come forward" in Ndebele, the second major language in Zimbabwe.[1] Founding members Maria Moyo,[2] Jenni Williams, and Magondonga Mahlangu established WOZA to fight for the rights of women and to confront massive human rights abuses in Zimbabwe. Using a nonviolent approach to social change, WOZA interrogates inept policies of the state advocating gender-sensitive policies and negotiating women's rights and freedoms. WOZA members now include men who share the vision of enabling Zimbabweans to make independent decisions and actively participate in their community's development. WOZA is increasingly recognized as an organization that not only champions women's rights but also as one that addresses political, social, and economic justice issues. The movement is certainly among the strongest community-based activist organizations in Zimbabwe.

WOZA is concerned with the impact of the conflict between ZANU PF and MDC on women and their families. This decade-old conflict has resulted in socioeconomic regression and political degeneration, a state of affairs that was only temporarily curbed by the signing of the Global Political Agreement (GPA) between ZANU PF and the two MDC formations on September 15, 2008. During the height of the conflict, WOZA members participated in demonstrations, signaling their derision of the status quo. The police often responded by arresting and detaining the protesting WOZA members. Since its formation in 2003, WOZA has led more than 50 protests, and more than 2,500 women have spent time in police custody as a result of their activism (WOZA 2008). However, WOZA remains undeterred by the state-directed violence and continues to champion women's rights using various strategies.

In line with the argument by Mohanty (1991) that for too long women in the third world have been considered not as agents of their own destiny but as victims (Mohanty 1991, 56), the WOZA case study is a refreshing departure from the previous fixation on women as victims. Extant literature (Becker 2003; Lihamba 2003; Mathey et al. 2003; Ngongo-Mbede 2003; Ntahobari and Ndayiziga 2003; International Crisis Group 2006) identifies an array of women's organizations in African countries such as Burundi, Liberia, Congo, Namibia, Tanzania, Sudan, and Uganda, where women have moved beyond victimhood, becoming active agents for social change, despite their very difficult circumstances. In Zimbabwe, the role of women in confronting protracted conflict has been identified earlier by scholars such as Ranger (1992) and Schmidt (1997). Such earlier experiences by Zimbabwean women could have possibly influenced WOZA leaders to establish such a formidable social movement.

WOZA is both a broad social movement and a women's movement. Wilson (1971, 8) defines a social movement as a "conscious, collective, organized attempt to bring about or resist large-scale change in the social order by non-institutionalized means." Hannigan (1985) distinguishes social movements from other social forms on the basis that the former exist outside the everyday institutional frameworks and that they are oriented toward a degree of social change. An important dimension of social movements is that they are "committed to empowerment of the marginalized …," and seek to "challenge the hegemonies of dominant groups and institutions that are key to revitalizing democracy today" (Hackett and Carroll 2004, 1; Toronto Star 2000). Kevin (2008) contends that social movements "offer an alternative view of society, economy and polity that is grounded in protagonists' experience and struggle." WOZA seeks to change inimical elements of the social structure in Zimbabwe by interrogating the impact of the socioeconomic and political crisis. The leaders in WOZA have successfully mobilized a constituency with a view to influence the political system, particularly the state.

WOZA is also conceived as a women's movement. Ngoma (2006) asserts that women's movements have a role to play in impacting public policy and the political situation. As a women's movement, WOZA seeks to support women's rights and needs by challenging attitudes and practices that seek to preserve the inequalities between men and women. The WOZA membership is open to women and men from all backgrounds. In their campaigns, WOZA members encourage people to exercise their democratic choice and choose a candidate who stands for social justice regardless of political affiliation. Using a case study from Zimbabwe, the objective of this chapter is to identify factors and processes that are critical for successful social movements.

The Context of WOZA's Operation

Located in southern Africa, Zimbabwe is a landlocked country of an estimated 13 million people. A former British colony previously named Rhodesia, the country obtained independence in 1980 and has been under the leadership of President Robert Mugabe and the ruling party, ZANU PF, for more than 30 years. Zimbabwe had previously been hailed as one of the most prosperous and promising sub-Saharan countries (Herbst 1990; Nhema 2002, Meldrum 2004; Kriger 2003, 2005, 2006), a status it enjoyed from independence until the mid-1990s. During that period, the country enjoyed a booming postindependence economy and a robust agricultural industry that allowed Zimbabwe to export food to its neighbors in the Southern African Development Community (SADC) and earning it the label, "the bread basket for Southern Africa." Since 1999, however, Zimbabwe has been deeply affected by a protracted political and socioeconomic crisis. By 2008, Zimbabwe was an economic disaster with more than 80 percent unemployment (Bird and Prowse 2008), a hyperinflation rate exceeding 230 million percent (Hanke 2008), and high levels of poverty. Zimbabwe's economic problems were accompanied by political challenges including internal repression, challenged institutions, diminishing civil rights, and widening social divisions. WOZA emerged in the early post-2000 era in response to the more than decade-long crisis and has continued its activism.

However, after lengthy negotiations, on September 15, 2008, protagonists ZANU PF and the two MDC formations agreed to the Global Political Agreement, which ended the political stalemate and paved way for a political transition and economic recovery process. Although the GPA presented opportunities for curbing inflation, halting violence and addressing the challenges of legitimacy that confronted Zimbabwe, the Government of National Unity is still affected by its own set of challenges. Three years after the negotiated agreement and subsequent inclusive government, the parties ZANU PF and MDC still disagree ideologically and on practical issues of governance. Although the situation in Zimbabwe has changed since the Global Political Agreement, WOZA continued with its activism to champion women and people's rights.

A History of the Women's Movement in Zimbabwe Movement

Ferree and Martin (1995, 2) posit that women's movements are "outcomes of situationally and historically specific processes. In each time and place, feminism reflects its history and prior developments, as well as present opportunities and constraints." Women's movements are not new phenomena in Zimbabwe. Schmidt (1992, 145) notes the length, breadth, and depth of the trajectory of women galvanizing and mobilizing for social change, pointing out that it dates back to the colonial era. Schmidt notes that the earliest women's groups in southern Rhodesia were largely church related and included such organizations as the Wesleyan Women's Groups. Gaidzanwa (1992) observes that women began to challenge patriarchy during the anticolonialist struggle in Zimbabwe when many women joined their male counterparts as combatants in the guerilla war. Campbell (2003) notes how the women's movement was revitalized in early postindependence Zimbabwe wherein women made demands for gender equity and continued to assert themselves in the political space. Cheater and Gaidzanwa (1996, 197) explain the rise of the women's movement in Zimbabwe as a response to the patriarchal state where "tradition was employed in the first decade of Zimbabwe's independence to spread the general message of women's resubordination ... " After independence, women's movements in Zimbabwe addressed their demands to the state, challenging existing patriarchal gender relations and cultural norms. Subsequently, women in postindependence Zimbabwe collected tangible gains in the form of legislation such as the Legal Age of Majority Act (LAMA),[3] the Matrimonial Causes Act[4], and the Equal Pay Regulations.[5] Campbell (2004, 301) acknowledges that,

> African women, especially those connected to the various organized movements for democracy and women's rights, have emerged as the force with the strongest claim for a new liberation process in Zimbabwe.

At the heart of the social movement literature is the social strain and break-down theory (Messner and Rosenfeld 1994), whose roots are in nineteenth-century Durkhemian sociology as well as in writings by Merton (1938) and Cohen (1965, 1977). Durkheim regards social breakdown as a prerequisite of collective action, arguing that social movements are a product of exter-nal conditions that drive the need for challenging the status quo. In the case of Zimbabwe, social breakdown and strain became manifest in the form of heightened levels of violence, severe economic decline, loss of political space, and the destruction of social capital. This has produced a situation that WOZA labeled a "complex emergency" (Williams 2008a). Despite the complexities, the emergency in Zimbabwe presented "political opportuni-ties" (1989; Jacquette 1989), which prompted the rise of what Tarrow (1998) labels "repertoires of contention." Schock (2005) addresses this idea through a discussion on the "repression-dissent paradox," a situation where politi-cal repression catalyses the emergence and galvanization of protest. Apart from WOZA, several social movements emerged in Zimbabwe during the political crisis including the National Constitutional Assembly (NCA), the Zimbabwe Election Support Network, the Crisis in Zimbabwe Coalition, and the Movement for Democratic Change. In Jenni Williams's words, "WOZA was founded because of the oppressive regime of Mugabe and, in spite of him, it grew into a massive organization," (Williams 2008). As such, the repressive regime in Zimbabwe unintentionally created the space for women to mobilize, thus giving WOZA the opportunity to emerge as a solution to, not a symptom of, the Zimbabwean crisis.

WOZA's activism is an arduous task as they seek to address a state that has increasingly employed brute power to respond to protest. Over the past decade, political engagement with the ZANU PF state has been systematically eroded by the counterrevolutionary sentiments from the party that equates any challenges of the status quo to antinationalism. As such, since its incep-tion, WOZA members have often been harassed, arrested, and detained by police when they participate in demonstrations and other forms of activism. Despite the closed political space, WOZA have remained undaunted as they continue to table their demands for women's rights to respective authori-ties. The undeterred activism of WOZA in the face of the structural violence confronting Zimbabwe can be understood in the writing of Galtung (1969) who argues that inimical structural arrangements in society frustrate people and predispose them to engage in conflict behavior. Habermas (1983) con-tends that social movements arise to retain endangered lifestyles. WOZA's goal is to teach Zimbabweans to defend themselves against repression and to enhance women's participation in social and economic transformation processes. WOZA personifies the involvement of women in leadership of peace-building initiatives.

What Makes WOZA So Resilient?

This section analyses the factors that have helped shape, define, and enable WOZA to manifest and nurture its cause. WOZA is notably resilient and manifest in the Zimbabwean socioeconomic and political arenas because the movement members successfully use their role as mothers to champion their cause. The social movement has been able to maintain a strong grassroots base and effectively use the media to create and maintain social networks. Furthermore, the packaging of WOZA's cause in human rights discourse has resulted in sympathy and support by similar minded organizations. Lastly, the WOZA movement cannot be adequately understood without examining the role of its leaders, Jenni Williams and Magodonga Mahlangu.

WOZA's Narrative: Packaging the struggle

Smithey (2009) argues that tactics and strategies define the successful orchestration of any social movement's set goals. The framing of issues determines whether social movement groups remain relevant and active in articulating their issues. WOZA's determined protests reflect a great deal of similarities with similar nonviolent struggles such as Ukraine's Orange Revolution, the Otpor movement in Serbia, and the Women in Peacebuilding Network of Liberia. Like the Otpor movement, WOZA uses symbolic gestures and powerful words to portray their message. Using the narrative of tough love, WOZA members candidly demand better governance and leadership while emphasizing their nurturing feminine roles. WOZA members are convinced that, as mothers, they have to be soft yet tough with politicians by relentlessly pressing for discipline and accountability from the governing élites. In some protests, WOZA women take to the streets making an L-shaped gesture using their thumbs and fingers, a symbol they call the love spear. Since 2002, WOZA members have held demonstrations on Valentine's Day, distributing roses to underscore the belief that their protest is based on love for people and for the nation. In their 2005 Valentine demonstrations, the WOZA banners read: "The Power of Love can conquer the Love of Power."

Symbolism is an integral part of any social movement, thud, during some of their demonstrations, WOZA women would hold brooms in their hands, symbolically washing away corruption and bad governance, while banging on empty pots to signify food shortages. Sometimes they would march in silence to support censored independent media. In other demonstrations, WOZA members would march with children clad in school uniforms to draw attention to drastic hikes in school fees of more than 1,000 percent. One of WOZA's renowned activities was the Bread and Roses March in 2008 when WOZA members took to the streets demanding bread and roses, with bread representing food and roses representing dignity.[6] On April 12, 2010, WOZA members in Bulawayo marched to the offices of the government electricity provider, the Zimbabwe Electricity Supply Authority (ZESA), to deliver "yellow cards"[7] to ZESA for poor service and high tariffs. WOZA women protested the exorbitant tariffs for electricity usage that were being charged by the government-owned electricity company, ZESA. Such high electricity bills were proving to be too costly and unsustainable. The use of such symbolism by WOZA has managed to draw significant attention to the serious issues confronting Zimbabwe. WOZA's use of these small and symbolic gestures in protest fit with the ideas in James Scott's ethnography, *Weapons of the Weak* (2005), which underscores how minute and pragmatic gestures of noncooperation allow ordinary people to draw attention to structural issues such as inequality, poverty, and injustice. Scott describes how poor people use gradual and small tactics of resistance to confront their difficult structural conditions and argues that such strategies will gradually erode a system. Schock (2005) concurs that compared to violence, nonviolent movement campaigns have a better chance of transforming authoritarian governments. For practical reasons, WOZA use the antithesis of violence during protests, being fully aware that soft power is the most credible alternative for women who are confronted with the unyielding brute state. In an analysis of third world women's movements, Lorber concludes that, "grassroots women's politics is practical, whereas middle class women's politics is feminist" (Lorber 1990: 294).

Tarrow (1998) discusses how successful social movements require innovation in terms of contentious activities. In this vein, WOZA members take advantage of internationally observed days to launch or highlight their campaigns. These include the International Day of Women, Human Rights Day, and the Day of the African Child, among others. A report from the online newspaper AllAfrica.com, quoted by PeaceWomen, notes that in November 2007, approximately 1,000 WOZA members participated in demonstrations to observe the 16 days of activism against gender violence (PeaceWomen 2007). On International Women's Day, March 8, 2008, WOZA held a demonstration in Bulawayo, demanding an end to political violence in Zimbabwe.

According to the WOZA reports, more than 50 WOZA members were arrested, detained, and beaten by the police (Amnesty International 2008a) after this protest, although this did not deter the movement from continuing to advance its cause.

Addressing Practical and Strategic Gender Needs

By seeking to address both practical and strategic gender needs of men and women, the WOZA movement has not only significantly filled the void between the governors and the governed but has also brought to the fore some hidden nuances and actors related to the conflict. While the focus on Zimbabwe's crises has tended to be on the political arena, other areas, such as the experience of women in the conflict, have been ignored. While the major political parties have been embroiled in power wrangles and ideological debates, WOZA has been engaging in campaigns for basic social service provision such as access to treatment for those who are HIV positive as well as access to affordable basic commodities. In addition to their focus on livelihood and women's issues, WOZA is concerned with issues of economic recovery, democratic transition, and governance in Zimbabwe. WOZA has, for example, campaigned against the Public Order and Security Act (POSA), which significantly restricts freedom of assembly.

Offe (1985, 820) observes that contemporary social movements challenge "the boundaries of institutional politics" by rupturing the traditional dichotomies between private and public life and between politics and civil society. Thus, during negotiations of the GPA, WOZA repeatedly criticized the gender blindness of these talks, their delays, and the continued violence. In May 2008, WOZA members protested at the Zambian embassy in Zimbabwe, issuing a petition against the continued postelection violence in Zimbabwe. On October 27, 2008, during a protest, whose theme was Pedzai Hurukuro: Tafa Nenzara (Conclude the Talks: We Are Dying of Hunger), women from WOZA and their civil society partners, Women's Coalition in Zimbabwe (WCoZ), demonstrated outside the hotel where negotiations were being held. In similar fashion to the events in Ghana in 2003 during the Liberian peace talks, WOZA's actions reflected Zimbabwean women's fatigue and frustration with the delay by the political leaders in coming to a conclusive political agreement. Even though WOZA successfully raised awareness and mobilized sympathy about the negative effect of the stalemate on Zimbabweans, after this incident, scores of women were arrested for "harassing SADC leaders" (Cuthbert 2008). Despite such kinds of setbacks, WOZA members continue to politically engage in Zimbabwe, demanding accountability from the principals in the Government of National Unity.

Grounded in Femininity

Analysis of WOZA in action reveals a gendered expression of experiences of structural violence. McKay and Mazurana (1999) use a feminist analysis to review women's contributions to peace-building processes. Their study reveals that the ways women confront social injustices are significantly different from their male counterparts, yet they achieve the same goals. The struggle for WOZA is grounded in their roles as mothers, sisters, and women, because the crisis in Zimbabwe has affected women more poignantly. Jenni Williams, quoted by Elisabeth Day (2009) in *The Observer*, underscores WOZA's appeal to femininity, saying,

> We speak from the moral authority that we are the mothers of the nation ... and if your mother cannot speak out on your behalf then you have no one that will speak for you. So that is why we are committed to doing this: because we want a better future for our children.

One of the most notable campaigns used by WOZA was Stand Up for Your Child, in which women took their children to the streets encouraging other women to vote during the March 2008 elections. WOZA encouraged women to use their vote to make a statement against government inefficiency and injustice so as to protect the next generation's inheritance. This protest was appealing to women, especially mothers, since they are primarily responsible for protecting the welfare of their children. Thus, when women participate in social movements, the experience gives them the capacity to develop gender consciousness and make gender-specific demands (Berger 1992; Seidman 1993; and Sharoni 1995, 2001). As mostly female activists, WOZA members used their platform to make efforts to improve their communities and enhance the lives of their families. Amnesty International reports that in May 2005, WOZA members, with their children, demonstrated against the increase in school fees of up to 1,000 percent (Amnesty International Update 2009). The government responded by evoking repressive legislation, namely Section 7(c) of the Miscellaneous Offences Act, which accused the women of displaying behaviour that is "likely to materially interfere with the ordinary comfort, convenience, peace or quiet of the public." Like the protagonists in *Contentious Lives: Two Argentine Women, Two Protests, and the Quest for Recognition* by Javier Auyero (2002), WOZA's activism reflects both the struggle for survival as well as personal journeys toward gaining recognition, respect, and dignity. Wilson (1971, 5) observes people's participation in social movements and concludes that,

> [a]nimated by the injustices, sufferings, and anxieties they see around them, men and women in social movements reach beyond the customary resources of the social order to launch their own crusade against the evils of society. In so doing they reach beyond themselves and become new men and women.

This connection of women's issues with human rights reflects the notion that the personal is political.[8] As much as WOZA members are raising issues of their personal struggles as mothers in Zimbabwe's scarred socioeconomic and political landscape, these women are also confronting structural challenges of human rights abuse, the ineffective state, and a difficult economic environment. In accordance with the structuration theory by Anthony Giddens (1986), WOZA members are dialectically weaving structure and action together. Ultimately, the WOZA case study reveals an intricate connection between the macro and micro, the grand and the minor, as well as the personal and public issues. The personalization of the political is reflected in WOZA founding members and leaders, Jenni Williams and Magodonga Mahlangu, who reflect a fearless and astute demeanor. In a personal testimony titled *Jenni Williams' Voice*, which she read during the Durban Review Conference held in April 2009, the WOZA leader discusses the personal impact of the her experience as a human rights defender and acknowledges how this has helped her personal and emotional growth.

It is apparent that for WOZA members, the social movement has become a site for the struggle for "the reappropriation of time, of space, and of relationships in the individual's daily experience." By participating in WOZA activities, women can move beyond victimhood to active social transformation and reclamation of the public sphere. WOZA is among those case studies that demonstrate how women can mobilize as mothers around issues of peace and human rights in authoritarian regimes. Scholars such as Schirmer (1989), Waylen (1992), and Noonan (1995) have focused considerable attention on this subject matter. In addition, scholars recognize that women are highly motivated and committed to ending violence and working toward peace because of the huge impact of conflict on them (Becker 1995; Korac 1998; Fearon 2002). Indeed, women's movements across the world, including Palestine, Argentina, India, and Liberia have significantly evoked their motherhood and femininity as forms of political identity to package their causes. Through their appeal to their femininity and nonviolent resistance, WOZA members have succeeded in bringing the government to make concessions in response to their demands.

Grassroots Mobilization

According to Lederach (1997), peace building must occur at every level, including the grassroots level. Using the concept of multitrack diplomacy, Diamond and McDonald (1996) discuss the same theme, arguing for the involvement of multiple parties in the construction of peace. Lederach underscores that support from the grassroots is essential for any sustainable peace process. The French school of thought on social movements conceives that true social movements are consciously constructed by rank-and-file members and are the expression of the collective will (Touraine 1981, 1983). As such, one of the factors explaining WOZA's resilience is their participatory and grassroots-centered approach to effecting social change. WOZA members are ordinary women from various community-based organizations. WOZA has limited formal requirements for membership, so members of WOZA are those who believe in its cause. According to WOZA (2007), the movement made consultations in all of Zimbabwe's ten provinces, conducting more than 284 meetings and reaching approximately 10,000 rural and urban people to ascertain views and gain insights from Zimbabweans. The outcome was a People's Charter, a document outlining Zimbabweans' expectations of a new Zimbabwe and their vision on the economy, politics, constitution, elections, and freedom, among others.[9] These consultations have been able to connect WOZA with the community.

The Role of Leadership

Literature on social movements underscores the immense role played by leaders in generating movement and sustaining momentum. Lederach (1997) underscores the role of leadership in peace building and conflict transformation. Well-led civil society organizations have proved to be valuable vehicles for democracy and development. Leadership is inherently a communal process of persuasion to induce followers to take action. Leaders are continually engaged in relational processes of social change in order to make a difference. WOZA has grown in numbers and effectiveness under the visionary, courageous, and creative leadership of its cofounders. Arguably, WOZA leaders Jenni Williams and Magodonga Mahlangu employ the servant leadership model (Greenleaf 1970) or exemplary leadership, since they experience the same physical and structural dangers that follower members face, including arrest and detention.

In the same vein, *The WOZA Story* (2004), a report by Sokwanele, an activist civil society organization focusing on politics in Zimbabwe, said of one of the WOZA leaders Jenni Williams:

> It is impossible to write about WOZA without mentioning Jenni Williams, one of the founders and the ongoing inspiration of WOZA women. She is a visionary, driven by a remarkable energy, determined and brave, undeterred by threats and harassment and numerous arrests and uncomfortable nights in stinking police cells.

Similarly, the cofounder of WOZA, Magodonga Mahlangu, is also esteemed for her leadership qualities. During an award ceremony in recognition of WOZA's winning of the 2009 Robert Kennedy Award for Human Rights, President Barack Obama also highlighted Mahlangu's courage and resilience against violence and adversity.

Social Networking

The WOZA case study demonstrates the importance of creating networks and coalitions among civil society for the success of social movements. Barnes (2006) aptly notes that local people are often unable to address all the dimensions and drivers of conflict on their own, especially under conditions of severe power imbalances. Similarly, Durkhemian sociology posits that social networking is pivotal in the success of social movements because it allows groups to maintain social consciousness and social ties through regular gatherings. Tarrow (1998) also underscores how "diffuse social networks" enhance the capacity of social movements to articulate their needs and gain audiences with important stakeholders. In this regard, WOZA has pursued strategic alliances with influential partners including organizations in the diaspora such as the Zimbabwean Exiles Forum (ZEF). On October 28, 2008, South African feminists and civil society organizations issued a press statement in support of WOZA, expressing their concern over the impasse of power-sharing negotiations between ZANU PF and MDC. The South African activists also launched what they called a "roll-out campaign of action in solidarity with Zimbabwean women" (AWID 2008). Other WOZA partners and sympathizers include Amnesty International (AI), Africa Action, and Human Rights Watch. These organizations have produced a number of reports that draw the attention of the international community to WOZA's plight. After the arrest of WOZA leaders Williams and Mahlangu on October 16, 2008, AI urged the Zimbabwean authorities to immediately and unconditionally release them. On March 25, 2009, AI organized a reception in Washington, D.C., to honor the two leaders for their brave struggle against injustice in Zimbabwe.

Effective and Creative Use of the Media

The role of the media, especially as a tool for activism and as a conduit for raising awareness, has been explored at length in social movement literature (Gamson and Wolfsfield 1993; Gamson 1995; Waterman 1998; Carroll and Ratner 1999; Castells 1989, 1996, 1997, 1998, 2000; Earl and Schussman 2003; Hackett and Carroll 2004; Jacobson 2004; Barker 2008). Hackett and Carroll (2004, 1) posit that social movements "greatly depend on the media to help them mobilize, and to validate their standing." WOZA uses media and technology in innovative ways to expose oppression, delegitimize brutality, and publicize the movement's agenda. Through a daily diary, the members chronicle their work, document the experiences of members in police custody, and share updates about their initiatives. WOZA also issues cyberpetitions, press statements, and open letters to public figures, voicing their concerns about particular issues. The WOZA Website and pamphlets provide names and contact information of those to whom appeals can be sent, including offices of the attorney general, police chiefs, and other influential external parties. WOZA also works with civil society partners such as Kubatana and Pambazuka News to relay messages about their activities. *Kubatana* is a Shona word meaning "togetherness." Kubatana is a network on NGOs and civil society actors in Zimbabwe. It is used as a platform for networking, information dissemination, and electronic activism. *Pambazuka* is a Swahili word that, when taken as a noun means "dawn," while as a verb, it means "to arise." Pambazuka is a Web forum for Africans interested in social justice issues. It is published for many civil society organizations and human rights activists in Africa. The publicizing of women's harassment at the hands of the police is a shaming strategy that has somewhat been effective in putting pressure on the state to observe the rule of law and afford women the right to justice and fair trials. Effective publicity work by WOZA has been important in articulating women's experiences, helping to transform public consciousness and legitimize WOZA's cause. Through various media outlets, WOZA has managed not only to highlight its cause but also to mobilize empathy and to galvanize support for various campaigns. Creative use of the media has enabled WOZA to transform fellow citizens from mere observers and bystanders to supporters and advocates in a common struggle.

Use of a Human Rights Discourse

Framing processes in social movements are a crucial dynamic in mobilizing supporters, recruiting sympathizers, convincing allies, legitimizing claims, consolidating a shared vision, and determining the overall character of the movement (Snow and Benford 1992; 1988; Gamson 1995; Benford and Snow 2000). The concept of the frame was propounded by Erving Goffman (1974) to describe an interpretive schema that people use to simplify, understand, create meaning, and make sense of their reality. Framing allows social movements to identify causes, translate local grievances into broader claims, and establish a course of action. The WOZA frames its cause in human rights discourse and identifies its initiative as a struggle for both human rights and women's rights.

The identity of WOZA as a human rights defender had been embraced by international organizations such as Amnesty International, Human Rights Watch, and Women Human Rights Defenders (WHRD), among others. In Zimbabwe, WOZA works closely with organizations such as Zimbabwe Lawyers for Human Rights (ZLHR), Law Society of Zimbabwe (LSZ), and the Zimbabwe Human Rights NGO forum (ZHRF). Such organizations assist WOZA with legal services, advocacy, and solidarity messages. Although the women's-rights-as-human-rights frame has been criticized for its universalizing tendencies (Friedman 1995), this narrative has nonetheless served WOZA well. In recognition of its role in defense of human rights, in 2006, WOZA was nominated for the Martin Ennals Award for Human Rights Defenders, which is awarded to individuals or organizations that demonstrate courage and resilience in confronting human rights abuses. In 2007, Jenni Williams was among ten women from around the globe who won the US State Department's International Women Courage Award. On September 15, 2009, WOZA received the 4th Annual Peace Award from the War Resisters' League for their use of nonviolent strategies to champion social justice and good governance.

Challenges for WOZA

WOZA operates in an environment where there is competition for recognition among various social movements and civil society organizations in Zimbabwe, including the Women's Action Group, Women's Trust, and

Women's Action Group. McFadden (1997) observes how the women's movement in southern Africa is challenged by numerous tensions among fellow women activists. The fragmentation of the women's movement has resulted in duplication of efforts and competition for space and recognition among social movements in Zimbabwe (McCandless 2005). Such a situation has ultimately resulted in a situation Masipula Sithole (1979) would label as "the struggle within the struggle." The fragmentation of any women's movement is not surprising since women have heterogeneous interests that are influenced by factors such as class, race, age, and status. Ray and Korteweg (1999, 66) conclude that,

> Relationships between women's movements and the state, between women's movements and other movements, and between women's movements themselves are extremely complex.

Leadership challenges have been identified as some of the key factors that compromise the vibrancy and democracy in most communities (Naidoo 2004). Despite the engagement of WOZA leadership in the organization's core activities and with the grassroots community, concerns have been raised about the nature of leadership in this social movement. WOZA has been criticized for having an oligarchic nature wherein Jenni Williams and a few key people control WOZA activities. This is risky in terms of organizational growth and sustainability, as there is limited room for capacity building of other members. The concern is that oligarchic institutions face the threat of a leadership vacuum in the event of the loss of the top leaders. Nonetheless, it seems common for strong resistance movements like WOZA to have oligarchic and centralized leadership as a survival strategy.

Another criticism for WOZA is that their strategy is characterized by confrontation and protests. In an opinion article, Wilson Johwa (2003) points out that WOZA critics are worried that Jenni Williams is "... pre-occupied with ad hoc demonstrations at the expense of a more holistic fight for the rights of WOZA members, most of whom are black working class women ..." While protesting is a democratic right, its overuse may derail processes of dialogue and other approaches to centered communication. Mugo and Ali (2009) observe that WOZA protests " ... always, provoke hostile and violent reactions from the state agents who send their security forces to disperse the women violently." WOZA protests are often followed by detentions, which usually complicate the lives of ordinary, vulnerable women, especially those with young children to take care of. Since these detentions are often controversial, the media often focus more on the arrests than on the issues that prompted the protests. During an interview with Inter-Press News Agency in 2008, Jenni Williams defended the use of nonviolent protests, arguing that it provides WOZA with the opportunity to publicize their struggle and expose the violence that characterizes state-run institutions as prisons. In apparent agreement with this reasoning, Smith et al. (2001: 14010) argue that "in order to gain media attention, activists must partake in dramatic and often controversial activities." Indeed, WOZA's protests and subsequent arrests have attracted media attention, raised awareness, and galvanized support for the movement and its causes.

Conclusion

This chapter provides an analysis of a social movement led by women in Zimbabwe, and it challenges the stereotype of women as only victims. Much work remains to be done to strengthen WOZA to enhance the social movement's capacity to continue making meaningful changes to the status quo. WOZA has managed to reinvigorate political conversation about people's rights and human needs and also to reignite debate on the state and its responsibilities. WOZA remains one of the few voices in Zimbabwe that are championing change despite the dramatic economic limitations and the limited political space. The WOZA case demonstrates that women's movements can be powerful forces for change and nonviolent response to conflict. Although there is little significant shift in the political climate and state behavior in Zimbabwe, WOZA continues to engage with the state, demonstrating that, despite difficult circumstances, women can build strong coalitions to fight for their personal and community needs.

References

Amnesty International. 2008a. "WOZA Activists Released on bail in Zimbabwe." November 6, 2008.

Amnesty International. 2008b. "Jenni Williams and WOZA: Determined to be free: Individuals at Risk." January 9, 2008.

Amnesty International. 2007. "Zimbabwe: Between a Rock and a Hard Place: Women Human Rights Defenders at Risk." July 2007.

Africa News. "Hundreds Demonstrate Outside Summit on Zimbabwean Deadlock." *Africa News*, October 27, 2008.

Auyero, J. 2002. *Contentious Lives: Two Argentine Women, Two Protests, and the Quest for Recognition*. Durham, N.C.: Duke University Press.

AWID. "Press Release and Statement: In Solidarity with Zimbabwean Women." Association for Women in Development, October 28, 2008.

Barker, Michael. 2008. "Mass Media and Social Movement: A Critical Examination of the Relationship between Mainstream Media and Social Movements." *Global Research*, April 22, 2008.

Barnes, C. "Agents for Change: Civil Society Roles in Preventing War and Building Peace." *Global Partnership for the Prevention of Armed Conflict*, Issue Paper 2, September 2006.

Becker, H. 2003. "Women, Politics and Peace in Northern Namibia," in *Women and Peace in Africa* (pp. 47–73). Paris: UNESCO Workshop.

Benford, R., and D. A. Snow. 2000. "Framing Processes and Social Movements: An Overview and Assessment." *Annual Review of Sociology*, 26, 611–39.

Bird, K. and Prowse, M. 2008. "Vulnerability, Poverty and Coping in Zimbabwe", UNU-WIDER paper No. 41.

Burton, John. 1987. *Resolving Deep-rooted Conflict: A Handbook*. Lanham, Md.: University Press of America.

Campbell, Horace. 2003. *Reclaiming Zimbabwe: Exhaustion of the Patriarchal Mode of Liberation*. Cape Town, South Africa: David Phillip Publishers.

Carroll, William, K. and R.S. Ratner. 1999. 'Media Strategies and Political Projects: A Comparative Study of Social Movements." *Canadian Journal of Sociology*, 24(1), 1–34.

Castells, Manuel. 2000. "Toward a Sociology of the Network Society." *Contemporary Sociology*, 29(5), 693–99.

Castells, Manuel. 1998. *The End of the Millennium: The Information Age: Economy, Society and Culture*, Vol. III. Cambridge, Mass.: Blackwell.

Castells, Manuel. 1997. *The Power of Identity, the Information Age: Economy, Society and Culture*, Vol. II. Cambridge, Mass.: Blackwell.

Castells, Manuel. 1996. *The Rise of the Network Society, the Information Age: Economy, Society and Culture*, Vol. I. Cambridge, Mass.: Blackwell.

Castells, Manuel. 1989. *The Informational City: Information Technology, Economic Restructuring, and the Urban Regional Process*. Oxford, UK, and Cambridge, Mass.: Blackwell.

Cheater, Angela, and Rudo. 1996. "Gaidzanwa, Citizenship in Neo-Patrilineal States: Gender and Mobility in Southern Africa" *Journal of Southern Africa Studies*, 22(22), 189–200.

Cohen, A. 1977. "The Concept of Criminal Organization." *British Journal of Criminology*, 17, 97–111.

Cohen, A. 1965. "The Sociology of the Deviant Act: Anomie Theory and Beyond." *American Sociological Review*, 30, 5–14.

Day, Elizabeth 2009. "The Woman Who Took on Mugabe." *The Observer*, May 10.

Diamond, Louise, and John MacDonald. 1996. *Multi-Track Diplomacy: A Systems Approach to Peace*. Bloomfield, Conn.: Kumarian Press.

Earl, Jennifer and Alan, Schussman. 2003. "The New Site of Activism: On-line Organization, Movement Entrepreneurs, and the Changing Location of Social Movement Decision Making," in P.G. Coy (ed.), *Consensus Decision Making, Northern Ireland and Indigenous Movements*. San Jose, CA: JAI Press Inc. Elsevier Science Ltd.

Ekiyor, Thelma. Aremiebi and Leymah. R. Gbowee. 2005. "Women's Peace Activism in West Africa: The WIPNET Experience," in van Paul Tongeren, Malin Brenk,

Marte Hellema, and Juliette Verhoeven l. (eds), *People Building Peace II: Successful Stories of Civil Society.* Boulder. Colo.: Lynne Reinner Publishers.

Fearon, Kate. 2002. "Institutionalizing a Political Voice and Ensuring Representation: the Northern Ireland Women's Coalition," in Catherine Barnes (ed.), *Owning the Process: Public Participation in Peacemaking.* London: Conciliation Resources.

Ferre, Myra, M. and Patricia. Y. Martin. 1995. "Introduction: Doing the Work of the Movement," in Ferre, M.M. and Martin, P. Y (eds), *Feminist Organizations Feminist Organizations: Harvest of the New Movement.* Philadelphia: Temple University Press.

Flacks, R. 2004. "Knowledge for What? Thoughts on the State of Social Movement Studies," in J. Goodwin and J. Jasper (eds), *Rethinking Social Movements: Structure, Culture, and Emotion* (pp. 146–7). Lanham, Md.: Rowman and Littlefield Publishers.

Friedman, Elisabeth. 1995. "Women's Human Rights: The Emergence of a Movement," in Peters, J. and A. Wolper (eds), *Women's Rights, Human Rights: International Feminist Perspectives.* London and New York: Routledge.

Galtung, Johan. 1996. *Peace by Peaceful Means: Peace, Conflict, Development and Civilization,* London: Sage.

Galtung, Johan. 1969. "Violence, Peace and Peace Research." *Journal of Peace Research,* 6(3), 167–91.

Gamson, W. A. 1995. "Constructing Social Protest," in H. Johnston and B. Klandermans (eds), *Social Movements and Culture* (pp. 85–106). London: UCL Press.

Gamson, W. A. and G. Wolfsfeld. 1993. "Movements and Media as Interacting Systems." *Annals of the American Academy of Political and Social Science,* 528, 114–25.

Gavin, Michelle D. 2007. "Planning for a Post-Mugabe Era." Council on Foreign Relations, CSR. Paper No. 31, October.

Giddens, Anthony. 1986. *Social Theory and Modern Sociology.* Cambridge, Mass.: Polity Press.

Giddens, Anthony. 1984. *The Constitution of Society: Outline of the Theory of Structuration.* Cambridge, Mass.: Polity Press.

Giugni, Marco. G. 1998. "Was It Worth the Effort? The Outcomes and Consequences of Social Movements." *Annual Review of Sociology,* 24, 371–93.

Goffman, Erving. 1974. *Frame Analysis.* New York: Harper.

Greenleaf, Robert K. 1974. *Servant Leadership: A Journey into the Nature of Legitimate Power.* New York: Paulist Press.

Guma, Lance. 2007. "WOZA Members Blame Police for Death of Founding Activist," *SW Radio Africa,* November 13.

Habermas, Jurgen. 1983. *The Theory of Communicative Action,* Vol. I, Cambridge, Mass.: MIT Press.

Hackett, Robert. A. and William K. Caroll. 2004. "Critical Social Movements and Media Reform." *The World Association for Christian Communication.*

Hanke, Steve. H. 2008. "Zimbabwe: From Hyperinflation to Growth." *Development Policy Analysis,* No. 6, Cato Institute, Washington DC.

Hannigan, John. A., Alain Touraine, and Manuel Castells."Social Movement Theory a Critical Appraisal." *The Sociological Quarterly,* 26(4), 435–54.

Hassim, Shireen. 1993. "Family, Motherhood and Zulu Nationalism: The Politics of the Inkhatha Women's Brigade." *Feminist Review*, (43), 1–25.

Herbst, Jeffrey. 2000. State *and Power in Africa: Comparative Lessons in Authority Lessons in Authority and Control.* Princeton, N.J.: Princeton University Press.

Herbst, Jeffrey. 1990. *State Politics in Zimbabwe*, Los Angeles: University of California Press.

International Crisis Group. 2006. "Beyond Victimhood: Women's Peace Building in Sudan, Congo, Brussels and Uganda." Africa Report No. 112 (June 28).

Interpress News Agency. 2008. "Zimbabwean Women Have Had More Trauma after Independence: Interview with Women of Zimbabwe Arise (WOZA) National Coordinator Jenni Williams," *Inter Press News Agency*, September 13.

Jacobson, Robin. 2004. "Internet Identities: Social Movement Organizations and On-line Activism." Paper presented at the annual meeting of the Western Political Science Association, Marriott Hotel, Portland, Oregon, March 11.

Jacquette, Jane. 1989. *The Women's Movement in Latin America: Feminism and the Transition to Democracy.* Winchester, Mass.: Unwin Hyman.

Johwa, Wilson. 2003. "Zimbabwe: Activist Using protest PR to Change the World," *International Press Service*, December 6.

Jovanovic, Milja. 2005. "Rage Against the Regime: The Otpor Movement in Serbia," in van Tongeren, Paul, Malin Brenk, Marte Hellema, and Juliette Verhoeven l. (eds). *People Building Peace II: Successful Stories of Civil Society.* Boulder, Colo.: Lynne Reinner Publishers.

Kevin, Gillan. 2008. "Understanding Meaning in Social Movements: A Hermeneutic Approach." *Social Movement Studies*, 7(3), 247–63.

Korac, Maja. 1998. *Linking Arms: Women and War in Post-Yugoslav States.* Uppsala, Sweden: Life and Peace Institute.

Kriesberg, Louis. 2003. *Constructive Conflicts: From Escalation to Resolution* (2nd edn.). Lanham, Md.: Rowman and Littlefield.

Kriger, Norma. 2006. "From Patriotic Memories to 'Patriotic History' in Zimbabwe, 1990–2005." *Third World Quarterly*, 27(6), 1151–69.

Kriger, Norma. 2005. "ZANU PF Strategies in General Elections, 1980–2000: Discourse and Coercion." *African Affairs*, 104(414), 1–34.

Kriger, Norma. 2003.*Guerrilla Veterans in Post-War Zimbabwe: Symbolic and Violent Politics, 1980–1987,* Cambridge, UK: Cambridge University Press.

Kriger, Norma. 2000. "Zimbabwe Today: Hope Against grim Realities," *Review of African Political Economy*, 27(85), 443–50.

Lederach, John. P. 1997. *Building Peace: Sustainable Reconciliation in Divided Societies.* Washington: United States Institute of Peace.

Lihamba, A. 2003. "Women's Peace Building and Conflict Resolution Skills, Morogoro Region, Tanzania," in *Women and Peace in Africa* (pp. 111–31). Paris: UNESCO Workshops.

Lorber, Judith. 1990. "From the Editor: Special Issue on Women and Development in the Third World." *Gender Sociology*, 4(3), 293–95.

Mathey, M.J., T. Dejan, M. Deballe, R. Sopio, A. Koulaninga, and J. Moga. 2003. "The Role Played by Women of the Central African Republic in the Prevention and Resolutions of Conflicts," in UNESCO, *Women and Peace in Africa* (pp. 35–46). Paris: UNESCO Workshop.

McCandless, Erin. 2005. "Rights versus Distribution: Strategic Challenges Facing Zimbabwean Social Movements." Paper presented at the annual meeting of the American Political Science Association, Marriott, Loews Philadelphia, and the Pennsylvania Convention Center, Philadelphia.

McFadden, Patricia. 1997. "The Challenges and Prospects for the African Women's Movement in the 21st Century." *Women in Action*, (1), http://www.hartford-hwp.com/archives/30/152.html

McKay, S., and D. Mazurana. 2004. *Where Are the Girls? Girls in Fighting Forces in Northern Uganda, Sierra Leone, and Mozambique: Their Lives During and After War*. Montreal, Canada: International Centre for Human Rights and Democratic Development.

Meldrum, Andrew. 2004. *Where We Have Hope: A Memoir of Zimbabwe*. New York: Palgrave Macmillan

Melucci, Alberto. 1996.*Challenging Codes: Collective Action in the Information Age*. Cambridge, UK: Cambridge University Press.

Melucci, Alberto. 1988. *Nomads of the Present: Social Movements and Individual Needs in Contemporary Society*. London: Hutchinson.

Meredith, Martin. 2002. *Our Votes, Our Guns: Robert Mugabe and the Tragedy of Zimbabwe*. New York: Public Affairs.

Meredith, Martin. 2002. *Robert Mugabe: Power, Plunder and Tyranny in Zimbabwe*. Johannesburg, South Africa: Jonathan Ball.

Messner, S. and R. Rosenfeld. 1994. *Crime and the American Dream*. Belmont, Calif.: Wadsworth.

Mohanty, Chandra T. 1991. "Under Western Eyes: Feminist Scholarship and Colonial Discourses," in Mohanty, Chandra T., A. Russo and L. Torres (eds), *Third World Women and the Politics of Feminism*, pp. 51–80. Indianapolis: Indiana University Press.

Mugo, Cynthia and Ali, Sadia. 2008. Review of Counting the Cost of Coutrage: Trauma Experiences of Women Human Rights Defenders, "Researching for Life: Paradigms and Power." *Feminist Africa*, (11), 145–50.

Naidoo, K. 2004. "The End of Blind Faith? Civil Society and the Challenge of Accountability, Legitimacy and Transparency." *Accountability Forum*, 2, 14–25.

Ngoma, Agnes, L. 2006. *Social Movements and Democracy in Africa: The Impact of Women's Struggles for Equal Rights in Botswana*. London: Routledge.

Ngongo-Mbede, V. 2003. "The Traditional Mediation of Conflicts by Women in Cameroon," in *Women and Peace in Africa* (pp. 27–34). Paris: UNESCO Workshops.

Nhema, A. 2002. *Democracy in Zimbabwe: From Liberation to Liberalization*. Harare: University of Zimbabwe Publications.

Noonan, R. K. 1995. "Women against the State: Political Opportunities and Collective Action Frames in Chile's Transition to Democracy." *Sociology Forum*, 10(81), 81–111.

Ntahobari, J., and B. Ndayiziga. 2003. "The Role of Burundian Women in the Peaceful Settlement of Conflicts," in *Women and Peace in Africa* (pp. 11–26). Paris: UNESCO Workshops.

Nzou, Cuthbert. 2008. "Over 40 Women Arrested over Zim Talks." *Zimonline*, October 27.

Offe, C. 1995. "New Social Movements: Challenging the Boundaries of Institutional Politics." *Social Research*, 52(4), 817–28.

Oliver, Pamela E. and Hank Johnston. 2000. "What a Good Idea: Ideas, Frames and Ideologies in Social Movements Research." *Mobilization*, 5(1), 37–54.

Osirim, Mary J. 2003. "Crisis in the State and Family: Violence against women in Zimbabwe." *African Studies Quarterly*, 7(2), available online at http://web.africa. ufl.edu/asq/v7/v7i2a8.htm.

Osirim, Mary J. 2000. "Making Good on Commitments to Grassroots Women: NGO's and Empowerment for Women in Contemporary Zimbabwe." *Women's Studies International Forum*, 24(2), 167–80.

Paley, Julia. 2001. *Marketing Democracy: Power and Social Movements in Past-Dictatorship Chile*. Berkeley: University of California Press.

PeaceWomen. 2007. "Zimbabwe: 1000 Women Mark 16 Days of Activism against Gender Violence," *PeaceWomen*, November 27.

Inter Press News Agency. 2008. "Q&A: Zimbabwean Women have had More Trauma after Independence: Interview with Women of Zimbabwe Arise (WOZA) National Coordinator Jenni Williams," *Inter Press News Agency*, September 13.

Ranger, T. 1992. "Afterword: War, Violence and Healing in Zimbabwe." *Journal of Southern African Studies*, 18(3), 698–707.

Ray, R., and A. C. Korteweg. 1999. "Women's Movements in the Third World: Identity, Mobilization, and Autonomy." *Annual Review of Sociology*, 25, 47–71.

Robert Kennedy Center. 2009. "Leading Zimbabwe Human Rights Defender and Movements Wins RFK Award." Robert Kennedy Center Press Release, September 16.

Schirmer, J. 1993. "The Seeking of Truth and the Gendering of Consciousness: The Comadres of El Salvador and The Conaviuga Widows of Guatemala," in S.A. Radcliffe and S. Westwood (eds), *'Viva' Women and Popular Protest in Latin America*, London and New York: Routledge.

Schirmer J. G. 1989. "Those Who Die for Life Cannot Be Called Dead: Women in Human Rights Protest in Latin America." *Feminist Review*, 32, 3–29.

Schmidt, H. 1997. "Healing the Wounds of War: Memories of Violence and the Making of History in Zimbabwe's Most Recent Past," *Journal of Southern African Studies*, 21(2), 301–10.

Schmidt, E. 1992. *Peasants, Traders and Wives: Shona Women in the History of Zimbabwe, 1870–1939*. Portsmouth, N.H.: Heinemann.

Schock, K. 2005. *Unarmed Insurrections: People Power Movements in Non-democracies*, Minneapolis: University of Minnesota Press.

Schulz, Markus. 1998. "Collective Action Across Borders: Opportunity Structures, Network Capacities, and Communicative Praxis in the Age of Advanced Globalization." *Sociological Perspectives*, 41(3), 587–616.

Scott, J. 1985. *Weapons of the Weak: Everyday Forms of Peasant Resistance*. New Haven, Conn.: Yale University Press.

Seidman, Gay W. 1993. "No Freedom without the Women: Mobilization and Gender in South Africa, 1970–1992." *Signs*, 18(2), 291–320.

Serbin, Andrés. 2005 "Effective Regional Networks and Partnerships," in van Tongeren, Paul, Malin Brenk, Marte Hellema, and Juliette Verhoeven l. (eds), *People Building Peace II: Successful Stories of Civil Society*. Boulder, Colo.: Lynne Rienner Publishers.

Sharoni, Simona. 2001. "Rethinking Women's Struggles in Israel-Palestine and in the North of Ireland," in Caroline Moser and Fiona Clark (eds), *Victims, Perpetrators or Actors: Gender, Armed Conflict and Political Violence* (pp. 85–98). London: Zed.

Sharoni, Simona. 1995. *Gender and the Israeli-Palestinian Conflict: The Politics of Women's Resistance*, Syracuse, N.Y.: Syracuse University Press.

Sibanda, E.M. 2005. *The Zimbabwe African People's Union 1961–87: A Political History of Insurgency in Southern Rhodesia*. Trenton, N.J.: Africa World Press.

Sita, R.N. 2006. "Gender Politics and the Pendulum of Political and Social Transformation in Zimbabwe." *Journal of Southern African Studies*, 32(1), 49–67.

Sithole, Masiphula. 1979. *Struggle within the Struggle: 1957–1980*, Gweru, Zimbabwe: Rujeko Publishers.

Smith, Jackie, John D. McCarthy, Clark McPhail, and Bogulsaw Augustyn. 2001. "From Protest to Agenda Building: Description Bias in Media Coverage of Protest Events in Washington, D.C." *Social Forces*, 79(4), 1397–423.

Smithey, Lee. 2009. "Social Movement Strategy, Tactics, and Collective Identity," *Sociology Compass*, 2(4), 658–71.

Snow D.A., and R.D. Benford. 1988. "Ideology, Frame Resonance, and Participant Mobilization." *International Social Movement Research*, 1, 97–218.

Snow, David A.E., Burke Rochford, Steven K. Worden, and Robert D. Benford. 1986. "Frame Alignment Processes, Micromobilization, and Movement Participation," *American Sociological Review*, 51, 464–81.

Tarrow, Sydney. 1998. *Power in Movements: Social Movements and Contentious Politics*. Cambridge, UK: Cambridge University Press.

Touraine, Alain. 1981. *The Voice and the Eye: An Analysis of Social Movements*, Cambridge, UK: Cambridge University Press.

Waterman, Peter. 1998. *Globalization, Social Movements, and the New Internationalisms*. London: Mansell.

Waylen, George. 1992. "Rethinking Women's Political Participation and Protest: Chile 1970–1990." *Political*, 40(2), 299–314.

Williams, Jenni. 2009. *Voice, Voices*, April 21.

Williams, Jenni. 2008. "A Moment in History: Mobilizing People Power-Opportunities for Change in Zimbabwe." A paper presented at the Nordic Africa Days, Copenhagen, Denmark, October 9.

Wilson, John. 1971. *Introduction to Social Movements*. New York: Basic Books.

WOZA. 2008. "The Effects of Fighting Repression with Love," August.

WOZA. 2008. "Counting the Cost of Courage: Trauma Experiences of Women Human Rights Defenders in Zimbabwe," August.

WOZA. 2007. "Defending Women—Defending the Rights of a Nation," A Preliminary Report on the Violence Against members of Women of Zimbabwe Arise, September.

CHAPTER NINE

Engendering Recovery: Rwanda

Peace Uwineza and Vanessa Noël Brown

Introduction

Rwanda, located in the Great Lakes region of central Africa, is home to one of the most devastating examples of intrastate violence in the twentieth century. Tensions erupted between the Hutus and Tutsis, Rwanda's two major ethnic groups, after the assassination of President Juvénal Habyarimana (a Hutu) in April 1994. This, in turn, unleashed an allegedly government-backed plan to exterminate the Tutsis. While the cause of the president's plane crash remains disputed, historians agree the event triggered the now infamous genocide against the Tutsis in Rwanda. Controversy also surrounds the total number of genocide victims with estimates ranging from 500,000 to 1 million Rwandans killed within a 100-day period (Semujanga 2003), with the victims largely being Tutsis and moderate Hutus. The Rwanda government's 2001 official census puts the number at 1,074,017 people, while others set deaths at 1.5 million people. The genocide followed a four-year war between Rwandan government forces and the Rwandese Patriotic Front (RPF) rebels. As the RPF advanced its war against the genocidal government, many Rwandans—the majority of them male—fled the country. By the time the killing spree concluded in 1994, gender demographics had significantly shifted due to the large number of men who had either died, were in prison as suspects to the genocide, or had fled the country fearing arrest or revenge as a result of their role in the genocide. *ProFemme*, the umbrella organization for all Rwandan women associations, estimates that immediately after the genocide six out of every seven Rwandans were female or upward of 88 percent of the population.

Authorities imprisoned approximately 130,000 Rwandan men on suspicion of genocide-related crimes until January 2003, at which time roughly half the detainees were released (Johnstone, forthcoming). Eventually those men who had fled the country returned, and many imprisoned men obtained release once the justice process began to run its course. By 2002, a national census found that out of a total population of 8,128,553 Rwandans, women accounted for 4,249,105, (52.27 percent). The demographic picture of women-to-men ratio in Rwanda provides a glimpse into major societal shifts in women's agency in the aftermath of the genocide.

Widowed or abandoned women were left highly traumatized as a result of physical assaults and widespread instances of rape and sexual enslavement during the years of protracted conflict. These same women found themselves shouldering the burden of reuniting surviving children, relatives, and friends and in some instances, taking on the roles as primary caretakers once the violence subsided. According to the United Nations Population Fund's 2002 survey, the predominance of the female population characterized Rwanda's turn-of-the-century demographics, with women comprising 54.4 percent of the total population. The 2002 survey noted that females were head of 34 percent of households, which highlights the civil war's impact not only on demographics but also shifted women's societal roles.

The genocide resulted in the death and displacement of millions of Rwandans and left many households' source of income destroyed, leaving behind a decimated social economic fabric. The genocide decimated traditional communal and extended family connections and devastated protection mechanisms. Government infrastructure and systems, once relied on by the population, were also left in tatters.

To rebuild, the postgenocide government of national unity made a conscious effort to view women not only as victims of a tragedy but also as catalysts for peace building. Structural changes grounded in legal and political decisions paved the way for women's advancement in the politics and decision-making levels of the country.

As a result, Rwandan women have toiled tirelessly to construct a better future for the next generation in the aftermath of the tragic conflict. Women rounded up surviving orphans and elderly via grassroots associations. They assumed nontraditional roles in performing manual labor, managing businesses, and heading families. When government officials sought to include women in the postgenocide political processes, Rwandan women rose to the challenge and increased their capacities as leaders, thus successfully distancing themselves from their traditional "minor" status. Rwanda in the twenty-first century provides an inspiring illustration of women effecting a positive transition in a post-conflict setting and leading the country's evolution from a time of trauma into an era marked by socioeconomic and political gains. Women in this small African country offer striking examples of leadership in both public and private spheres, where their efforts have collectively repositioned the traditional gender narrative from women as solely victims of tragedy to women as leaders of positive societal change.

This chapter explores how a catastrophic ethnic conflict proved to be a catalyst in many women's lives. Rwandans emerged from the tragedy with the motivation to create a stronger social fabric for the next generation. It explores the socialcultural aspects of the postgenocide era that facilitated the advancement of women in society and provides examples of creative female leadership in business, politics, and psychosocial initiatives. The Rwandan conflict was a transformative event through which significantly shifted following a cataclysmic period of intrastate violence. This chapter explores why the ongoing empowerment of women is a critical factor in Rwanda's continuing upward trajectory. It also considers current challenges that remain for Rwandan women amid such significant gains. The narratives provide a case study of how Rwandan women's agency propelled dramatic social progress that has led to Rwanda being cited as a twentieth-century example not only of tragedy but as one of the success stories of women's leadership in Africa.

Rwandan Women's Status in the Twentieth Century

Rwanda has a unique historical trajectory against which women's most recent gains can be considered. In African societies, women's roles are typically subservient to longstanding patriarchal structures. However historians contend that women in precolonial Rwanda were well respected and protected with a particular reverence to their role as mothers. Rwandan traditional sayings, proverbs, and folklore provide evidence of women's status in the precolonial era, including *"Ukurusha umugore akurusha urugo"* or "With a great woman, a great home is assured" and *"Umutima w'urugo"* or "the heart of a home," which presents a woman as the source of livelihood for a family (Uwineza and Pearson 2009). In 1960, a Belgian government report to the U.N. General Assembly commented, "One also easily perceives the importance and the majesty accorded to women in this country in their role as the bearers of life, the fertility of the race. One witnesses the great respect given to women, especially if she is the mother of a number of children" (translated from French; Uwineza and Pearson 2009). The Kinyarwanda word *"mabuja"* is a term of endearment used by husbands when referring to their wives and also exemplifies a woman's role as the manager of the family. *Mabuja* also denotes respect for someone with whom you consult before making a decision (Rutayisire 2008).

The colonial era, in contrast, saw women's place in Rwanda shift into that of an increasingly marginalized group. Colonial rule (1899–1962) marked an era of discrimination against women in socioeconomic and political spheres, which dismantled Rwandan traditional ways of life in the Rwandan culture. A decline in women's perceived status and related opportunities in society resulted when sociocultural values shifted to a monetary economy and European education became the driving force behind progress and human value. Mutamba and Izabiliza (2005, 14–15) note how the colonialist influence shaped women's positions in society:

> The abrupt shift from subsistence to a monetary economy based on paid employment and a formal education system, weakened women's position relative to that of men. In particular, it weakened their bargaining position on matters concerning their access to, and control over resources and the degree of their level of participation in the development process.

Thus with the advent of colonialism, women became increasingly marginalized as the normative roles central to indigenous traditions began to erode. The introduction of a monetary economy and formal education— both colonial-era structures that excluded women—resulted in an access to leadership that sidelined women. Such a decreased status of women remained even after the colonialist government departed.

Rwanda's postcolonial regime perpetuated divisionism and exclusionism that did not spare women. By the time the genocide occurred, women had largely come to accept their second-class status in society. During this period, authorities marginalized anyone considered weak or irrelevant. This included the Tutsis, people from the south (related to regional segregation based on the north-south divide) and women. Structural mechanisms that guaranteed inequality were firmly in place: Rwandan family law designated the man as the exclusive head of a household. Women could not own a business, open a bank account, or decide to live in a particular location unless one's husband authorized it (United Nations Population Fund and the Ministry of Gender and Women in Development 2002, 32). A woman's survival depended on support from one's husband, father or another male relative. Access to credit was nonexistent. Sexual harassment in the workplace was common, and speaking out against such treatment went against social norms. Husbands often received and managed their wives' salaries. Women's second-class status is the social backdrop from which the postgenocide change in women's status emerged. The years of intrastate conflict saw the opening up of space for women to take on increased responsibilities during wartimes.

Rose Mukantabana worked as a secretary in assorted government ministries in the 1980s, during which time she noted that women never rose above the position of secretary. In the Ministry of Natural Resources, only one woman had a managerial position, in the loans section of the finance department. Mukantabana said this was usually the case in other ministries, where women did not receive promotions beyond secretarial positions or archival management (June 2009 interview conducted by Uwineza). She would later rise to turn that standard on its head in the 2008 national elections by becoming the first elected female speaker of parliament in Africa's Great Lakes region.

The 1990s genocide was not the first incident of conflict amongst disparate Hutus and Tutsis. Intervals of violence in the 1950s and 1960s resulted in thousands of Rwandans seeking refuge in neighboring countries. These periods of conflict provided space for women's contributions. While in exile, Rwandan women adapted to new conditions and began to cultivate the land and grow food in order to support their families. Women in exile joined the Rwandan Patriotic Front (RPF) struggle and contributed to its success (the RFP became Rwanda's ruling party in July 1994). Powley (2003) offers the analysis that the RFP's policy of including women was influenced by its exposure to gender equality in Uganda, where many RFP members spent years in exile. John Mutamba, former representative of the Ministry of Gender Affairs, concurs: Men who grew up in exile know the experience of discrimination ... Gender is now part of our political thinking. We appreciate all components of our population across all the social divides. (Mutamba and Izabiliza 2005, 12)

During the RPF's struggle in the early 1990s, women's involvement in the resistance was highly pronounced. Leaders such as Inyumba Aloisea, head of RPF's finance section, were instrumental in encouraging other women to view themselves as equal partners with much to contribute. The RPF enlisted able-bodied men and women for the frontline while the less-able formed groups to coordinate contributions:

> Almost all these groups were run by women. They dealt only in cash because of the clandestine nature of their work, but their coded records were scrupulously detailed and there was never a case of embezzlement. (Kinzer 2008, 82)

Taking on such responsibilities prepared women for future opportunities in coalitions that have shaped postgenocide policy and reforms.

The postgenocide era at the turn of the twenty-first century has proved to have the sharpest upward trajectory to date for women's increased levels of leadership. Both the Rwandan government and international supporters of Rwanda's post-conflict stabilization have emphasized the need for women's involvement in the reconstruction process as a development strategy. This approach helped empower Rwandan women, who in turn increasingly view themselves as active participants in the affairs that affect their lives and those of the people under their care. Rwandan women took advantage of new opportunities while society at large reconsidered women and men's roles and relationships. Grassroots efforts have had a major role in providing psychosocial assistance to women as well as playing a role in the creation of economic avenues for women.

Grassroots Initiatives in the Aftermath of Genocide

Since the genocide, women have been working across a spectrum of classes and sectors to build a strong social fabric that is now the foundation of a new era in Rwanda. Educated women are taking the lead in sensitizing and encouraging rural women to become leaders and take part in the affairs of their lives, their homes, and their nation. Their efforts include the formation of NGOs, grassroots associations, and educational and training programs to bring disenfranchised women into the political life of the country.

Many grassroots organizations led by Rwandan women arose in order to provide support amid the conflict's immense trauma and personal and economic losses. Grieving women who witnessed their loved ones' brutal murders created Avega-Agahozo, a genocide survivors' association. Many of the founder members were tortured, wounded, and raped. Newly established grassroots nongovernment organizations (NGOs) helped women get access to government and international donor support, which subsequently propelled association members into becoming viable social economic actors. Numerous cooperatives helped rural, uneducated women, formerly culturally relegated to the backyard, to evolve into viable businesswomen.

Sisters Janet Nkubana and Joy Ndungutse founded Gahaya Links, a grassroots organization that assisted women left widowed by the genocide. Nkubana states that, in the past, society had not viewed women as able business managers but recent years, "have proved that women can be, and perhaps can even do it better than men" (quoted in September 1, 2008, Inter Press News Service). One such example is the basket weavers, who have become international exporters of their traditional handicrafts. With support and guidance from the urban educated women, the rural women were able to take advantage of the 2000 African Growth and Opportunity Act (AGOA), a US trade pact that provided a means through which Rwandan women transformed rural handicraft specialists into basket weavers. Together urban and rural women successfully created profitable co-operatives that export baskets and other traditional ornaments worldwide.

Amid the economic gains achieved by Rwandan women, men are increasingly more positive toward women's advancement, with many Rwandan women noting the support they enjoy from their husbands as they seek work outside the home. While many Rwandan men previously dismissed weaving as women's work with no real benefits, their attitudes later changed. In recent years, when men observed the success of weaving co-operatives headed by local women, some joined the weaving classes. The psychosocial impact of fine crafts training emerges from the transformation of a traditional pastime activity into a lucrative business, which has raised the status of women as breadwinners within their family units. Further evidence of the repositioning of traditional gender roles is thus evident through the evolution of grassroots efforts such as weaving co-operatives.

Women weavers offered the following anecdotes that point to a repositioning of gender norms. One noted that in a recent weaving training class, 4 of the 37 students were men. Such statistics represent a shift in the role of Rwandan women as the primary breadwinners in their marriage. Sarafina Mukaruberwa a leader of a weaving group in Kigali stated during an interview:

'I usually spend two to three months in Kigali training other women, leaving [my] children under the care of my husband.' In years past this was unheard of as women were the ones expected to stay at home as men went out to work. 'Men now see the benefits,' as she went on to say, '… my income is much higher than my husband makes, this makes him accept my disappearance from home as he knows that when I come back, I will bring money to complete the construction of our house or to pay for other family expenses.' (July 2008 Interview conducted by Uwineza)

Leading households and entrepreneurships has afforded women better social status and self-esteem, resulting in a new storyline for women in Rwanda. Priscilla Kankindi, another young single woman from the Muhanga district, proffered this point of view:

I now have property of my own which I control and use as I wish. I have my own cows, a piece of land, and money to spend on personal needs. I also help my parents by buying household needs and helping my younger brothers and sisters with school requirements. Because I have my own income, I have resisted early marriage. I am happy and contented, no man can confuse me with gifts like money, a mobile telephone etc, which they use to get other girls. (September 2008 interview conducted by Uwineza)

Children raised in the postgenocide era may be more likely to carry attitudes of equality between the men and women into the next generation. Youth born in the era of exile bore witness to single mothers functioning as the head of the family. They understand that women were the first to meet their material and psychological needs. These children went on to assume leadership roles in post-conflict Rwanda, armed with increased appreciation for women's capabilities and recognition of the importance of women's empowerment

Grassroots efforts have offered financial means to Rwandan women. However such initiatives' benefits are not limited to simply making money to support one's family. Such efforts have also encompassed the psychosocial benefits with women demonstrating their motivation to support one another across former dividing lines that defined the era of genocide.

Healing and Reconciliation in the Postgenocide Era

While traditional cultural norms did not see Rwandan women called up for active service in times of war, the 1990s genocide included examples of women involved in the killings, with 2.3 percent of genocide suspects being women (Powley 2003, 2). Rwandan nuns implicated in the genocide crime include Sisters Benedict and Bernadette (Lakiya 1995, 919). Other instances of women perpetrators include teachers and mothers who purportedly killed children and fellow women (Mutamba and Izabiliza 2005, 8). Such acts added to the trauma and distrust among Hutu and Tutsi neighbors who had formerly lived together peacefully.

Women-led initiatives at all levels have also helped transform ethnic divisions that were well entrenched at the close of the 1994 genocide. In the postgenocide era, women on both sides of the ethnic divide have demonstrated a keen interest in reconciliation processes. This is evident in all the associations and cooperatives where women have overcome ethnic differences, working together to uplift their well-being (Mutamba and Izabiliza 2005, 42–43): "Multi-ethnic associations involving both Hutu and Tutsi reemerged recognizing their need to live together again and to find ways of supporting themselves through collaborative activities, Hutu and Tutsi women sought to overcome the mistrust spawned by the war and genocide" (Newbury and Baldwin 2000, 1–2).

Weaving groups designed to foster economic opportunity for rural women have had a dual benefit in providing a setting for building connections across formerly drawn ethnic lines. When trainees enroll in craft training, organizers do not require information about participants' background (ethnic or otherwise). Participants come together with a single purpose of learning how to make items that are marketable. In the evenings when the weaving work is finished, trainees discuss different issues including their relationships. Outside experts are invited who engage participants in debates on issues such as HIV/AIDS, reconciliation, and other topics of the day.

Emphasis on commonality of cause both among men and women and also among women from different backgrounds, which originally were conflictual, became a powerful tool in ensuring that Rwandan society views women's empowerment positively. Moghadam highlights the notion of commonality of interest through her concept of global feminism, which asserts that women have more in common than divides them. "As historical victims of patriarchy, they are naturally united across history; they must now transcend political and cultural divides that are contemporary effects of traditional patriarchal politics" (Moghadam 2005).

Harré and Moghaddam (2007) also describe how people use narratives to position themselves and others. The following case study is an example of Rwandan women emerging from a tragic conflict to reposition their role in society as peace-seeking leaders. Storylines within one's community contribute to this repositioning, with one such example in this chapter being the emergence of women as national leaders. The Honorable Rose Mukantabana, Rwanda's highest female elected official, and Zaina Nyiramatama, executive secretary of the women's association HAGURUKA, also offer alternative narratives to the preconflict era of women as subordinates, sharing their narratives that demonstrate women's agency in structural and legal reforms in the postgenocide era.

Rose Mukantabana and Zaina Nyiramatama have been affiliated with the women's association HAGURUKA since its inception in pregenocide years, with the latter currently serving as executive secretary. At the start of HAGURUKA's formation in July 1991, Rwanda was a nation at war with a rebel movement. There were many internally displaced people in the country, mostly from northern Rwanda where the war was concentrated at the time. These people were living in terrible conditions in camps at Nyacyonga, a village close to Kigali City. This inspired HAGURUKA's formation, as there was a need to address the many challenges faced by women and children in those camps. The major issues were violence against women and women in illegal marriages with children who were not legally recognized, something particularly problematic when family conflicts arise as is often the case in war and suffering. HAGURUKA ensured that the law recognized children as legally belonging to a man, hence enjoying all accruing rights from such legal standing, even in situations where the mother is not legally married to the man (June 2009 interview conducted by Uwineza).

The 24 founding members of HAGURUKA, which means "stand up" in Kinyarwanda, included 18 women and six men. They recruited men and women who were willing to challenge the status quo of the time and advocate for women's rights. Zaina Nyiramatama, one of HAGURUKA's founding members, explained that from its inception HAGURUKA targeted all ethnic groups and women from across Rwanda as they wanted the group's work to be free of the divisions of the time. They recruited men who were vocal and willing to challenge the status quo. HAGURUKA, in its early years and still today, recognizes that the first step in assisting women is to offer psychological counseling followed by legal interventions (May 2009 interview conducted by Uwineza).

Prior to the genocide, inheritance and family-related rights favored men. HAGURUKA then came into existence to help create awareness about these issues among top leaders. Just as the association was beginning to take shape, the 1994 genocide erupted, distorting even the limited social cohesion and legal order that existed. During the height of the genocide, HAGURUKA struggled to retain its cohesiveness as members began to side with disparate political parties. By 1994, HAGURUKA had lost many of the members of its extended network: Many died, some joined the killing spree, and others fled into exile. For a time the organization simply disintegrated (May 2009 interview conducted by Uwineza).

After the war, HAGURUKA reestablished itself. It began by assessing the impact of mass violence on women, many whom were widows or whose husbands were imprisoned. A major issue was the loss of control of family property to male relatives. Mukantabana described HAGURUKA's foci as conceived at its December 1994 relaunch (June 2009 interview conducted by Uwineza):

—At the time, there was no functioning legal system and all organizations became involved in emergency assistance. HAGURUKA focused on the needs of the many orphaned children or those separated from their parents. It reunited families and placed those children who were unable to reconnect with relatives into foster homes.

—Working with UNHCR, HAGURUKA also got involved in helping women restart their lives by providing basic needs such as access to cooking utensils, food, and farm implements.

—In 1996, with the situation slowly improving, HAGURUKA returned its focus to its legal mission. It engaged in advocacy for the challenges faced by women; identified loop holes in the law; proposed bills of law to address the disparities; and, where new laws got enacted, trained and sensitized women on their rights and how best to address them—legally. It also provided free legal services to vulnerable women.

—The main issues were to do with ownership of family property in the case of orphans and widows, both of which had no legal rights to such property.

HAGURUKA's modes of assistance have continued to expand and evolve into the postgenocide era while continuing to operate on the principle that boundaries do not separate the commonalities women face, such as poverty and gender-based violence (GBV). The mutual concerns of women in the region, displaced or otherwise, form a common platform that transcends the cultural and ethnic divisions among them. This, in turn, provides a foundation for peace and social justice (Women's Commission for Refugee Women and Children 2001). Grassroots efforts to advance socioeconomic opportunities and provide psychosocial support networks constitute an important factor in efforts to foster reconciliation and build security in the Great Lakes region, while structural reforms have also been essential in creating increased space for women's participation in decision making.

Rwanda's Institutional Framework

Rwanda offers a unique example of leaders earmarking gender as a targeted development strategy. President Kagame has been a frequent advocate of women being key to achieving sustainable peace and development:

The [societal norms] introduced by colonialism played a key role in restructuring gender relations to the disadvantage of women. These imbalances are not only an obstacle to the country's development but constitute a form of social injustice. It is imperative to our lawmakers, policy makers and implementers to have an objective and correct analysis of the gender question in order to design appropriate corrective policies and programs. The question of gender equality in our society needs a clear and critical evaluation in order to come up with concrete strategies to map the future development in which men and women are true partners and beneficiaries. My understanding of gender is that it is an issue of good governance, good economic management and respect of human rights.—Paul Kagame addressing a 1999 gender training workshop for Parliamentarians. (Mutamba and Izabiliza 2003, 8)

Although Rwanda has institutionalized some gender reforms at the executive level since the 1980s, it was only after the genocide that the government established the Ministry of Gender.

Prior to the genocide, a subdivision in various ministries including the social affairs ministry, and the family ministry, among others, addressed gender issues. The Ministry of Gender and Family Promotion, which later became the Ministry of Family and Gender Development, came into being after the genocide. The latter marked a shift in understanding gender at the central level of policy making.

One of the primary tasks of the Ministry of Family and Gender Development is to ensure that gender is mainstreamed at all levels of government and in all institutions. More recently, the Ministry of Gender has been downsized once again, functioning only as a small organ in the prime minister's office. Although this change has been met with some criticism, the feasible explanation is that gender has been effectively mainstreamed via gender desks in all ministries, in the police, army, and at all levels of administration. A gender observatory body, provided for in the 2003 Constitution, was also instituted and became functional in 2008 to monitor all governmental and nongovernmental organizations for gender disparities and due compliance.

Women's committees appeared at all decentralized levels of governance in order to ensure that women were included in the political mainstream and in line with the minimum 30 percent constitutional requirement. These structures have helped women to establish themselves as elected representatives at all levels of governance. A quota system that assigned 24 seats in parliament to women has helped ensure the attainment of a critical mass of women representatives. Following elections in 2008, women comprised 56 percent of the legislature. The real impact is evident once women actually take office. Elected women serve in the same governance structures as men, ensuring that their presence is not merely a token appointment. At the same time, the general elections do not exclude women, thus they are active competitors with their male counterparts for the remaining governance posts. Due to this concerted effort to include women, Rwanda has achieved the world's highest percentage of women serving in its parliament.

At the executive level, women held 38 percent of the cabinet ministers' seats as of July 2010. The president of the supreme court and the executive secretary of the Gacaca courts were also women. Five out of 12 supreme court justices were women (41.7 percent) in 2010. Women's leadership initiatives have not only provided new means of self-esteem and much-needed material support, it has shifted perspectives on men and women's relative positions in society.

Ongoing Challenges Faced by Rwandan Women

As with all changes taking place in society and, in spite of all the support women enjoy from a progender balance government, Rwandan women still face a multitude of challenges. The Honorable Rose Mukantabana acknowledged that "Some traditions die hard." She notes that resistance from some men remains in both rural and urban areas. She also notes that rampant poverty is still a challenge. "Poverty and violence are inseparable." Many women still depend on men for their survival. Such women may fail to get out of an abusive relationship due to fear of survival and an uncertain future. Some get married at a young age out of necessity. In such a situation, men abuse the women simply because they know that they are their source of livelihood (Hon. Rose Mukantabana). In response, HAGURUKA started a microfinance initiative in addition to the legal services to help the most vulnerable women begin income-generating activities which may give them the confidence, empowerment, and freedom to transform their economic situations (June 2009 interview conducted by Uwineza).

According to Nyiramatama, an area that still needs to see progress includes the attitudes of men, many of who remain resistant to the changes in social norms. Some Rwandan men still view sexual issues and property rights as areas where they retain the primary right to decide. Mukantabana also adds that cases are known where a man refuses to drive or be driven in his wife's car acquired after she becomes a high-ranking government official. Some women have found doors locked on them after leaving a late meeting at the office. The solution is joint sensitization sessions, which will change the attitude that gender is just about women (June 2009 interview conducted by Uwineza). Gender is closely tied to power and control of resources and freedom. Mukantabana notes that local leaders also seem to resist the changes, at times resorting to old ideas such as encouraging women to return to their husbands and to submit as tradition demands instead of encouraging them to seek legal and professional help (May 2009 interview conducted by Uwineza).

Violence against women and children also continues to be a widespread phenomenon 15 years after the genocide. Although gender-based violence has always existed in Rwandan society, including wife beating and other forms of abuse, in past decades it rarely included murder. Traditionally, an abused woman would return to her parents, remarry, or simply persist by involving elders who would often reconcile the couple. One of the biggest challenges that remain in postgenocide Rwanda is thwarting gender-based violence. In the past decade, GBV has impacted both urban and rural women in unprecedented proportions. The Rwanda National Police stated that there were 6,440 reports of GBV-related crimes committed against women and children during 2002–2004, with more than 75 percent of crimes reported being against children 18 years or younger. The police also reported that 259 husbands murdered their wives and there were more than 2,000 rape cases reported to police between 2006 and 2009 (Kagame 2009). These numbers do not reflect unreported cases, making the number of victims of GBV likely much higher.

Achieving justice for sexual crimes remains elusive. This was the case with the many women who were gang raped, making it hard for their rapists to be identified and tried. To date, rape cases continue to prove challenging to the justice system. While some women may be able to identify their tormentors, many fear to do so as this exposes them to the social stigma rape brings. Others may not be able to identify their perpetrators or stand the rigors of court cross–examination, where the woman is expected to graphically explain how the rape was conducted, or stand the "open trial" Gacaca system, where prosecution and cross examination are done not only in public, but in a local community where the woman and perpetrator are well known. The Gacaca court is part of a system of community justice inspired by tradition and established in 2001 in Rwanda; even HAGURUKA has not yet successfully addressed this challenge. In every criminal case, there is the accuser and the accused. Failure to identify these two parties implies failure to get a fair trial and thus no chance for reparations and restitution (June 2009 interview conducted by Uwineza).

Educated women, especially those who may have attained high positions of leadership, sometimes face harassment and abuse from husbands who may feel threatened by their wives' success, a response resulting from inferiority complexes. Some married women misunderstand the feminist message of women initiatives, interpreting it as simply overturning the status quo and having women control the men. HAGURUKA emphasizes that such empowerment programs are complementary to existing gender roles rather than creating competition within families. Women also still lack the required training and experience to favorably compete with their male counterparts.

Many women among the rural poor are still unfamiliar with the new laws and lack the knowledge to utilize them. Rural women sometimes complain about the new gender advancements and changing roles of men and women, claiming that this erodes Rwandan culture. Ignorance and poverty are therefore major setbacks to women's advancement, as some women prefer to ignore advancements out of fear of losing their male relations, whom they feel are their source of livelihood. HAGURUKA's efforts to educate women about their rights have been conducted in tandem with legal changes that afford women more control over their families and livelihoods. Recent family law reforms are an important aspect in repositioning women's status in Rwandan society.

Improving access to education for girls and women remains critical to advancing opportunities across all aspects of society. Ignorance of the law remains a problem, according to Mukantabana. There is need for continued and concerted efforts to educate and disseminate the laws and general knowledge on women's rights (June 2009 interview conducted by Uwineza).

Women's Agency in Legal Reforms

Women's collective actions in the aftermath of war have in effect repositioned women as leaders rather than simply victims of tragedy. There is a clear trend in Rwandan women rising to the task not only in the economic sector but also in the policy-making arena. Structural reforms have also institutionalized legislation that addressed discrepancies in the laws that previously discriminated against women. The qualitative impact of women's leadership, in addition to their quantitative representation, warrants closer examination.

In developed democracies in the West, change can result from pressure organized by an engaged civil society including activists and lobbyists. Change can also result from an electorate that understands the power of its vote, forcing those in power to consider the needs of those who put them there. This explains why women movements in the West advocated for the right for women to vote, knowing well that once they established political participation, those running for office would more seriously consider women's grievances. The US women's liberation movement of the 1960s serves as a powerful precedent for furthering women's freedom to choose their role in society and participate in public life. However, one should not forget that this great call for social change was particular to the traditional American woman's experience.

Such citizen advocacy is often impossible in conflict-ridden societies where those in power manipulate the concept of democracy. As long as self-serving leaders control the machinery that keeps them in power, supported by a few conspirators to share in the spoils, average people face significant odds in advancing an alternative agenda. Conflict dynamics often leave citizens marginalized and treated as the "enemies" of the state and the status quo when they try to claim their rights. Amid the transition from the genocide, however, many Rwandan women have challenged the status quo and undertaken an active role in redefining their place in society.

Legal reforms in Rwanda have led to significant gains for women in the years since the genocide. Rwanda's 2003 constitution guarantees: "the equality of all Rwandans and between women and men reflected by ensuring that women are granted at least 30 percent of posts in decision making organs." The 1995 Beijing Platform for Action, which endorsed the 30 percent quota for decision-making positions, was also adopted by several African countries including Cote d'Ivoire, Eritrea, Mali, and Mozambique (Pearson 2008). Rwanda's success story is unique in that the agency of women is evident not only in their quantitative representation but also in their qualitative impact. This likely could not have been achieved without the various legal and institutional reforms that have been deliberately adopted by the government and which Rwandan women actively supported and utilized.

Women parliamentarians demonstrate the importance of working in solidarity in their pursuit of advancement. These women leaders tirelessly advocate for changes in the laws that are not gender sensitive. Women have worked as one united force to initiate new laws and reforms. Although the women parliamentarians' call for unity draws on their political affiliations, it also enables interethnic collaboration as women fight for the same cause. In 1996, female parliamentarians formed the multiparty and multiethnic Forum of Rwandan Women Parliamentarians (FFRP), which works across party lines on issues of common importance to women (Powley 2008a, 8). Women lawmakers have been purported as less likely to take bribes and are more inclined to promote public works projects that matter most to women. In recent years, Rwandan women legislators have led parliamentary efforts to eliminate discrimination, enhance human rights protections, and combat gender-based violence.

The 2003 elections saw Rwanda rank as the number one nation in women's representation in national level government seats, with females claiming 49 percent of seats in parliament and 38 percent in the cabinet (executive branch–level department heads) (Powley 2003, 2). The September 2008 parliamentary elections reaffirmed Rwandan women's status with even greater returns:

Women contesting in Rwanda's second parliamentary elections since the 1994 genocide held September 15 [2008] have secured 45 out of the 80 seats available (56.3 percent), making the incoming parliament the first in the world to have women in the majority—(UNIFEM 2008)

On October 6, 2008, another milestone occurred when the new parliament swore in the Honorable Rose Mukantabana, who was the first elected speaker of parliament in Africa's Great Lakes region. This is the third-highest-ranking position in the Rwandan government after the president of the republic and the senate president. She won a landslide victory over her opponent, Abbas Mukama, after she won the votes of 70 members of the 80-seat house. In a parliament where women's issues are often tabled with laws being revised and new ones enacted in favor of women, a female speaker of parliament is a positive development for the women who wish to see change moving even faster. The FFRP, in particular, has worked collaboratively to achieve other major legal milestones including addressing discrimination against women in nationality and citizenship laws and securing women's rights to inheritance and land ownership (Gomez and Koppell 2008).

A notable achievement in gender-focused legislation is the law against gender-based violence that the Rwandan government established on July 17, 2008. This was widely celebrated not only because it addresses a key violation but also because it was the first substantive piece of gender law in Rwanda that the legislature initiated rather than the executive branch. Additionally, women parliamentarians initiated it through their cross-party, interethnic Forum of Rwandan Women Parliamentarians. The new law defined and penalized previously uncharacterized forms of GBV. With the new protective laws and sensitization campaigns calling on women to fight for their rights, abused women often react by suing their husbands or asking for divorce, both of which results into the sharing of the family property. The law assures women custody of their children up to the age of seven years with child support paid by the father.

The right to inherit property was another particularly significant gain for women in Rwanda's post-conflict era as most survivors of the genocide were female and as such could not lawfully claim ownership of the property left behind by their husbands and/or parents. Traditionally women had no right to inherit property under the assumption that their husbands, fathers, brothers, or another male relative would support them. Following the war and genocide, women remained in homes absent of close male family members; distant male relatives often returned and claim ownership, forcing the women off the property. In many instances, uncles or any other male who could claim kinship forced young girls into marriage in order to prevent females from inheriting their parents' property. As a result of the new family law, women now have access to their parents' and husbands' properties, which in turn has furthered their economic empowerment. HAGURUKA demonstrates how women-focused programs have evolved from the pregenocide era to meet the challenges that remain for women and families.

HAGURUKA cofounder Zaina Nyiramatama commented: "[Much] has been achieved— everything has changed—the benefits far outweigh the challenges." In addition to highlighting the family law reforms, which give women the right to inheritance, she also mentions the law giving foreign spouses of Rwandan women and their children the right to Rwandan citizenship (which was formerly not the case) and a change in business law that prohibited women from starting businesses without their husbands' consent. She added that there is a notable "change of attitude among the men— they support their wives attending local meetings, joining associations and becoming leaders all unheard of just before 1994" (May 2009 interview conducted by Uwineza).

In recent years, HAGURUKA has expanded its work to include socioeconomic services. Today HAGURUKA has six branches in Rwanda, which utilize 383 paralegals who advise women on legal issues and on their rights and provide related counseling. HAGURUKA has 16 lawyers working full time to offer free legal services to needy women (May 2009 interview conducted by Uwineza). Its multifaceted approach of advocating for women-friendly reforms at the policy level while advising them of their rights has continued since its early founding, despite interruption during the genocide. Today the organization sees the positive impact of women's agency at high levels of decision making. At the same time, it continues with the approach of counseling women on their rights and providing legal assistance regardless of women's income or educational level.

HAGURUKA is preparing a translation of laws that impact women into Kinyarwanda and into simpler, more accessible language. Group members will disseminate the abridged laws and train local leaders who typically deal with the gender-related court cases. The organization is also engaged in training and sensitization campaigns on the new law against gender- and sexual-based violence (GSBV). Through Rwanda's decentralization system, GSBV committees were established at the grassroots level to address GSBV-related cases before they resort to the courts of law. Plans are under way to build "safe havens" for the women who need shelter from abusive family members (May 2009 interview conducted by Uwineza). Women's legal rights remain at the forefront of the organization's work.

HAGURUKA is presently engaged in a survey to identify, analyze, and compile data on cases concluded in court but for which the court decisions were ignored especially in those instances when men are required to give compensation to women. In some cases, women face barriers even after settling a case in court: Men still refuse to give the women what is due to them and seek to drag out a court case indefinitely. HAGURUKA intends to lobby the higher authorities especially officials in the Ministry of Justice to address this issue, using the data and analysis collected. National leaders are eager to receive the survey's results so as to act on them, a sign that cofounder Nyiramatama finds encouraging (May 2009 interview conducted by Uwineza).

In Rwanda's postgenocide era, among the many ills left unaddressed by pregenocide governments, gender has been a major agent of change for the present government. With such support and confidence freely given, women also took the initiative to study existing laws for gender disparities and went on to propose new ones and then inform the rest of the population about these laws. The shift from Rwandan women's former place as the secondary gender occurred in large part due to grassroots initiatives and structural reforms with the support of the country's postgenocide institutional framework.

Lessons for Other Post-Conflict Societies

In seeking solutions to the post-conflict challenges Rwandan women opted to frame gender as an issue for national development. They avoided a so-called feminist struggle with men and instead endeavored to involve men in their fight. While debating proposed bills of law to protect women's rights in parliament, leaders framed women in the affirmative, as "our mothers, sisters and wives." This helped Rwandan men to see the importance of supporting such bills rather than feeling confronted with disempowerment. Other post-conflict societies might also emulate this strategy: not alienating men but instead incorporating them in gender integration efforts. The presentation of gender mainstreaming as beneficial to the socio-economic welfare of the entire family and to the nation as a whole—not just as special access for women—will support the realization of women's equality as the accepted norm.

When discussing women's agency, Mukantabana points out that a wrong understanding of the concept of gender can at times increase conflicts rather than mitigate them. The solution, she believes, is awareness-raising campaigns that engage both men and women. Mukantabana notes that gender is a tool for development with men and women working in partnership, but if perceived otherwise, gender can become viewed as a problem and not a solution (June 2009 interview conducted by Uwineza).

The Honorable Mukantabana offered the following reflections in response to the question of how Rwandan men's attitudes toward women have evolved in the pregenocide and postgenocide era:

—Most men, especially those in leadership … have realized that gender is a tool of development and security and that an empowered wife is a resource to the family.
—As a result, most men are supporting and encouraging their wives to further their education, and many are supportive of their wives' promotion and salary increments, which in turn benefit their families.
—Men are increasingly respecting and giving value to the women.

Post-conflict leadership should embrace gender as an integrated development and post-conflict stabilization strategy so that women are better empowered to lead their family's recovery and to participate in social and economic revitalization. Women must be involved in all levels of decision making in order for such an approach to effect lasting change. Governments should recognize the need for institutional and legal reforms that would not be achievable in a post-conflict setting without true political will.

Women elites must recognize the importance of working closely with their less advantaged counterparts as a means of increasing their weight and legitimizing their cause. Women who organize as a cohesive voice can better advocate for pressing issues. By making it their mission to empower and uplift their fellow women, they increase the power of their voice.

Promoting women's involvement in decision making need not be limited to numerical representation in leadership positions. Ensuring gender mainstreaming in other sectors such as education and business is the only way of ensuring sustainability for women's achievements. Gender mainstreaming also needs to target key areas such as law enforcement, the military, and other agencies that are in charge of post-conflict situations.

Conclusion

Rwandan women are not merely passive recipients of the patriarchal traditions they inherited. Women's agency created a turning point in the aftermath of crisis, effectively repositioning women's role in Rwandan society. Historically, the range of decision-making positions as the head of households and businesses available to Rwandan women was severely limited. However, amid significant losses in Rwanda's male population, the conflict proved to be a catalyst for positive change as Rwandan women took on constructive leadership roles in their society. The authenticity of women's status in society materialized in part due to the quantity of both rural and urban women taking on new responsibilities and leadership roles and by structural changes including legal reforms supported by both male and female political leaders in Rwanda.

As Rwanda increasingly expands women's rights, there is a need to acknowledge potential backlashes against women from those who object to women as equals rather than as secondary to men. Raising the awareness of both men and women that increased participation in public life and decision-making positions need not destroy family relationships or subordinate men is also crucial.

The narrative of Rwandan women can empower others to approach conflict not only as a tragedy but as a vehicle for transforming lives for the better. "We live in a world that is a network of stories ….Power is operationalized within language, through both stating itself and being active when spoken …." (see Harré and Moghaddam 2003). The necessary conditions to change a normative position, in this case the role women can and do play in society, involves shifting those narratives that were embedded within a society's historical storyline. Disseminating the success stories of Rwandan women solidifies an alternative narrative to the notion that women in conflict are but victims. In this case, women along with their male supporters are the champions who overcame much tragedy to establish a new narrative for Rwandan women in the twenty-first century.

Keywords

institutional reforms, traditional cultural norms, gender mainstreaming, political will, commonality of cause, Rwandan family law, gender-based violence, grassroots initiatives, postgenocide era, normative gender roles.

Discussion Questions

1. How is Positioning Theory applied to this case study?
2. Which grassroot initiatives enabled Rwandan women to shift the narrative of women from that of "victims" to peace-building and post-conflict reconstruction actors? How were these complemented by policy reforms?
3. How can the advancement of women go beyond numbers in decision-making positions to transformation of the well-being of the majority of the women?

4. How can other historically patriarchal societies draw on traditional culture practices to promote gender equality? Provide examples from other cultures.
5. How did economic empowerment of Rwandan women contribute to gender mainstreaming in society at large?

To what extent can national leadership contribute to gender mainstreaming as a tool for peace building and national development?

References

Beijing Platform for Action. Beijing: United Nations Fourth World Conference on Women, 1995, available at http://www.un.org/womenwatch/daw/beijing/platform/decision.htm.

Belgian Government. 1960. *Rapport soumis par le Gouvernement Belge a l'Assemblee Generale Des Nations Unies au Sujet de l'Administration du Rwanda-Burundi, pendant les années 1959,* Bruxelles, Imprimerie Fr. Van Muysewinkel, pp. 23–27, Rue d' Anethan.

The Constitution of Rwanda, adopted by referendum on May 26, 2003. En.wikipedia.org/wiki/constitution_of_Rwanda.

Gomez, Jessica and Carla Koppell. 2008. *Policy Brief: Advancing Women's Caucuses in Legislatures.* Hunt Alternatives Fund.

Harré, Rom, Fathali Moghaddam, and N. Lee. (eds). 2007. *Global Conflict Resolution Through Positioning Analysis.* New York, NY Springer.

Harré, Rom and Fathali M. Moghaddam (eds). 2003. *The Self and Others: Positioning Individuals and Groups in Personal, Political, and Cultural Contexts,* Westport, Connecticut Praeger Publishers.

Hunt Alternatives Fund. 2008 Inclusive Security—Women Waging Peace. papers drawn from the 2005–2007 Rwanda Project in Kigali, available at http://www.huntalternatives.org/pages/478_rwanda_project.cfm.

Johnstone, Ralph. *A Time for Peace.* Institute of Research and Dialogue for Peace, Forthcoming.

Kagame, George. 2009. "Gender Monitoring Office," *The New Times,* November 27.

Kagame, President Paul. Official Speech, 1999.

Kinzer Stephen, 2008. *A Thousand Hills: Rwanda's Rebirth and the Man Who Dreamed It.* Hoboken, N.J.: John Wiley & Sons.

Moghaddam, M. Valentine, 2005. *Globalizing Women: Transitional Feminist Networks.* Baltimore: John Hopkins University Press.

Mutamba, John and Jeanne Izabiliza. 2005. *The Role of Women in Reconciliation and Peace Building in Rwanda: Ten Years after Genocide 1994–2004,* Kigali, Rwanda: National Unity and Reconciliation Commission, Kigasli May. at : http://www.nurc.gov.rw/documents/researches/Role_of_women_in_peace_building.pdf

Newbury C. and H. Baldwin. 2000. *Aftermath: Women's Organizations in Postconflict Rwanda.* Center for Development Information and Evaluation, USAID, Washington, DC, July.

Omar, Rakiya and Alex de Waal. 1994. "Bertolt Brecht Rwanda: Death Despair and Defiance." *Review of African Political Economy*, 21(61), September, 471–3.

Pearson, Elizabeth. 2008. *Demonstrating Legislative Leadership: The Introduction of Rwanda's Gender-Based Violence Bill.* The Initiative for Inclusive Security, April.

Powley, Elizabeth, 2008a. *Defending Children's Rights: The Legislative Priorities of Rwandan Women Parliamentarians.* The Initiative for Inclusive Security, April.

Powley, Elizabeth, 2008b. *Engendering Rwanda's Decentralization: Supporting Women Candidates for Local Office*, The Initiative for Inclusive Security, April.

Powley, Elizabeth, 2003. *Strengthening Governance: The Role of Women in Rwanda's Transition.* Hunt Alternatives Funds, p. 17.

Semujanga J. 2003. *Origins of Rwanda Genocide.* New York: Humanity Books.

SFCG: Search for Common Ground, Chapter 2 "Understanding Change" Designing for Results: Integrating Monitoring and Evaluation in Conflict Transformation Programs, 2006.

UNIFEM. 2008. "Rwanda Briefing to the International UNIFEM Network," September 19.

United Nations Development Program. 2007. "Turning 2020 Vision into a Reality: From Recovery to Sustainable Development—National Human Development Report Rwanda," available at http://hdr.undp.org/en/reports/nationalreports/africa/rwanda/rwanda_2007_en.pdf.

United Nations Population Fund and Rwanda's Ministry of Gender and Women in Development. 2002. "A Study of Beliefs, Attitudes and Socio-Cultural Practices in Rwanda," May.

Uwineza, Peace and Elizabeth Pearson. 2009. *Sustaining Women's Gains in Rwanda: The Influence of Indigenous Culture and Post-Genocide Politics.* Hunt Alternatives Fund.

Women's Commission for Refugee Women and Children. 2001. "You Cannot Dance If You Cannot Stand: A Review of the Rwanda Women's Initiative and the United Nations High Commissioner for Refugees' Commitment to Gender Equality in Post-conflict Societies" available at http://www.peacewomen.org/resources/Rwanda/dance.pdf.

CHAPTER TEN

Rebuilding the Gulf: United States

Terra Tolley

The Gulf of Mexico is riddled with accounts of tragedy in the wake of Hurricane Katrina and the BP oil spill. Stories of environmental and economic devastation and loss of life dominate the narrative. One aspect of that narrative that has been underrepresented in media, academic, and government reports is the extraordinary story of survival. Rebuilding the Gulf of Mexico is an extensive and comprehensive process. This chapter represents the role of bayou women in reconstructing the gulf through environmental security, cross-cultural communication, capacity building, economic opportunity, and trauma healing. It examines human resiliency and the psychological need to survive and rebuild. It also considers the important role of historical narratives for victims of trauma. The stories that follow are stories of human agency applied under the weight of circumstance. They are offered as an example of women's strength and capacity for coping.

This chapter was inspired by field research conducted in more than 100 coastal communities throughout Alabama, Florida, Louisiana, Mississippi, and Texas. Interviews began in September 2005 following Hurricane Katrina and continued throughout the events preceding and following the BP oil spill in April 2010. Four common narratives surfaced from the interviews, particularly among women working symbiotically with the waters of the gulf: economic opportunity, survival, trauma healing, and hope. Older women spoke of their previous experiences with Hurricane Betsy in 1956. Vietnamese American women shared their experiences escaping southern Vietnam in the 1970s and early 1980s. Younger women discussed their futures, community, and how to survive economically when their most lucrative opportunities lie in seafood, oil, or the industries that support them.

The Gulf of Mexico: History and Economic Opportunity

Water flows through every aspect of bayou culture, literally and symbolically. The Gulf of Mexico is the ninth-largest body of water on the planet and supports a diverse range of human and marine life. The original indigenous communities of the bayous lived off marine culture by using reeds and coastal trees to build homes and consuming marine life for food. Residents along the Mississippi Delta and the Gulf of Mexico have been dependent on the land and waterways since the early seventeenth-century European settlements. Much of the bayou culture identifies with the untamable spirits of Spanish pirates, American Indian, and Creole ancestors—with a focus on historical trades such as fishing and water navigation, which continue today.

The region's major industries include oil and gas, fishing (shellfish, shrimp, finfish, and recreational), tourism, and shipping. These industries contribute to making the Gulf of Mexico the 29th-largest economy in world (if the United States and Mexico region of the gulf were considered a single economic entity), bringing in more than $234 billion a year in economic production (Hargreaves 2010). Each of these industries relies directly on the environmental health and navigation of the Gulf of Mexico, making the region especially vulnerable to both natural and manmade disasters.

Natural disasters are an environmental threat to the gulf region as the natural resiliency of the ecosystem is compromised by more than a century of harvesting diminishing natural resources such as oil, gas, and timber. Manmade canals, land salination, and the deforested coastlines all contribute to the storm exposure of the people and wildlife. Geographic vulnerability to natural disaster is exacerbated by environmental disaster, which compounds erosion, land degradation, invasive species, and deforestation. Structurally, the Gulf of Mexico is challenged with a history of political corruption, poor education systems, gang violence, a culturally diverse and at times conflicting population, and poverty. At the same time, its unique cultural identity—its folklore, music, art, and food—all add to its resiliency. There is much to preserve in the Gulf of Mexico, and as the stories here demonstrate, even the largest natural and manmade disasters in US history cannot extinguish the tenacious innovation and hope of the region's people.

The written history of the gulf predominately reflects the evolution of men—as pirates, oil entrepreneurs, and fishermen in the area. Many Cajuns continue to subscribe to the mentality and symbolism of pirates and are the first to defend their identity and territory from elements or ridicule. Cajun fishermen often refer to themselves as the "cowboys of the sea" (T. Tolley, personal communication, October 21, 2005–March 5, 2007) who report only to the tides.

In reality, women also play a crucial role in the region. While women may not spend as much time at sea, they broker shrimp prices, maintain docks, rent recreational boats, run motels, cook at crab shacks, and clean foundations used for rebuilding. Frequently, it is the women who run the homes and businesses, and it is the women who author the narratives of survival and hope when disaster strikes. Immediately following the storms, "women were at the center of most households' emergency management" (Vaill 2006, 12). Hence, this chapter is about the evolution of those women—the "cowgirls of the sea." What follows is their story.

Survival

There is little sound left. The noise of the insects, birds, animals, and engines has disappeared. When the wind rises, there is a slight whistle of reeds, a crash of a wave, and a scratching of a mangled broom scraping on concrete. When Katrina's winds ceased blowing and the chaos of sound and motion stopped, a solitary activity pierced the stillness—that of a woman sweeping the remains of her home—which for most residents of the bayou was a concrete slab. Though it is an image of devastation in the face of calamity, the only viable option is to carry on and rebuild. That is what women in the bayous know. As a result, they are rarely idle; rather they are industrious, hardworking, shrewd, and compassionate. They are businesswomen who know how to survive. Women are often found working together to rebuild their communities in the aftermath of disastrous events that threaten their economy and even their culture.

Hurricane Katrina

In five years of interviews with women in the Gulf of Mexico, the most common narratives that surfaced were stories of survival. For the elder women of the bayou, their first experience was during Hurricane Betsy in 1956. For Vietnamese American women, it was escaping southern Vietnam.

These previous experiences informed the critical role of women after Hurricane Katrina and, later, the BP oil spill. They provided evidence and understanding that life would be preserved—that it would go on in the face of destruction. Bayou women were the first to transcend cultural, economic, and religious differences to build and maintain peace and social and economic capital, while satisfying the basic human needs of their families in times of recovery (T. Tolley, personal communication, October 21, 2005–August 15, 2010). They communicated their needs among one another and were able to articulate their experiences through remembrances and often through prayer. This particular ability to interpret history and to incorporate and adapt to its lessons dramatically increased the women's capacity to carry on and maintain a posture of moving forward. This was true after Hurricane Katrina; it was also true after the BP oil spill.

The Oil Spill

On April 20, 2010, North America's largest manmade disaster poisoned the water and economy that residents of the Gulf of Mexico rely on. An explosion on Transocean's Deepwater Horizon drilling rig caused the death of 11 people, and by the first weekend of May, endangered sea turtles began to wash up on the Mississippi coast. The BP oil spill directly infiltrated the economic lifeline and symbolic identity of coastal residents, just as they were re-emerging from five years of rebuilding from Katrina. By mid-July, multiple attempts to cap the oil had failed, and it seemed too many that the crude oil would go on gushing forever. As the probability of an immediate solution faded and the ecological and economic fallout increased, the time between the disasters seemed to collapse, inducing what felt like continuous despair. Ten days after the Deepwater Horizon explosion, a third generation oyster-catcher seethed, "Get rid of oil. By the time we done drilling it we won't be able to breathe. Now we have no food to eat. Watch what the bible says. We now live in the Black Gulf of Mexico" (T. Tolley, personal communication, May 1, 2010).

After more than 100 days of gushing pipelines, the ruptured well was finally capped on September 19, 2010. By that time, every level of the ecosystem had been affected by the spill, as pelicans, sea turtles, dolphins, shrimp, oysters, crab, and thousands of other species washed up—dead—along with the hope and economic livelihood of the local populations.

Historical Narratives

However, as hope fell, the narratives that inspire it began to rise, just as they had in the aftermath of Katrina, and it was primarily the women telling the stories. Historical narratives are essential elements of healing for people experiencing trauma, especially for groups that have experienced multiple or episodic traumatic events over generations. The women of the bayou seem to resonate with this understanding, and they instinctively reach to their reservoir of narratives in times of natural and manmade disaster, as an antidote for hopelessness and a reason for rebuilding—again. Through their stories, they remind one another of the strength of women everywhere; their narratives are testimonies to the resilience of women, the ability to transcend trauma, overcome hardship, and to live symbiotically with the land, water, and the diversity of life and culture that they call home.

Media

The media played an interesting role in representing the people of the bayous and in their comparison between Hurricane Katrina and the BP oil spill. For example, when describing her experiences with Katrina and BP, a marina owner in St. Bernard Parish in Louisiana described her perception of the media: "Sometimes it seems like national media makes it worse for people down here by showing people when they are drunk, or ignorant, and vulnerable. Next media will be asking 'Why did the government let us back down here after Katrina? Why didn't they just make it a reserve'" (T. Tolley, personal communication, May 1, 2010)?

The evolution of the media's portrayal of the BP oil spill also demonstrates the roles of women in rebuilding the gulf. The initial appearance of BP's post spill advertisements portrayed the response of traditional, wealthy, white males in powerful decision-making positions through the image of former CEO Tony Hayward (BP 2010). After his attempts at consoling the nation were ineffective, marketing teams started to promote the face of BP as an approachable, unintimidating, maternally natured, non-white woman from Louisiana. Iris Cross, the BP community response director is in multiple video clips in which the Houston-based director promotes a sense of calm and peace in the BP cleanup effort by holding hands with relief workers, standing side by side with fisherman, and saying, "I was born in New Orleans. My family still lives here. BP is going to be here until the oil is gone, and the people and businesses are back to normal—until we make this right" (BP 2010). Iris Cross is represented on the BP Website much more than former president Tony Hayward was, because she portrays the new public relations approach for the company and the media seemed to respond favorably to the image and message she was presenting.

While interviews for this chapter were being conducted, media frenzy was at its peak in the anticipation of President Obama's first visit to Venice, Louisiana. Venice was a victim of Hurricane Katrina. It was also the closest fishing port to the Deepwater Horizon explosion. On April 30, 2010,

BBC News, *The Financial Times*, *National Geographic* and hundreds of other media representatives swarmed the Venice marina. The levels of cynicism showed when a charter fisherman explained to a *BBC* reporter that he had a dead baby seal in the back of his truck and this was an Al Qaeda conspiracy. The reporter was ready to follow the dazed fisherman to his truck, until an American colleague stopped him and explained that the man was playing a joke on him because he was disillusioned with the media, government officials, and other curious outsiders. While awaiting the arrival of the National Oceanic and Atmospheric Administration (NOAA) director for a briefing on initial fishing closures, a gregarious woman swept through the charter boat captains, sending her greetings and supporting a reporter from *The Financial Times*. This was one of the few females present, and she introduced herself as Women of the Storm's Pamela Pipes. Organizations such as Women of the Storm are prime examples of groups of women who gathered after Hurricane Katrina to rebuild their communities and to educate people about the realities of disaster in the Gulf of Mexico.

Trauma and Healing

When analyzing the events and aftermath of Katrina and the BP oil spill, several issues emerge. The violence of hurricanes and oil spills is an additive to the other historical challenges that citizens in the gulf region endure including structural violence, regional conflicts, and issues of identity, ethnic violence, and religious differences. Carolyn Yoder (2005) accurately describes how disasters illuminate inequalities and trauma: The ongoing violence of poverty and systems that make people unable to meet basic needs such as healthcare is called structural violence and is a cause of trauma. Often these structural-induced traumas go unnoticed until an event such as Hurricane Katrina graphically exposes what has existed all along. These dynamics are helpful in discussing the role of women in trauma and healing in the Gulf of Mexico. Such tragedies result in women revisiting previous traumas. For boat people of the bayous, their history of survival provided evidence that they had the strength to move on, rebuild, and become agents of change and progress.

Survival

I was ten when I came here. The night before we left my brothers and I were sat down by our parents and told we were leaving for America. We were told to pretend to go to school the next day, we just took our school bags from the house, and we got on a boat that was owned by a friend of my father's. The first night out in the water we were marauded by Thai pirates. There were about 25 men on the boat, two women with young children, an 18-year-old girl and myself. The first boat of pirates kidnapped the teenage girl while her fiancé watched helplessly. A second boat came, robbed everyone and took all the women into the cabin of the boat to violate us. Something happened, and the pirates went to the deck. After the next three days, three Malaysian pirate boats attacked. They had tricked our captain by flying an American flag. They wanted all we had left, which was the boat itself. They took us to a tiny Malaysian island that was filled with Vietnamese refugees. We ended up living there, in diseased, cramped refugee camps for 18 months before we were placed in Louisiana.

(T. Tolley, personal communication)

For Mai, a businesswoman living in Louisiana, the hurricane evoked post-traumatic stress from her journey from Vietnam to the United States in 1979. Mai's story is highly representative of Vietnamese leaving the Saigon area during the war. During Katrina, she lost her home and relocated to live with family in Texas. She commutes back to Louisiana to check on her home and to communicate with the fishermen she worked with for many years, as well as the insurance companies, banks, and emergency agencies that slowly surfaced after the storm.

Mai is a member of the Vietnamese group often referred to as boat people. The boat culture is a symbol of economic viability for coastal Vietnamese Americans. For those who left the demise of Saigon, it is also a symbol of disaster, disease, loss, and eventual freedom. From 1975 to 1983, thousands of refugees from Vietnam took up residence in ragged boats with little more than hope for a better life. Boats left for Hong Kong, Indonesia, Malaysia, Thailand, and the Philippines. Those with family in North America were desperately trying to reach the East Coast.

The United Nations High Commissioner for Refugees estimated that more than 250,000 boat people died during passage (at least a third of those who escaped), and more than 160 people died on the refugee island of Kho Kra from disease, malnutrition, and physical violence. Kho Kra's tragic tale echoes conditions on the island where Mai waited for a year and a half for resettlement. According to the Boat People's Website there are more than "1.6 million boat people scattered throughout the United States, Australia, Canada, France, England, Germany, Japan, Hong Kong, South Korea, and the Philippines" (Boat People 2010).

Vietnamese immigrants to the United States found a natural transition to the fishing industry in the gulf—especially shrimp fishing. Since the 1980s, there have been many opportunities for Cajun and Vietnamese women to work together in the region to keep the fishing industry and gulf society afloat. Evidence of the capacity for cooperation among women can be seen in the fishing industry, in churches and temples, in schools and community organizations, and, post-Katrina, in relief organizations. As an example, one Mississippi oyster factory, run by a third-generation fishing woman, hires Latinas and Vietnamese American women for shucking as a way of providing a stable income for women whose husbands are fishermen. There were also a number of Federal Emergency Management Agency (FEMA)–sponsored dialogues, attracting fishing women from all backgrounds to discuss the future of the industry and the region. The Red Cross recruited thousands of women to help distribute food, clean water, medical supplies, and other needs.

It should be noted that there were vast differences between the experience of Cajun women who were survivors of Hurricane Katrina and women who had immigrated, fleeing the violence in Southeast Asia, only to encounter hostility in their new host country. Since the fall of Saigon in the late 1970s, when refugees from Vietnam, Laos, and Cambodia began to migrate to the United States, tension has existed between Cajun fisherman and Southeast Asian refugees. This tension became evident when Vietnamese fishermen became involved in the shrimp industry, which is also abundant in southern Vietnam. Many southern Caucasian and African American families lost family members in the war in Vietnam. Some of these families, still reeling from that tragedy and fostering an image of the Southeast Asians as the "enemy," viewed the refugees, turned competitors, as a threat and a reminder of the families' painful losses. Generally, the refugees that fled the war-torn region were victims of the Viet Cong—the United States' actual opponent in that war. Unfortunately, enemy stereotypes once instilled tend to persist until a new image is presented that challenges them. In 2007, some Vietnam veterans were still referring to Vietnamese Americans in the gulf in hostile and derogatory terms such as *gooks* and *chinks*, blaming them for a war that devastated the American psyche.

Identity

Identity is in important element of survival rhetoric for people who have experienced trauma, including those in the Gulf of Mexico where Cajun, African American, and Southeast Asians have all struggled with issues of historic trauma, structural violence, and the often perplexing question of what it actually means to be an American" while balancing values and traditions from the country of origin.

One impressive attribute of Southeast Asian identity is the attention paid to intergenerational caretaking. There is high social value accorded to the old taking care of the young, and the middle aged taking care of the old. Each generation has a role in society and is treated with respect and reverence. During Hurricane Katrina, hundreds of senior citizens died in flooded respite homes. Caretakers did not have the assistance or resources to transport physically disabled patients out of facilities. Stories of people's parents being abandoned in senior homes and drowning are common in the gulf. The majority of those who died as a result of the storm were senior citizens. The loss of elders is seen as a tragedy for Southeast Asian families, as the knowledge passed down generationally is believed to build strength and family cohesion.

The stories of survivors tell of the strength and pain of multiple generations. These traumatic experiences can either empower the mentality of survival and industry or they can create generations of victimhood narratives that create an "us versus them" mentality that perpetuates misunderstanding and opposition (Volkan 1997). Because of the masculine connotations of war, the pride and warfare identity still lingers with men and creates more obstacles for them to cross cultural divides. Though women are deeply victimized in war, through rape, deprivation, and the devastation of being wives, mothers, and daughters who lose loved ones in battle, five years of interviews point to a reluctance on the part of the men in the gulf region, especially those that fought or fled from the Vietnam War, to overcome their cultural differences and negative stereotypes to work together. On the other hand, Vietnamese, African American, Caucasian, Cajun, and Latina women who share similar historic and cultural narratives were more immediately willing to come together to rebuild under of the weight of the overarching goal of survival.

Understanding how people and societies interpret the past illuminates emotional traditions and narratives of events and cultures (Ross 2007). When interviewing Vietnamese fishing people, it became apparent that the integration of their experiences relative to their immigration to the United States influenced their response to trauma in the face of Hurricane Katrina. When asking about the ability to recover economically, psychologically, and physically, some female informants offered narratives on how they have always been "survivors." These narratives discuss their experience as the boat people of Vietnam. Thus the idea of survivor was added as an aspect of their identity that functioned to increase their resiliency. The way that people remember the past influences their identity and their ability to survive in the present, offering hope for their future.

Cajun Culture

Lillian, a fourth-generation fisherwoman, describes the history of her people, the changes in the land and government politics, and the relationship with the Vietnamese community in her 40 years of experience living in Mississippi:

> If federal government helped us with restoration we could survive. They messed up the canals... I don't know if there is any hope. The culture of this bayou is gone. The history of this Good Earth, the reason people came here originally is the wealth of the land. The Indians came here in the summer months to find food, and furs for winter. They then went back to Baton Rouge for the winter storms. There were Indian mountains in the prairies, but then they were all taken out and sold for dirt. Can you believe that? The white people drove them out.

When Lillian was initially interviewed in 2005, she openly expressed the relative deprivation felt from Cajun communities in comparison with Vietnamese American fishermen.

> Vietnamese came in late 70s and early 80s, they got 3 percent interest to buy boats while we were paying 28 percent interest. Now they own bigger boats, and all sleep on boats, only thing they contribute to community is the water, ice and rice they buy. Sometimes they buy one house, and three or four families move in to one home.... The hurricane devastated most people here and they don't want to come back. People are looking to clean house and sell.... If I get insurance money [I] will repair, not rebuild. This business will end with my son. Five generations at least will end." (T. Tolley, personal communication, November 5, 2005)

When speaking with Lillian in May 2008, she was still slowly repairing and had been working with some of the Vietnamese businesswomen in southern Louisiana to allow fishermen to offload their catch onto the docks and to raise the price of the shrimp market. The extent of their loss from the hurricanes encouraged women to overlook past feelings of inequality to preserve the economic capital of the industry.

Religion

Religion is an important aspect of the culture and identity for many women in the gulf. Working and living intimately with the element of water lends to their faith, as does the historic nature of the communities and residents. Across time, different religions have interpreted the significance of natural disasters in a variety of ways. Deism and natural law philosophy provides another element to the analysis of natural disaster. Deists believed that "God does not interfere with nature. He gave man reason to enable him to cope with life on earth and to learn the laws of nature and natural disasters are governed by natural forces that man can learn about and tame. Disasters are a challenge to spur us to the study of natural forces" (Hutchison 2005). Some New Orleans churches said that God unleashed the floods to purify the filth and crime of the city.

Following the onslaught of Katrina, the streets of Biloxi and New Orleans were emblazoned with signs of "Why God, Why?" Some believed that God was washing the sins of New Orleans away, literally and figuratively. Other religious leaders tempered their response with historical perspectives. For example, a Vietnamese Baptist reverend in Pascagoula, Mississippi, commends the rebuilding response of the local people and of federal agencies and nonprofits. The reverend explained that if a hurricane had hit like this in Vietnam there would be no government support whatsoever. He also expressed how the fatal floods and landslides in 2004 in the mountains of Vietnam killed thousands of people and the Vietnamese government did not respond while the international community barely blinked an eye. The same scenario seemed to be in play in summer 2008 with the devastating floods and the high loss of life (BBC News 2008, para. 1). However, the local religious communities responded, and African American and Vietnamese women, pulling together, were at the heart of Christian church recovery movements.

BP hired Catholic charities in Louisiana to continue operating after the BP oil spill, since they were the first responders on the scene. Their relief effort was predominately composed of female volunteers. The same is true for the Buddhist temples that were some of the first buildings open in Biloxi after Hurricane Katrina. Reverend Tran of Biloxi described how his church would still be in ruins if "the women of Biloxi had not scraped money and building materials together to provide shelter for those of us who lost our homes" (T. Tolley, personal communication, February 9, 2006). Similar stories surfaced in 2010 after the BP oil spill. Women and men fought to keep marine life and economic opportunity, and as one female marina owner stated; "This is our home, every bird, marsh and boat is part of our community, and we are going to protect it" (T.Tolley, personal communication, May 3, 2010).

Although women and children suffer disproportionately during wars, natural disasters, and economic crises (CARE International 2010), they are deemed as "front-line caregivers" who take on the responsibility to support members of their community and play a significant role in emotional- and behavioral-oriented programs during disaster recovery (Clarke 2003). Economically challenged people also suffer disproportionately during disasters. Environmental studies indicate that "poor people are more likely to be subjected to environmental contaminants," and statistically, impoverished residents tend to reside near pollutant centers and facilities such as chemical and hazardous waste sites (134). As an example, there is an 80-mile stretch called Cancer Alley running along the banks of the Mississippi from New Orleans to Baton Rouge. It is evidence of a structural form of "environmental racism," where residents living below the poverty line are constantly exposed to the byproducts of petrochemical plants in predominately African American communities (133).

Although women, particularly those of low income, bear the brunt of discrimination and structural inequality, in the case of Hurricane Katrina, these women were able to supersede the cultural, economic, and historical constraints of their narratives—the same constraints that seemed to shackle the "cowboys of the sea"—and work together to create economic opportunity and harmony. Clarke (2003) also stated how "out of bad things good things can grow. Disasters are rarely complete disasters. Even worst cases can lead to social betterment" (135). In some very tangible ways, the challenges to the human condition that resulted from back-to-back disasters in the gulf presented potential for people in the bayou to come together to create a new society, an improved environment, and a richer cultural community that they can thrive in. Women were particularly skilled in doing this and seemed inherently more able and willing to communicate their immediate and long-term needs to one another. This is especially illustrated in those instances when women overcame physical and structural violence and became agents of rebuilding gulf society by maintaining the social and economic capital of the sea.

From Violence to Action

Conflict-resolution literature shows that natural disasters commonly gives rise to collective violence (Gurr 1970), as desperate times can lead weary traumatized people to engage in chaotic behavior. The aftermath of Katrina chaos gave rise to riots in the streets surrounding development meetings, insurance conferences, and political discussions about what citizens were to do. Like Katrina, the BP oil spill damaged people psychologically, economically, emotionally, physically, and culturally. In spite of this, the women united to promote rebuilding, economic security, and healing. As they transcended religious barriers and economic competition, they worked collectively to hold the region together and to keep the men fishing. This was particularly evident when observing community forums where participants included female FEMA representatives, Vietnamese American business owners, and female social scientists problem solving together.

Although negotiation styles tend to differ between cultures, genders, varying constructions of identity, and the interpretation of psychocultural narratives, the local women's negotiation styles and capacities to communicate with one another reflected sensitivity to culture, gender, age, profession, and experience, all variables essential to successful negotiation (Cohen 1991). For example, Nyugen, the manager of a fishing house in western Louisiana, explains the ability of the Vietnamese community to work together to maintain culture and a successful seafood industry: "Vietnamese people know how to trust; we are patient and we have togetherness. We work with Chinese too. All Asian people know how to confront disaster. We will feed you, lend you our hands, but we will not necessarily show you our business. Our work is private. We make it through trust and honesty. It is the way of the people. Work is trust" (T. Tolley, personal communication, October 15, 2005). Mary, a Buddhist Vietnamese mother of seven and owner of a major shrimp boat and offloading port in central Louisiana, completely reconstructed her business without the assistance of insurance companies or federal agencies. She was one of the first operations open after the hurricane hit, despite experiencing extensive economic and physical damage. Mary and her family worked tirelessly to rebuild the offloading center because "the fishermen rely on us. They have worked with us for 25 years and they have to survive. People don't know what to do. They have lost their homes, family members and their livelihood. I have to do all I can to carry on" (T. Tolley, personal communication, September 23, 2005). Mary is a devout Buddhist who works 18 hours a day, cooks three meals a day, supports hundreds of fishermen, and is impeccably dressed, with freshly painted red nails and shrimp boots as she wades through 2 tons of rotted debris from her seafood operation.

After five years, Mary says she is tired of fighting insurance companies that refuse to support her rebuilding efforts. She considered taking her insurance company to court but feels that the law is rarely on her side—as a woman, a Vietnamese American, and in a time when thousands of people are taking claims to the scales of justice. Perhaps she is right. When looking at the law and the language in the courtroom, John M. Conley and William M. O'Barr discuss the relationships between gender, power, and the illusion of equal rights in the courtroom: "[T]he ideal of equal rights may be illusory in the sense that the rights being offered are not equally relevant to the different social circumstances of men and women" (Conley and O'Barr 1998, 62). Mary's experiences working with FEMA, attorneys, and the local parish government proved unproductive and disheartening. "I need help now. I am going to have to get it from my people. Fishermen are relying on me" (T. Tolley, personal communication, October 23, 2005). She received support from donations from members of her Buddhist temple, which were organized and distributed by the women of the organization, but three years after the storm she still had seen little aid from her insurance company or the government.

Other female shrimp loaders in Mississippi and southern Louisiana pooled resources to help one another rebuild. People traded construction materials, ice, and fuel and helped one another to get back to viable production levels. When the government neglected to provide the support they needed, the women of the bayou organized among themselves and took their case to Washington to demand recognition and recovery assistance:

Women of the Storm, a delegation of 140 Louisianans, and a group that is supported by the Ms. Foundation for Women, took blue tarp umbrellas to Capitol Hill in Washington and called for increased support for post-Katrina recovery: raising Louisiana's share of revenue from coastal oil drilling, strengthening levee protection, restoring Gulf coastline, and wetlands, and supporting to buy out flood-destroyed homes at 60 percent of their value. The women, a diverse group including civic leaders and activists from New Orleans' Vietnamese community, combined a news conference on the Capitol steps with persistent networking to gain access to key congressional committee members, top aides to President Bush, Laura Bush's chief of staff, as well as sessions with House Democratic Leader Nancy Pelosi and a top aide to House Speaker Dennis Hastert. (Vaill 2006, 6)

Hope

Hurricane Katrina drastically disrupted the culture, economy, and environment of the Gulf of Mexico. In addition to accelerating the demise of an already fading seafood industry, it reminded people of historical grievances. The "cowboys of the sea," who already viewed themselves as the final wranglers of the rugged waves, felt like they were witnessing the dismantling of their industry—an industry that had already been crippled by the weakened US economy. Yet the "cowgirls" fought to maintain their cultural identity and preserve the economic and social capital of the gulf, throwing their lassoes wide enough to draw the people of the region together. Their efforts will likely continue to create stability and economic and social viability, even if they are confronted with future disaster.

Historical narratives of past survival can be interpreted in ways that lend strength and resiliency to communities, enabling them to come together and to carry on in the face of disaster, whether the origins of those disasters are manmade or natural. Women tend to maintain those narratives and the foundations of industry, home, and culture in societies. As a result, they can become active agents—creative authors—narrating not only the survival of the community but also its potential to flourish.

Keywords

Hurricane Katrina, BP, oil spill, women, fishing, Gulf of Mexico, seafood industry, trauma, survival, rebuilding

Discussion Questions

1. Do the roles of women transform after a disaster in your community?
2. What incidents of trauma survival can be used to empower and inspire rather than perpetuate a sense of helplessness?
3. Are the experiences of refugees in the United States different from American-born citizens during the recovery period following natural disasters?

References

"BP Oil Spill." 2010. *BP Global*, June 5, available at http://www.youtube-nocookie.com/watch?v=ZF64SPueNtw

Clarke, Lee. 2003. *Worst Disasters: Terror and Catastrophe in the Popular Imagination.* Chicago: The University of Chicago Press.

Conley, John M., and William M. O'Barr. 1998. *Just Words: Law, Language and Power.* Chicago: The University of Chicago Press.

"Gulf of Mexico Response." 2010. *BP Global.* October 13, available at http://www.youtube.com/bpplc

Hargreaves, Steve. 2010. "Gulf Oil Spill: What's at Stake." *CNN Money.* May 30, available at http://money.cnn.com/2010/05/26/news/economy/gulf_economy/index.htm

Hutchison, Fred. 2005. "Hurricane Katrina and the Culture War: Can Natural Disasters Change Worldviews?" *RenewAmerica*, September 7, available at http://www.renewamerica.us/analyses/050906hutchison.htm

"Making it Right: Communities." 2010. *BP Global.* August 20, available at http://www.youtube.com/watch?v=6YJ7Rugl3eI&feature=player_embedded

Ross, Marc Howard. 2007. *Cultural Contestation in Ethnic Conflict.* Cambridge, UK: Cambridge University Press.

Vaill, Sarah. 2006. *The Calm in the Storm: Women Leaders in Gulf Coast Recovery.* New York and San Francisco: Women's Funding Network and Ms. Foundation for Women.

"Vietnam Floods Leave 100 Dead." 2008. *BBC News.* August 11, available at http://news.bbc.co.uk/2/hi/asia-pacific/7553797.stm.

CHAPTER ELEVEN

Conferencing Serious Crime: United States

Jennifer Langdon

Whatever people's image and thought is about this city and what the statistics are, there are still human beings who live here who are capable of resolving their own conflicts and their own criminal cases in really effective ways, just with each other.

Lauren Abramson (in Mirsky 2004, 2)

The city of Baltimore, Maryland, is ranked among the most violent in the United States. While some sources rank it as the tenth most dangerous city (Johnson 2010) and others as the eleventh (Sutherland 2010), there is no doubt that Baltimore, like many other urban centers, is plagued by an epidemic of crime. In Baltimore (and elsewhere) the traditional approach to addressing crime and violence is to declare war. That is, to declare war on those who are perceived to be perpetrating the violence—drug dealers, prostitutes, unsupervised teenagers, and the like. As a society, we look to the police and prosecutors to be frontline soldiers in this war on crime. Police and prosecutors strategize a variety of tactics to defeat the criminals—from zero tolerance to community policing. Reflecting this militaristic metaphor, "The War Room" is the name of a recent Baltimore state's attorney's strategy to combat repeat violent offenders (Ericson 2010).

Of course not all crime in Baltimore is violent in nature. Many of the crimes that negatively affect the quality of life in the city, like vandalism and petty theft, are not violent per se, yet they still evoke a sense of insecurity among residents. Combat-oriented strategies are frequently utilized to fight these crimes as well—often to little or no avail. The failure of traditional modes of fighting crime has certainly been the case in Baltimore. Citizens have seen a string of police commissioners come and go in the last two decades, as well as political scandals involving the (now-former) mayor and other citywide elected officials. As a result, Baltimore is still very much a city that is struggling with crime as its national rankings indicate.

In the midst of this ongoing war between police, prosecutors, and criminals, there has emerged a small group of women who are conflict-resolution practitioners using a different approach to addressing Baltimore's crime problem. Led by Dr. Lauren Abramson, the executive director and founder of the Community Conferencing Center in Baltimore, these practitioners offer a nonhierarchical and collaborative intervention in cases of urban crime and conflict. Instead of the traditional adversarial approach to addressing crime, Abramson and her colleagues employ a restorative approach to crime and conflict, called community conferencing. Community conferencing provides a forum and process in which those affected by the crime address the consequences of and solutions to the incident. Community conferencing has proven to be extremely successful, in that 95 percent of conferences held in Baltimore reach agreements that are accepted and followed through on (Spivack 2010).

Abramson and the community conferencing facilitators that she leads are women waging peace in a violent city. Abramson brought the practice of community conferencing to Baltimore, the first urban environment in which conferencing has been implemented on a wide scale. Over the course of the last 15 years, Abramson and her colleagues have developed and enhanced both the theory and practice of community conferencing, providing a model of best practices for the state and beyond. In this chapter, I depict Abramson and her colleagues as agents of positive change in an urban conflict zone. I detail their work, explain how the practice of community conferencing works, and explore the gendered aspects of both the theory and practice of community conferencing.

An Accidental Activist

Lauren Abramson (2010) never planned to run a nonprofit organization like the Community Conferencing Center or any other organization for that matter. Abramson (2010b) describes her career and life path as unfolding "organically." She was always interested in how the body worked and originally studied to be a dentist like her father. However, she was also drawn to liberal arts and ended up studying psychology as an undergraduate. She was particularly interested in biopsychology, a subdiscipline that focuses on the physiological mechanisms that underlie mental processes. Abramson went on to study biopsychology and animal behavior as a graduate student. Her graduate school mentor introduced her to the work of Silvan Tomkins, the creator of affect script psychology. Affect script psychology, or affect theory, is an explanation of human motivation that is based on an understanding of nine basic emotions or affects (Kelly 2009). Abramson was intrigued by affect theory, later met Tomkins at a lecture in Detroit, and collaborated with Tomkins in the last years of his life.

It was her interest and expertise in Tomkins's affect theory that led her to community conferencing. In 1994, Abramson attended a presentation about community conferencing given by Australians David Moore and John MacDonald. The men had traveled to the United States to tell of their successes with this restorative justice practice imported from New Zealand. Abramson immediately started to make connections between Tomkins's affect theory and the practice of conferencing. This was the spark of connection between theory and practice that resulted in Abramson's bringing conferencing to Baltimore and to her founding the Community Conferencing Center there. Before sharing Abramson's compelling story of activism and positive social change, it is important to detail the process and history of community conferencing itself.

The Practice of Community Conferencing

Described as "elegantly simple" (Casciani 2010), community conferencing is a conflict transformation practice that "provides a space and structure for people in conflict to have a conversation with each other"(Abramson 2004, 1:4). The process involves gathering all of the people who have been affected by a conflict, sitting in a circle with no table, and asking the participants to share their answers to three questions: "(1) What happened? (2) How have people been affected? (3) How can the harm be repaired and future occurrences prevented?" (Abramson 2004, 1:4). The process is facilitated by a trained practitioner who impartially prepares each of the participants for the conference, convenes and conducts the conference, and then follows up with the participants to monitor compliance with the agreement (Abramson 2004). Although each conference is unique to the set of circumstances, in Baltimore many conferences involve young people who have violated the law—minor violations as well as serious ones. For example, the Community Conference Center routinely receives referrals from schools. One such case involved 17 high school students—both girls and boys—involved in two separate but related melees that could only be broken up by police officers (Community Conferencing Center 2010). The students faced suspension as well as possible assault charges. All the involved parties, their parents, and guardians as well as school staff and police were interviewed and prepared for the conference. A total of 43 people attended the conference, where it was revealed that the fights stemmed from a disagreement over one dollar that was owed by one student to another. The conference ended with apologies being exchanged and a written agreement being signed. The students were not suspended, as the principal who participated in the conference was confident that the conflict had been resolved (Community Conferencing Center 2010). This is an example of one of the 98 percent of conferences that end with the parties arriving at an agreement (Community Conferencing Center 2010).

While community conferencing is often associated with juvenile justice, its origins are actually in child welfare reform. Community conferencing originated in New Zealand in the late 1980s. Family group conferencing, as it was called in its original New Zealand form, was developed as a culturally sensitive reform addressing decision-making processes in child and family welfare cases (Alder and Wundersitz 1994). The practice was institutionalized by the passage of the Children, Young Persons, and Their Families Act in 1989 (Alder and Wundersitz 1994). Family group conferencing, in its original form, allowed for the families of youth offenders to meet in private after hearing of the impact of the wrongdoing on the victim to determine an appropriate punishment and/or reparation for the offense. The consequences suggested by the offender's family were then discussed, negotiated, and agreed on by the victim and others attending the conference (Maxwell and Morris 1994). The practice was seen as culturally sensitive to the traditional family decision-making practices of New Zealand's indigenous Maori population (Daly 2001). The involvement and empowerment of the family in the process was an innovation in the processing of juvenile offenders in New Zealand.

The relative success of family group conferencing in New Zealand generated interest among police and youth workers in Australia, and a modified version of conferencing was developed and implemented in that country in the early 1990s (O'Connell and Moore 1994; Moore 2004). Referred to as the "Wagga model" after the New South Wales city, Wagga Wagga, in which it originated, conferencing in Australia was developed by police as a "cautioning scheme" for youth offenders (O'Connell and Moore 1994). In the Wagga model, the conference is facilitated by a police officer. Also, there is less emphasis placed on private decision making by the offender's family than in the New Zealand model (Daly 2001). The Wagga model is the predominant conferencing model to have been adopted in the United States (Umbreit and Bazemore 2002). While the Wagga model of restorative conferencing is associated with criminal offenses (predominantly perpetrated by juveniles), community conferencing, as adapted and modified by Abramson and her colleagues, has application to a wider set of conflicts.

Community conferencing is an effective intervention in both criminal and noncriminal conflicts. It is interesting to note that Abramson defines crime as a form of conflict. Like conferencing itself, Abramson's definition of conflict is "elegantly simple." She defines conflict as "a general state of negative feelings" (Abramson and Moore 2001, 323). The emphasis placed on emotional transformation is what sets conferencing apart from the more commonly known conflict resolution practice of mediation (Abramson and Moore 2001). It is also this focus on emotion that has been Abramson's primary contribution to the development of the theory of community conferencing. There is clearly a gendered aspect to the focus on emotion in the theory and practice of conferencing. This gendered aspect will be discussed in a later section of this chapter.

Abramson is not alone in making the connection between conflict and crime. Nils Christie (1977), Norwegian criminologist, in his landmark article "Conflicts as Property," describes how the criminal justice system has "stolen" the handling of crime from those directly involved in the conflicts. Similarly, Howard Zehr (1990), father of restorative justice, in his seminal text *Changing Lenses* advocates for us to reframe our image of crime from one of lawbreaking to one of interpersonal conflict. The field of restorative justice is founded on the reconceptualization of crime as interpersonal conflict.

Abramson (2010b) differs from Zehr and other restorative justice advocates in that she sees justice as a limiting frame. Abramson and her colleagues have used community conferencing not only for cases of crime (called "undisputed harm") but also for neighborhood and workplace conflicts (Abramson and Moore 2001). While many define community conferencing as a restorative justice practice, Abramson terms it a conflict transformation process (Abramson and Moore 2002). By defining conflict in such a simple manner, the use of conferencing is virtually limitless when those involved in any incident are experiencing negative feelings. Abramson has been instrumental in emphasizing that community conferencing is more than just a restorative justice process. Her use of community conferencing in Baltimore has been versatile, ranging from juvenile offending to complex community conflicts to serious crimes such as murder and rape.

Bringing Conferencing to Baltimore

Abramson learned about community conferencing while working as an assistant professor at Johns Hopkins University in Baltimore. She was doing research, influenced by Tomkins's affect theory, on how emotions affect health. She was introduced to conferencing at a presentation given by Transformative Justice Australia and immediately saw a strong connection between the emotional aspect of the transformation that takes place during a community conference and Tomkins's affect script psychology (Abramson 2010).

The following year, Abramson attended the first community conferencing training in the United States. Afterward, Abramson set about bringing community conferencing to Baltimore. She began to spread the word about the power of conferencing to her contacts in the community, juvenile services officials, and potential funders. Abramson also developed a professional collaboration with David Moore and began to publish on the connection between Tomkins's affect theory and the practice of community conferencing (Abramson 1998). It is Abramson's activism on both the levels of social practice and theory development that makes her story as an agent of positive change so compelling.

On the local and practical level, Abramson and her colleagues at the Community Conferencing Center have involved more than 8,000 people across the city in conferences, resulting in a 60 percent lower recidivism rate among juveniles who participated in a conference (Community Conferencing Center 2010). The Community Conferencing Center also serves as the statewide leader for the practice of conferencing in Maryland, having been instrumental in spreading the use of community conferencing to other jurisdictions in the state. Abramson has also risen to national prominence for her leadership in the area of social innovation technology. She was recently awarded a prestigious 2010 PopTech Social Innovation Fellowship (Spivack 2010).

Of course, Abramson did not rise to national prominence overnight or by herself. After attending the community conferencing training in 1995, Abramson met with leaders of Baltimore's juvenile justice community, gained some interest, and then arranged an informational meeting for others from the city community who were interested (Abramson and Moore 2001). The meeting was conducted by Transformative Justice Australia and had 40 or so participants from both the government and private sectors (Abramson and Moore 2001). For instance, Patricia Jessamy, Baltimore City state's attorney, was an early supporter of the conferencing (Abramson 2010b). The meeting sparked interest and generated the funding to conduct community conferencing training in Baltimore. Abramson received grant funding to oversee the development of citywide community conferencing programs (Abramson and Moore 2001). Meanwhile Abramson was working on developing community conferencing in Baltimore on her own time, maintaining her research duties at Johns Hopkins University. Abramson (2010) has stated that her original intent was to plant the seeds about conferencing in Baltimore and "till the soil," not to be a leader per se; so this arrangement suited her well, at first.

The initial strategy for bringing community conferencing to the citizens of Baltimore was "top-down" as "top officials within the police department and juvenile justice expressed strong support for a Community Conferencing program" (Abramson and Moore 2001, 329). However, Abramson soon learned that implementation was not uniformly supported at the frontline level. While some juvenile probation workers facilitated conferences themselves with great success, others would not use the system for referrals (Abramson and Moore 2001). While she worked to improve the communication and referral system within the juvenile justice system, another method of implementing a community conferencing program emerged. This model, funded through the state's crime prevention agency, focused on four neighborhoods, termed "hot spots" because of their high crime rates. Abramson coordinated this program as well, providing support to the community-based coordinators (Abramson and Moore 2001). This decentralized model also presented challenges for implementation. Quality assurance was a significant issue, as each neighborhood had different criteria for hiring facilitators (Abramson and Moore 2001). Abramson observed that "neighborhoods without special funding for conferences have begun to use the process for the widest variety of cases and in the most creative ways" (Abramson and Moore 2001, 331). That is, the neighborhoods that were not targeted for the funding were not limited by the criminal justice framing that went with the grant.

In 1998, Abramson was awarded an 18-month Open Society Institute Fellowship to support her work in developing community conferencing in Baltimore. During this time, referral sources expanded to include schools, community organizations, and neighborhoods. Abramson was also learning what makes a good facilitator. In line with the belief that humans have the innate "capacity to resolve their own conflicts," conferencing facilitators do not have to have certain educational degrees or certifications (Abramson 2004, 1:3). Facilitators have to be comfortable with people expressing strong emotions and be able to remain neutral during the preparation and the convening of the conference (Abramson and Moore 2001). Another significant lesson that Abramson learned during this time was about the ability to use volunteers as community conferencing facilitators. She found that many of those who had been trained as facilitators could not commit to the time it takes to prepare and convene a conference (Abramson and Moore 2001). Conference preparation often involves home visits with the primary participants and their families, as well as extensive phone contact with all other participants in order to schedule the conference. In short, preparation is labor intensive and made it difficult to maintain a core group of trained volunteer facilitators.

With the demand for conferences increasing, and with the decentralized structure of implementation offering serious obstacles, Abramson founded the Community Conferencing Center in 2000 as a nonprofit organization and hired her first staff person as a facilitator. At this early stage in the development of community conferencing in Baltimore, almost all of the facilitators were women. For example, Misty Fae, a facilitator who is still active in the work, joined the organization shortly after the inception of the center. Fae was instrumental in locating the physical space for the center and in developing a database program to track cases and evaluate results (Abramson 2010b). Women were also instrumental in helping to secure funding for the organization. One such woman was Cheryl Casciani, from the Baltimore Community Foundation, who connected Abramson with interested private funders at the crucial time when Abramson's OSI fellowship was ending. To this day, although there are men who facilitate conferences, almost all of the facilitators are women. Citing the work of Carol Gilligan (1993), both Abramson and Casciani conjecture that the overrepresentation of women in the population of conference facilitators may have to do with women's tendency toward an ethic of care (Abramson 2010b; Casciani 2010). While the gendered aspect of conferencing will be explored in more detail, it is important first to share the other innovative modifications to conferencing practice that Abramson and her colleagues have achieved.

Innovation in Practice and Design

Abramson and her colleagues at the Community Conferencing Center have modified the Wagga model of conferencing somewhat. The most significant modification is that they do not use police officers as community conferencing facilitators. The CCC trains volunteers and professional staff to conduct community conferences. As discussed in the previous section, over the years the CCC has relied more heavily on professional staff because the task of preparation can be labor intensive and therefore not conducive to staffing the program with all volunteers.

The other significant modification that Abramson and her colleagues have made to the Wagga model is to use the conferencing script (a more specific version of the three questions used to structure a community conference) as a template to guide the ordered sequence of the conversation that goes on during a conference. In the Wagga model, the facilitator of the conference reads from the script word for word. Those facilitators trained under the "Baltimore model" are taught to rely on the script in the beginning of their practice, but the focus is on learning the principles and guidelines of community conferencing instead of how to follow a "recipe" (Abramson 2004). The training manual offers the following metaphor: "Community Conferencing facilitation is like jazz. You will improvise" (Abramson 2004, 1:2).

This principle-driven focus on community conferencing practice is central to developing a skilled set of professional facilitators and a community of practitioners. The principles of conferencing that Abramson (2004) communicates are that we all "have the capacity to resolve our own conflicts"— that we do not need professionals to solve them for us. She also states that people need a safe environment and a structure in which to work with others to solve their conflicts (Abramson 2004). The expression of emotion is also a central principle underlying the practice of conferencing (Abramson 2004). This last principle is directly related to Tomkins's affect theory, as well as to the gendered nature of conferencing practice. Abramson not only teaches these principles in facilitator training, but she also practices these principles in the workplace.

For example, the physical layout of the CCC office supports the principle-driven practice of community conferencing. The office is characterized by its open space where facilitators can easily learn from others by listening to their colleagues prepare conferences by talking to participants over the phone. Abramson (2010b) describes the CCC as a "learning organization" that is committed to practicing the principles of conferencing inside the organization as well as with participants in a conference. Abramson and the staff of the CCC are intentional about creating a workplace that is a safe environment for facilitators to process the often emotionally difficult work that they do. She describes the practice of "campfire," where a facilitator who is struggling with a particularly difficult case or participant is able to call "campfire" and have an open meeting and gather support and advice from her colleagues (Abramson 2010b).

The design of the center is open and welcoming is other ways as well. Just as one of the principles of community conferencing is to create a safe environment for participants, a safe and supportive environment is also created for facilitators. Fae (2010) describes the workplace as very family friendly. For example, it is not unheard of for mothers to bring infants with them to work and to nurse their infants throughout the day. The center is also open to those who are still in the early stages of learning how to facilitate a conference. New facilitators from other community conferencing programs across the state are welcome to come and observe intake and conference preparation.

Perhaps it is this commitment to what Abramson (2010) calls "parallel process" that has made the Community Conferencing Center into the thriving and vibrant organization it is today. Not only has Abramson received national recognition for her work, but the Community Conferencing Center itself was recognized as the Best Non-profit Organization of 2009 by the *Baltimore City Paper* (*The City Paper* 2009). Awards, of course, are just one measure of success. The positive impact that community conferencing has had on the communities and neighborhoods in Baltimore is the most important measure for success. A recent editorial in *The Baltimore Sun* lauds both the effectiveness and cost efficiency of community conferencing. At a cost of $900 per youth, conferencing offers a viable alternative to detention centers (Ferebee 2010). This figure is one-tenth the cost of sending a young person to court (Abramson 2010a). The Community Conferencing Center, since its inception in 2000, has served more than 8,000 people and has documented a 60 percent reduction in recidivism rates for those youth who participate in a community conference (Community Conferencing Center 2010).

In addition to the high agreement compliance rate and the low recidivism rate that characterizes community conferencing, the stories of transformation that come out of conferences are perhaps the most compelling evidence of its effectiveness. Many of the stories are posted on the center's Website or in other promotional material for the center. Other stories have been disseminated in the news media. One such account is captured in a 2002 *Baltimore City Paper* article, titled "A League of Their Own" (Sullivan 2002). The article features the local football league that was started as a result of a community conference. After hundreds of calls to the police and even more angry exchanges between adult residents and kids playing in the streets and alleys of a southeastern Baltimore neighborhood, the Community Conferencing Center was contacted and asked to convene a conference. The conference was prepared and convened by Misty Fae. Much larger than the "average" conference, 44 people, 13 of whom were children, attended the conference. The emotions ranged from anger, with yelling and screaming, to a quiet realization that the kids in the neighborhood had nowhere safe to play and this is what led them to play in the streets and alleys. The next moment in the conference was the pivotal one:

> (Don) Ferges, one of the most vocal complainants at the conference, offered a simple solution. He agreed to accompany a group of kids to

Patterson Park for a couple of hours at a time so they could play with adult supervision. The day after the conference, 13 kids showed up to go with him to the park. The next day, 24 kids showed up. Within two weeks, he had 60 kids who wanted to take part in his field trips to the park, and Ferges helped them organize informal football games (Sullivan 2002 under "Feud").

The conference effected change not only in those present at the conference but community wide. It is community conferencing's potential for building communities and social capital in communities that makes it so powerful.

While the football league story is one that is often repeated to demonstrate the power of conferencing, it is not the only community-changing success story of conferencing. Abramson and Moore (2002) share the account of another neighborhood transformed in the article "The Psychology of Community Conferencing." In this case, the conference was originally convened in relation to an identified "problem residence" but evolved to address other community issues such as vacant houses and teens hanging out on the corner. As a result of the conference, among other things, GED classes were organized at a local center, and a plan was devised to address the problems of a vacant house on the block (Abramson and Moore 2002). Once again, as this account shows, the impact of a community conference has the potential to be community wide.

Stories about successful community conferences like the two recounted above are plentiful, but they emphasize only one aspect of the compelling nature of Abramson's positive social activism. She has not only been a positive agent of change on the local and practical level, she has also influenced the field of conflict resolution and restorative justice on the theoretical level as well. Abramson has theorized crime as a form of conflict. She has also emphasized the importance of emotional transformation in successfully addressing conflict. Her application of Tomkins's affect script psychology to the theory of conflict resolution practice is highly instructive. It is this aspect of Abramson's innovation that will be the focus of the following section of the chapter.

Innovation in the Theory of Practice

Community conferencing is most often categorized as a restorative justice practice by scholars and advocates in the field. The predominant theory of practice in the field of restorative justice is John Braithwaite's (1989) theory of reintegrative shaming. Braithwaite highlights shame as an important

concept in the explanation of why conferencing works. He provides a sociological explanation for shame, distinguishing between stigmatizing shame
and reintegrative shame. Reintegrative shaming is "when the person's
behavior is condemned but their self-esteem and confidence are upheld
through positive comments about them and gestures of forgiveness and (re)-
acceptance" (Barton 2000, 54). Societies that employ reintegrative shaming
are reported to have lower crime rates than those that stigmatize offenders
(Braithwaite 1989). Following this theory, the community conference acts
as a ceremonial forum in which the offender takes responsibility for his or
her behavior and yet is offered the opportunity to be reintegrated into his or
her community by way of offering an apology and complying with mutually
agreed-on consequences for the wrongdoing.

When Abramson attended her first community conferencing training,
the theory of reintegrative shaming was the predominant (if not the only)
theory of conferencing practice. Abramson (2010b) describes participating
in the training and making connections with Tomkins's affect theory. By
then, Abramson's knowledge of the theory was second nature. She brought
the applicability of affect theory to the attention of David Moore, a trainer
from Transformative Justice Australia. This connection began a professional
collaboration that has proposed and demonstrated the usefulness of affect
theory when applied to community conferencing (Abramson and Moore
2001; 2002).

Affect theory applies an interpersonal lens to understanding the role of
shame in relationships. Tomkins identified shame as one of the nine affects,
or primary emotions, that humans experience (Kelly 2009). Tomkins points
to shame as a physiological mechanism that "is experienced whenever there
is a sudden, temporary reduction in positive affective experience" (Moore
and McDonald 2000, 151). However, shame is but one of the affects that
Tomkins identifies in his theory (Abramson 1998). Applied more generally,
affect theory provides a psychological explanation for the emotional transformation that is purported to occur during a community conference.

Abramson and Moore (2002) describe this transformation as largely an
emotional process that follows four stages—from anger, fear, and contempt;
to disgust, distress, and surprise; to deflation and collective vulnerability;
to finally interest and relief during the agreement stage. The four stages
of emotional transformation are prompted by questions in the conferencing script. The conference begins with a brief introduction offered by the
facilitator that reminds participants of the purpose of the conference. (It
is important to note that substantial preparation with each participant has
been conducted by the facilitator, so this is not the first time the participants

have been informed of the purpose of the conference.) The facilitator then introduces everyone in attendance and begins the conference by asking the person responsible for the harm to describe the incident and what he or she was thinking at the time. The victim then has his or her turn to speak about the effect that the incident has had. The narrative prompts in the conferencing script are specifically designed to evoke emotion from the participants. As Abramson and Moore (2002, 136) describe, "Participants typically move from more distancing and toxic negative emotions (contempt/anger/fear), through the less distancing negative emotions (sadness and shame), and finally to positive feeling (joy and interest) about oneself and others." By moving through this emotional transformation together, participants in the conference are brought back into relationship with one another. Once the group experiences this shift, it is then able to focus on how to repair the harm that has been done and how to prevent future occurrences.

As Abramson (2010) observes, the power of the emotion expressed in a conference is proportional to the power for positive change. In the two conferences recounted in the previous section, the emotion was extremely high, perhaps because the situations had been going on for so long without any resolution. This observation is instructive for the application of community conferencing in other conflict zones.

Gendered Aspects of Conferencing

The overrepresentation of women in the population of conference facilitators and the central part that emotion plays in the conferencing process are two aspects in which the practice of community conferencing is gendered. What I mean by the term *gendered* is that community conferencing is associated with social characteristics that have been constructed and construed as feminine. As feminist political scientists Sjoberg and Gentry (2007, 7) describe, "Established gender norms portray women as naturally nurturing, emotionally sensitive and domesticated." Following this line of argument, one might hypothesize that women are drawn to practice community conferencing more so than men because conferencing is an emotionally sensitive process and emotional sensitivity is expected of and rewarded in women in our society.

This gendering of community conferencing as feminine is supported by the work of psychologist Carol Gilligan. Gilligan (1993), in her research on moral development, observed that girls and women more often used the lenses of care and relationship when they approached ethical problems. Boys and men more often used what she called an "ethic of justice"—that is, applying logical rules to the analysis of ethical problems. Gilligan contended that women tend to reason differently than men and that one method of ethical reasoning is not superior to the other. Gilligan's "ethic of care" concept was further developed by feminist ethicist Nel Noddings (1984), who argued that the ethic of care, or what she termed "relational ethics," was preferable to the ethic of justice.

It is interesting to note that Abramson referred to the work of Gilligan when I inquired what connections she made between gender and community conferencing. In a followup communication, Abramson (2011) also noted that the design of the office of the CCC is also feminine in the sense that it is "designed explicitly for collaboration and learning." Fae (2010), another leader in the Baltimore community conferencing community, makes this point even more emphatically:

> It's not a coincidence that this process—which is centered around affect/feeling/emotion—is championed by women. Women are both biologically bent and socially conditioned to be emotionally aware. We understand the transformational power of emotion.

Fae goes on to make another observation that is echoed by Sjoberg and Gentry in their discussion of gendering. Fae writes that "processes that reflect the way women work, or encompass values that are thought to be feminine are devalued." Similarly, Sjoberg and Gentry (2007, 7) state that "qualities associated with women and femininity have been traditionally characterized as inferior to those associated with men and masculinity."

These observations lead us to shift to considering community conferencing as a feminine process using a feminist lens of analysis. The fact that feminine characteristics are devalued in our societies may answer the question why community conferencing has not been adopted more widely by institutions in Baltimore and beyond. The Community Conferencing Center boasts and documents an impressive agreement and compliance rate, and it is far more cost effective than the traditional methods employed for addressing crime and conflict, yet it is marginalized in the criminal justice and conflict resolution professional communities. A feminist analysis emphasizes how the gendering of community conferencing as feminine must be understood within the social context of gender subordination—that is, the assumed superiority of the masculine over the feminine.

Still, Abramson and her colleagues at the Community Conferencing Center have made significant positive impact in Baltimore and beyond. Abramson has emerged not only as a leader in the city of Baltimore, but also in the state of Maryland as well as nationally. She has advanced not only the practice of community conferencing, creating what I term the "Baltimore model" of community conferencing, but she has also advanced the theory of practice for community conferencing emphasizing the often overlooked role of emotional transformation in conflict-resolution processes. These advancements solidify her categorization as an agent of positive change.

Conclusion

Abramson's work in Baltimore offers at least two important applications for conflict resolution practitioners around the globe. First, by defining crime as one of many different forms of conflict, Abramson broadens the potential effective uses of community conferencing. While conferencing is practiced in a variety of settings worldwide, it is almost always used in a setting where an undisputed harm (or crime) has occurred. While Abramson and her colleagues at the Community Conferencing Center use conferencing in this way, they also demonstrate that community conferencing has a much broader range of uses. Conflict-resolution practitioners should recognize community conferencing as one of the potential social interventions available to them in their work.

The second aspect of Abramson's contribution to the practice of conflict resolution is her development of affect script psychology as a theory that explains conflict-resolution practice. While Abramson and her colleagues have focused their attention on affect theory as informing community conferencing practice, the theory may not be so limited in its application. While other conflict resolution scholar-practitioners have offered emotion as an adjunct to "more serious" theories of conflict, Abramson is the first to place emotional transformation at the heart of a theory of conflict resolution.

What makes Abramson's story most notable is her ability to effect positive change at both the level of practice and at the level of theory. While many in the field may argue that one is more important than the other, Abramson manages to maintain a near perfect balance between innovations on both levels. For this reason, she should be considered a remarkable woman who is waging peace in Baltimore and beyond.

Keywords

crime, urban violence, conflict transformation, affect script psychology, community conferencing, emotion, theory of practice, ethic of care.

Discussion Questions

1. Do you agree with Lauren Abramson that crime is a form of conflict? Why or why not?
2. Why do you think women are overrepresented in the population of community conferencing facilitators? On what assumptions do you base your answer?
3. In what other social contexts can you see community conferencing being effectively applied?
4. How could you use community conferencing for offenders of violent crimes?

References

Abramson, Lauren. 2011. Baltimore, January 4.

Abramson, Lauren. 2010a. "Better Justice," available at www.poptech.org.

Abramson, Lauren. 2010b. Interview by author. Baltimore, December 10.

Abramson, Lauren. 2004. *Community Conferencing: Facilitator Training Manual.* Baltimore, Md.

Abramson, Lauren. 1998. "Keeping It Restorative: Focusing on All Emotions and Not Just Shame." *Correctional Psychologist*, 30, 2–3.

Abramson, Lauren, and David Moore. 2002. "The Psychology of Community Conferencing," in *Repairing Communities through Restorative Justice*. Lanham, Md: American Correctional Association.

Abramson, Lauren, and David Moore. 2001. "Transforming Conflict in the Inner City: Community Conferencing in Baltimore." *Contemporary Justice Review*, 4(3–4), 321–40.

Alder, C., and J. Wundersitz. 1994. "New Directions in Juvenile Justice Reform in Australia," in C. Alder and J. Wundersitz (eds), *Family Conferencing and Juvenile Justice*. Canberra: Australian Institute of Criminology.

Barton, Charles. 2000. "Theories of Restorative Justice." *Australian Journal of a Professional and Applied Ethics*, 2(1), 41–53.

Braithwaite, John. 1989. *Crime, Shame, and Reintegration*. Cambridge, UK: Cambridge University Press.

Casciani, Cheryl. 2010. Interview by author. Baltimore, Md., December 14.

Christie, Nils. 1977. "Conflicts as Property." *British Journal of Criminology*, 17(1), 1–15.

The City Paper. 2009. "Best Non-Profit Organization: Community Conferencing Center." September 16, 2009.

Community Conferencing Center. 2010. Available at http://www.communitycon-ferencing.org.

Daly, K. 2001. "Conferencing in Australia and New Zealand: Variations, Research Findings and Prospects," in A. Morris and G. Maxwell (eds), *Restorative Justice for Juveniles: Conferencing Mediation and Circles*. Portland, Ore.: Hart Publishing.

Ericson, Edward. 2010. "Room for Improvement: Celebrated Crime Control Measure Actually a Flop, Former Chief Reveals." *The City Paper,* available at http://www2.citypaper.com/news/story.asp?id=20418.

Fae, Misty. 2010. December 20.

Ferebee, Hathaway. 2010. "A Prescription for Juvenile Justice." *The Baltimore Sun,* December 16.

Gilligan, Carol. 1993. *In a Different Voice: Psychological Theory and Women's Development.* Cambridge, Mass.: Harvard University Press.

Johnson, Priya. 2010. *Most Dangerous Cities in the United States,* available at http://www.buzzle.com/articles/most-dangerous-cities-in-the-united-states.html.

Kelly, Vernon. 2011. *A Primer of Affect Psychology,* available at www.tomkins.org.

Maxwell, G., and A. Morris. 1994. "The New Zealand Model of Family Group Conferences," in C. Alder and J. Wundersitz (eds), *Family Conferencing and Juvenile Justice.* Canberra: Australian Institute of Criminology.

Mirsky, Laura. 2004. *The Community Conferencing Center: Restorative Practices in Baltimore, Maryland,* available at www.restorativepractices.org/library/cccbaltimore.html.

Moore, David. 2004. "Managing Social Conflict—The Evolution of a Practical Theory." *Journal of Sociology and Social Welfare,* XXXI (1), 71–91.

Moore, David, and John McDonald. 2000. *Transforming Conflict.* Sydney: Transformative Justice Australia.

Noddings, Nel. 1984. *Caring: A Feminine Approach to Ethics and Moral Education.* Berkeley: University of California Press.

O'Connell, T., and David Moore. 1994. "Family Conferencing in Wagga Wagga," in C. Alder and J. Wundersitz (eds), *Family Conferencing and Juvenile Justice.* Canberra: Australian Institute of Criminology.

Sjoberg, Laura, and Caron Gentry. 2007. *Mothers, Monsters, Whores: Women's Violence in Global Politics.* London: Zed Books.

Spivack, Emily. 2010. "Lauren Abramson: Resolving Conflict with a Handshake, not Handcuffs," available at www.poptech.org.

Sullivan, Erin. 2002. "A League of Their Own." *Baltimore City Paper,* November 13.

Sutherland, J.J. 2010. *The Annual List of Most Dangerous Cities Is Out, Does It Mean Anything?* available at http://www.npr.org/blogs/thetwo-way/2010/11/22/131513907/the-annual-list-of-most-dangerous-cities-is-out-does-it-mean-anything.

Umbreit, Mark, and Gordon Bazemore. 2002. "A Comparison of Four Restorative Justice Conferencing Models by the Office of Juvenile Justice and Delinquency Prevention," in J. Perry (ed.), *Repairing Communities through Restorative Justice.* Lanham, Md.: American Correctional Association.

Zehr, Howard. 1990. *Changing Lenses: a New Focus for Crime and Justice.* Scottdale, Pa.: Herald Press.

SECTION IV

Women Sustaining Peace

CHAPTER TWELVE

Promises of Justice: Uganda, Democratic Republic of Congo, and Sudan

Susan F. Hirsch

Introduction

International criminal prosecution is increasingly pursued in conflict and post-conflict situations with the goals (among others) of punishing perpetrators, providing recourse and remedy to victims, and preventing future instances of the world's worst crimes. The establishment of the International Criminal Court (ICC) through the Rome Statute in 1998 has brought new international attention to the victimization of women through genocide, crimes against humanity, and war crimes. Relatedly, the approach taken by the ICC has also directed attention to gender violence and sexual violence, which affect women in disproportionate numbers in situations of mass atrocity. The groundwork for the ICC's innovative legal approach to gender was laid by the International Criminal Tribunal for the Former Yugoslavia (ICTY) and the International Criminal Tribunal for Rwanda (ICTR), as well as through developments in international humanitarian and human rights law. Efforts to institutionalize legal recognition for the particular kinds of suffering that women have faced and to support gender-sensitive approaches to crimes, procedures, and remedies are routinely understood as offering women new forms of legal agency. For instance, the recognition of rape as a tactic of genocide allows victims of rape to make legal claims, demand a variety of services, and obtain recognition and restitution in a manner quite different from those who suffered such violations in the past. In the logic of the liberal legal framework that tends to dominate international law, these changes in the law are purported to increase women's agency by investing them with the entitlements of a new legal subject position. Reformers who supported the initiatives that resulted in these changes to international law and legal practice laud them as a triumph for women's empowerment and increased agency, even in the aftermath of extreme violent conflict.

At the same time, the new attention to gender in international criminal law has generated considerable controversy. The concerns expressed are quite varied, such as charges that the development of international law has lacked input from a wide diversity of women's and feminist perspectives. Other critics note the potential for the new legal remedies to be viewed as illegitimate in the event that they are ignored or inappropriately applied. Still others note the possibility of privileging women's suffering over men's that could result from particular uses of the laws in conflict situations. Some of most significant and compelling criticisms allege that the new legal arrangements place limits on women's agency by, for instance, configuring them as gendered victims. In this same vein, other critics have argued that women's involvement in legal processes might circumscribe their participation in other initiatives, such as efforts at reconciliation. Intervention into conflict using law is itself controversial and has sparked debates over what is sometimes referred to as the "peace versus justice dilemma." The growing tension over whether the legal developments mentioned above offer women the advantages they promise prompts the explicit consideration in this chapter of women's agency in relation to international criminal law.

The recent legal developments and the ensuing controversies beg a simple question: Does the increased use of gender-sensitive legal mechanisms at the international level increase or decrease women's agency in conflict and/or post-conflict settings? Related questions include: What are the implications of new legal subject positions for women's agency in conflict and post-conflict settings? What will be the effects, especially for women? The International Criminal Court has just begun holding trials, and thus the empirical evidence required to answer these questions is quite limited. However, it is possible to reason from similar developments in domestic law, from the results of the ad hoc international tribunals, and also from the initial evidence of ICC involvement. Based on this material, the argument offered herein is as follows: Including women as a special category of victim in situations of mass atrocity offers contradictory messages about women's capacity for agency and yet also establishes a diverse array of opportunities for women's exercise of agency as individuals and groups. The discussion introduces the concept of "law-inspired agency" and thus offers an innovative way of conceptualizing agentive acts in relation to law. The proposed approach gets around intractable debates, such as whether the legal subject position of "victim" possesses agency and whether the option of law itself precludes the agentive pursuit of other remedies, such as reconciliation.

The following section describes the changes in international criminal law that have afforded women increased recognition as victims of crimes, including crimes of gender violence in conflict settings. A subsequent section explores the debates over women's agency sparked by these legal innovations and further delineates the reconceptualization of women's agency as legal subjects that is advanced in this chapter. Later sections address preliminary evidence of how women have exercised law-inspired agency in several conflicts currently receiving the attention of international legal bodies, specifically northern Uganda, the Democratic Republic of Congo, and the Darfur region of Sudan. The conclusion insists that analysts must look not just *at* law but *in relation to* law to appreciate how openings for women's agency in the legal domain spark additional opportunities for agency.

The Recognition of Gender in International Criminal Law

Attention to women as a category of person who might deserve special treatment in international law has grown considerably. Earlier efforts at the ad hoc tribunals that focused on crimes committed in the former Yugoslavia and Rwanda resulted in some gains for recognition of the crimes that affect women disproportionally (Green et al. 1994). For instance, the category of rape in international humanitarian law began to be established through the victims who testified about their experiences at the ICTY. The *Akayesu* trial held during the ICTR gained the first convictions for rape as an act in furtherance of genocide (Askin 2005). In the 1990s, many activists and legal reformers contributed to the explosion of attention to sexual violence as international crime (for reviews of this history, see, e.g., Bedont 1999; Halley 2008). Despite the many gains made with respect to legal recognition, crimes of sexual violence are not recognized as grave harms under the Geneva Convention, a goal some activists continue to pursue in order to trigger universal jurisdiction (Engle 2005).

In tandem with the changes described above, the development of the Rome Statute that established the International Criminal Court also included new recognition of crimes that affect women disproportionally (e.g., rape and sexual slavery) (*Rome Statute of the International Criminal Court* 2002). Also endorsed was explicit recognition of the special attention that women as victims of violence might warrant, such as protection or trauma counseling. The Women's Caucus for Gender Justice (WCGJ) played an important role in furthering a feminist agenda during the planning and development of the ICC, as did other NGOs and advocacy groups with interests in gender (Oosterveld 1999, 2005; Copelon 2000; Halley 2008; Spees 2003). Their gains were many, including recognition of the gender dimensions of war crimes, crimes against humanity, and genocide; gender-sensitive procedural rules; a nondiscrimination policy; and the inclusion in the ICC statute of a progressive definition of gender that asserts its culturally constructed character (Oosterveld 2005).

The success of the WCGJ and other feminist efforts represented an unprecedented exercise of agency on the part of women determined to bring mainstream attention to gender in international criminal law.[1] The feminist writing that led to these efforts decried the impunity for crimes of gender violence that had characterized conflict situations (see, e.g., Askin 1997; Chesterman 1997). Committed legal reformers fought hard to eradicate impunity by forcing legal recognition of gender-based crimes as constituting grievous harm on a par with other offenses of mass atrocity (for a review of earlier efforts, see e.g., Engle 2005). The resulting developments in international law constituted a new approach to crimes related to gender and to the treatment of women as a special class of victims in situations of extreme conflict (see, e.g., Bedont 1999). Another intended result was that women who had been victimized as a consequence of their gender should expect more concerted attention to the harms they had suffered. Legal recognition as a victim of sexual violence provided women with, for instance, avenues to participate in prosecution, pursue other legal action alongside a criminal proceeding, seek assistance for their psychophysical injuries, and claim reparations.

The recognition afforded women in the Rome Statute was achieved as part of the general expansion of attention to victims in ICC statutes and procedures (Amnesty International 1999; International Criminal Court 2005). The Rome Statute allows for victims' needs and interests to be addressed by the court in ways that go beyond previous initiatives in international criminal justice by granting them the rights to participation, protection, and reparations, which all entail specific acts of agency (see, generally, International Criminal Court 2005a,b; War Crimes Research Office 2007).[2] For instance, victims are encouraged to provide the court with information about crimes committed against them and are entitled to receive information about the court's activities with respect to investigation and prosecution, including notification of trial, deferments, terminations, judgments, and appeals. As well, victims may participate directly in the trial process, and, if they so request, can be granted assistance in retaining counsel. For the first time in an international criminal proceeding, legal representatives of victims spoke at the war crimes trial of Thomas Lubanga, accused of crimes related to the conflict in the Democratic Republic of Congo, which is discussed in more detail below (IBA 2009). At trial, victims may act on their personal interests to put forward claims or question witnesses (for commentary, see Garkawe 2003). All victims are entitled to receive protection and assistance, including for trauma, and can make claims for reparations. Various offices of the court address victims' issues (e.g., the Office of the Prosecutor, Victim Witness Unit of the Registry, the Office of Public Counsel for Victims, and the Victims' Participation and Reparations Unit), and victims of sexual assault or abuse receive special attention as do minors and those with limited means. The needs of female victims are mentioned specifically in the procedural rules that define the ICC's approach to victims (Bedont 1999).

The gendered nature of women's legal subjectivity as a result of the recent attention to women as a particular class of victim is key to the argument made in this chapter that the new legal initiatives increase women's opportunities for agency. Women who have suffered in situations of mass atrocity gain standing through legal recognition that interprets their harm as specifically gendered. That recognition underpins and thus makes possible certain acts of gendered agency on their part (e.g., seeking a remedy in court). Perhaps the strength of the argument linking legal recognition to new forms of women's agency lies primarily in its converse: the previous lack of legal (and political or public) recognition of gender-related crimes (or the refusal to treat these crimes as seriously as other forms of violence, such as murder) precluded the agentive actions of women qua women in, for instance, making claims or seeking remedies. In effect, prior to the history of legal reform outlined above, women's suffering was erased or diminished in part through its lack of recognition in law. That erasure dampened possibilities for gendered agentive action on the part of those harmed. In making a plea for support for the International Criminal Court that reflects her belief in its ability to assist women, Corcoran argues: "Trials, even if they take years, not only hold perpetrators accountable, but also provide victims with a voice they otherwise would not have had" (Corcoran 2008: 225–26).

With respect to both domestic and international contexts, the expansion of the role of victim in criminal law is a potentially powerful form of recognizing legal subjects and institutionalizing avenues for agentive action on their part, which might include getting a voice, seeking reparations, or other remedies. From this theoretical perspective, legal recognition serves to constitute subjects who are then invested with particular options for agency (see, e.g., Minow 1991; Hirsch and Lazarus-Black 1994; Coutin 2000). In criminal law, "victim" is a familiar legal subject position, which has been invested with varying degrees of agency depending on the time, place, and politics of the legal system. As Cole (2006) has argued cogently, the figure of victim has always been double edged. The tendency to "blame the victim" is evidence of a negative strain in the conceptualization of harmed subjects, especially when they assert collective victimhood. Even as this tendency operates to disempower victims, they are also entitled to and capable of acts of agency as well as tremendous symbolic power (see also Lamb 1999). The double-edged quality of victimhood makes it problematic to posit a predictable link among legal subject position, victims' agency to make claims, and the receipt of a satisfying remedy without asking how this process works in particular contexts or for particular categories of victim (Constable 2005; Cole 2006; Clarke 2009; Hirsch 2009). Although a deeper discussion of the subject position of victim lies beyond the scope of this chapter, the concern with the limits and opportunities for women victims given their new subject positions in international law is revisited in a subsequent section. The point relevant for this discussion is that the position of victim is more complex than the conventional notion that victims lack power or agency. The emergence of new and complex subject positions with recognition at the global level, including victims, thus demands a reconceptualization of the gendered agency offered through and inspired by the law recently available to women.

Implications of Legal Recognition for Women's Agency

A number of authors have drawn attention to potential negative implications of women's special recognition in international criminal law and legal proceedings. Although these criticisms reflect a variety of perspectives, the focus in this section is on two distinct approaches to questioning the attributions of women's agency associated with these developments. The first type of criticism suggests that women's actual treatment in legal proceedings might diminish rather than increase their agency. The second is a broader indictment of the entire effort to deploy international criminal law to address gender-specific harms. As the discussion below suggests, both of these criticisms are compelling, and their applicability to these early years of the operation of the ICC is considered in a later section.

In an influential article, Julie Mertus argues that women's agency might be undermined when they participate in adversarial legal processes at the international level. She cites the treatment of women who, in choosing to testify at the International Criminal Tribunal for the former Yugoslavia, were quite purposeful in their approach to law: "They did not view themselves as passive recipients of assistance, but as active agents of change who knowingly chose to use international advocacy as a personal and political tool"

(Mertus 2004, 111). But, in the course of participation, even women with a strong sense of purpose experienced limits on their agency through legal discourse and procedures that prohibited them from fully expressing their experiences of suffering. Mertus concluded that "[a]lthough women still may exercise agency in the context of the adversarial process, their ability to do so is stunted. In the words of one Kosovar survivor of wartime rape: 'it is like shouting from the bottom of a well.' War crime trials serve useful goals, but they do not adequately meet the needs of survivors" (Mertus 2004, 113). As Mertus claims, the procedural requirements of an adversarial process mean that women are offered an inadequate context to express their experiences of violence. This conclusion leads her to propose supplements and alternatives to adversarial justice, such as truth-telling exercises and therapeutic story-telling, that might better support women's agency toward "creating a record, achieving justice, remembering or forgetting" (Mertus 2004, 124). Dembour and Haslan (2004) make the point more generally with respect to victims and witnesses at the ICTY that the experience of testifying can be unsatisfying or traumatic and can fail to offer an adequate context for representing victims' stories (for a similar argument, see Fletcher and Weinstein 2002; Danieli 2009). Other research shows that witnesses who testified at the ICTY came away with a variety of perspectives about the experience, and many were left feeling ambivalent about the degree to which they had exercised agency through participating in the proceedings (see also Stover 2005).

The courtroom context can be even more daunting for those who endeavor to testify about their experiences of rape or sexual assault. With respect to domestic courts, rape victims routinely report a sense of revictimization that can include loss of control over presenting their perspective. As Mertus argues, even though rape shield protections in use at the ICTY minimized the extent to which defense attorneys could question witness' prior sexual behavior, individuals were impugned through the proceedings (Mertus 2004). Attention to the problem of revictimization led to strengthening the procedural safeguards during the development of the International Criminal Court. For one, prior sexual history of the victim is not permitted as a defense. As another, provisions are made for victims who choose to testify *in camera* rather than face the defendant in open court. Also, counseling and support are supposed to be available to victims and witnesses. These provisions represent major advancements in international law and also in comparison to many domestic jurisdictions and should, in theory, operate to increase women's ability to participate.

Another major change brought about through the Rome Statute and its implementation addressed the issue of consent, which has long been linked to women's disempowerment in legal contexts. Specifically, victim's consent is no longer a relevant factor in determining a defendant's culpability for sexual violence. The act of sexual penetration (carried out in various ways) is a crime by virtue of the circumstances of coercion that were part and parcel of the conflict setting or the climate of violence in which it occurred. In prosecuting crimes of sexual violence in many conflict situations, it now must be assumed that consent was impossible given the coercion and control characterizing the context. Thus, a victim of rape or sexual assault need not demonstrate resistance or refusal in order for the violation to be proved against the accused. Accordingly, in an ICC prosecution, victims of sexual violence will not need to face cross-examination about whether their actions constituted lack of consent. The difference between this approach to consent and previous approaches in international and domestic law is quite stark. Women have always found the courtroom a difficult context for demonstrating lack of consent to gender violence. In an article that explores the interrelations among violence, gender, and subjectivity, Veena Das links this difficulty to the tendency to define the sexual violation of women as a violation of those men who hold power over them (i.e. fathers and husbands). Das argues:

> Legal reasoning then works to punish those men who have violated the rights of men, especially those who can be placed in a higher position as compared with the alleged perpetrator (Kannibaran & Kannibaran 2002) and to display publicly the distinction between good women and bad women by pronouncing upon whose "no" to sex can be converted to "consent" because of their sexual history. (Das 2008, 292)

Although a variety of changes in international law explicitly detach the harm of rape from notions of honor (individual or familial) and thus overtly reject perspectives on sexual violence that follow this line of thinking, it may be difficult to ensure that these culturally salient understandings will have no place in court. The longstanding role of the law in supporting the logic described by Das means that it may be especially difficult to effect this change.

The question remains: Will these changes, in fact, empower women in international proceedings? The preliminary answer is that the results may be mixed. For instance, successfully eliminating the egregious act of having to prove one's lack of consent in a prosecution for sexual violence may have another, unintended impact on women's agency. Specifically, the actions of the perpetrator become the centerpiece of the primary narrative presented in court. Thus, it is only the perpetrator's action that "matters." Women's agency—in their actions at the time of the assault or in recounting the events—is not particularly crucial to the outcome of the trial, even if they can narrate their own strong resistance to the assault. Perhaps diminishing women's agency in this way can be justified against the gain of freedom from scrutiny of their actions; however, women themselves may have a clear sense of what should be aired in public. From another perspective, Beltz (2008, 166) is among those who express concern that "special procedural safeguards for victims of rape and sexual violence who chose to testify before the ICC and other war crimes tribunals" will be needed to protect women above and beyond what has already been anticipated and implemented. The final sections return to this concern by examining initial evidence from three conflict situations.

A second, more abstract area of criticism of the developments around gender in international criminal law is offered by law professor Janet Halley who demonstrates that the legal reforms of the 1990s are rooted in "a structuralist understanding of male domination and female subordination" (Halley 2008, 2). According to Halley, this perspective views the sexual harms suffered by women in conflict settings as "universal in their scope" and emphasizes criminalization, prosecution, and incarceration as appropriate remedies that are also responsibilities of the global community (Halley 2008, 60). Noting that the feminist activists who put forward this approach were largely, though not completely, successful in grounding international criminal law in a structuralist perspective, Halley criticizes the approach on several grounds, including for emphasizing a "carceral" approach to gender relations and "inviting feminists to forget about having a positive vision of human, or female, life well lived" (Halley 2008, 121). Her concerns have implications for gendered agency. For one, the theoretical positioning of women as universally dominated shares the problem with earlier radical feminism of offering no options for women to gain effective agency or to work in concert with men (as well as no vision of the good life). A legal approach grounded in that lack of possibility could scarcely be expected to foster women's agency. Secondly, Halley notes that by using international criminal law women must subordinate their own agency to that of the state and to rely on "state forms of power to the exclusion of more dispersed ones, ones that might actually lie within the reach of actual women—and men— leading their everyday and their wartime lives" (Halley 2008, 121). Certainly those women who advocate "local" approaches to justice or healing as remedies after sexual violence (rather than criminal prosecution) would be limited in their efforts. But Halley's greatest fear is that the new laws create an obligation for action under international humanitarian and criminal law that she, many other feminists, and many other women find unacceptable. She argues that the new approach "involves a – to me absolutely chilling – indifference to the suffering and death of men" (Halley 2008: 123). As other commentators have also claimed, international humanitarian law sets up a "matrix of rules for privileged killing" that could also be used by international criminal law to trigger military interventions. Halley asks: "War as legally justified vengeance for the intensely illegal rape of women? It has happened before and, if the Rome Statute has the moral grip on the world that its proponents want it to have, it will happen again—but now with the new possibility that feminist labors may stoke the fires of war" (Halley 2008: 123). Such criticisms have opened up a debate over whether the turn to international criminal law harnesses the power of domestic and international institutions to further women's legitimate claims to legal agency, or whether it severely limits women's options for responding ethically and effectively to the harms that they experience disproportionately.

The criticisms outlined in this section point to areas that warrant examination as the ICC's investigations and prosecutions move forward. The new gendered legal subject positions constituted through the ICC's operation have been used in only a few conflict contexts and, even in those contexts, have had little time to make an impact. Accordingly, sufficient data to assess whether women achieve agency through these constructs, or whether their agency is limited in the ways suggested by Mertus, Halley, and others, does not yet exist. However, it is possible to undertake a preliminary assessment of the actions that women can and have taken in particular contexts where these legal categories and processes have been deployed. Case studies of Uganda, Congo, and Darfur later in this chapter offer evidence that developments in international criminal law produce contradictory messages about gendered agency and also multiple opportunities for agentive acts on the part of women as well as some limitations on women's agency along the lines articulated by Mertus and Halley. In the next section, I offer a reconceptualized perspective on women's agency in relation to the law by directing attention to the wide range of opportunities for agency brought about through the new international legal subject positions, including law-inspired opportunities.

Agency and Legal Subjectivity Reconceptualized

Long before formal proceedings in a legal institution begin, individuals thought to have suffered harm are designated as potential victims by representatives of the international community. They need not have taken any action at all to become "victims." That designation, which is deployed by humanitarian agencies and legal personnel, opens up multiple opportunities for agency. For instance, many individuals in Uganda, the Congo, and Darfur have been offered the chance to describe what happened to them or their loved ones during their respective conflicts. Arguably, the production of a story of harm—witnessed by others and told without coercion—can be viewed as an act of agency that follows from the designation of victim and at the same time constitutes the teller as such. To the extent that the individual narrates a story for consumption by witnesses who represent the international community, the new position from which to take agentive action is perhaps more powerful by virtue of its global reach (Hirsch 2009).

In each of the three conflict contexts discussed below, international organizations have conducted outreach and investigations. Their attention to gender—mandated by the Rome Statute—means that they have necessarily engaged victims as gendered subjects. Thus these outreach and investigative interactions encourage attention to categories of self and social role, such as widow, mother, female abductee, and female rape victim, that recognize gender. The instantiation of gendered subject positions might have the effect of channeling agency in particular ways. For instance, female abductees in northern Uganda may be encouraged to express their experiences of abduction differently than males by, for instance, discussing fears and/or experiences of sexual slavery or forced pregnancy. Or the claims made by mothers about the loss of children might be given special attention as emotional harm. The recognition of gendered roles at the international level can, at least in theory, give rise to a consciousness of agentive possibilities that has not been available previously. An obvious example would be the provision of rights associated with the category of victim, such as the rights to protection and remedies. Gaining access to a rights discourse is a potentially transformative experience not least because of the openings for agentive acts, such as making claims. The entitlements that ensue through involvement in a criminal process draw their power from a global discourse of rights that many of those harmed by conflict might not have previously encountered. Women, in particular, may have had less experience with entitlement through rights discourse than men. Specifically, the right to make claims as a result of sexual violence may be a relatively new idea (Merry 2006). Relatedly, the ability to make claims through the gendered, legal role of "widow" in the aftermath of violence might also be novel in the many contexts where widows have had limited entitlements (e.g., with respect to inheritance).

In theory, legal and humanitarian organizations reach out to women victims to afford them the opportunity to act on these rights and entitlements.

Their ability to do this depends on the degree and type of outreach offered and may never result in agency in the form of actual claims or remedies. Even though many women victims lack the support and knowledge needed to act on their legal options, their very constitution as gendered legal subjects might make them aware of several factors crucial to acting agentively in the future. For instance, women victims of conflict may learn that telling their story of harm can have multiple functions and effects, such as gaining sympathy or offering evidence toward a claim. They might also come to appreciate the fact that stories can be produced across different venues with different purposes and results. Of course, as the story of harm becomes disembodied through repeated tellings and retellings by others for purposes unknown or unacceptable to the victim, an individual victim can lose control of the story and might perceive an erosion of agency. Anthropologist Kamari Clarke asserts that victims' position in the early operation of the ICC is spectral—a figment of the court's political whim—rather than a coherent subject position (Clarke 2007). This is a reminder that the agency derived from telling one's story or any other agentive act associated with the law can be undermined by the politics of the legal process.

Interaction with international law is perhaps more potentially transformative for women than for men. Women, who have often been generally disenfranchised, may find their new perspective on rights and entitlements useful in contexts other than criminal prosecution. The encounter with international legal outreach may offer women new tools for understanding their subject position. For instance, learning that they have legal recognition by virtue of victimhood could be useful to those women who seek to address their special plight as widows, a category often invested with limited rights or limited channels for acting on rights in local settings (Emorut 2009). Such opportunities could be enormously consequential for women, particularly in a war-torn context where damages to social networks make flexibility in conceptualizing one's position a key to survival.

My point is not a normative one in support of international legal intervention or, relatedly, of raising women's rights consciousness, but rather I speculate, with some limited evidence, that the ideas underpinning gendered legal subject positions might invest women in conflict settings with ways of thinking about their position that could be more broadly useful. As Stover's interviews with witnesses at the ICTY demonstrate, awareness of entitlement and positioning that lie outside one's immediate surroundings can be a life-changing option for some persons who may previously have had much more circumscribed understandings of their social roles (Stover 2005). For people who have already had the life-changing experience of conflict and violence, such a break with prior experience might introduce refreshing options. Perhaps among the most important aspects of a gendered legal subject position is the recognition that one shares an alliance with other women locally, nationally, regionally, and globally. The experiences of gendered collectivity and of entitlement as a gendered group are at least first steps toward perceiving and acting on new forms of agency. Such experiences can, however, be double edged as collective groups of victims are often viewed as threats (Cole 2006). Thus, women's agency as a result of legal entitlement can have, in the several ways mentioned, both negative and positive effects, as can be seen in the case studies discussed in the next section.

Preliminary Observations of Gender and Agency with Respect to Law

The differences among the three case studies of Uganda, Democratic Republic of Congo, and the Darfur region of Sudan are many, although they are all situated in the same region of Africa and have geopolitical interrelations. (For general discussion of the effects on gender of new prosecutions in Africa, see Oko 2008.) The discussion below offers preliminary observations linking the gendered legal subjectivity associated with international criminal law to women's agency in each context. In the course of outreach and investigation in each context, many women were interviewed by humanitarian and legal organizations, and subsequently some became involved in ongoing legal processes. It is entirely possible that through this experience some women gained new perspectives on self and social position, rights discourse, legal positioning, entitlement, and the link between making claims from a position and the receipt of recognition and remedy. The cases begin to demonstrate the argument that law might open up or inspire new possibilities for women's agency, including collective action. As well, the case studies below show instances of the limitations on agency, as predicted by Mertus (2004) and Halley (2008).

Northern Uganda Region

The situation in northern Uganda was the first to be referred to the International Criminal Court for investigation. This decades-long conflict has pitted the government of Uganda against a series of rebel movements, including the Lord's Resistance Army (LRA). People in the northern region—particularly the Acholi ethnic group—have suffered extensive displacement of population, murder, abduction, the conscription of child soldiers, and rape. In 2005, the ICC issued an indictment for five rebel leaders, including LRA commander Joseph Kony. None of the accused have been captured; two are no longer alive. The ICC's involvement has generated tremendous controversy. For one, critics have alleged that the moves toward prosecution have endangered ongoing peace talks at crucial moments. Also, many have charged that victims prefer local responses (e.g., rituals of reconciliation and restorative justice) over international prosecution. In many ways the controversies, and the delay caused by the ICC's inability to arrest the suspects, have meant that Ugandan women have had considerable opportunity to become aware of and pursue a variety of avenues for agency.

Well before indictments were issued, humanitarian organizations and the ICC had conducted extensive outreach and recorded many accounts from women and girls who had experienced conflict. Among the victims were girls who had been abducted by the LRA and forced into sexual slavery. The controversy over the ICC's involvement has resulted in close attention to the interests of victims by the ICC and many international actors. Numerous reports have been written about victims' interests and several large-scale polls have been conducted (see, e.g., Liu Institute for Refugee Law Project 2004; Global Issues 2005; Office of High Commissioner for Human Rights 2007). The extensive research on victims and their stories has provided repeated opportunities to acquaint victims with ways of understanding their own subject positions, including those that emphasize gender and the law. Some victims have registered their interest in appearing in court should those indicted be captured and put on trial in The Hague or through newly developed national courts with jurisdiction over the conflict. Repeated contact through research and outreach has served to shape some victims' views of their options and thus their potential agency.

As a result of the controversy and the delay in justice, some women have organized into interest groups, such as the Greater Northern Women's Peace Initiative, or joined groups convened by local and international NGOs. As groups, victims have confronted both rebel perpetrators and the government in their search for peace and/or accountability. Betty Bigombe, a major female leadership figure, has taken a prominent role in the controversy over the ICC's involvement. Bigombe has long served as a chief mediator between the government of Uganda and the LRA, and she represents a role model of women's capacity for agency in a conflict setting. She has raised concerns about the possibilities for establishing peace with the ICC indictments looming. In the debate over what Ugandan, and particularly Acholi, victims want, women have expressed a variety of views, although Bigombe has tended to emphasize local remedies, which include several reconstituted rituals designed to reintegrate soldiers and reconcile factions within the population (Allen 2006; Clarke 2009; Hirsch 2009).

Whether women support the prosecutions or seek alternative responses or both, the ICC's intervention has had several effects: It recognizes female victims as gendered legal subjects; it brings a global perspective into deliberations; and it offers a discourse of rights, including gendered rights. Each of these potentially sets a new ground for a variety of agentive acts on the part of Ugandan women. It is important to note that this potential could be operative even in situations when the women themselves support an approach to justice other than ICC involvement. The controversy over replacing international prosecution with local remedies or national prosecution also has a gender dimension. Some Ugandan women have become concerned about the role of traditional male leaders, whose power has become more entrenched with the elevation of rituals of reconciliation, and consequently reject what they see as a return to patriarchal values. This leads these women to ally themselves either with the international court or with efforts to pursue justice in the national courts. This is another instance of women's agency in reaction to the law, that is, law-inspired agency undertaken through a gendered subject position.

My point is that women coming together even to protest laws is also an agentive act, although it is hard to say for certain the extent to which the gendered nature of their opposition was attributable to the developments in international law. The case is a reminder of the importance of monitoring the variety of effects on agency of new legal developments.

The Democratic Republic of Congo

During the mid- to late 1990s, the Democratic Republic of Congo (DRC) was the scene of a civil war that also involved neighboring nations. More than three million people were killed, and at least 10,000 were raped (Human Rights Watch 2002). In 2004, the DRC government referred cases to the International Criminal Court for investigation with the result that Thomas Lubanga, a former rebel leader, became the first defendant transferred to The Hague to face trial. In January 2009, the ICC began its first-ever trial, which focused on war crimes allegedly committed by Lubanga, including the forced conscription of child soldiers allegedly deployed to kill and rape other combatants and civilians. Estimates are that more than 30,000 children were conscripted in the Congo conflict (Human Rights Watch 2002). Two defendants, accused of operating military offensives in the Ituri region, were also transferred to The Hague, where they await trial on war crimes and crimes against humanity.

Humanitarian organizations have documented that, during the DRC conflict, sexual assault against women and girls was extensive and undertaken by all parties to the conflict (Puechguirbal 2003; Pritchett 2008). One organization alleged that the targeting of females warranted the conclusion that the Congo was experiencing a "war within a war" (Human Rights Watch 2002). Accordingly, commentators questioned why the chief prosecutor of the ICC failed to charge Lubanga with rape (or other sexual violence crimes) and whether this constituted "selective justice" (Pritchett 2008).[3] The chief prosecutor explained that his office can only charge a defendant with crimes that can be proved. Perhaps this controversy led the Lubanga Trial Court judges to show great concern over the special position of women and girls by questioning witnesses pointedly about the specific issue of the rape of girl soldiers (IBA 2009, 29). Eventually, the repeated mention of rape throughout Lubanga's trial led attorneys for victims to request that the court add the charge of sexual slavery to the counts against the defendant (Institute for War and Peace Reporting 2009).

Many people provided information that, throughout the civil war in the Congo, women, girls, and a smaller number of boys were assaulted sexually. One hundred victims have chosen to be party to the Lubanga case, which entitles them to offer statements and to pose questions of the defendant and witnesses through their legal representatives. Hundreds more made application to the court as victims (Bingold et al. 2009). These acts of agency, made available through law, have been undertaken by Congolese women as well as men. Given that victims are participating in the adversarial proceeding, the concerns raised by Mertus, as discussed in a previous section, with respect to potential limits on women's agency are relevant. Will these women feel that they are "shouting from the bottom of a well," as did the victims of rape who testified at the International Criminal Tribunal for the Former Yugoslavia? As for the experience of victim/witnesses in the court proceedings, an International Bar Association (IBA) report suggests that, in the initial proceedings of the Lubanga case, the dignity and privacy of witnesses was respected (for general reports on the trial, see "The Lubanga Trial at the International Criminal Court" http://www.lubangatrial.org/). Those who have chosen to testify have been permitted to with considerable protections, including the option to obscure their identity and to avoid eye contact with the accused. Certainly, such accommodations allow the participation of women and others who might have feared facing the defendant directly or felt too embarrassed to appear in open court. Also, their testimony can include long, unbroken stories that resemble how people talk about such incidents in conversations with friends or family. Although testifying in court remains a difficult and awkward process, it is possible that some of Mertus's conclusions as to the limits on women's agency might not be warranted. The IBA report expresses concern that airing some testimony only on closed-circuit television, while protecting witnesses, might limit the degree to which victims' messages, and those of the trial itself, circulate publically (IBA 2009). Thus, a woman's decision to retain anonymity might facilitate some aspects of her agency (e.g., telling her story) while limiting others (e.g., publicizing her perspective).

The Lubanga prosecution also opened up another unanticipated area of agency for women. In June 2008, Lubanga's trial was postponed while the court addressed a charge that the ICC prosecutor had mishandled evidence. Observers were stunned at the prospect that Lubanga might be released, although this did not ultimately occur. In the capital of the Congo, many people, including male and female victims, protested the delay and the possible release. They protested as victims, with a vested interest in the international case, and thus became politically active as gendered victims. I bring this up not as evidence that those in the Congo preferred the international legal prosecution of Lubanga and others over some other kind of remedy but rather to note the multiple forms of agency generated in relation to international law. Most importantly, these protests took place on both national and international stages. The victim deserving of global justice demanded that justice in new ways, thereby exercising forms of political agency that had previously been unavailable.

Darfur, Sudan

For decades the Sudanese nation has been engaged in a civil war pitting the northern national government against the southern oppositional movement. In 2003, conflict broke out in the western Darfur region, where disputes over land and government neglect of the region's population had been brewing for years. Rebel forces clashed with Sudanese government troops and their alleged surrogates in the form of militias called *janjaweed*. The conflict has had devastating effects, particularly on the Fur ethnic group: the deaths of a half million people and the displacement of four times that many (Amnesty International 2004b; Hagan 2008). Rape and sexual assault have been committed extensively, and women and girls have been seriously affected in multiple ways (Amnesty International 2004a). Ethnic violence is a feature of the conflict, although whether the conflict constitutes genocide is the subject of debate. For the first time ever, the United Nations Security Council voted to refer the Darfur situation to the ICC for investigation. Indictments have been issued against several leaders of the violence, including Omar Al Bashir, the president of Sudan. The charges include crimes against humanity and war crimes, such as rape and pillaging.

Outreach by human rights organizations, particularly in the refugee camps, and by the US State Department, which commissioned 1,000 interviews in 2004, has offered many women the chance to describe their experiences of conflict. Yet, much of the area, including the camps, remains so highly insecure that outreach has likely not accomplished enough to have an impact on many women's understandings of their subject position as relates to international law. Many victims who have been recognized as deserving of justice have never encountered anyone who might offer them a perspective on that designation. The insecurity and violence that make outreach almost impossible in some areas also undermine the ability of women who are aware of their legal position to invest it with much relevance. Any sense of legal agency that might ensue from the ICC recognition of victims is challenged by the recurrence of attacks against them. It is one thing to ask victims to wait for a trial, as in the case of northern Uganda, where justice has been delayed, but for victims deserving of global justice to endure repeated violations against them tests belief in the efficacy of international justice, as noted by Corcoran (2008). Moreover, Sudanese officials in Darfur have also turned to law as a weapon in the conflict. Under the guise of maintaining security, suspected rebels and many civilians have been apprehended and severely punished, even executed (Amnesty International 2009). The extraordinary insecurity experienced by Darfurians necessarily works against viewing law, including international law, as a source of effective agency.

That said, some Darfurians have expressed support for the ICC and its efforts to prosecute Bashir and others. A group of local Darfurian lawyers, including several women, have been outspoken in their desire to use the law as a response to the conflict and have gone through training outside Sudan to provide them with the capacity to assist victims (Cox and Roth 2008). Although they have expressed hopes for the ICC to punish the most serious violators, they are equally concerned about conducting trials locally. Writing about the lack of gender violence justice with respect to Darfur, Schneider argues that this might be precisely an approach that female victims could find satisfying:

> There is much to be said for holding liable under command responsibility those leaders responsible for the commission of atrocities, and that must

be done where appropriate through the ICC, but there are critical reasons to hold those actually committing gender violence also liable, whether that is done at the ICC or on the national level. Victims and survivors might derive more satisfaction and healing from participation in trials leading to convictions of their actual torturers and rapists; they might find greater catharsis from seeing such persons in the dock than from seeing their commanders—usually strangers to those victimized—who gave impersonal orders or encouraged such crimes generally. (Schneider 2008, 973–74)

Many commentators on this and the other conflicts discussed above speculate on the needs and desires of victims, particularly their interest in local justice, without recognizing the great difficulty in knowing what victims want and how their interests might change over time and over the life of a conflict (Hirsch 2009). Asking them directly is especially difficult in situations where outreach to provide information about options and to learn victims' views must cross national, linguistic, legal, and cultural barriers.

Ascertaining the remedy that women in Darfur might prefer is also complicated by the lack of agreement on the crimes they have suffered. Their experiences are the subject of a debate over whether the rapes and assaults on them constituted genocide. At present, genocide is not a charge leveled by the ICC, although many commentators have voiced their criticism of ICC reticence and offered evidence to show otherwise (see, e.g., Corcoran 2008; Hagan 2008; Schneider 2008). Darfurian women's words and actions are interpreted and reinterpreted by researchers and legal personnel to prove that the crime of genocide has taken place. The experiences of these women lie at the center of several geopolitical conflicts involving international bodies, various nations (e.g., China, the United States, and others), and lawyers, humanitarian workers, and feminist NGOs. I raise this to emphasize the complexity and tentativeness of the subject position occupied by women who might have little knowledge of the debates swirling over them. Yet these debates are consequential in determining how women are constituted as victims.

In an article subtitled "Saving the Women of Darfur," Corcoran holds the international community accountable for the continued violations against women and girls in Darfur. In her reasoning, the world's nations are fully aware that Darfurian women are being victimized through rape and other violence and have failed to act to protect them (Corcoran 2008). She and others have called for military assistance in capturing those indicted and securing the region. This provocative demand, which turns on the enforcement of international law and the protection of victims for its rationale, returns us to the criticism leveled by Janet Halley (2008). She was especially concerned that enforcement of international law would be used to sanction invasion and that feminist thinking, advocacy, and aims would have fueled such incursions. For Halley, this use of feminist agency is questionable, particularly given the lack of debate among feminists and women more generally over whether protecting particular women from sexual assault justifies exposing men to combat deaths. Corcoran's insistence on "saving the women" is a powerful symbol not the least because it emphasizes Darfurian women's lack of agency and their dependence on others. But at the same time, erasing any possibility that Darfurian women could act agentively under the circumstances makes it difficult for them to participate in a debate over the fate of their region. It may be especially important to view agency broadly when such debates are undertaken.

Conclusion

> Women generally do not start wars. They do not commonly perpetuate them, nor do they predominate in fighting them. Women are underutilized in the prevention of wars, and underrepresented in planning to end them. Therefore, it is a particularly cruel injustice that women should be deliberately targeted for such suffering in war.
>
> (Schneider 2008, 994).

Notwithstanding the truth of Schneider's quote, women exercise agency in many ways in relation to conflict. This chapter has endeavored to direct attention to the ways in which recent considerations of gender in international criminal law has expanded women's options for agency with respect to mass conflict and its aftermath. For instance, crimes that have a disproportionate effect on women, such as sexual assault and rape in furtherance of genocide, have gained new recognition as international criminal law develops to address mass atrocity. Moreover, special attention to gender and the gendered nature of victims is also reflected in the forms of criminal investigation and procedure that have emerged from the ICTY, ICTR, and ICC. Critics of such developments point out the many ways in which women are constrained from acting in their own interests, especially in formal legal settings. However, it is difficult to deny that more recognition of women's experiences by international criminal law, particularly the constitution of new gendered legal subject positions, despite association with the concept of "victim," offers the possibility for novel enactments of agency by women caught in the midst of conflict and its aftermath.

As this chapter has attempted to demonstrate, the gendered legal subject positions available to women influence their thoughts and actions within and alongside legal institutions give rise to acts of agency that would not otherwise occur. The examples from Uganda, the Democratic Republic of Congo, and Sudan illustrate the wide variety of women's enactments of agency in relation to international criminal law. For instance, through their identification as victims recognized as deserving of justice under international criminal law, women may find that they are encouraged and enabled to recount their experiences of conflict, and many have done so both in and out of legal settings. Relatedly, women may gain agency to act on their claims of harm as the legal discourses that confirm their rights as victims of conflict become familiar to them. Claims to rights are powerful acts of agency in the neoliberal contexts of most conflict and post-conflict settings; thus, women may find that they have acquired a language with which they can pursue a variety of initiatives and concerns. Finally, not all women are interested in acting on the legal subject position in which they find themselves through the remedies offered by international law. At the same time, they are drawn into a politics of law that may result in them embracing that position or rejecting it; both acts are expressions of their agency inspired by international law.

It is too early to determine the extent to which women's agency will be manifest in conflict and post-conflict settings in relation to the new legal options, although researchers and advocates would do well to be attentive to women's law-inspired acts of agency and, at the same time, the limits of law as a response to conflict.

Keywords

justice, International Criminal Court, tribunals, victim, International Criminal Tribunal for the former Yugoslavia (ICTY), International Criminal Tribunal of Rwanda (ICTR), Women Caucus for Gender and Justice (WCGJ), Rome Statute, revictimization.

Discussion Questions

1. How has international criminal law changed to include women's experiences of conflict? What are the most significant criticisms against these changes?

2. What are the contradictory messages about women's capacity for agency that result from their special recognition through international law?
3. What is the difference between legal agency and law-inspired agency? What forms does each take for women who have experienced conflict?
4. What are the pros and cons of using the term *victim* to describe those who have experienced conflict? Is it more or less problematic to apply this term to females as compared with males?
5. Does gaining agency through law have particular advantages for women? Disadvantages?

References

Allen, Tim. 2006. *Trial Justice: The International Criminal Court and the Lord's Resistance Army*. London and New York: Zed Books.

Amnesty International (AI). 2009. Amnesty International Report 2009, Sudan.

Amnesty International (AI). 2004a. Sudan: Darfur: Rape as a Weapon of War: Sexual Violence and Its Consequences.

Amnesty International (AI). 2004b. Sudan: Darfur: Too Many People Killed for No Reason.

Amnesty International (AI). 1999. The International Criminal Court: Ensuring an Effective Role for Victims.

Askin, Kelly D. 2005. "Gender Crimes Jurisprudence at the ICTR." *Journal of International Criminal Justice*, 3, 1007–18.

Askin, Kelly D. 1997. *War Crimes Against Women: Prosecution in International Tribunals*. The Hague: Martinjus Nijhoff.

Bedont, Barbara C. 1999. "En-Gendering Justice: The Statute of the International Criminal Court in a Gender Perspective." *Human Rights in Development* 1999–2000, 137–62.

Beltz, Amanda. 2008. "Prosecuting Rape in International Criminal Tribunals: The Need to Balance Victim's Rights with the Due Process Rights of the Accused." *Saint John's Journal of Legal Commentary*, 23, 167–209.

Bingold, Elizabeth, Michael H. Huneke, and Don Shaver. 2009. "International Criminal Law." *The International Lawyer*, 43, 473–87.

Chesterman, Simon. 1997. "Never Again ... and Again: Law, Order, and the Gender of War Crimes in Bosnia and Beyond." *Yale Journal of International Law*, 22(2), 229–79.

Clarke, Kamari Maxine. 2009. *Fictions of Justice: The International Criminal Court and the Challenges of Legal Pluralism in Sub-Saharan Africa*. New York: Cambridge University Press.

Clarke, Kamari Maxine. 2007. "Global Justice, Local Controversies: The International Criminal Court and the Sovereignty of Victims," in M. Dembour and T. Kelly (eds), *Paths to International Justice*. Cambridge, UK: Cambridge University Press.

Cole, Alyson M. 2006. *The Cult of True Victimhood: From the War on Welfare to the War on Terror*. Stanford, Calif.: Stanford University Press.

Constable, Marianne. 2005. *Just Silences: The Limits and Possibilities of Modern Law.* Princeton, N.J.: Princeton University Press.

Copelon, Rhonda. 2000. "Gender Crimes as War Crimes: Integrating Crimes against Women into International Criminal Law." *McGill Law Journal*, 46, 217–40.

Corcoran, Rebecca. 2008. "Justice for the Forgotten: Saving the Women of Darfur." *Boston College Third World Law Journal*, 28, 203–38.

Coutin, Susan Bibler. 2000. *Legalizing Moves: Salvadoran Immigrants' Struggle for U.S. Residency.* Ann Arbor: University of Michigan Press.

Cox, Genevieve A., and Jerome C. Roth. 2008. "Seeking Justice for Victims in Darfur: The Darfur Legal Training Program." *Fordham International Law Journal*, 31, 816–26.

Danieli, Yael. 2009. "Massive Trauma and the Healing Role of Reparative Justice," in C. Ferstman, M. Goetz and A. Stephens (eds), *Reparations for Victims of Genocide, Crimes Against Humanity and War Crimes: Systems in Place and Systems in the Making.* Leiden and Boston: Martinus Nijhoff.

Das, Veena. 2008. "Violence, Gender, and Subjectivity." *Annual Review of Anthropology*, 37, 283–99.

Dembour, Marie-Benedicte, and Emily Haslam. 2004. "Silencing Hearings? Victim-Witnesses at War Crimes Trials." *European Journal of International Law*, 15, 151–79.

Emorut, Francis. 2009. "Uganda: Kadaga Urges MPs to Defend Rights of Widows, Orphans." *New Vision*, July 2.

Engle, Karen. 2005. "Feminism and its (Dis)Contents: Criminalizing Wartime Rape in Bosnia and Herzegovina." *American Journal of International Law*, 99, 778–816.

Fletcher, Laurel, and Harvey Weinstein. 2002. "Violence and Social Repair: Rethinking the Contribution of Justice to Reconciliation." *Human Rights Quarterly*, 24, 573–639.

Garkawe, Sam. 2003. "Victims and the International Criminal Court: Three Major Issues." *International Criminal Law Review*, 3(4), 345–67.

Green, Jennifer, Rhonda Copelon, Patrick Cotter, Beth Stephans, and Kathleen Pratt. 1994. "Affecting the Rules for the Prosecution of Rape and Other Gender-Based Violence before the International Criminal Tribunal for the Former Yugoslavia: A Feminist Proposal and Critique." *Hastings Women's Law Journal*, 5(2), 171–221.

Hagan, John. 2008. *Darfur and the Crime of Genocide, Cambridge Series in Law and Society.* Cambridge, UK: Cambridge University Press.

Halley, Janet. 2008. "Rape at Rome: Feminist Interventions in the Criminalization of Sex-Related Violence in Positive International Criminal Law." *Michigan Journal of International Law*, 30, 1–123.

Hirsch, Susan F. 2009. "The Victim Deserving of Global Justice: Power, Culture, and Recovering Individuals," in K.M. Clarke and M. Goodale (eds), *Mirrors of Justice: Law, Power, and the Making of History* (pp. 149–70). Cambridge, UK: Cambridge University Press.

Hirsch, Susan F., and Mindie Lazarus-Black. 1994. "Introduction/Performance and Paradox: Exploring Law's Role in Hegemony and Resistance," in M. Lazarus-Black and S. F. Hirsch (eds), *Contested States: Law, Hegemony, and Resistance.* New York and London: Routledge.

Human Rights Watch (HRW). 2002. The War Within the War: Sexual Violence Against Women and Girls in Eastern Congo.

Institute for War and Peace Reporting (IWPR). 2009. "Lubanga Trial—Prosecution Wraps up Case." *Africa News*, July 17.

International Bar Association (IBA). 2009. "First Challenges: An Examination of Recent Landmark Developments at the International Criminal Court," in *International Bar Association Human Rights Institute Report*. International Bar Association.

International Criminal Court (ICC). 2005a. Victims and Witnesses, available at http://www.icc-cpi.int/victimsissues.html.

International Criminal Court (ICC). 2005b. Victims Trust Fund 2005, available at http://www.icc-cpi.int/vtf.html.

International Criminal Court (ICC). Rules of Procedure and Evidence, available at http://www.icc-cpi.int/.

Lamb, Sharon (ed.). 1999. *New Versions of Victims: Feminists Struggle with the Concept*. New York: New York University Press.

Liu Institute for Global Issues (UBC). 2005. *Roco Wat I Acoli: Restoring Relationships in Acholi-Land: Traditional Approaches to Justice and Reintegration*. Gulu District NGO Forum, Ker Kwaro Acholi. Vancouver: Liu Institute.

"The Lubanga Trial at the International Criminal Court." Open Society Foundations, available at http://www.lubangatrial.org/.

Merry, Sally Engle. 2006. *Human Rights and Gender Violence: Translating International Law into Local Justice*, in W.M. O'Barr and J. M. Conley (eds), *Chicago Series in Law and Society*. Chicago and London: The University of Chicago Press.

Mertus, Julie. 2004. "'Shouting from the Bottom of the Well': The Impact of International Trials for Wartime Rape on Women's Agency." *International Feminist Journal of Politics*, 6(1), 110–28.

Minow, Martha. 1991. "Identities." *Yale Journal of Law and the Humanities*, 3, 97–133.

Office of High Commissioner for Human Rights (OHCR). 2007. Making Peace Our Own: Victims' Perceptions of Accountability, Reconciliation and Transitional Justice in Northern Uganda. United Nations. Available at: http://www.unhcr.org/refworld/docid/46cc4a690.html.

Oko, Okechukwu. 2008. "Women, Children, and Victims of Massive Crimes: Legal Developments in Africa: The Challenges of International Criminal Prosecutions in Africa." *Fordham Universitiy School of Law*, 31, 343–414.

Oosterveld, Valerie. 2005. "The Definition of 'Gender' in the Rome Statute of the International Criminal Court: A Step Forward or Back for International Criminal Justice?" *Harvard Human Rights Journal*, 18, 55–84.

Oosterveld, Valerie. 1999. "The Making of a Gender-Sensitive International Criminal Court." *International Law FORUM du Droit International*, 1(1), 38–41.

Pritchett, Suzan. 2008. "Entrenched Hegemony, Efficient Procedure, or Selective Justice: An Inquiry into Charges for Gender-Based Violence at the International Criminal Court." *Transnational Law and Contemporary Problems*, 17, 265–305.

Puechguirbal, Nadine. 2003. "Women and War in the Democratic Republic of Congo." *Signs*, 28(4), 1271–81.

Refugee Law Project (RLP). 2004. "Behind the Violence: Causes, Consequences and the Search for Solutions to the War in Northern Uganda," in *Refugee Law Project Working Paper*. Kampala, Uganda: Refugee Law Project.

Rome Statute of the International Criminal Court. July 1, 2002, Available at http://www.icc-cpi.int/.

Schneider, Mary Deutsch. 2008. "About Women, War, and Darfur: The Continued Quest for Gender Violence Justice." *North Dakota Law Review* 83, 915–96.

Spees, P. 2003. "Women's Advocacy in the Creation of the International Criminal Court: Changing the Landscapes of Justice and Power." *Signs*, 28(4), 1233–54.

Stover, Eric. 2005. *The Witnesses: War Crimes and the Promise of Justice in the Hague, Pennsylvania Studies in Human Rights*. Philadelphia: University of Pennsylvania Press.

War Crimes Research Office. 2007. *Victim Participation Before the International Criminal Court*. Washington, DC: American University.

CHAPTER THIRTEEN

Engaging Legislation: Liberia and Chechnya

Ekaterina Romanova and Erica Sewell

Introduction

All the time the war lasted, we have endured in modest silence all you men did […]
We were far from satisfied […]; often in our homes we would hear you discussing, upside down and inside out, some important turn of affairs. Then with sad hearts, but smiling lips, we would ask you: Well, in today's Assembly did they vote for peace?
But 'Mind your own business!' the husband would growl […]
And we would say no more.

Lysistrata, Aristophanes

Women's voices in the peace-building process have continually been silenced, despite the fact that women bear the brunt of the effects of war. Driven by the desire to provide for their families rather than to make a political statement, women have been able to achieve unexpected success in conflict resolution and peace building. Women have a unique opportunity to address the needs of their war-torn communities, but their contributions are often neither recognized nor acknowledged. By comparing the two conflicts in Chechnya and Liberia, this chapter examines the stark differences in women's mobilization and addresses the question of what defines a women's peace movement and what hinders its broader recognition. The chapter arrives at the conclusion that the success of a women's peace movement cannot be measured by political advancement of women but rather should be assessed by the level of positive impact on the lives of people caught in the midst of violent conflict.

Background

War has been historically a form of human activity, where roles are strictly defined along gender lines. Most soldiers, militia members, or perpetrators have been men, while the majority of civilians have been women and children. As civilians, women suffer the effects of wars disproportionately. A 2000 United Nations report concluded that 90 percent of current war causalities worldwide are civilians, compared to a century ago when 95 percent of those who lost their lives were soldiers and military personnel (Ramsbotham et al. 2006). In 2003, it was reported that between 75 and 80 percent of refugees and internally displaced persons worldwide are women and children (Bello 2003). Sexual violence, a tactic used to humiliate the enemy and physically and morally destroy the base of communities, is continuously used as a weapon of war. Recent atrocious examples of mass rapes, where women are the predominant victims, include conflicts in the Democratic Republic of Congo, Sudan, Liberia, Uganda, Peru, Sri Lanka, Cambodia, Somalia, Rwanda, Chechnya, Bangladesh, and the former Yugoslavia (Tomasevic 1995; Frederick 2001; OHCHR/MONUSCO 2010).

Considering the scale of women's sufferings, one cannot discuss peacebuilding without recognizing the harsh reality and disregard of women's experiences. Sixty years have passed since the adoption of the Universal Declaration of Human Rights, which recognizes equal rights of men and women. However, the de facto equality is not yet achieved. Women remain largely excluded from the official peace-building process though women are often in the best position to address the needs of their communities.

This chapter examines two examples of women's mobilization as a result of armed conflict. The case studies, Liberia and Chechnya, represent two different types of conflict, with dissimilar root causes and sociopolitical contexts. The two examples vary significantly in the mode, type, and outcome of women's mobilization. Yet these significant disparities allow one to see the striking similarities in the aspirations of women and their willingness to mobilize, which is seen through the examination of what helps or hinders the success of a women's movement. In Liberia, the women mobilized for peace using a variety of collective action methods and demanded that their voices be heard. They insisted on having a seat at the final peace negotiations table. Chechnya differed as the women's activities never gained momentum, nor were women able to translate their initiative into a broader form of political mobilization. While women in Chechnya did not strive for political representation, they were the first to reach across the ethnic divide, to address the needs of communities and to deal with the devastation of the two consecutive wars. The contrasts between the two selected cases emphasize the challenges that any women's peace movement faces and the obstacles it has to overcome.

Defining a Women's Movement

A women's movement is a form of collective action that encompasses a variety of formal and informal actions that take place periodically or consistently throughout a certain period of time. What distinguishes it from any other movement is that it is initiated and carried out by women. The US women's suffragette movement in the late nineteenth and early twentieth centuries and the women's rights movement of the 1960s are some of the well-known and most successful efforts that were able to achieve significant results in advocating for women's rights. A women's movement offers a broad platform for women to mobilize and oftentimes does not aspire to challenge the male-dominant status quo or to pursue a political agenda. It can consist of dispersed women's groups focusing on different sets of priorities but working for the benefit of their local communities or an overarching goal of improving the lives of people worldwide. In brief, a women's movement can be described as a diverse "spectrum of people who act in an individual way" or "organizations or groups who are working to ameliorate diverse aspects of the gender subordination on the basis of sex" (cited from Kerr 2007, 119). Women's peace movements are a variation of a women's movement, which pursues a strictly defined goal of ending a conflict, advocating for peace, and assisting civilians in war zones and during post-conflict reconstruction.

Liberia: From War to Peace

The case of Liberia is particularly interesting in terms of women's mobilization, because the women's peace movement gained international recognition and became a powerful force in bringing peace to Liberia.

Liberia is a country slowly recovering from more than a decade of perpetual violence. The first phase of the civil war occurred between 1989 and 1997 and concluded with the election of former president Charles Taylor. The fragile peace could not be sustained during the second phase of the civil war spanning from 1999 to 2003. Human rights abuses were rampant, rape was frequently used as a tool of war, and every person, regardless of age or gender, was at risk. It has been estimated that, by 2003, more than 150,000 people had been killed and half of the country's three million citizens displaced (Hammer 2006).

In times of war, gender roles are often stereotyped with women as victims, while the men are the fighters and later the peacemakers. Throughout the civil war in Liberia, the women defied their caste roles. From the start of the civil war on December 24, 1989, women engaged in community peace-building activities and did not waver from their goal for peace until the Comprehensive Peace Agreement was signed on August 18, 2003 (Levitt 2005). Over the years of civil unrest and war, the women's movement progressed, coalesced, and ultimately turned into one of Liberia's most powerful nongovernmental voices. The women's movement illustrates how the women broke away from the "victim" paradigm to move their country forward. The women were actively engaged in the peace-building process as agents of change, utilizing nonviolent direct action methods. They fought with words rather than guns.

It is essential to recognize the elements that caused the women to mobilize, how their mobilization efforts strengthened, and the effect that the movement had on bringing a sustainable peace to Liberia. The women's movement grew out of the continuous inhumane violence against women and deteriorating societal conditions. One leader of the movement, in an interview with the author of this chapter, stated that it was "the sexual violence against women. Women were being used as sex machines by soldiers. Women wanted to live again and through that the women rose up" (Sewell[1] 2007, 16).

Women's advocacy and political activism helped to solidify their agenda and push the movement onward. As the women gained more recognition, they were empowered to create a unified voice, but they had to redouble their efforts to continue to be heard. The women were often not invited to the peace conferences but would pay their own way to attend.

Opportunities such as the women's participation in the United Nation's Fourth World Conference on Women in 1995, where a large delegation from Liberia including Mary Brownell and Ruth Cesar attended the conference, provided them with an opportunity to network with other women in the global arena. They attracted international attention to their fight for peace through their nonviolent activities such as demonstrations, sit-ins, and mass prayer campaigns. A key component to the success of the women was the role of the international community. The women received financial assistance and were able to participate in capacity-building training workshops. Some organizations involved included the United Nations, Catholic Relief Services, and the National Endowment for Democracy. The women mobilized both locally and regionally because they knew that, to achieve peace in Liberia, leaders in Guinea and Sierra Leone had to be involved. The Mano

River Women's Peace Network (MARWOPNET) is an organization composed of women from Liberia, Guinea, and Sierra Leone that was formed as a regional network. Sister Mary Laurene, administrator at Stella Maris Polytechnic University in Monrovia, stated "the mobilization of women seemed to strengthen as the women gained more recognition and support" (Sewell 2007, 16).

On June 4, 2003, the peace talks that eventually led to the signing of the Comprehensive Peace Agreement (CPA) began in Accra, Ghana. MARWOPNET served as the official organization chosen to represent the women. A milestone was achieved when MARWOPNET was honored with the 2003 United Nations Prize in the field of human rights. This award was a major step forward, because it proved that women are essential and important actors in the peace-building process; they are agents of change, rather than victims of social conditions.

Chechnya: Two Wars and Silent Suffering

Chechnya is an example of a significantly different type of conflict and social mobilization effort. Since the dissolution of the Soviet Union in 1991, Chechnya, a republic in the northern Caucasus Mountains, went through two brutal wars, experienced tremendous devastation, and lost an estimated 15–20 percent of its population (HRVC 2008). It is estimated that approximately 800,000 people had been displaced by the two wars in Chechnya, and by 2009, 80,000 people still remained internally displaced (IDMC 2009).

The first war in Chechnya started in 1994 with the Russian government militarily trying to reinstate its control and prevent the secession of the republic. Two years later, the negotiated peace agreement postponed a decision on Chechen independence and forced the Russian army's withdrawal. In the years to follow, the situation in Chechnya continued to deteriorate. The republic was plagued with violence, kidnappings, political instability, and economic devastation (Tishkov 2004, Ware 2005). By 1999, violence was no longer contained within the borders of the republic. Following a series of terrorist attacks claimed to be carried out by Chechen rebels in a number of cities in Russia including Moscow, the second Chechen campaign started in the fall of that year.

Since the beginning of the second military campaign in 1999, the war progressed from an active military operation to civil war and finally to negative peace. The newly established government, headed by President Ramzan Kadyrov, achieved significant progress in bringing stability to that war-devastated part of the northern Caucasus. But there was little recognition of the work done by different organizations composed mostly of women that were active in providing the basic necessities to the civilian population during the two wars and interwar period. At that time, the devastating human rights situation and the disregard to the civilian's basic needs by authorities, military personnel, and militias brought the women together. Even though the women were addressing the dire humanitarian situation, they were later excluded from the official negotiations and post-conflict reconstruction processes.

Peace-building measures organized by women in Chechnya and response to such forms of mobilization reflect on a broader context of civil society in the post-Soviet Russian Federation. Civic activism in the country remains largely marginalized. In Sperling's words, it is "still closer to dissidence (individual forms of protest and action) than to the mass mobilization and institutionalization characteristic of civil society" (Sperling 2006, 161). Grassroots initiatives have been significantly restrained by the limited domestic support, strict government control, lack of funding, and civilian reservations.

In the early 1990s the cultural as well as political environment of the Russian Federation did not allow women to assume political leadership roles. Instead, the role of a mother had a greater appeal and produced a broader resonance in society. Women's grassroots organizations advocated for their maternal right to know the fate of their family and community members and for the right to provide for their basic needs. The mothers' movement has become the most prominent antiwar advocate in the country and includes, but is not limited to, such groups as the Mothers of Chechnya, the Committee of Soldiers' Mothers (CSM), and the Mothers' Rights Foundation.

Groups uniting through their role as mothers have been able to bridge ethnic and religious divides utilizing the common interest of maternal love and human rights. Women have organized marches, such as Mothers March for Peace in 1995, and vigils that brought Russian and Chechen mothers together and have enabled the establishment of social services and education centers for children and elders (Mothers of Chechnya 2006). Women's groups have served as advocates for stopping sexual violence and abuse inflicted by the military, law enforcement, or militia. They have carried out small and large scale humanitarian actions by providing food, distributing clothes to civilians and refugees, and rebuilding schools and day-care centers.

Unfortunately, the progress and effectiveness of women's organizations have been limited by strict government control and regulations regarding nongovernmental activities in Chechnya and in the Russian Federation. As a result, women's initiatives have been often sidelined, marginalized, and lacked networking capability. While grassroots groups managed to significantly contribute to the lives of local communities, they have been unable to transform into a larger peace movement or become a considerable political force due to the constricting societal limitations.

Two Cases Compared: Liberia and Chechnya

The two cases seem strikingly different, but there are strong parallels between the two movements. In both countries the movements evolved in response to the tremendous suffering caused by military actions, constant violence, and abuse. They both began through humanitarian action by providing food, clothes, shelter, and social services to their communities, regardless of cultural, socioeconomic status and ethnic or religious background. For example, in Liberia, educated and uneducated women worked side by side to address the needs of their communities. In Chechnya, the women united with Russian women and found common ground through their strong and powerful love for their children that spanned the divide produced by the war.

The ability of women's groups to build bridges and establish a strong and supportive networking provides sustainability and visibility to women's activities. The broader the influence the groups have on the local, regional, and international arena, the stronger their impact. In Liberia, the regional coordination and collaboration of women's groups strengthened the movement and helped achieve the goal of a sustainable peace. The networking created stable financial, educational, and training support. This contributed to the visibility of the activities, which in turn provided a significant level of legitimacy and credibility to the groups among the civilians, authorities, and international community. As a movement gains momentum, it has a powerful effect on the women, who previously might have been silenced by traditional gender assumptions, cultural norms, and political structures.

The political and traditional culture of the community and civil society is an important prerequisite for a sustainable women's movement. During times of turmoil and war, peace movements face many more challenges, and without openness to grassroots activities, the women's groups fall prey to political games. In Chechnya, women's peace movements remained repressed and marginalized and failed to find an explicit constituency that would allow them to expand and guarantee continuity. Awareness of the common challenges is a mechanism that brings people together and helps them organize. It takes a strong and committed leadership to pursue the goals of the movements, which often consist of different dispersed groups. The ability for a movement to find its own strong and unified voice assists in making it stand out among other activists in society. Leaders help contribute to public awareness about the problems and visibility of the group activities. Substantial achievements were made in Liberia because the women took ownership for their initiatives.

The women's groups in Chechnya were not as successful in the political arena. Perhaps it was the result of their leadership conformity, ineptitude, or lack of political experience. Chechnya's grassroots organizations, however, were able to help civilians despite the physical threat of the ongoing military operations. What did assist was the women's use of the role of mother that is deeply rooted in Russian and Chechen cultures. This helped to unite women of different backgrounds. Such partnerships proved to be a strong force in carrying out the mission of protecting children, elders, and communities.

International recognition is crucial in determining the success of any movement. The international community can assist by providing training, education, and financial resources for women's groups to empower women and support their mission. Today, the international community bears responsibility for the inability to predict, prevent, or stop a conflict. The commitment of international organizations provided a high level of support for the women's peace movement in Liberia.

In Chechnya, the ideological perception that a second campaign was a part of a larger Global War on Terror that threatens global security muffled reports of human rights abuse and ignored signs of the unbearable situation of the civilians and refugees (Hill et al. 2005). The international community elected not to pressure the Russian government to address the human rights situation in Chechnya. At the same time, other human rights organizations were being denied access to Chechnya. Their work was limited to working with refugees along the borders of Chechnya, while the needs of civilians living in the center of military operations were not recognized or acknowledged. The Chechen government's inflexible and suspicious attitude to international relief, human rights organizations, religious missions, and international observers, coupled with the inability of the international community to assist those trapped in the heart of the conflict did nothing to reduce the human tragedy. This led to the women not being able to participate in any training or gain financial resources, each of which is critical to a movement's success.

Table 13.1 illustrates the factors that either contributed to or hindered the women's movement in Liberia and Chechnya. Table 13.2 outlines the components that either assist or hinder the success of women's movements.

Table 13.1 Factors Shaping the Women's Movement in Liberia and Chechnya

Factors	Liberia	Chechnya
Agenda	Stop violence and abuse of women, provide basic needs to the devastated communities, and be represented at the peace negotiations	Stop abuse by the military and violence against civilians, search for disappeared relatives, and provide basic needs to the devastated communities
Bridging class, ethnic and religious differences	Brought together women of different socioeconomic, ethnic and religious backgrounds	Brought together women of different ethnic and religious backgrounds
Local/regional collaboration	Strong collaboration and networking among Sierra Leone, Guinea, and Liberia	Dispersed groups working in local communities with limited collaboration across borders
Leadership	Strong leadership— Mary Brownell and Ruth Cesar, to name a few. Women were educated and ready to lead	Poor leadership of a women's political faction and strong leadership of various mothers' groups
Determination	Constant engagement in local capacity building and ending violence and active participation in the political processes	Search for missing people, advocacy for soldiers and civilians who experienced abuse
Support of local/federal government (political system in the country)	Relative openness to grassroots activities	Strong control of civil society by the government and limited access of international organizations to the region
International attention to the conflict and the movement	Strong commitment to the peacemaking process	Silent about human rights abuses
Support of international community/financial support/capacity building (transnational women's cooperation)	Strong support	Support limited to the border region

Table 13.2 Components of a Successful Women's Movement

Positive	Negative
Mobilization of women from different socioeconomic, cultural, religious, and ethnic backgrounds—embracing the whole society	Fragmented mobilization, the lack of a unified voice and dispersed and uncoordinated activities
Collaboration among women (local, regional, international) and strong networking	Poor networking
Local initiative and ownership of projects and activities, which are grounded in the local culture and the needs of the communities	Lack of skills, capacity, and resources (financial and human) to carry out activities
Strong and committed leadership	Poor leadership, dominance of self-interest and personal political/economic gains rather than addressing the needs of communities
Political culture open to grassroots activities, tradition of civil society and receptiveness of the communities to grassroots initiatives	Lack of civil society history, poor grassroots initiative culture, lack of explicit constituency
Support of the international community, capacity building, funding, and a commitment to advocating for human rights	Authoritarian political structure, strong dominant and powerful central government
Long-term commitment to conflict resolution and building sustainable peace	Inadequate commitment and willingness of the international community

Conclusion

A successful women's peace movement is not required to be a strong, centralized, and well-coordinated movement with a political agenda. Rather, the assessment of women's activities should be based on the ability to achieve a particular set of goals. Recognition of factors influencing the successes and failures of women's peace movements can be used by both the international community and women's organizations as methods to increase their effectiveness.

The women's mobilization in Liberia is viewed as a movement because of the political aspirations of the movement's leaders and their political agenda. In Chechnya, the women's activities were localized and achieved some political recognition. The traditional role of women in society limited activities of women's groups in the political sphere but also helped gain public support.

It provided a broader context for achieving their goals of taking care of their children and communities in times of war and interwar periods.

The women's mobilization efforts in Chechnya never succeeded in becoming a movement. The traditional definition of a movement is characterized by political aspirations, which does not apply to isolated activities of women's groups. Women's initiatives, whether dispersed, localized, temporal, or consistent over time, if unified, can weave a canvas of intense activities that contribute to the improvement of people's lives and thus become a movement. Women's groups working in a time of war typify a peace movement.

The two cases illustrate women's movements, differing in sociopolitical contexts and aspirations. The two movements with their own successes, failures, constraints, and capacity have consistently worked to achieve the overarching goal of assisting those trapped by conflict. Their initiatives and efforts need to be recognized and acknowledged, which becomes the first step in mainstreaming women's activities, experiences, knowledge, and perhaps expanding the concept of a movement.

Recommendations

In order to provide global security and assure the dignity of human life, there is an urgent need for people to work together (whether organized in a broader movement or in dispersed smaller groups) with a commitment to sustainable peace.

Understanding the factors that advance women's activism is important in forming adequate policies that will ensure recognition of women's peace-building efforts. Accordingly, to build a strong and effective women's movement it is important:

- to encourage mobilization of women across societal divides;
- to support and assist women in building sustainable and effective networking mechanisms;
- to recognize the needs of local communities and promote local initiatives that would provide ownership of various activities;
- to take into consideration the cultural aspect of societies where the movement is developing;
- to provide support through capacity-building initiatives, funding, and training by international and domestic organizations;
- to make a long-term commitment to support the activities the women will need to succeed.

Keywords

• Activism, Chechnya, collective action, Liberia, networking, peace movement, peace-building, war, women's groups, Women's movement.

Discussion Questions

1. Are women's peace movements different from other forms of collective action?
2. Does women's activism challenge or conform to gender stereotypes?
3. How do political, social, and cultural contexts shape women's peace movements?

References

Aristophanes. 1987. *Lysistrata*. Edited by Jeffrey Henderson. Oxford: Clarendon Press.

Bello, Carolina Rodriguez. 2003. "Refugees and Internally Displaced People." Women's Human Rights Net. Accessed on March 22, 2008. http://www.whrnet.org/docs/issue-refugees.html.

Frederick, Sharon. 2001. *Rape: Weapon of Terror*. Paramus, N.J.: Global Publishing.

Hammer, J. 2006. "Healing Powers: African Women Are Starting to Take Charge—Making New Laws, Changing Old Attitudes, Inspiring Others to Follow Their Lead. Who Will Help Them Mend a Broken Continent?" *Newsweek*, 147, 15–30.

Hill, Fiona, Anatol Lieven, and Thomas De Waal. 2005. "A Spreading Danger: Tone for a New Policy Toward Chechnya," *Policy Brief* 35 (March), Carnegie Endowment for International Peace.

Human Rights Violations in Chechnya (HRVC). 2008. Accessed on April 8, 2008. Available at http://www.hrvc.net/main.htm.

Internal Displacement Monitoring Center (IDMC). 2009. "Russian Federation: Monitoring of IDPs and returnees is still needed." Accessed on November 20, 2010. Available at http://www.internal-displacement.org/8025708F004CE90B/(httpCountries)/CA9F7ECE2BA5EB86802570A7004CA481?OpenDocument.

Kerr, Joanna. 2007. "Second Fund *her* Report: Financial Sustainability for Women's Movement's Worldwide." Association for Women's Rights in Development (AWID). Accessed March 23, 2008. Available at http://www.awid.org/go.php?cid=530.

Levitt, Jeremy. 2005. *The Evolution of Deadly Conflict in Liberia*. Durham, N.C.: Carolina Academic Press.

Mothers of Chechnya. 2006. *The Current Situation in Chechnya: the Mothers of Chechnya on the Problem of Missing Persons and Human Rights Violations*. The Mothers of Chechnya and Swedish Peace and Arbitration Society.

OHCHR/MONUSCO (Office of the High Commissioner for Human Rights/United Nations Organization Stabilization Mission in the Democratic Republic of Congo), 2010. Accessed November 20, 2010. Available at http://monusco.unmissions.org/Default.aspx.

Ramsbotham, Oliver, Tom Woodhouse, and Hugh Miall. 2006. *Contemporary Conflict Resolution* (2nd edn). Cambridge, UK: Polity Press.

Sewell, Erica. 2007. "Women Building Peace: the Liberian Women's Peace Movement." *Critical Half*, 5(2), 14–20.

Sperling, Valerie. 2006. "Women's Organizations: Institutionalized Interest Groups or Vulnerable Dissidents?" in Alfred B. Evans, Jr., Laura A. Henry, and Lisa McIntosh Sundstrom (eds), *Russian Civil Society: A Critical Assessment* (pp. 161–78). Armonk, N.Y.: M.E. Sharpe.

Tishkov, Valery. 2004. *Chechnya: Life in a War-torn Society.* Berkeley and Los Angeles, CA: University of California Press.

Tomasevic, Dragana. 1995. "On Using Women," Translated by Slobodan Darkulic. *Freedom Review*, 26(5), 38–9.

Ware, Robert Bruce. 2005. "A Multitude of Evils: Mythology and Political Failure in Chechnya," in Richard Sakwa (ed.), *Chechnya: from Past to Future* (pp. 79–117). London: Anthem Press.

CHAPTER FOURTEEN

Challenging Patriarchy: Pakistan, Egypt, and Turkey

Saira Yamin

Each country interprets women's rights under Islam somewhat differently, and within each country social class is a determining factor in the way in which women's personal rights are treated.

—*Suha Sabbagh 1996, XV*

She is the personification of "honor". He is the custodian of "honor": a male member of the clan, a father, brother, husband, son, or other relative. She represents the honor of the family, the tribe, and the community. He must guard, protect and preserve that honor. It is his prerogative. He must uphold the traditions and customs of the forefathers. Honor must never be violated. A woman who shames her community must not live.

Women are perceived as symbols of "honor" in many cultures across the globe. Honor killings represent this cultural paradigm. The practice may be defined as the systemic killing of a girl or a woman in accordance with social custom. I refer to it as cultural femicide: an instance of culturally induced violence against women, with death as the intended outcome. Girls and women in various parts of the world, even today, are vulnerable to honor killings at the mere possibility of an illicit relationship, for marrying outside the clan or without family approval, for electing to abandon a marriage, for interacting with the opposite sex. The list goes on.

Another instance of cultural violence against women, in the defense of honor, is the practice of vaginal circumcision, also referred to as female genital mutilation (FGM). The procedure may be performed in infancy, childhood, or at a later stage in a girl's life. It is designed to restrain her sexual desires and behavior. This chapter explores the injustice against women in the name of honor in Pakistani, Egyptian, and Turkish subcultures.

Context

The gendered intersection of religion, culture, and development in Pakistan, Egypt, and Turkey is a highly complex one. It perpetuates violence against women. I shall reflect on the environment of oppression in a comparative context across these societies. Additionally I shall examine women's capacities to cope as well as their contributions to women's movements. These three countries, while different in many ways, have certain characteristics in common, especially pertaining to the rights of women. Women's agency in these countries is constrained by low literacy levels, patriarchal religious interpretations, gender inequality, and uneven patterns of development, as well as cultural practices inhibiting women's growth, development, and welfare. Women belonging to the poorest socioeconomic levels of society—rural and urban—are especially vulnerable.

A state's inability or unwillingness to introduce and implement policies empowering women, especially in extending human rights without discrimination, is a cause for concern. Though trends in globalization, civil society mobilization, and international conventions and agreements have contributed remarkably in advocating and promoting legislation in favor of women, I shall demonstrate that the incidence of violence against women remains high, and legislation continues to be highly ineffective in providing protection to women. Their participation in legislative processes may be gauged by their representation percentage, approximately 15, in the world's legislative bodies. (Farzana Bari 2005, 1). With reference to Pakistan, Egypt, and Turkey, I shall explore how literacy levels and discriminatory judicial structures contribute to the lack of women's awareness of rights that do exist.

Domestic violence and honor killings continue today in Egypt, Pakistan, and Turkey, practices that are entrenched in centuries-old pre-Islamic traditions. It remains uncommon today for women to report rape or other instances of sexual violence, as there are stigmas attached to such publicity, even for victims. Access to laws is also complicated by the existence of tribal, religious, and secular parallel judicial systems, as I shall illustrate. The high cost of litigation, the lack of access to legal aid, sexual harassment by law enforcement agencies, and gender-biased and unfair judicial structures and personnel are merely some of the additional factors that discourage women and their families, regardless of socioeconomic backgrounds, from seeking legal retribution. Moreover, conditions in women's shelters are usually deplorable and therefore not considered an option by most women.

A key to the advancement of gender equitable societies is an environment that facilitates women's access to justice. Patriarchal traditions, structures, and norms, often upheld in violation of women's rights, reflect the asymmetrical relationships that exist among women and men in many parts of the world, these three countries included. Ziad Majed (2005, 9) speaks of the dilemma of cultural dualism "where values such as freedom, democracy, rationalism, and women's rights are pitted against a patriarchal culture that is not in tune with the spirit of equality." The gendered inequality in the balance of power is also evident in women's disproportionate representation in governance and decision making (United National Development Program UNDP 2005), as well as in discriminatory wages, laws regulating the ownership of property, and patterns of inheritance (International Center for Research on Women 2005), among other considerations. The resultant inequity is overcome when women claim their voices—in legislative and judicial institutions, in advocating their rights, in acquiring safe opportunities for economic empowerment and social development, and, above all, in educating themselves (and members of their communities).

Political and legal institutions can contribute to the marginalization of women, as can the dynamics of class and culture. Women's access to justice is inextricably tied to their socioeconomic backgrounds. Women living in affluent and educated communities are relatively better positioned, though still vulnerable, and not fully capable of defending themselves and coping with sexual violence. Education helps wear away oppressive values and fosters social harmony and justice within the family and community. Because cultural values and religion are frequently used to oppress women, Islam is often misinterpreted and misrepresented to maintain a gender-based hierarchy to control women in public and private spaces (Jamila Hussain 2004, 29–30).

Islam clearly confers a status of equality among women and men in a number of ways. Two passages from the Quran cite the following:

1. I shall not lose sight of the labor of any of you who labors in My way, be it man or woman; each of you is equal to the other. (3, 195)
2. The believers, men and women, are protectors one of another; on them will Allah pour His mercy. (9, 71–72)

Embedded in its tradition, every kind of violence against women is strictly forbidden in Islam. In reality, however, culture often trumps religion. Consider the practice of honor killing, where a woman is treated as a commodity associated with family and tribal honor. Women are killed in the name of honor for what is deemed immoral behavior. Women are also used to settle disputes. Honor as a concept is reified. Empirical data suggest that honor killings are a cross-cultural practice, and many variations have been reported in non-Muslim states as well, such as Italy, India, Israel, Sweden, Brazil, Ecuador, and Uganda (Hillary Mayell 2002; Naima El Moussaoui 2007).

Despite strong evidence of women's political leadership in Pakistan, Egypt, and Turkey, vis-à-vis other Muslim countries, empirical data reveal that Egyptian, Pakistani, and Turkish women lag the furthest behind in terms of gender equality. In 2005, the World Economic Forum's (WEF) *Global Gender Gap Index* evaluated women's economic participation and opportunity, political empowerment, educational attainment, and health and well-being in 58 countries. It placed the three countries at the bottom of the list (Association for Women's Rights in Development 2008). Tracking women's progress in 2007, WEF's *Global Gender Gap Report* assessed 128 countries. Egypt and Turkey ranked 120 and 121 respectively; and Pakistan stood at 126 (WEF 2007). More recently, the WEF *Global Gender Gap Report* (2008) evaluated 130 countries, placing Turkey, Egypt, and Pakistan at 123, 124, and 127, respectively. The indicators used by WEF provide a succinct explanation for women's agency (or lack thereof) in navigating the social, cultural, political, and economic spaces in their countries.

Although statistics paint a bleak picture, it is important to note that women in these three Muslim societies who have access to opportunities for personal growth and development have been active in various realms, ranging from politics and academics, to sports, culture, arts, and the sciences, among others. Pakistan and Turkey have produced world leaders—Benazir Bhutto and Tansu Cillar, both former prime ministers of their respective countries. Similarly Egyptian women have been recognized as the most independent women in the region since Pharaonic times, (Elizabeth Warnock Fernea 1998, 240–41). Fernea notes that Egypt remains the birthplace of the first Arab women's movement and that the country produces more women engineers than Europe. In the past century, Egypt provides far more liberal opportunities for women than most Arab countries. Compare this situation with Saudi Arabia, for example, where women do not drive or appear in public unless covered from head to toe and generally remain invisible in society. On the other hand, consider the tradition of belly dancing in Egypt, where it is culturally acceptable for entertainment divas to perform in public venues, clad in revealing hip scarves and halter tops.

The UNDP provides quantitative indicators of global gender inequality in the Human Development Index (HDI), in its *Human Development Report* for 2007/2008. The HDI's conclusions are presented in its Gender Development Index (GDI) and the Gender Empowerment Measure (GEM). The GDI compares female and male health and longevity, literacy levels, and income potential. The GEM measures the disparity between women and men on such variables as political and economic participation, decision making, and control over economic resources. The GDI ranking of 177 UN member countries places Turkey at 84, Egypt at 112, and Pakistan at 136. These ranks resonate with the pessimistic WEF findings cited above.

What follows are insights into women's marginalization in these three societies, particularly, their vulnerability to sexual violence and honor killings. There are parallels between the three cases with respect to poverty, adherence to archaic patriarchal values, and the inequitable distribution of the benefits of development. The women's movements in these countries, including the impact on women's rights and the welfare of citizens in general, are discussed, as is the commonly distorted interpretation of Islam—often at the expense of women, through oppression and exploitation.

Women's Rights and the Notions of Honor and Shame

According to custom, she has no rights. That is how I was raised, no one ever told me that Pakistan had a constitution, laws and rights written down in a book.

—*Mukhtaran Mai 2006, 29*

The status of women in Pakistan varies across the divides of class, region, and rural/urban settings. The positioning of the state vis-à-vis feudal structures and primitive cultural norms and the inequitable distribution of rights and resources is important. In Pakistan "gender and class determine the extent to which individuals can claim the full benefits of a citizenship. State practices do not provide impoverished women equality of rights or protection" (Shahnaz Khan 2003, 96). Charles Lindholm emphasizes that, despite the provisions in the constitution giving rights to women, "nothing is stronger than custom" (1996, 25).

The women of Pakistan are slowly and steadily progressing toward better political representation. The number of reserved seats held by women in the national assembly has increased to 17 percent, and in the local legislative assemblies to 33 percent (Pakistan Elections 2007/2008). Though this is a significant accomplishment, several development organizations stress that affirmative action alone cannot address the gender inequality that permeates the social fabric. Women in decision-making positions operating in patriarchal cultures are generally co-opted by men, and there is little evidence to suggest that increases in quotas as a stand-alone strategy can create a gender equitable environment. Pakistan's slain former premier Benazir Bhutto, it is speculated, complied with her feudal husband, Asif Ali Zardari's demands in official matters while in office. Zardari was also appointed minister for investment during her tenure as the country's premier, in an obvious display of nepotism.

The Stockholm-based Institute for Democracy and Electoral Development (IDEA) notes that women politicians are expected to navigate a "masculine model" of politics, where women have yet to find the space to accommodate their values and even their lifestyles (Gumisai Mutumi 2004). This explains the attitudes and behaviors of world leaders such as Britain's former prime minister Margaret Thatcher, nicknamed "the Iron Lady"; India's former prime minister Indira Gandhi, also known for her hawkish temperament; and Hillary Clinton, former US senator and now Secretary of State. Clinton wore pantsuits like a uniform in the US Senate in an apparent effort to, what many believe, appear masculine.

Legislation and advocacy on violence against women is imperative for rooting out gender-insensitive and feudalistic cultural norms in Pakistan. *The Guardian* (Saeed Shah 2008) and other media, for example, reported the burying alive, in the name of honor, of three teenaged girls and two middle-aged women of the Umerani tribe of Balochistan Province, a heinous act flagrantly defended by a member of parliament. An article in a prestigious Pakistani daily *The Nation* reported that Senator Israr Ullah Zehri, a feudal, like many members of the national assembly, went on record on the senate floor, in support of honor killings in the name of centuries-old "Baloch customary laws and traditions" (Khalid Aziz 2008).

Mukhtaran Mai, from the remote rural town of Meerwala in the Muzaffargarh District of Pakistan, is probably among the thousands of women raped every year to settle tribal disputes. The independent Human Rights Commission of Pakistan (HRCP) notes that "rape continues to be the most taboo human rights violation and is therefore the least reported in the news and to the HRCP" (Human Rights Commission of Pakistan 2007). According to the HRCP, "a woman is raped every two hours and gang raped every eight hours" (US Department of State 2007). The truth is that there are no reliable statistics on the number of women who are victimized in the name of honor. The practice is endemic in tribal cultures across Pakistan. In most cases, incidents are unreported because of the immense shame and humiliation associated with it. Disclosure could also evoke the honor killing of the victim to preserve the dignity of the family and clan. Mukhtaran was gang-raped by the orders of a local tribal council in June 2002, to settle scores between rival groups. In her memoirs, Mukhtaran states, "like many illiterate women, I knew nothing about the law—and so little about my rights that I didn't know I have any" (Mai 2006, 28). Many women, married and unmarried, observes Mai in her book, feel so disgraced by rape that they are prompted to commit suicide. Mukhtaran had also considered doing the same.

Mukhtaran's story was covered widely by the media and caught the attention of the Pakistan government and the international press. Mukhtaran, subsequently dubbed the "Bravest Woman in the World" by *Glamour* magazine in November 2005, mustered the extraordinary courage to share her atrocity, despite the shame that such publicity brings to her and her family. Shame is such an inhibiting and humiliating cultural dynamic that the ordeals of countless women are neither told nor ever will be.

Among other debilitating factors, Mukhtaran, in her exposé, speaks to women's inability to read and write. She recalls that, upon reporting her rape, she signed a blank piece of paper at the request of the police. A false report was fabricated and filed on her behalf. Mukhtaran was unable to hire a lawyer until she received a large sum of money from the government of Pakistan as a token of sympathy (Mai 2006, 59). Mukhtaran donated a substantial amount of her compensation money to public welfare. She used part of it to start a school and eventually a shelter for girls and a school for boys as well. Mukhtaran believes the school for boys will play an important part in changing the minds of men (Chiade O'Shea 2004).

Mukhtaran continues to champion the cause of poor communities in a hostile feudal village system. Donations from around the world have poured in to support Mukhtaran and her initiatives. She is, writes Nicholas Kristof (2009) every so often in the *New York Times*, one of his heroes. Mukhtaran's story builds on the complexities inherent to the parallel legal systems of the government, religion, and tribe. As Mukhtaran has stated, "each tribe has its own rules that completely ignore the official law, and sometimes even religious law," (Mai 2006, 97).

Until recently, the possibility of incarceration or death by stoning under the Hudood Ordinance remained a facet of institutionalized discrimination against female victims of rape. *Zina* laws governing adultery, fornication, rape, and prostitution, under the Hudood Ordinance, required a woman to produce four witnesses if she reported sexual violence. Failure on her part to do so was interpreted as guilt. Hence, she could face capital punishment (for adultery) and imprisonment (for fornication), if she sought justice in a court of law without witnesses.

The *zina* laws were enacted in 1979, a feature of military dictator General Zia ul Haq's so-called Islamization process (Khan 2003, 76). The discriminatory legislation was essentially the trump card played by the general to win favor with religious constituencies, thereby consolidating his rule. In one of the darkest moments of General Zia's bitterly remembered military rule, the context of the following verse of the Quran was distorted, marking the institutionalization of inhumanity against women:

> And those who launch a charge against chaste women and produce not four witnesses (to support their allegations)—flog them with eighty stripes; and reject their evidence ever after: for such men are wicked transgressors. (Surah Al Nur 24, 4)

This Quranic injunction speaks clearly in favor of women, protecting them from sexual accusation by men at the cost of a stringent penalty for failure on the man's part, not the woman's, to provide evidence. The requirement to produce four eyewitnesses to prove a sexual allegation against a woman is an onerous one. Khan (2003, 76) notes that *zina* laws under the Hudood Ordinance were treated as an offense against the state. Mukhtaran attests that, for many a rape victim in Pakistan, it is difficult to prove the offense—since the only witnesses are usually the criminals themselves (Mai 2006, 56). In Mukhtaran's case, however, there were witnesses. She was gang-raped in front of the village, including her father and other relatives. Unfortunately for Mukhtaran and other victims, the system favors those who can bribe and use their influence with law enforcement agencies and the judiciary.

In a dramatic, yet less than perfect development, the Hudood Ordinances were repealed in 2006 and have been replaced by the Women's Protection Act (WPA), enacted in 2007. Asma Jehangir, a lawyer who is known for championing women's rights in Pakistan, suggests (2006) that, under the new amendments introduced in this act, *zina* (illegal sexual intercourse or all sex outside marriage) remains "an offence but the procedure for its complaint has been made stricter and those making an accusation of rape cannot be punished for zina. Thus, false accusations of zina will dramatically drop." The road to this remarkable milestone was paved through rigorous lobbying and campaigning by women's rights groups in Pakistan, with the invaluable support of the Pakistani print media and the English press, in particular. Unfortunately, however, due to lack of awareness and understanding of the WPA by law enforcement agencies, the law has failed to deliver on its promise. A *Daily Times* article states that women still find it difficult to report sexual violence in police stations (Amin Akhtar 2008).

Defence of Honor by Female Genital Mutilation

Gender, or women's oppression is inseparable from class, race and religious oppression. The patriarchal class system propagates the idea that the oppression of women and the poor is a divine law and is not man-made.

—Nawal El-Saadawi 1997, 15

The oppression of women, when the practice is deeply embedded in patriarchal structures, is deemed the natural social order. This is true in Egypt, just as much as in Pakistani society. Born in 1931, El-Saadawi was circumcised at the age of six in accordance with Egyptian custom. Her father was an official in Egypt's Ministry of Education and believed in educating all his eight children, daughters and sons. Although they were a traditional family, yet they were progressive. Later in El-Saadawi's life as a medical doctor and Egypt's director of public health, she was persecuted and jailed by government authorities, in view of her controversial stance on women's rights and advocacy against FGM (Malti-Douglas Fedwa 1995). El-Saadawi is now best known for her bold feminist activism at the rural, urban, and international levels. El-Saadawi has written extensively on women's issues and has more than 20 books to her credit. Her writings have been translated into many languages.

It is worth mentioning that Egypt's 1956 civil code gives women a constitutional status equal to that of men. Hatem (Sabbagh 1996, 172) writes that the constitution grants equality of opportunity to all Egyptians, male and female, without discrimination. Jobs are also guaranteed by the state to women who possess the requisite skills. Hatem adds:

> Labor laws were changed to insure and protect women's equal standing in the labor force. This entitled women to 50 days of paid maternity leave, and it obligated employers to provide day-care services where 100 or more women were employed. Finally it forbade employers to fire pregnant women while on maternity leave. (Sabbagh 1996, 173)

Unlike most Arab countries and particularly those in the gulf region, Egyptian women are distinguished by their active and uninhibited public participation in economic activities. Unlike many conservative Muslim cultures, Egyptian women go about their business in such public roles as government employees, street vendors, saleswomen, and guides. Official statistics on the women's labor force, writes Fernea (1998, 276), understate women's actual contributions. Fernea ascribes women's greater visibility in public spaces to the success of feminist activism in Egypt. She describes Egyptian women as working in "factories, shops, offices, airline offices, farms … in professional places like Egypt's Television Corporation, where fifty percent of the employees are women" (ibid.).

Egyptian films and television broadcasts are extremely popular in the Middle East. Portrayal of women in popular media appears to draw its inspiration from Western cultural models. Egyptian women are often the envy of other Arab women, who do not enjoy many of the same freedoms. The cross-currents of Arab and Western cultures are apparent in Egyptian television productions. Many of the themes are borrowed from Western celebrities such as Oprah Winfrey. Flashy music videos on Egyptian television feature female performers dressed provocatively and dancing like MTV superstars. Mute the sound of the regional music and the Arabic lyrics, and one might think the imagery is that of a hip hop or rock video.

Yet while Egyptian women continue to radically challenge traditional norms and practices through the media, political campaigns, and grassroots advocacy, Egyptian society remains mired in tensions arising from cultural heterogeneity and social polarization. Honor killings and FGM are still prevalent, despite reforms in Egypt's family and nationality laws (Fernea 1998, 275). Female circumcision has been traced back to Pharaonic times, predating Islam and Christianity. Both Muslim and Christian communities in Egypt have subsequently adopted this practice, however. Female circumcision is by and large an East African tradition practiced along the Nile River and not known to be as common in most Arab and Muslim countries other than Egypt, Sudan, and Somalia (Sabbagh 1996, 13; Dale Eickelmann 1998; Fernea 1998, 269). Elsewhere in Africa, female circumcision prevails in paganism and other cultures that are neither predominantly Muslim nor Christian (Fernea 1998, 254). Communities subscribing to female circumcision maintain that it preserves a girl's chastity by curbing her sexual instincts while she is unmarried (Harick and Marston 1996, 80).

Advocacy against FGM and its harmful effects by experts, clerics, and the civil society in Egypt has been in vain. Harick and Marston (1996, 82) note that female mutilation has been banned in Egypt since 1979, but the law has been difficult to enforce. In 1994, the practice was shown on television in Cairo, eliciting strong public reaction. In June 2007, the Egyptian government announced a complete ban on FGM in response to public outrage over the death of a 12-year-old who died while being circumcised in Upper Egypt. The practice is more common in rural than urban areas, however it is surmised that more than 90 percent of Egyptian women are circumcised (Magdi Abdel Hadi 2007).

Given the strong presence of conservative religious elements in Egypt, the airing of a weekly talk show on the subject of sex, called *The Big Talk*, is a remarkable feat for any woman in a predominantly Muslim country. Dr. Heba Kotb, also known as Egypt's Dr. Ruth, hosts the weekly talk show broadcast via satellite. Kotb appears on the airwaves wearing a *hijab*, the Muslim headscarf symbolizing modesty. She addresses questions related to marital sex within the parameters guided by Islam, in the light of the Quran. The show is very popular in the Middle East and speaks volumes about women's capacity to have a voice in Egypt, despite the controversy surrounding such issues.

Public discussion of subjects such as conjugal love is taboo in most Muslim cultures. The talk show is undoubtedly a first in the Muslim world. Quoting heavily from the Quran, Kotb offers insights concerning homosexuality, healthy marital sexual relations, and women's rights in this regard. The broadcast begins by Kotb inviting the attention of her audience in a straightforward manner: "Sex. Don't be afraid. Join me to talk about sex without shame" (Aneesh Raman 2007). One hopes that voices of women like Kotb would develop enough credibility to advocate against FGM and other forms of sexual violence against women, not uncommon in Egypt even today.

Although on the decline, honor killings are also practiced in rural areas and small towns in Egypt. Honor killings in both Egypt and Pakistan are guided by the same dynamic—cultural traditions are portrayed as religious (Sabbagh 1996, 12). As Fatima Mernissi (163) argues, "men seeking power through religion and its revivification are mostly from newly urbanized middle- and lower middle-class backgrounds." Mernissi's thesis resonates with the notion that patriarchal influences often associated with low levels of socioeconomic development in rural areas become infused in urban cultures as a result of the high rate of rural to urban migration.

Mernissi's observations are validated by El-Saadawi (1997) in her exploration of social disarray in Egyptian society stemming from uneven development. El-Saadawi suggests that the perpetuation of discriminatory patriarchal norms in otherwise modernized urban communities is the contagion from adjacent, rural, relatively undeveloped localities. The Global South, argues El-Saadawi, is still in delayed stages of development, existing side by side in various regions, and is still far from achieving cultural homogeneity, and still witnessing history "living before our eyes" (El-Saadawi 1997, 35).

Saadawi successfully deconstructs the complexities of uneven development, especially as they contribute to systemic and cultural violence against women. Women's welfare and progress in countries with uneven patterns of development are challenged by the primacy of primitive cultural dynamics. Inequitable distribution of the benefits of development hinders the advancement of women's rights and thereby their security. In regions where women remain unaware of their rights, men continue to subjugate them. The potential of the spillover of repressive values in contiguous geographic milieus remains. Development in urban centers and the associated liberation of women creates tensions within social, political, economic, and cultural structures and institutions. Threat to cultural values and traditions is often strongly resisted by patriarchs and clan elders, sometimes resulting in extreme levels of social and cultural polarization and frictions among Islamic and secular constituencies.

Family Honor above Individual Rights

Law, tradition, pleasure, indulgence, property, power, appreciation, arbitration… are all favorable to men.

—*Aynur Demirderik 1999, 78*

El-Saadawi's thesis on the complexities associated with poverty and uneven development in Egypt are equally relevant to Turkey. Turkey lies at the interface between Europe and Asia. It has close ties with Europe and is a candidate for membership in the European Union. While its population is predominantly Muslim, the government of Turkey has maintained a strongly secular tradition since the foundation of the republic in 1923 by Mustafa Kemal Atatürk. Diba Nigar Goksel (2007) writes that although the penal and civil codes introduced in the 1930s were designed along a European model—Italian in this case—a half-century later, reforms had not penetrated deep into Anatolia in the eastern part of the country.

Honor killings were widespread, many girls were not sent to mandatory primary school, and they were married off at a very young age, sometimes into polygamous marriages. Goskel (2007, 21) sheds light on the incidence of forced marriage requiring rape victims to marry the perpetrators of the crime. At the end of the twentieth century, Goksel (2007, 1) observes that Turkish women still did not have equal status with men under the civil and criminal law. The husband was the head of the household, and the penal code was based on family honor (not individual rights).

The cultural disparities among regions and especially those apparent in rural and urban settings are quite stark in Turkey. To borrow Pinar Ilkkaracan's insight:

Turkey is one of the countries most seriously affected by problems resulting from regional differences in socio-economic conditions, which are progressively worse as one moves from West to East. The West of Turkey consumes most of the private and public sector resources and is also highly urbanized, while most of the population in the East lives in rural areas. (1998, 67)

The rural-urban differential classifies Turkey as a microcosm of uneven development and cultural heterogeneity. In establishing a nexus between underdevelopment and the salience of primitive cultural influences in eastern Turkey, Ilkkaracan (1998, 66) notes that a woman may not legally seek a divorce from her husband on the grounds of adultery on his part. However, she may be killed in the name of honor for a similar act of immorality. She argues that eastern Turkey's culture is rooted in semifeudal traditional foundations (ibid.). Like many patriarchal societies, the subjugation of women by men continues whereby customary and religious laws are used to control their sexuality.

Domestic violence is common in rural Turkey. As in Pakistan and Egypt, women are not usually known to report sexual and domestic violence to law enforcement agencies. Despite a municipality law passed in 2004 providing for shelters for victims of domestic violence, few women have turned to them for protection. Most Turkish municipalities have not created shelters for women, as required by law (Goskel 2007, 29), and victims of domestic violence often do not know where to seek refuge. The conditions are generally uncongenial, due to inadequate funding in shelters that do exist (Goskel 2007, 27).

Rural-to-urban migration, driven by economic factors and the spillover of the Islamic revival in a secular urban culture, has stirred up tensions in political and social institutions. Political unrest over the ban of the headscarf in academic institutions is a manifestation of ideological polarization in contemporary Turkish society. As observable in Egypt and Pakistan, the issue of class is often tied to that of gender inequality in Turkey. Fernea (1998, 223) quotes from an interview referencing Aytan, a maid: "The majority of Turkish women are just like Aytan, village women now living in the city. They've brought their values with them. That complicates things."

Both women and men migrating to Turkish urban centers from rural areas share primitive cultural values that are unfavorable to women. These migrating communities often live in poverty and do not have the opportunities to afford modern education for their children. Fernea (1998, 220) brings into sharp focus the socioeconomic dimension in positioning urban Turkish culture. She notes that one-third of Istanbul's population in 1987 lived in *gecikondus*—squatter settlements. Half of them were poor working-class women. The United Nations report *State of the World Cities: Globalization and Urban Culture* (2004, 68) asserts that half of Istanbul's population lives in slum conditions. Meltem Muftuler-Bac (1999, 313), a leading Turkish scholar, suggests that

> the seemingly bright picture – Turkey as the most modern, democratic, secular Muslim state that also secures women's rights – is misleading in many ways. In fact, I propose that this perception is more harmful than outright oppression because it shakes the ground for women's rights movements by suggesting that they are unnecessary.

Turkish history is replete with examples of the struggle of women in securing their rights. One such name is that of an intellectual Fatima Aliye, who died at the age of 72 in 1936. Aliye was the daughter of a bureaucrat and a historian. She rose to fame as the first female novelist and newspaper columnist. Her works are known as the first to highlight women's issues in Turkish society. Aliye was at the forefront of activism during the Turkish nationalist movement after World War I. Her writings challenged conservative influences in Turkish society by exploring women's education, role in society, and right to follow Western trends in fashion (Aylin Gorgun-Baran 2008, 136). As a tribute to her legacy, Aliye is the first woman in Turkish history to appear on a banknote, the 50 lira bill introduced in 2008.

Halide Edip Adivar is another name fondly remembered by secular groups in Turkey. Adivar was instrumental in pioneering women's rights. She is considered the most liberal champion of women's rights during Turkey's struggle for independence. Like Aliye, Adivar emerged as a leading activist in Turkey's nationalist movement. She was a novelist and an orator. Her speeches and writings were an inspiration to both women and men. Adivar died in 1964 at the age of 82 (Gorgun-Baran 2008, 136).

Other more recent prominent female activists include academics such as Deniz Kandiyoti and Sirin Tekeli. Kandiyoti is a sociologist and has written extensively to raise awareness about the status of women in Turkish society since the 1970s. A range of themes is discussed in her works covering the life of rural women, women's social movements in Turkish history, women's social mobility, Islam, and state policies, among others (Katharina Knaus 2007, 7–8). Tekeli is a political scientist by profession and has produced several books on issues concerning women since the 1980s. Her analytical writings draw on the significance of state feminism and women's political participation, among others (Knaus 2007, 9). Tekeli also helped institute the Women's Library and Information Center in Istanbul in 1990. The library was established to preserve documents relating to the women's movement in Turkey (Knaus 2007, 10).

Over the years, feminist and political activism on the part of women has steadily increased in Turkey. The last nearly three decades have witnessed a renewed vigor in feminist activism. The latest wave of the women's movement, albeit culturally diverse, represents the core of Turkish civil society. It constitutes professional women: scholars, journalists, doctors, students, and ordinary Turkish women. Nadje S. Al-Ali (2002, 24) suggests that, unlike Egyptian feminists, Turkish women have been successful in creating solidarity networks, especially in advocating against domestic violence.

The print and popular media have been effective channels of information dissemination for Turkish feminists. Women's journals and magazines raising social and legal awareness about problems such as domestic violence and sexual harassment abound (Al-Ali 2002, 25). Along with these efforts, women writers in Turkey have organized to promote feminist activism through the production of historical narratives on women's voices, since the times of the Ottoman Empire in the nineteenth century. The period laid the foundations of women's social and legal emancipation (Knaus 2007, 2).

Women's movements in Turkey, Egypt, and Pakistan have been vociferous in campaigning for democratic reforms in political institutions. Of the Turkish women's movement, writes Knaus (2007, 2), it "has been one of the most influential players within civil society on the Turkish political scene."

Reflections

Challenged by poverty, patriarchal belief systems, and institutionalized discrimination on the part of the state, women navigate through their society against all odds. They are marginalized, alienated, and oppressed. They have been killed, maimed, and mutilated in the name of honor for centuries. Statistically, they are not a minority. Yet they are fundamentally underrepresented in policy making. They are treated as commodities. In many cultures, they are deemed incapable of making rational decisions.

In Pakistan, Egypt, and Turkey, a newborn's fate is often defined by its gender. The birth of a baby girl is often frowned upon if she is the first baby in the family. She is yet more unwelcome if there are daughters before her and no sons. A daughter is perceived as an economic and social burden. A woman who is not able to produce sons is considered unworthy. There are immense social pressures associated with her fertility. Her life is governed by patriarchal customs and worldviews.

In the event of sexual harassment, which is quite common, it is typically considered her fault. Common reactions to sexual harassment elicit reactions such as: "she must not have been modest in her attire," "she must cover up properly so as not to invite temptation," "the color of her gaudy clothes was asking for attention," "she carries herself inappropriately," "she wears much makeup," "she is always dolled up," and "her intent is to attract men."

Social norms demand that a woman should be discreet in her demeanor, often to the point of being virtually invisible. She must not speak in the company of men. In such cultures, a woman is considered wise when silent. Pakistani women are constantly reminded of the notion of *aurat aur chaar deewari*, meaning that a woman's rightful place is within the confines of four walls. The issue of women's segregation in public and private spaces is deliberated in social and political discourses, within and across Pakistani society: in the media, the mosque, and parliament. Al-Ali's narrative on women's movements in Egypt and Turkey (2002, 8) suggests that traditional thinking in these societies resonates with Pakistani perceptions "in terms of women's seclusion, veiling, women belonging to the private sphere (while men are seen to belong to the public sphere), sexual modesty and the concepts of honor and shame."

Women's Movements and Social Change

Egypt

Ray and Korteweg (1999) identify two important preconditions for women's mobilization. The first (52) suggests that advances in industrialization, urbanization, and education precipitate women's movements. The second proposition (55) holds that anticolonial and nationalist struggles in the third world have created the space for broader feminist negotiation. Ray and Korteweg (58) add that revolutionary patterns observed in nationalist struggles are akin to a contemporary religious renaissance in the Middle East and South Asia. They argue that the emergence of Islamism has given rise to a new form of gender activism in Egypt.

Ray and Korteweg acknowledge Azza Karam's (1999, 58) commentary on three coexisting forms of feminism in Egypt: secular (liberal), Islamist (fundamentalist), and Muslim (pragmatist and progressive). Sabbagh (1996, 14–15) suggests that Egyptian women have been most politically active in the Arab world. Recalling women's participation in mass-based political, anticolonial, and nationalist movements, she writes that women have been able to position themselves as political players and activists, with a degree of independence that most Arab women from other countries do not enjoy. Feminist leaders such as Huda Sharawi, founder of the first Egyptian Feminist Union, will be remembered in the annals of Arab feminist history for symbolically removing her face veil upon returning from an international women's conference in Rome in 1923. "Sharawi's 'unveiling' was marked as a watershed in Arab women's movements" (Fernea 1998, 241).

Others on the forefront of the feminist movement in Egypt include Dr. Nawal El-Saadawi, known for her advocacy on women's health and sexual rights, discussed earlier in the chapter. Her speeches and writings reflect her brave stance against FGM and have led to her own persecution. Dr. Saadawi established the Arab Women's Solidarity Association (AWSA), based in Egypt, in 1982, with branches in other Arab countries (El-Saadawi 1998, 38). Many Egyptian feminist organizations have emerged since the late 1970s, many of them urban, but some are also present in rural areas.

Turkey

In recent years a forceful civil society has emerged in Turkey. Evidence of this development is observed in the mushrooming of hundreds of socially and politically active women nongovernmental organizations (NGOs). Since 2001, Turkey has undergone a series of historic reforms in the civil and penal codes. The new laws governing marriage, divorce, and property ownership give men and women equal rights. Female sexuality is now an individual right rather than an aspect of family honor (Goksel 2007, 2). Goksel writes that these reforms represent a monumental turn of events in favor of women, ever since the abolition of polygamy in the 1920s.

Yesim Arat (1998, 117–18) notes that feminist organizations have been engaged, since the mid-1980s, in setting the agenda for women's rights through advocacy. The feminist movement in Turkey is organized in two independent secular and faith-based groups (ibid. 122) that have visibly challenged existing social and political power structures. Among notable achievements are the campaign against domestic violence in Istanbul and the establishment of Purple Roof Women's Shelter Foundation in 1990, providing counseling and shelter for victims (Arat 1998, 120). More recent accomplishments by the feminist movement in Turkey include the 2004 amendment to the constitution, which states that "women and men have equal rights" and "the state is responsible for taking all necessary measures to realize equality between women and men" (Article 10). Goskel (2007, 2) adds that the Turkish Civil Code introduced in 2001, reforms in the laws governing employment and family courts instituted in 2003, as well as a "completely reformed penal code" (2004) have brought about comprehensive changes to the legal status of women."

Pakistan

In Pakistan, the launch of the women's movement may be attributed to the Women's Action Forum (WAF) established in 1981. The organization is secular in ideology and publishes several newspapers in major Pakistani cities. The group emerged in the wake of General Zia's Islamization process, which restricted women's visibility and interactions in public and private spaces. WAF has inspired the formation of a vast network of women rights organizations across the country, working on such issues as service delivery, rights-based advocacy, lobbying, capacity building, and research. Many of these organizations work in coordination with community-based organizations (CBOs) extending their outreach to Pakistan's rural areas. Women's rights have taken center stage in many organizations including relief agencies, human rights, and international nongovernmental organizations (INGOs). Some local NGOs thrive on international donor support, while many tap local sources of funding.

Organizations such as the AGHS Legal Aid Cell for women, run by the internationally recognized human rights activists and lawyers Asma Jehangir and Hina Jillani; Progressive Women's Association, headed by another fearless women's rights activist Shahnaz Bukhari; Aurat Publication and Information Service Foundation; Shirkat Gah, Women's Resource Center; Pattan Development Organization; Bedari for the promotion of women's and girls' human rights; Human Rights Commission of Pakistan (HRCP); and Kwendo Khor Women and Children's Development Program, among many other national NGOs, have been at the forefront of rights advocacy and service delivery for women. Many of these organizations provide free legal aid, shelters, vocational training programs, counseling services, and crisis centers for women.

Milestones reached by the Pakistani women's movement include the institution of the National Commission on the Status of Women, initiating a process to repeal of Hudood Ordinances, and reserved seats for women's representation in Parliament. There have been other successful policy initiatives, though, including the adoption of a National Plan of Action, in response to the Beijing Platform for Action, outlining 184 actions in 12 areas of concern; the National Policy for Women's Development and Empowerment (2002); and the creation of the First Women's Bank Limited, advancing a twofold development and commercial mandate. It is entirely staffed by professional women bankers and caters to women clients, including poor women without collateral (Shaheed and Hamdani 2004).

Lessons Learned

Reforms in legislation are critical for structural and systemic change favorable to the status of girls and women. However on its own, legislation cannot address the underlying socioeconomic, cultural, and political causes of gender inequity. Women can elevate their own socioeconomic status through education and skill building, support empowerment through legal institutions, and promote a shift toward development for the entire community. International standards for gender empowerment must be enforced for these countries to compete in a global environment. Incentives by donor countries could be helpful in this regard. At the policy level, resources must be mobilized toward gender mainstreaming. Best practices and models such as gender budgeting, a strategy to monitor the allocation of funds for gender empowerment, in government departments and ministries may be replicated.

Development agendas must be designed to reach out to women, especially in rural and remote areas where violence against women continues unabated. Governments and civil society organizations should link up in creating economic opportunity structures for women. There are resources and expertise at both levels that could be better utilized through concerted efforts. Access to primary, secondary, and higher education for girls and women is particularly important. Similarly, educating boys and men would be a key intervention in mitigating the causes of violence. Education broadens the mind and liberates societies from the clutches of inhumane cultural traditions. The long-term benefits of universal education can address the gap in uneven development across Pakistani, Egyptian, and Turkish societies.

Awareness-raising programs through curricular inputs, as well as media campaigns, are useful for information dissemination on women's rights and for women's access to the legal system. It is important to share narratives about women's role in history. They serve as replicable models and affirm the movements for women's rights. Low-budget initiatives such as radio broadcasts should be actively pursued, especially as this medium often has the widest outreach in developing countries. Street theater and television programs have been successful in modeling social behavior in many parts of the world. Such initiatives should be supplemented with community education programs centered on themes that promote the notion of equality of all human beings, women and men.

Conclusion

The conflation of Islamic and patriarchal values remains a bane for women in most Muslim countries. Separating the cultural from the religious is a key challenge for women's rights groups, particularly as men craft religious laws with skewed interpretations of Quranic verses. Parallel legal systems complicate access to and provision of justice. Turkish, Pakistani, and Egyptian societies continue to experience extreme levels of sociocultural polarization developing in the wake of trends in globalization and the Islamic renaissance of recent decades.

Despite these obstacles, secular and religious actors, particularly in the cases of Egypt and Turkey, have evolved their own feminist constituencies. Al-Ali makes an apt observation in regard to the dynamics of women's movements in the Middle East. She writes,

> The coexistence of diversity and similarity also holds true for women's movements: specific historical trajectories as well as current ideas and practices account for variations between women's movements in different nation states. Women's movements in the Middle East are similar in that they share several historical and political factors, such as their links to nationalist movements, their links to processes of modernization and development, and tensions between (2002, 9).

On the other hand, while Muslim women in prepartition British India were at the forefront of the struggle for an independent Pakistan, political activism did not merge with feminist movements in the aftermath of independence in 1947. It must be acknowledged, however, that presently the women's movement in Pakistan is a liberal prodemocracy constituency that is as politically active as the feminist camps in Turkey and Egypt. However, to the disadvantage of the relatively young Pakistani women's movement, strong linkages with Western donors and the absence of a hard to penetrate, broad grassroots base have undermined their credibility and hence their capacity to create greater change.

The women's movement in Pakistan is in its evolutionary stages still. It has neither sought solidarity with religious women's groups nor found common grounds with them. Unlike Egypt and Turkey where feminist activism has a secular as well as faith-based constituency, women's religious groups in Pakistan have not demonstrated an inclination for prowomen advocacy. Many of the organizations have been opposed to the reformation of the aforementioned Hudood Ordinances. The feudal lobby in Pakistan's parliament has moved to hinder many positive resolutions tabled by liberal parliamentarians, female and male. Most legal and political institutional reforms in favor of women may be attributed to the secular women's rights networks in Pakistan, as well as the policy formulation in line with international conventions and agreements.

Feminist campaigns in Pakistan, Egypt, and Turkey are frequently modeled along similar initiatives in other parts of the world. However, many women's organizations funded by Western donors are deemed controversial for carrying forth "donor-driven agendas." Nonetheless, the positive impact of Western donor support and international conventions must be noted for their contribution to the institutional presence of feminist movements in Egypt, Pakistan, and Turkey. Al-Ali (2002, 10) emphasizes that the United Nations Decade for Women ushered in a productive era fostering dialogue on women's issues and the growth of a vibrant NGO culture.

Women's movements in these three countries draw their inspiration from one another and members have learned from the successes of other development and neighboring states. With revolutionary advances in information technology, there is an unprecedented level of networking among women's rights groups in various parts of the world, as well as within and across states. International protocols and treaties governing women's rights have engendered a global environment that acknowledges, creates awareness for, and supports the rights and needs of women. Exchanges between activists at these conferences have been invaluable in terms of learning, innovating, networking, and creating local, regional, and international support systems.

Women's movements in all three countries have benefited from the production of feminist knowledge and awareness through fiction, nonfiction, and poetry. Popular and print media have been effective tools in information dissemination and women's rights campaigns. The creation of women's networks, international conferences, and global governance have boosted the momentum, bolstering feminist activism at the national level. The movements in these countries face enormous challenges, but the lessons of history teach us that women have earned their rights. The importance of remembering history is therefore very important in the context of women's movements. All along, women have been vehicles of change for women, children, and humankind.

References

Abdel Hadi, Magdi. 2007. "Egypt Forbids Female Circumcision." BBC online (June 28). Available at http://news.bbc.co.uk/2/hi/middle_east/6251426.stm.

Akhtar, Amin. 2008. "Women's Protection Law Fails Rape Victims." *Daily Times*, March 30. Available at http://www.dailytimes.com.pk/default.asp?page=2008%5C03%5C30%5Cstory_30-3-2008_pg7_34.

Al-Ali, Nadje S. 2002. *The Women's Movement in Egypt with Selective Reference to Turkey.* Civil Society and Social Movements Programme Paper Number 5. United Nations Research Institute for Social Development (April).

Arat, Yesim. 1998. "Feminists, Islamists and Political Change in Turkey." *Political Psychology* 19 (March). pp.117–131.

Association for Women's Rights in Development. 2008. *A Review of "Women's Empowerment: Measuring the Global Gender Gap."* Available at http://www.awid.org/eng/Issues-and-Analysis/Library/A-review-of-Women-s-Empowerment-Measuring-the-Global-Gender-Gap/%28language%29/eng-GB.

Aziz, Khalid. 2008. "Senator Defends Honor Killing." *The Nation*, August 30. Available at http://www.nation.com.pk/pakistan-news-newspaper-daily-english-online/Politics/30-Aug-2008/Senator-defends-honourkilling

Bari, Farzana. 2005. "Women's Political Participation: Issues and Challenges." United Nations Division for the Advancement of Women, Expert Group Meeting: "Enhancing Participation of Women in Development through an Enabling Environment for Achieving Gender Equality and the Advancement of Women," Bangkok, Thailand, November 8–11.

Demirderik, Aynur. 1999. *Deconstructing Images of 'The Turkish Woman..'* Edited by Arat Zahra. New York: Palgrave.

Eickelmann, Dale. 1998. *The Middle East and Central Asia: An Anthropological Approach.* Englewood Cliffs, N.J.: Prentice Hall.

El-Saadawi, Nawal. 1997. *The Nawal el Saadawi Reader.* New York: Zed Books.

Fernea, Elizabeth Warnock. 1998. *In Search of Islamic Feminism: One Woman's global journey.* New York: Doubleday.

Foundation for Sustainable Development. *Women's Empowerment.* Available at http://www.fsdinternational.org/devsubject/womensempowerment.

Goksel, Diba Nigar. 2007. "Sex and Power in Turkey: Feminism, Islam, and the Maturing of Turkish Democracy." Berlin: European Stability Initiative. Available at http://www.esiweb.org/pdf/esi_document_id_90.pdf.

Gorgun-Baran, Aylin. 2008. "A Sociological Analysis of Leadership in Turkish Women." *American-Eurasian Journal of Scientific Research*, 3, 132–8.

Government of Pakistan. *Pakistan Elections 2007/2008.* Available at http://www.elections.com.pk/contents.php?i=9 (accessed February 2, 2009).

Harik, Ramsay M., and Elsa Marston. 1996. *Women in the Middle East.* New York: Moffa Press.

Hatem, Mervat F. 1996."Economic and Political Liberalization in Egypt and the Demise of State Feminism. Arab Women Between Defiance and Restraint." Suha Sabagh (ed.), pp. 177–93. New York: Olive Branch Press.

Human Rights Commission of Pakistan. 2007. Trend Analysis of Human Rights Violations 2005–2006. Available at http://hrcpblog.wordpress.com/2007/11/23/trend-analysis-of-human-rights-violations-2005–2006/.

Hussain, Jamila. 2004. *Islam: Its Law and Society.* Sydney: Federation Press.

Ilkarracan, Ipek, and Sevil. 2007. "Who Cares Determines Who Participates in the Labor Force and Who Does Not: The Institutional and Social Determinants of

Female Labor Force Participation in Turkey." *International Conference in Istanbul Technical University and Women for Women's Human Rights—New Ways.* Istanbul.

Ilkkaracan, Pinar. 1998. "Exploring the Context of Women's Sexuality in Eastern Turkey." *Reproductive Health Matters*, 6(12), 66–75.

International Center for Research on Women. 2005. *Property Ownership for Women Enriches Empowers and Protects.* ICRW Millenium Development Goal Series.

Jehangir, Asma. 2006. "Protecting Women." *Daily Times*,November 26. Available at http://www.dailytimes.com.pk/default.asp?page=2006%5C11%5C21%5Cstory_21–11–2006_pg3_5.

Khan, Shahnaz. 2003."The Moral Regulation of the Pakistani Woman." *Feminist Review*, 75, 75–94.

Knaus, Katharina. (2007). "Turkish Women: A Century of Change." *Turkish Policy Quarterly*, 6(1), 47–59.

Kristof, Nicholas. 2009. "Mukhtar Mai's Case in Pakistan." *New York Times*, March 2. Available at http://kristof.blogs.nytimes.com/2009/03/02/mukhtar-mais-case-in-pakistan/.

Lindholm, Charles (ed.) 1996. "The Swat Pakhtun Family as Political Timing." *Frontier Perspective: Essays in Contemporary Anthropology* (pp. 17–27). Karachi: Oxford University Press.

Mai, Mukhtaran. 2006. *In the Name of Honor.* Translated by Marie-Therese. New York: Atria Books.

Majed, Ziad. 2005. *Building Democracy in Egypt.* International Institute for Democracy and Electoral Assistance (IDEA) and the Arab NGO Network for Development (ANND).

Malti-Douglas, Fedwa. 1995. *Men, Women, and God(s).* Los Angeles: University of California Press.

Mayell, Hillary. 2002. "Thousands of Women Killed for Family 'Honor'." *National Geographic*, February 12.

Meltem, Muftuler-Bac. 1999. "Turkish Women's Predicament." *Women Studies International Forum*, 22(3), 303–16.

Mernissi, Fatima. 1996. *Arab Women Between Defiance and Restraint.* Edited by Suha Sabbagh. New York: Olive Branch Press.

Moussaoui, Naima El. *Talking about Honor Killings.* Common Ground News Service. December 18, 2007. Available at http://www.commongroundnews.org/article.php?id=22317&lan=en&sid=1&sp=0.

Mutumi, Gumisai. 2004. "Women Break into African Politics." *Africa Renewal.* Available at http://un.org/ecosocdev/geninfo/afrec/vol18no1/181women.htm (accessed on February 2, 2009).

Raman, Aneesh. 2007. "Egypt's Dr. Ruth: Lets Talk Sex in the Arab World." CNN.com (April 26). Available at http://edition.cnn.com/2007/WORLD/meast/04/25/muslim.sextalk/.

O'Shea, Chiade. 2004. "School Hope for Rape Victim." BBC online (December 7). Available at http://news.bbc.co.uk/2/hi/south_asia/4042941.stm.

Shah, Saeed. 20008. "Pakistan: Three Teenage Girls Buried Alive in Tribal 'Honour' Killing." *The Guardian*, September 1. Available at http://www.guardian.co.uk/world/2008/sep/01/pakistan.

Suha, Sabbagh (ed.). 1996. *Arab Women: Between Defiance and Restraint.* Brooklyn, N.Y.: Olive Branch Press.

UN-HABITAT. 2004. "State of the World Cities: Globalization and Urban Culture."

United Nation Development Program. 2007/2008. *Human Development Report.*

United Nation Development Program. 2005. *Human Development Report.*

US Department of State. 2006. "Pakistan." Country Reports on Human Rights Practices. Bureau of Democracy Human Rights and Labor. Available at http://www.state.gov/g/drl/rls/hrrpt/2006/78874.htm.

World Economic Forum. 2008 "The Global Gender Gap Report."

World Economic Forum. 2007. "The Global Gender Gap Report."

CHAPTER FIFTEEN

Organizing the Disenfranchised: Haiti and Dominican Republic

Yves-Renée Jennings

Peace goes with justice and equal treatment for all based on the level of trust and truth that allows people who are interdependent to talk honestly about problems while creating the mental, emotional and social space for everyone to be heard in order to engender the level of respect that promotes and maintains good and constructive relationships. And it is difficult to achieve that although this is my goal in the work that I am doing.
—Interview with Colette Lespinasse in July 2008

I dream of the day when there will be no discrimination against Haitians and Haitians born in the Dominican Republic because for best or worst the two people are linked and are interdependent. As a Haitian-Dominican who has had the help of many good-hearted Dominicans in order to have an education and to be in a position to help others, I want to continue my work with Dominicans who believe in the humanity of all. This is to ensure that Haitian-Dominicans can view positively their Dominican culture and equally recognize their Haitian heritage while they always remember that they are human beings deserving the full respect of others and the right to live with dignity.
—Interview with Sonia Pierre in July 2008

In summer 2008, while researching women's work within the context of social change in the Caribbean region, I met and interviewed Colette Lespinasse and Sonia Pierre. Both have emerged as social change agents. Because of their commitment to advocacy and service and their determination to help disenfranchised Haitians and Haitian descendents in the Dominican Republic, they have found a voice and become aware of their potential. A year later, curious about both women's motivation, I decided to go to the Dominican Republic and Haiti and to learn more about their work. I found out that both Colette and Sonia have served as catalysts for positive social actions that can bring about constructive social transformation in the lives of the disenfranchised and with particular regard to the Haitian migration and human rights issues in the Dominican Republic and Haiti. As servant-transformational leaders, who willingly put the needs, aspirations, and interests of those they deliberately choose to serve first while providing them the space to develop their potentials as free and self-sufficient individuals, Colette and Sonia have endeavored to help the disenfranchised better their lives as they struggle against inequality and discrimination and renew their resilience to survive daily. In this chapter, I refer to both women's agency as a positive social change catalyst, provide a few examples of their work, and point out their respective efforts to help Haitians and Dominicans improve their relationships on the island of Hispaniola, which both peoples have shared since the 1800s.

As a scholar-practitioner in the field of conflict analysis and resolution, I also highlight the interrelationship between the work of human rights advocates such as Colette and Sonia and that of conflict resolution practitioners. This interrelationship makes a case for professionals in the field of human rights advocacy and conflict resolution to partner as they seek to help others achieve constructive social change. In my view, although the paradigms and interventions of both fields differ, they each strive toward the same goal, ensuring that humans' rights are respected and humans' needs met, thus making our world a better place.

Women as Social Agents

Across the world women have endeavored to contribute to positive social change despite patriarchal or social hindrances that have often erected deep-rooted systemic barriers and limited their participation in the constructive transformation of their societies. Their involvement in state, society, or community affairs during recent decades has changed the patriarchal discourse about women's ability to be full social agents and contributors who can positively influence policy decisions that promote societal transformation. Highlighting the importance of female agency and women's contribution to social transformation around the world, Maja Mikula (2005) articulates that, throughout history, women have initiated social actions that have secured the well-being of their family, community, race, class, or ethnic group based on their natural orientation to serve and help others. She notes that their boldness and strong beliefs in the humanity and dignity of others have often allowed them to advance social change in what is yet a predominantly patriarchal world.

Emphasizing the need for women's contribution and leadership in regard to conflict prevention, conflict resolution, peace building, and positive social change, in an address to the US House Committee on Foreign Affairs, Subcommittee on International Organizations, Human Rights and Oversights, Helen Hunt (2008) asserts that "Women are [now] at the forefront of good governance efforts and often serve as a bridge between government and civil society, working across political lines to achieve important policy priorities" (1). Therefore, their ability to lead, contribute, and make the best use of limited resources often complements their knowledge and experience of caring for and helping others while simultaneously giving them a voice. These efforts have helped women leaders worldwide raise societal awareness about inequality and human rights violations, while empowering the disenfranchised so they can live with dignity, reach their potential, and feel inspired to constructively contribute to their society.

As social agents, Colette and Sonia have helped create, respectively, in Haiti and the Dominican Republic a dynamic and evolutionary social change process that not opens a space where the disadvantaged can learn about his/her rights but that can also influence the policies and laws necessary for societal transformation of inequality and discrimination in both countries. In this context, an unwavering passion for positive change and a compassion for the disenfranchised have guided both Colette and Sonia as servant-transformational leaders to help others with purpose and commitment based on a foundation of positive social values. Such determination rests on a constructive service and empowerment culture, which Kuzmenko et al. (2004) believes links both servant and transformational leadership styles.

Servant-Transformational Leadership

Based on his work experience and his interpretation of prior literature on leadership, Greenleaf (1997) posits that servant leaders are individuals who put others' needs, aspirations, and interests above their own. Greenleaf (1997, 2003) further emphasizes that, while servant leaders deliberately choose to serve, they also provide those they serve with the opportunity "to grow healthier, wiser, freer, more autonomous, and more likely themselves to become servants" (13–14). Within this frame, Greenleaf's (1997) paradigm asserts that servant leaders are chiefly concerned with serving others because of their natural service orientation, and they only lead in order to effectively serve. Farling, Stone, and Winston (1999) support this view, as they conceive that it is important for leaders to understand that serving others is one of their primary functions. Complementing this view, Russell and Stone (2002) also believe that service is one of the core attributes of servant leadership, a fundamental goal that rests on collaboration.

Thus, through collaboration, servant leaders create environments where people can learn how to trust one another and work together based on common visions sustained by courage, commitment, hope, and principles of justice and truth as well as the determination to prevent destructive interactions. While servant leaders usually become the voice of those they serve and help them learn how to constructively claim their rights, they also empower the individuals they seek to help. In this context, servant leaders help those they serve acquire an enhanced level of consciousness about their potential to also become constructive social change agents. However, Spears (2002) cautions that servant leaders need to adopt a long-term transformational approach in order to help those they serve achieve the "potential for creating positive change" (9) because a "quick fix" (10) approach does not result in constructive societal transformation.

James M. Burns (1978) also helps make the linkage between servant and transformational styles of leadership as he argues that leaders who become engaged in helping others can motivate them to become confident about their potential to improve their lives based on sustained efforts and values anchored in hard work, while building their capacity to achieve a better future. Thus, transformational leaders inspire those they serve to strive for goals rooted in positive social values and to contribute to the betterment of their lives and society. Taking transformational leadership further, Purdue (2001) asserts that leaders with transformational qualities can serve not only as motivators for personal development but also as social catalysts for institutional change and progress.

A Context for Social Action

Since the 1800s, as neighboring nations with significantly different ethnic backgrounds, the Dominican Republic and Haiti have occupied the island of Hispaniola located in the Caribbean Basin. Dominicans are of a mixed African, Taino Indian, and Spanish descent, while Haitians are predominantly of African heritage. Despite their proximity, relations between the two people have always been contentious because of their historical past and the racial differences that have led to what Ernesto Sagas (1994) calls the *antihaitianismo*. This epithet encapsulates the Dominicans' antagonistic attitudes toward Haitians. Such attitudes are rooted in the Haitian conquest and control of the Dominican Republic during the 1820s and the Dominicans' proclaimed racial dissimilarities and the resulting prejudice toward Haitians. Such prejudice contributes to racial tension and acrimony between the two peoples despite their economic interdependency. In this respect, Deine and McDougall (2007) assert that the Dominican *antihaitianismo* has led Dominicans to denigrate and ostracize not only the Haitians but also other Dominicans who merely look like Haitians.

In regard to their interdependence, not only do the two peoples share the same island, they have also maintained significant economic relations for the last two centuries. Older Haitians who migrated to the Dominican Republic attest that, even before the 1950s when the two countries entered into an accord that allowed Haitians to seasonally migrate to work in Dominican sugar cane plantations, Haitians migrated to the Dominican side of the island, and many never returned to Haiti. Such accords provided jobs to Haitians and complemented the Dominicans' lack of manpower in cane plantations. Referring to the two countries' willingness to ratify their interdependence in the case of the cane plantations, James Ferguson (2003) notes that:

> Bilateral agreements or convenios [were drawn up] between the rulers of the two countries, under which, Haitian labourers or braceros were brought across the border for specified periods of work on sugar plantations. After Trujillo's 1952 convenio brought in 16,500 workers, more convenios were signed between Trujillo and his Haitian counterpart "Papa Doc" Duvalier (10).

With the downward-spiraling poverty and instability in Haiti during the last few decades, in addition to documented seasonal cane cutters and other Haitians who have obtained legal residence in the Dominican Republic or who have been admitted to Dominican universities, a significant influx of undocumented poor Haitians has also entered the country through its porous border. These undocumented Haitian migrants usually find work either in the Dominican cane plantations during the *zafra* (sugarcane harvest), coffee and citrus harvests, or in the construction sector. Because of their willingness to accept low wages, undocumented Haitian workers compete with native Dominicans for employment.

The resulting push-and-pull relationship has led to an asymmetric power relationship between poor Haitian undocumented migrants and wealthy Dominican employers. Meanwhile, through its institutionalized structures, the Dominican Republic has endeavored to rid the country of undocumented Haitians whenever they create social problems, when their influx reaches a certain level, or as a safeguard to prevent jobs from being taken away from Dominicans and to avert the haitianization of the country (Lamson 2007). It is within this historical and social context that two women with different backgrounds but similar passions have emerged as agents of social change.

Colette Lespinasse

Born in Haiti, Colette Lespinasse earned her bachelor's degree in business administration from Universite Quisqueya in 1999 and continued with coursework in human rights, journalism, and international law in Canada, Haiti, and Italy. As a human rights advocate, Colette has benefited from numerous training programs in social identity, human rights, and democracy in Haiti and abroad. A distinguished journalist, Colette has worked with Radio Soleil and has been involved with radio programs at Radio Kiskeya where she produces a weekly program related to women issues about various topics. Her professional life has also included serving as the coordinator for advocacy activities, while acting as a public relations director and overseeing fundraising activities. Colette's impetus to help the disenfranchised emerged in the early 1990s when Haitian migration to the Dominican Republic became a significant problem for both the Dominican Republic and Haiti.

Motivation

Colette's passion to help others and her determination to give them a voice has motivated her to work with disenfranchised Haitian migrants and Dominicans who looked Haitian during their mass deportation in the 1991. During this memorable expulsion, Colette recalled that deportees were transported out of the Dominican Republic and dropped off at Plateau Central, an area in the northern part of Haiti. Most of them did not have a place to go or did not know anyone in Haiti because they were born or were living in the Dominican Republic's *bateys* (shanty towns where cane cutters live) for many generations. Deportees who had families in Haiti came from distant places such as Les Cayes, a town in the southern part of Haiti, and had no means to reach home. This mass deportation convinced Colette that she needed to help build a foundation that promotes constructive social change to benefit disenfranchised Haitians working in the Dominican Republic.

Colette shared the source of her ability to carry out her work in an interview in July 2008:

> My knowledge to do this work come from my training in Haiti and abroad (Canada and Italy) based on different topics related to identity and human rights and democracy, and my instinct to help people exchange their views so they can get to know each other and build better relations. I have a deep passion for what I do because I want to help women know that they have a voice, that they can and need to participate in the affairs of their country because without them Haiti would not be still here. Furthermore, I have used my life experience to help Haitian women who have been undermined, marginalized and not given any value or recognition by men and our society while they have been responsible and have worked hard to provide for their families without any real socio-economic means. I truly believe that Haitian women need to learn how to constructively be part of their society, become educated, and knowledgeable about how policies and laws impact them. I want them to understand that their voice matters and they can significantly contribute to what needs to be done to help our country come out of its impasse. However, they need to know their socio-economic rights so they can become empowered and improve their life so our country can also improve. (Interview with Lespinasse in July 2008)

In the early 1990s, Colette started the Support Group for Refugees and the Repatriated (GARR) to help address the various problems that Haitian deportees were encountering because no support system existed in Haiti to address them. Based on friendly cultural exchanges that she had maintained with various networks in the Dominican Republic and with the help of Oxfam International, Action Aid, other international and local NGOs, and Dominican religious organizations, Colette and other Haitians created a *centre d'hébergement* (housing center) to welcome the continuous flow of deportees from the Dominican Republic. Through GARR and with the support of both Haitians and Dominicans, Colette put in place a crisis management project to help reintegrate expulsed or repatriated families and individuals. Her organization provided the deportees with services that allowed them to secure proper legal documents and vital papers—which many did not have. Colette also provided them with food and shelter as well as basic health care for pregnant women, children, and elders. She also offered them language translation services and ensured that deported children went to school.

Contribution

Through GARR, Colette provides support to Haitians migrating to the Dominican Republic and to Haitian deportees at different Haitian border towns during intermittent expulsions from the Dominican Republic. For instance, she has created a welcome center in Belladères where Haitian refugees or migrant workers deported from the Dominican Republic receive a wide range of services and assistance upon arrival and until they get settled. These services are essential not only for immediate assistance but also as a conflict prevention measure. The flow of deportees often creates significant tension within border communities where many families and individuals often attempt to settle because of the absence of a better life in other parts of Haiti.

As a speaker at Radio Kiskeya in Haiti, she broadcasts programs to provide a forum for Haitians to talk and debate gender and women's issues, so that Haitian women become aware that they have rights and need to positively participate in the affairs of their country by ensuring that their voices are heard. In this respect, Colette has endeavored to help Haitian women because she believes that they have been disenfranchised, undermined, marginalized, and not given any value or recognition within Haiti's male-dominated society. She remains determined to help Haitian women understand the need to have a seat at the peace-building and governance tables and to seek opportunities to constructively contribute to sustainable social change in Haiti. Colette also helps Haitian women by providing them with training opportunities where they learn how to participate in positive social change and contribute their voices to the formulation of policies and laws impacting women, Haitians, and the country as a whole. Colette remains committed to raising the awareness of Haitian society as well as policy and lawmakers about the migration problems between the two countries.

In addition, Colette assists Dominicans coming to Haiti, as she wants to promote friendly exchanges between Haitians and Dominicans. She is completely committed to helping Dominicans and Haitians cultivate more harmonious relationships while they learn how to respect one another and work collaboratively and peacefully. She is determined to help create a safe space to allow both peoples to come together and enter into dialogues so they can learn how to deal with their deep-seated hatred, rancor, and acrimonious past. In this regard, Colette contemplates launching cultural and social activities at different border towns to ensure that Dominicans and Haitians learn together how to achieve strong mutual respect and human relations. To support her work, Colette has developed partnerships with other Dominican and Haitian nongovernmental organizations based on her belief that bilateral initiatives can help achieve sustainable stability on the island, while creating a window of opportunity for Dominicans and Haitians to help each side understand the other, given their interdependency. In this respect, Colette pointed out:

I have invested a great deal for the achievement of peace within the border communities so that both peoples along the border can have respect for each other, get rid of their mutual prejudice, work toward justice and respect toward each other. However, I strongly believe that the Dominican Republic alone cannot resolve the migrant problem and Haiti needs to be an active participant so both countries can find together a lasting solution that allows migrants to be treated respectfully and as human beings who have a right to aspire to a better future. (Interview with Lespinasse in July 2008)

As she strives to bring the two peoples together, Colette also participates in bilateral annual meetings between concerned citizens on both sides of the island during partnership gatherings that periodically bring together an equal number of Haitians and Dominicans in border towns or cities. During such encounters, both sides usually discuss ongoing bilateral projects while everyone contributes their ideas about what actions can be taken. Both sides also report on activities that have helped improve relations between border communities or address undocumented migration issues in border towns. Colette recounts her contributions as she has collaborated during bilateral meetings. For instance, she explains how she collaborated in summer 2008 in meetings where both Dominicans and Haitians designed and discussed a proposal for submission to both governments recommending the establishment of a joint commercial and trade accord. This accord will help formulate operating rules and policies pertinent to border markets and commercial interactions between Dominicans and Haitians and will benefit both countries while protecting the rights of Haitians who have been abused or extorted by border patrols.

Challenges

Haiti's realities remain difficult. Although social agents like Colette work tirelessly to lay the groundwork to help resolve the migration problems between the two countries, no sustained progress has been realized in regard to protecting undocumented Haitian migrants against the discrimination and inequality they meet in the Dominican Republic. Although Colette helps many deportees who would otherwise have no place to turn, she believes that more support from the two governments could help improve the migration situation and border trade issues that still persist. Currently, issues of vendor taxes related to border markets, or the formulation and implementation of a bilateral agreement to clearly specify the conditions under which commercial exchanges should take place in various border towns, have not been dealt with effectively by either government. The absence of bilateral agreements and pertinent regulations and a push for a fail-safe implementation system often leads border patrols to require the payment of market taxes more than once from Haitian vendors who go to the Dominican Republic on market days to cities such as Dajabón. Taking into account Haiti's rampant poverty and the plight of disenfranchised Haitians, Colette sees as her biggest challenge the difficulty of convincing many individuals to find other means to build a better future in Haiti instead of accepting the discriminatory ways to which they are often subjected in the Dominican Republic. With sadness, Colette points out that:

> No matter how many training programs I have put in place and implemented through GARR to convince Haitians who think about going to the Dominican Republic to work without any social benefit, they still risk facing discrimination and acrimony to cross the border to work in the Dominican Republic. My biggest challenge is to convince them that they can use their abilities in Haiti to build a better future while they learn how to voice their grievances constructively about the human rights and needs. Regardless of discussions and forums I have held with disenfranchised Haitians to help them have a vision for a better future, they still cannot fathom such life as they are in a constant mode of survival and live only for 'today'. (Interview with Lespinasse in July 2008)

Hope for the Future and Vision

Colette's vision for Haiti and the Dominican Republic is to find ways to help the two peoples become more responsible about living together peacefully while respecting one another. She also wants to see the two countries arrive at a mutually sustainable solution to the migration situation. She hopes that with the help of nongovernment organizations, both countries could bolster the willingness to address their age-old acrimony and rancor and to put an end to their hatred and race-based politics. As she looks toward the future, she reiterates:

My hope is for disadvantaged Haitians to have a life where they live and are treated as respected and deserving human beings and for the people of Haiti and the Dominican Republic to learn how to accept and respect their differences and use their interdependency to build a peaceful co-existence on the island that they will share against all odds. Furthermore, my vision is for Haitian women to know their rights. (Interview with Lespinasse in July 2008)

Thus, Colette believes that the achievement of peace within border communities, the realization of better relations between the two peoples, the eradication of their mutual prejudice, and the respective recognition of one another's rights are critical to the attainment of peace on Hispaniola. She envisages that disenfranchised Haitians will become inspired through the help that her organization and others like hers are providing and that they will learn how to claim their rights. She also dreams that, with sustained support, Haitian women can constructively participate in the affairs of the state and positively voice their views in order to become full participants in stabilizing Haiti.

Sonia Pierre

Sonia Pierre was born in a Dominican *batey* where she lived with her parents and others in a one-room portion of a barrack. Like many other children of Haitian descent born in the *bateys*, Sonia had no sustained access to social benefits. However, she was able to attend school until the age of 10, at which time she was sent to Villa Altagracia for further schooling thanks to good-hearted Dominican women who wanted to help her reach her potential. Sonia experienced deep-rooted racism, discrimination, and dehumanizing segregation for the first time at Villa Altagracia. She recalled being ostracized and demonized by Dominicans and was disheartened when her teachers told atrocious stories about Haitians. She would go home sad, confused, and lost, asking her mother why she was born of Haitian parents. Her mother responded that Haitians were proud people and that she should feel blessed that she had Haitian parents.

Witnessing many human rights violations being committed against Haitian migrants who came to the Dominican Republic as cane plantation laborers, at the age of 13 Sonia became an advocate for Haitian migrants who were being abused. She started her journey as a social change agent in her early teens by serving as a translator for *batey* Haitian migrants who did not know enough Spanish to voice their grievances about how they were being abused, and Sonia would translate for them during labor negotiations. As the *porte-parole* of the *bateys*, she was arrested during her teens for stepping up and being a voice for the disenfranchised. As she became older, relentlessly determined to serve *batey* communities, she joined various student social movements and became involved in social work for women. She became the protégé of older Dominican women who believed in the humanity of all human beings and who helped her receive an education while they trained and mentored her in how to be a constructive human rights advocate.

Motivation

Her motivation came from the realization that there was something wrong with the abject poverty within which Haitians lived in the *bateys* and/or were badly treated in the *bateys* by Dominican foremen. Also troubled about women who were giving birth to children who had no future and would likely end up in the *bateys* with the same fate as their mothers, Sonia was always deeply concerned about children who died due to the pervasive lack of hygiene and health care. She also wanted to help older Haitian migrants who spent their lives at the *bateys* but had to live as indigents in their old age, and ensure that children of Haitian descent born in the *bateys* learned about their Haitian ancestry. Among the many poignant recollections she shared when I interviewed her in July 2008, Sonia mentioned that:

> Even an early age, I thought there was something wrong with the abject poverty within which Haitians lived in the bateys and/or were badly treated in the bateys by Dominican foremen or chiefs. The batey chiefs would tell the migrants that their lives depended on them and sometimes would beat them up for no reason. When I left the batey where I was raised, I could not believe how other parts of my country, the Dominican Republic were different as I could not find the poor living that I was used too. However, as a child born in the Dominican Republic from Haitian parents, I was right away reminded that I was inferior and not considered as human. I could not believe how Haitian-Dominicans were ostracized by most Dominicans in the schools that I attended outside the bateys. I became very upset about all the bad things that Dominicans were saying about Haitians. I was shocked and confused because my mother always told me good things about Haiti. I even started to question why I was born Haitian. So, when I became a teen, I started joining social movements carried out by students and became involved in social work for women. (Interview with Pierre in July 2008)

Sonia became a full-fledged activist around the age of 13 when she decided to help Haitians who could not speak Spanish voice their grievances about their seasonal contracts as cane cutters on the *batey* plantations. She also started to help women who were being abused by men. Sonia was determined to make a difference because *batey* women, at the time of her childhood, needed men to sponsor them to get into the *bateys* and they had to accept harsh conditions just so they could have a better chance at improving their lives. Later, Sonia had the opportunity to become part of a cultural center founded by a Dominican sociologist and where she worked with children of Haitian descent born in the Dominican Republic and assisted *batey* women, children, and elders. Sonia believes that:

> What I lived through and witnessed during my childhood became my motivation to help others first started when I came to the realization that there was something wrong in terms of how people in the bateys were being treated. Moreover, seeing the devastating and abusive conditions of batey women, who were the backbone of the bateys, along with other children of Haitian descent, in the 1990s, along with others, I started the Movement of Dominican-Haitian Women (MUDHA) to help and serve disenfranchised women and other batey community members. (Interview with Pierre in July 2008)

Contribution

During her teen years, in addition to serving as the translator for male Haitian migrants who wanted to claim their rights for better living conditions as cane cutters, Sonia decided to also help *batey* women, who were often depressed. When those women arrived at the *bateys* from Haiti, they thought that they would find a better life in the Dominican Republic. Instead, they quickly found out that life was harder than when they were in Haiti because, in addition to the grueling plantation work, they were abused by men. When she realized that some husbands were forcing their wives to be with other men, Sonia decided to stay close to these women thinking she could protect them. Often she ended up taking them to the hospital because their husbands or partners would beat them. She also helped women and children during trauma workshops in which they learned how to deal with abuses sustained from their husbands, partners, or fathers.

As the director of MUDHA and a servant-transformational leader, with the support of and in collaboration with many Dominicans, Sonia has helped *batey* women become empowered by creating opportunities for them to have access to literacy, small businesses, and vocational training. Building such capacity opens up economic outlets for these women and provides them with independence. With the support of Dominican doctors, psychologists, lawyers, and sociologists, Sonia has found opportunities for children of Haitian descent to attend the university and learn about human rights so they can constructively contribute to the Dominican society. With the assistance of Dominican and international doctors and professionals of Haitian descent born in the Dominican Republic, she has instituted AIDS awareness and HIV-care programs. She has provided sexually transmitted disease prevention training sessions to the youth and gender violence mitigation workshops to both men and women.

Sonia assists Haitian descendents with legal issues related to their citizenship and vital legal identity papers, because the Dominican Republic has decided in the last decade that children born of undocumented Haitian parents, who migrated from Haiti to work on Dominican cane plantations, could not be Dominican citizens. This has created significant demand for MUDHA services. Sonia has managed to assist Haitians in the *bateys* with support from the Pan American Development Foundation, an affiliate of the Organization of American States, organizations in Great Britain and the United States, universities in Puerto Rico, and nongovernmental organizations in Haiti, the Dominican Republic, and other countries.

Challenges

The challenges to Sonia's work are enormous. Nationalist Dominicans have not understood her vision that children of Haitian descent born in the Dominican Republic should have the opportunity to reach their potential so they, too, could contribute positively to the country. There are many court struggles related to citizenship issues of children of Haitian descent born in the Dominican Republic. MUDHA's efforts are significantly constrained, because Sonia does not have sufficient funding to help older migrants and disenfranchised *batey* Haitians who live near poverty level.

MUDHA remains cautious about accepting funding from politically based sources in order to preserve its independence and protect its vulnerability as a humanitarian and advocacy organization that strives to help disenfranchised Haitians in a country where discriminatory practices and race politics against Haitians are prevalent. Furthermore, since MUDHA's employees are predominantly Dominican, Sonia has to continuously ensure that they understand MUDHA's goals and objectives, which aim to help empower children of Haitian descent so they can constructively endorse their responsibility to the country. According to Sonia, her contribution to constructive social advocacy encompasses various aspects as she recalls that:

> Through MUDHA, I work with other local, regional, and international organizations and groups to build schools, and provide education, healthcare, psychological service to deal with depression, family planning, housing, legal counseling, assistance to get sick people to the hospital, and help reduce illiteracy in batey communities. Such efforts are rooted in my determination to help ensure that Haitiano-Dominicans have the education and a level of awareness that help them live as proud and empowered people although they are being ostracized in their own country. In this context, I want to help form well-educated professionals who have the sound knowledge that they need so they can constructively contribute to their country as Dominicans. Now I am helping many migrants who have been here for many years and whose citizenships are being revoked based on the rationale that the DR made a mistake by awarding them citizenship. When batey children (or Haitiano-Dominicans) become educated they can have a better hope to improve their lives, and help the government understand that they are not the Haitian problem. (Interview with Pierre in July 2008)

Hope for the Future and Vision

As a servant-transformational leader, Sonia envisions a better future for Haitian descendants in the Dominican Republic, with sustained support of *batey* women's education and the establishment of gender-based violence prevention programs to help both men and women. She wants to implement programs that help people in the *bateys* not only with employment, education, and health care but also to provide them with psychological counseling, feminine care, and geriatric assistance. She also desires to put in place programs to help mothers understand that they cannot favor boys over girls and that they need to change their mindset to encourage both boys and girls to become educated and respected individuals. Furthermore, she plans to help children of Haitian descent born in the Dominican Republic learn how to be civic minded and contribute to the Dominican Republic while also learning to be proud of their Haitian heritage. When asked how she sees the future, Sonia envisages that:

> I want to continue to promote the education of women in the bateys; change how they are treated; and help mothers understand that they

cannot favor boys to girls and they needed to change their mindset to push both as human beings who have God-given potentials. I also want to ensure that Haitiano-Dominicans maintain their Dominican culture; and be proud of their Haitian origin against all odds. For me, this is very important because their origin is part of their identity. Furthermore, my vision is to continue to help build positively strong Haitiano-Dominican communities so community members can help the country develop and not to become a burden for the Dominican Republic. I want to have programs that can help people in the bateys not only with jobs and schools and healthcare but also emotionally. I want women to have access to feminine care and older people to geriatric care. I envision vibrant and well-developed Haitiano-Dominican communities where members are fully accepted by the country. (Interview with Pierre in July 2008)

Thus, Sonia wants to ensure that children of Haitian descent learn how to deal positively with the discrimination, ostracization, and rancor from nationalist Dominicans, while learning not to despise them regardless of their mistreatment. She is looking for effective ways to sensitize the Dominican diaspora about the plight of migrant Haitians in the Dominican Republic, given that they have also been migrants and understand the trauma of those who are being ostracized and discriminated against. One of Sonia's biggest dreams is to create a library where youth can regularly hold cultural discussions about their ancestry or meet to analyze a wide range of educational books about different topics.

The Two Caribbean Women's Efforts from a Leadership Standpoint

At times, individuals emerge as leaders to help others deal with a conflict or a social issue resulting from competing interests, values, and cultures and deep-rooted needs or identity issues. In regard to these two Caribbean women, although their goals and objectives are marginally different, that share a commonality: They want to help disenfranchised Haitian migrants. They have fashioned their interventions to espouse different platforms and viewpoints, which range from assistance with basic necessities such as food, shelter, and physical security to being the voice of the migrants while advocating on their behalf for a better life. Such interventions have the potential to help the disenfranchised achieve a level of confidence so they can transform their lives through hard work while feeling empowered to positively influence their own environment, society, and even country.

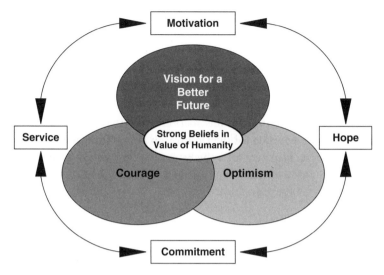

© Framework developed by Yves-Renée Jennings August 2008

Figure 15.1 Framework for Servant-Transformational Leadership Profile

As illustrated in Figure 15.1, the two Caribbean women's core values of motivation, commitment, hope, and service, anchored by strong beliefs in the value of humanity, have reinforced their courage, visions for a better future, and optimism as reflected in their efforts to influence the transformation of their respective countries' institutional systems as well as the personal transformation of the disadvantaged. Their advocacy, based on bilateral principles, for the formulation and implementation of equitable and effective migration policies in Haiti and the Dominican Republic to allow Haitians in that country to live with dignity—as residents, citizens, or seasonal workers—attests to their constructive leadership toward social change. Such leadership, if supported by both governments, could help establish mutually acceptable agreements that benefit their respective territorial stability and human security at different societal levels, while building a foundation to help both peoples overcome their old-age rancor and acrimony.

The Two Caribbean Women's Contribution as Servant-Transformational Leaders

These two Caribbean women leaders' determination to serve and inspire others through their contribution to constructive social change offers a firsthand view of their efforts to help communities at the grassroots level, while working with other civil society organizations to come up with policy recommendations that help both governments achieve stability on the island. Their commitment, motivation, vision, and courage have led to various positive social actions that have benefited the disenfranchised while effectively contributing to conflict prevention by helping to overcome the propensity for violence based on their old-age mutual rancor and antagonism. As servant-transformational leaders, these two women have helped others grow as individuals, while making them aware of their potential to become autonomous and contributing members of their society, thus giving them some hope for a better future.

In addition, they have also helped inform their respective societies, the policy makers and lawmakers involved in various sociostructural issues, in the hope that their actions will positively transform institutions while creating an empowering environment for the disadvantaged. Because of their strong beliefs, both leaders envisage a future where Haitian migrants can go to the Dominican Republic, under the auspices of bilateral agreements effectively implemented by both governments, and where children of Haitian descent born in the Dominican Republic can have their human rights respected and live with dignity and respect while their basic human needs are met. In addition, these tireless advocates yearn for an environment where both people will learn to accept one another's cultural and racial identities while they work together at different levels to develop and maintain the harmonious relationships needed to build a better future on the island of Hispaniola.

The willingness of these two Caribbean leaders to resolutely provide sustained assistance to the disenfranchised, while inspiring them to achieve the type of transformation that will allow them to become self-sufficient and plan for a better future, conforms to John Paul Lederach's (1997) view that transformation is a long-term engagement. As civil society leaders, these two women are helping at both the micro and the macro level. At the micro level, because of their strong beliefs and optimism, they have courageously given voice to the disenfranchised; at the macro level they have endeavored to influence both the Dominican and the Haitian governments toward constructive social change.

Within this context, this chapter has brought to light some of the work of two Caribbean women civil society leaders and featured their contributions to social change through human rights advocacy. These two women's stories illustrate how they emerged as servant-transformational leaders, despite the prevalent traditional, cultural, and patriarchal boundaries that exist in the Caribbean, to become social change agents. Their efforts to help address short-term human needs and long-term transformational needs at the institutional, group, and individual level can help promote better relationships between the two peoples and resolve and prevent violent conflicts between them.

Their efforts have yet to result in the enactment of laws or the formulation and implementation of policies that would recognize and help fulfill the human rights and basic human needs of the isenfranchised Haitians and Haitian descendants living in the Dominican Republic. Nevertheless, they have raised the awareness of both countries about the critical social issues that have significantly impacted the potential for peaceful relationships between the two peoples, in spite of the ontroversies that have resulted from their advocacy. Through their work and motivation, they have pointed out that, in order for the island to achieve stability, peace, and economic growth that can benefit both countries in light of their interdependence, Haiti and the Dominican Republic need to work together.

Their respective cooperation and partnership can help citizens of both countries overcome their contentious past and the race-based politics and mutual mistrust that have perpetuated rancor, hatred, discrimination, prejudice, and tension. In this respect, this chapter implicitly underscores that, without strong and proactive human rights advocacy toward constructive social change and consistent conflict prevention and resolution efforts, it is almost impossible for the Dominican Republic and Haiti to put an end to their perennial race politics and old-age antagonism. Nor is it possible without such advocacy for the people of these two countries to address their increasing mutual rancor and hatred, which otherwise can potentially lead to large-scale violence and even genocide in the Dominican Republic and Dominican-Haitian border towns.

Moving Forward

According to Colette, in the face of the significant disastrous impact of the earthquake on Haiti and its people, the Dominican Republic's demonstration of solidarity and support toward the victims and its Haitian neighbor holds the promise that this tragedy might have helped Dominicans realize that both their peoples share the same destiny on the island of Hispaniola. When I talked again to Colette after the 2010 earthquake, she stressed that this latest manifestation of how Dominicans helped (from the heart) their neighbors has given her hope that the two peoples one day will find ways to address their old-age antagonisms and mutual hatred and live in harmony while collaborating to protect Hispaniola and learn how to respect one another despite their differences.

During telephone conversations with Colette and Sonia after the 2010 Haiti earthquake, she pointed out the two peoples of Hispaniola have shown that they have the potential to come together and work for their common good, given the sign of solidarity demonstrated in the aftermath of the seismic disaster. Although tragic, the natural disaster that devastated Haiti in January 2010 seems to show that the two people (who are often referred to as two wings of the same bird) have become aware that their respective safety and security interrelate. Such an awareness provides unprecedented opportunity that human rights advocates like Colette and Sonia have been working toward.

Implications for the Field of Conflict Analysis and Resolution

Although many perceive that conflict resolution practitioners and human rights advocates see issues that impact the welfare of the individual through different lenses or employ dissimilar intervention strategies, both sides have the same basic goals. As these two women leaders' work illustrates, there are numerous opportunities for conflict practitioners to partner with human rights advocates to bring about constructive social change. For instance, in the case of the Dominican-Haitian migration situation, conflict practitioners could help these human rights advocates create a safe environment where opposing parties could enter into a dialogue about their issues. Furthermore, they could collaborate to carry out problem-solving processes to help Dominicans and Haitians learn to address their issues constructively.

They could also work together to help community leaders in Dominican-Haitian border towns and the Dominican capital of Santo Domingo design and develop identity-based programs that can help both peoples learn about one another as human beings. As these few examples show, despite their differing orientation, the work of both human rights advocates and conflict practitioners are complementary because both want to have all human beings' basic needs fulfilled and their rights met.

As stated in its series Human Rights Dialogue, the Carnegie Foundation believes that "Human rights advocates and conflict resolution specialists share a common aim—building stable societies based on mutual respect and the rule of law—and often work on the same conflicts, addressing closely related issues" (1). Therefore, the work of human rights advocates such as Colette and Sonia offer numerous opportunities for partnership with conflict resolution practitioners, particularly in regard to helping the communities they respectively work with learn how to constructively come together to voice their own grievances in ways that lead to positive social transformation. That social transformation, in turn, will allow them to have the same rights as other segments of their societies.

Keywords

advocacy, advocates, basic human needs, Caribbean region, commitment, conflict analysis and resolution, courage, dignity, discrimination, disenfranchised, Dominican Republic, Haiti, hope, respect, servant-transformational leader, service, social change, social change agents, social transformation, migration, motivation

Discussion Questions

1. What approach would you adopt to partner with Colette Lespinasse to develop a dialogue between Haitian and the Dominican officials on how to arrive at a mutually sustainable solution to the migration situation?
2. How would you help Sonia Pierre develop a training program to help Haitian-Dominican mothers understand that they cannot favor boys over girls?
3. What three main points would you make in a paper that argues that Haitian children born in the Dominican Republic should be considered as Dominican citizens, and how would you support such argument?

References

Burns, J.M. 1978. *Leadership*. New York: Harper & Row, p. 20.

Carnegie Foundation. 2002. "Introduction: Integrating Human Rights and Peace Work, Voice of Ethics for International Policy." *Human Rights Dialogues (1994–2005)*, Series 2, No. 7 (Winter 2002): 1–4. Available at http://www/cceia.org/resources/publications/dialogue/02_07articles/242.html.

Farling, M.L., Stone, A.G., and Winston, B.E. 1999. "Servant Leadership: Setting the Stage for Empirical Research." *The Journal of Leadership Studies*, 6, 49–72.

Ferguson, James. 2003. "Migration in the Caribbean: Haiti, the Dominican Republic and Beyond." Minority Rights Group International, pp. 1–44. Available at http://www.oas.org/atip/Regional%20Reports/MigrationintheCaribbean.pdf.

Greenleaf, R.K. 1977. *Servant Leadership*. Mahwah, N.J.: Paulist Press.

Greenleaf, R.K., Beazley, H., Beggs, J. and Spears, L.C. 2003. *The Servant Leader Within: A Transformative Path*. Mahwah, N.J.: Paulist Press, pp. 15–16.

Greenleaf, R.K., Spears, L.C., and Covey, S.R. 2002. *Servant Leadership: A Journey into the Nature of Legitimate Power and Greatness*. Mahwah, N.J.: Paulist Press, pp. 13–14.

Greenleaf, R.K., Spears, L.C., and Vaill, P.B. 1998. *The Power of the Servant Leader*. San Francisco: Berrett-Koehler Publishers, Inc., pp. 3–16.

Hunt, Swanee. 2008. Statement by Ambassador Swanee Hunt Chair, Initiative for Inclusive Security US House Committee on Foreign Affairs, Subcommittee on International Organizations, Human Rights, and Oversight on May 15, 2008, 1. Available at http://foreignaffairs.house.gov/110/hun051508.htm.

Jennings, Yves-Renée. 2008a. Interviews with Sonia, MUDHA (Movement of Dominican-Haitian Women), July 21, Santo Domingo, Republic Dominican, West Indies.

Jennings, Yves-Renée. 2008b. Interviews with Colette Lespinasse, GARR (Support Group for Refugees and the Repatriated), July 24, 2008, Port-au-Prince, Haiti, West Indies.

Kuzmenko, Tatiana N., Smith, Brien N. and Ray V. Montagno. 2004. "Transformational and Servant Leadership: Content and Contextual Comparisons." *Journal of Leadership and Organizational Studies*, 10(4), 1–12.

Lamson, Sara. 2007. *The Bitter for the Sweet*. UC Berkeley, Center for Latin American Studies, pp. 1–3. Available at http://socrates.berkeley.edu:7001/Publications/newsletter/ Fall2007/pdf/BRLAS Fall2007-PriceofSugar-standard.pdf.

Lederach, J. P. 1997. *Building Peace: Sustainable Reconciliation in Divided Societies*. US Institute of Peace.

Mikula, Maja (ed.). 2005. *Women, Activism and Social Change: Stretching Boundaries*. Routledge Research in Gender and Society. New York: Routledge/Taylor and Francis.

Purdue, D. 2001. "Neighbourhood Governance: 'Leadership Trust and Social Capital.'" *Urban Studies*, 38(12), 2211–24. Available at http://usj.sagepub.com/cgi/content/abstract/38/12/2211.

Russell, R.F. and A.G. Stone. 2002. "A Review of Servant Leadership Attributes: Developing a Researchable Model." *Leadership & Organization Development Journal*, 23(3), 145–57.

Sagas, E. 1994. "An Apparent Contradiction? Popular Perception of Haiti and the Foreign Policy of the Dominican Republic." Paper presented at the Sixth Annual Conference of the Haitian Studies Association, Boston, MA, Department of Latin American and Puerto Rican Studies, Lehman College, The City University of New York. Available at http://www.windowsonhaiti.com/esagas2.shtml.

Spears, L. C. 2002. "Tracing the Past, Present, and Future of Servant-Leadership," in *Focus On Leadership: Servant-leadership for the Twenty-first Century* (pp. 1–10). New York: John Wiley & Sons.

SECTION V

Conclusion

CHAPTER SIXTEEN

Challenging the Dominant Narrative

Sandra I. Cheldelin and Maneshka Eliatamby

Introduction

There are several misconceptions about women's roles and behavior during times of conflict, violence, war, and peace building. One of the common stories about conflict and violence is that women, more than men, are the victims. While women and children are often adversely affected during times of war and natural disaster, this argument discounts two major realities that hold true in such situations; first, that men are spared of victimhood and, secondly, that women's roles are limited to that of the victim.

Another misconception about women is that they are best suited for peacemaking—some believe that women have an inherent capacity to work collaboratively and bring parties that are in conflict together in dialogue with each other. Moreover, Manchanda (2010) goes further and in stating that "the flat assumption that women are for peace (is) because they are the worst sufferers in conflict." While this book acknowledges the truth behind these claims, from our own experiences in the fields of peace building and development, we know that this is not the entire truth—not the whole story. Rita Manchanda quotes Cynthia Cockburn as stating that "if women have a distinctive angle in peace, it is not due to women being nurturing. It seems more to do with knowing oppression when we see it" (Manchanda 2001, 17). Manchanda argues that women's experiences of being excluded and "inferiorized" gives them special insight into the root causes of conflict. In many cultures, women's socialization places them in inferior positions to their male counterparts. It is this disadvantaged vantage point that has shaped women's ontology and epistemology for millennia. This gender-specific paradigm has also given them the insight and ability to understand violent structures and the root causes of violence and to take actions to change the structures that give birth to and foster violence. Manchanda claims that women do not always delineate between domestic and public/political structures of violence and "are more likely to see a continuum of violence, because they experience the connected forms of domestic and political violence that stretches from the home, to the street to the battlefield" (Manchanda 2001, 17).

Popular rhetoric also often ignores how women's lives change as a result of war and traumatic experiences and how they forge strategies to survive these situations. Rarely do we hear stories of women that have demonstrated their capacities for agency—voice, action, retaliation, and intervention—in times of conflict and post-conflict reconstruction and how their adoption of new roles transforms gender dynamics in the societies from which they come.

Reflecting on our own work in the academy and in the field, we have come to recognize that women play a myriad of roles in the face of war and peace, in violence and intervention, in competition and collaboration—and that their roles are hardly monolithic. The multiplicity of women's roles is too often ignored both in academic teaching and research, as well as in practice. Through the stories of women's experiences in wartime and as part of peace building, we have attempted to fill this void, shed light on this multiplicity, and force acknowledgment of the variety of roles women play.

The chapters reveal that women are not always innocent bystanders in times of conflict—neither are their voices silenced in post-conflict times. This multiplicity of roles is illustrated in the themes that emerged from the cases in this book. Five themes stand out as most important: (1) there is a strong connection between violence and gendered identity, (2) gendered identities are influenced by social movements, (3) stopping violence depends on using social movement networks committed to sustainable peace, (4) peace requires access to broad-based educational opportunities, and (5) successful post-conflict reconstruction requires a commitment to gender-based mainstreaming and social justice issues. The stories presented in this book are evidence that women have successfully navigated the labyrinth of experiencing and making war and calling for, creating, and sustaining peace.

Women Waging War

Common discourse suggests that war is gendered. Men are the dominant players, and women are either the victims or the innocent bystanders. Francis Fukuyama even goes as far as stating that "males are genetically predisposed to violence" (Bouta et al. 2005, 11). Despite these mainstream views of gendered roles in violence and war, Bouta et al. (2005, 11), found that females were active participants in fighting forces and combat in 55 different conflicts. Mazurna and Carlson's review of women in the Sierra Leone conflict found that women's involvement in violence was a rather complex phenomenon, and that while they were often "captives and dependents... they were also involved in planning and executing the war" (Mazurana and Carlson 2004).Our book has explicated six such cases: Chechnya, Eritrea, Liberia, Nepal, Sierra Leone, and Sri Lanka.

Clearly, women do not always bear nurturing and nonviolent qualities in the face of war and peace. In such extreme cases as the Chechnyan and Sri Lankan female suicide terrorists, women were simultaneously victims and perpetrators, trapped in men's tactics of war. Strapping on explosives—becoming human bombs—in the name of their country or their group allowed them to redefine their gender role in society. When violence is experienced as a result of actions by the state, or when a country is under the control of a foreign power, it helps the propaganda efforts to recruit female suicide bombers. When there is control of a country by a foreign power, there will be increased cases of suicide terrorism, and the role of women in them will grow. One reason is the "shock effect" grounded in gendered stereotypes. Female-based aggression and violence violates cultural assumptions about women as weak and vulnerable, recasting them as violent, murderous, and destructive.

This tactic is especially enticing to women as a way to redefine who they are in society. In the chapters "Fighting for Emancipation" and "Dying for Equality," we see how women chose violence as a means of negotiating not only their wartime situation but their position in society as a whole. Women witness the elite status and privileges afforded to females in suicide cadres willing to carry out their missions. These women achieve a greater sense of equality with men and are granted heroine status with female militants. This is in stark contrast to their previous statuses and inequalities. In her chapter titled "Girls with Guns," Patricia Maulden states that "[I]n both Sierra Leone and Liberia the possession of an AK-47 or in some cases a machete produced an instant realignment of the traditional power structure" (Chapter 5). This appears to be the case in numerous other instances as well. In Turshen and Twagiramariya's book *What Women Do in Wartime*, authors Goldblatt and Meintjes write on women's experiences in South Africa and state that "[w]ar also breaks down the patriarchal structures of society that confine and degrade women. In the very breakdown of morals, traditions, customs, and community, war also opens up and creates new beginnings" (Turshen 1998, 20).

Various liberation and revolutionary movements have included women's rights and equality for men and women in their programs for political change (Manchanda 2001, 12–13). While these chapters shed light on glimmers of hope during dark times of war—situations sometimes providing unexpected opportunities for women to challenge the patriarchal structures that they come from—these wartime gains unfortunately do not necessarily translate into women's emancipation during post-conflict and peace times. Liberation achieved in battle is not always sustainable, and women are often required to return to prewar social norms. However, this concept is difficult to comprehend at the point when the AK-47 one is holding has begun to earn the respect of males on the battlefield and women begin to experience more freedom and emancipation than they ever had prior to taking up arms. Additionally, we recognize that while authors such as Manchanda (2010) have begun researching and writing on how women negotiate post-conflict and postwar situations, we recognize that this is an area that is still under-researched and undertheorized.

Gendered Identity and Social Movements

Women-led social movements are different from those that are led by men. Women's experiences give them a sense of agency and gender consciousness. They believe that, as a group, they can make gender-specific demands. The many examples of women's movements in this book provide insight into how they are organized, how they work, and how they are sustained. What seems most apparent is that women conceptualize of and organize social movements differently. This is particularly evident in Zimbabwe, where Women of Zimbabwe Arize (WOZA) has maintained a strong grassroots base and has created a broad-based network of support. Members used their role as mothers to champion their cause. The leaders set ambitious but relevant goals and grounded their work in traditional notions of femininity.

By seeking to address both the practical and strategic gendered needs of men and women, WOZA members were able to capture the attention of the entire community. They presented themselves as mothers, sisters, and women—those most affected in postwar cleanup—and they engaged in a Standup for Your Child movement. Women took their children to the streets, encouraged other women to vote during the March 2008 elections, claimed their vote as a mark against the government's inefficiency and injustice, and declared their role to be protectors of the next generation's inheritance.

Often members of women's movements established a human rights narrative. Connecting women's issues with human rights forced the personal to be political and the private domain (usually female) to be considered in the public sphere of influence, making women and children's issues relevant and worthy of attention. These women created coalitions of support among civil society groups, using media as a tool for activism and a conduit for raising awareness. They exposed oppression, brutality, and harassment by the police; pressured the state to observe the rule of law; and demanded women's rights to justice and fair trials. Framing their narrative as human rights issues provided them a shared vision and therefore made it easier to mobilize supporters and recruit sympathizers, locally and globally—some of these movements got the support of such organizations as Amnesty International, Human Rights Watch, and Women Human Rights Defenders. These women-led social movements are impressive examples of navigating the labyrinth by embracing and expanding on gendered identity.

Women Waging Peace

Stopping the war and making the transition to a state of peace—the public domain—is almost always limited to men. Women are seldom players in stopping war and ending conflict. During Sri Lanka's cease-fire negotiations conducted in the early 2000s, while the country had a female president and while women actively participated as combatants on behalf of the LTTE, there were no women at the negotiating table (the LTTE later included the female heads of the organization's political wing in one of the subcommittees overseeing an aspect of the negotiations). It was clearly the responsibility of both parties to the conflict, the Sri Lankan government and the LTTE as well as the negotiating teams made up of the Norwegian and Japanese governments, to ensure the inclusion of women, who according to statistics, makeup nearly 51 percent of the country's population. The stories of women's exclusion from these negotiations at the peace table are not endemic to Sri Lanka alone. This same story repeats itself in Nepal, Uganda, Liberia, Sierra Leone, and Guatemala, to name a few. Even in those cases where women have been included, their participation is often limited and minimized.

It is clear that steps toward including women at the negotiating table are greatly needed. This certainly was the vision and intention behind the United Nations Security Council Resolutions 1325 and its subsequent Resolution 1820, which are discussed later in this chapter.

Social Networks Committed to Sustainable Peace

Several cases presented demonstrate ways women's social networks made a commitment to peace as their dominant narrative. They employed numerous activities: (1) encouraged mobilization of women across societal divides, (2) supported and assisted women in building sustainable and effective net-working mechanisms, (3) recognized the needs of local communities and promoted local initiatives, (4) took into consideration the cultural aspect of societies where the movement was developing, (5) provided support through capacity-building initiatives (many were funded and trained by international as well as domestic organizations), and (6) made long-term commitments to support the growth and development of women.

While a woman's movement may initiate a peace process, sustainable peace ultimately requires a societal shift from hostility toward and disregard of half of its population to one of partnership and respect. Unfortunately, achieving peace becomes a public domain of work, and women are usually left out, as previously noted. Rwanda however, appears to be a success story. Its citizens have been able to sustain peace in its postgenocide war. They initiated a healing and reconciliation process—HAGURUKA, detailed in Uwineza and Brown's chapter titled "Engendering Recovery" (Chapter 9). When craft-making training programs were offered, the organizers focused attention on the purpose of the training—creating economic opportunities for women and their families—and not on the different backgrounds of the attendees. In this case, both Hutu and Tutsi women learned to make market-able crafts. In the evenings, however, trainees discussed various other topics, sometimes led by outside experts, about relationships, HIV/AIDS, reconcili-ation experiences, and the like. These trainings became a venue for women's economic empowerment and trauma healing.

This highlights that sustainable peace movements must embrace gender as an integrated strategy so that women are better prepared and empowered to lead their families in recovery. Women must participate in both social and economic revitalization. Ambassador Swanee Hunt identifies at least ten other indicators of progress in her successful network of peace. The range of activities reflected in her movement is broad and comprehensive and could be viewed as benchmarks for other successful programmatic efforts: policy makers speak regularly about the importance of women's involvement; net-work members have access to the most powerful government officials in the world; women leaders address key organizations such as the United Nations, the US Congress, the World Bank, and the European Union; network leaders are regularly sought after to present and discuss their issues; publications and dissemination efforts are often referenced; international conferences and organizations seek out leaders to advise; and documentary filmmak-ers and other media sources want to tell their stories. Creating partnerships with other organizations, human rights advocates, and conflict resolution specialists is critical to build stable communities based on mutual respect and the rule of law.

Post-Conflict Programs and Education

There are a number of lessons about post-conflict programming and the critical role of education in these chapters. An important one focuses on the reintegration of women and child soldiers and ways programmatic intentions that address boys' needs are different from the needs of girls. Youth Demobilization, Disarmament, Rehabilitation, and Reintegration (DDRR) programs in West Africa reflect a belief that boys and danger are linked, and therefore it is essential to move quickly to mitigate potential crises. That is, large numbers of male youth wandering aimlessly through their communities with little to do are likely to engage in violence. The danger element is informed by the male's behavior as a child soldier who killed or traumatized members of their own families and community members. Unfortunately girls are left out of programmatic offerings—based on the gendered assumption they were victims or that they are not, by nature, dangerous or a threat to reengage violence. As a result, these girls become further marginalized, as they are already without support from former wartime husbands and are not welcome in their families and communities. Some become violent and engage in girl-gang-related activities. The more than 17,000 girls and women who were engaged in the war in Liberia are a case in point.

This only highlights the essential task of providing educational opportunities to young women too. Teaching job skills to girls allows them a path out of poverty and powerlessness. So, too, do women need to learn of their legal rights. As noted in several situations, conflating Islamic and patriarchal values, especially in rural areas of some Islamic countries, can be particularly troubling. Women's rights groups find it challenging to separate the cultural issues from the religious ones, especially when there are parallel legal systems complicating women's access to justice. Women have demonstrated that awareness-raising programs through media campaigns are useful in informing women of their rights and ways to access their legal systems.

Support should be given to help women educate one another. The regional alliances that were formed in the women's movements in Pakistan, Egypt, and Turkey provide inspiration and offer success stories for other developing and neighboring states. As technology becomes more available, women's rights groups can access one another within their communities and countries as well as in regional and international arenas.

Our experiences in the field have also shed light on the fact that post-conflict training and education needs to go beyond the traditional DDRR processes, especially where women and girls have actively participated in warfare. Many of the traditional societies that these girls and women come from stigmatize and shun those returning from combat, especially the females who are considered to have violated social norms. For examples, many women who attempted to return to their homes in Eritrea were not welcome by their families and villages and were forced to create "female-only villages." Girls attempting to return to their schools in Sri Lanka's Eastern Province were ostracized even by their teachers—some of them gave up hope of proper reintegration and education. It is clear that the formal DDRR processes must also include training and education for the local populations these women and girls are returning to.

Mainstreaming, Social Justice, and Human Security

After years of violence and conflict, it is clear that retuning communities and societies to peace and prosperity requires intentional and well-supported mainstreaming efforts. These efforts must involve all stakeholders of peace, especially women, as they are the group most invested in family and community stability and most able to reweave torn communities—essential to the psychological, social, and economic welfare of their societies. Allowing women access to all levels of decision making forces governments to recognize the need for institutional and legal reform. It cannot be limited to numerical representation in leadership positions of government. Gender mainstreaming in other critical sectors such as education, business, security, and military is the only way of ensuring sustainability for their achievements.

The international legal system has set the stage to demand equal justice for women and men, especially through the passage of UN Security Council Resolutions 1325 and 1820 that are focused on gender mainstreaming. UN Security Council Resolution 1325, which was adopted in October 2000, calls for the implementation of gender perspectives in post-conflict reconstruction, focusing on the needs of women and girls during repatriation, resettlement, rehabilitation, and reintegration. This legislation was followed by UN Security Council Resolution 1820 in June 2008—in direct response to loopholes in UN Security Council Resolution 1325 pertaining to sexual violence prevention and response. UN SCR 1820 views sexual violence now as "unacceptable and preventable" and not merely as an inevitable feature of conflict—the previously dominant narrative. However, it should be noted that this legislation, too, is limited to the discussion of sexual violence against civilians during and in the aftermath of armed conflict—it does not include acts of sexual violence committed before the start of armed conflict.

The efficacy of these two resolutions is still to be determined. Rwanda and Liberia are often cited as success stories where women have been included both in negotiations for peace as well as in post-conflict governance. Liberia boasts Africa's first female president, Ellen Johnson Sirleaf, while Rwanda's parliament is made up of more than 51 percent women. While both of these cases indicate tremendous leaps toward achieving equal participation in government, it is still to be determined whether women holding leadership positions indicates and translates into women's empowerment at the grassroots and civil society levels. In 1960, Ceylon (now Sri Lanka) became the first country to have a woman elected as its leader, and India, Pakistan, and Bangladesh have elected women to the highest level of leadership since. However, in all of these cases, the election of a female head of state has not translated to women's emancipation at the grassroots level. Manchanda (2010, 1), in an article titled "Nepali Women Seize the Political Dawn," states that, while the new constitution of Nepal requires women's participation at the local and national governmental levels, in reality, much of the decision making in the country takes place among men behind closed doors. This begs the question, Have egalitarian legislations adopted by these countries' new constitutions changed women's daily lives? While it is beyond the scope of this book to evaluate the efficacy of UN Resolutions 1325 and 1820 from this standpoint, we recognize the need for such research.

While such legislations have set the stage to demand equal rights through the implementation of international laws, it is time for leaders around the world to be institutionally accountable in regard to gender crimes, providing gender equality in such social structures as education and health care and insisting on equality in social and political settings. We must work toward recognition of victims as people and not stigmatized cultural symbols and establish programs wherein women are valued beyond their reproductive capabilities. In societies where female gender identity has been limited to childbearing and rearing and where qualities gendered as "feminine" are given lower status, women likely will be the victims of violence. During wartime, when women are the victims of rape and torture, too often they are blamed for the violence. For real change to occur and be sustainable, the consequences of such violence need to be reframed and recontextualized so that women are not held responsible for their plight. Not being stigmatized would go a long way toward restoring a sense of dignity and rebuilding individual and community identity.

Again, the case of Rwanda provides an example where local laws changed the lives of the local population. Formed in 1991, HAGURUKA initially focused on the rights of women and children in Rwandan society. They began by assessing the impact of mass violence on women—many of whom were widows or whose husbands were imprisoned. One of the main issues focused on was the loss of control of family property to male relatives. However, as a result of the genocide and the lack of a functioning legal system, the organizations became involved in emergency assistance. In 1996, HAGURUKA returned its focus to its original mission, which led to the enactment of new laws pertaining to family property. The network's leadership and governance training framed gender as an issue for national development. They avoided a so-called feminist struggle with men and instead endeavored to involve men in their fight. While debating proposed bills of law to protect women's rights in parliament, leaders framed women in the affirmative as "our mothers, sisters and wives." This helped men understand the importance of supporting such bills rather than feeling confronted with disempowerment. The lesson here is not to alienate men but instead to incorporate them in gender integration efforts.

Imagining the Unimaginable

The cases we present in this book where women have participated in conflict and where they have been agents of peace clearly show how their gendered social roles are transformed as a result of trauma and violence. They have broken numerous societal barriers and changed their gendered roles and cultures. These women give the field of peace building the hope that there is room for forgiveness and positive transformation even in the most protracted conflicts. Women's stories of survival and hope also emerge in less violent, but equally troubling environments. This is reflected in the story of the Gulf of Mexico's experiences with Hurricane Katrina and the BP oil spill, and in the crime-ridden inner city of Baltimore, Maryland.

It is time to imagine what has historically been the unimaginable. For example, one way to address Schneider's (2008, 994) claim that it is particularly cruel to target women, especially when they are most often not the initial instigators of violence and war, is to hear President Nelson Mandela's call for violence against women to be recognized as a human issue—and not one limited to a woman's issue, a feminist issue, or an international development issue. There is legislation in place to provide the foundation to stop victimizing women (United Nations, 2010). It is now up to the citizens, including men, to isolate the perpetrators.

It is time to acknowledge that what women bring to the table enhances and expands the content and quality of the conversation and increases the likelihood of stopping violence and sustaining peace. Women already bridge the gap between the private and public spheres, and therefore the dominant narrative of a bifurcated private and public arena is not only a dishonest one, it also does the field of conflict resolution and the communities that we serve a disservice. It is dishonest because the stories of women's participation in the public arena—WOZA, the Gulf of Mexico, Rwanda, and the global inclusive security movement, to mention a few—demonstrate women successfully positioning themselves in both spheres. It is a disservice to the field because it limits our imagination of what is possible. Women's position in the private and public spheres uniquely places them as true representatives of inclusive human security.

A number of cases in the book suggest that, instead of viewing women solely as innocent bystanders of conflict, we need to acknowledge that thousands of women join armed groups and go into combat. Once we have acknowledged this and researched and comprehended the root causes of their violence, only then will we be successful in countering this trend. What we know about female suicide cadres and combatants is that the patriarchal cultures from which they come are contributing factors in their decision to adopt violence. The cases presented are about traditionally patriarchal cultures where women have lower status and where women see the adoption of extreme violence as a form of agency. When a culture has strict traditions and practices that subordinate women and ascribe their particular roles, women who do not fit into these roles are often ostracized and marginalized. When women are excluded, they are left with few options within their own societal structures. They then become more vulnerable to the option of taking up arms or joining a terrorist group.

Bouta et al. (2005, 9) state that "*[k]ey development challenges* are to acknowledge women's and men's participation in armies, and to target *all* women that joined the armies—with or without weapons—with assistance." Access to primary, secondary, and higher education for girls and women is particularly important. Similarly, educating boys and men is a critical intervention in mitigating the causes of violence. Education broadens the mind and liberates societies from the clutches of unfair and inhumane cultural traditions. Long-term benefits of universal education can address the gap in uneven development across societies, including in Egypt, Eritrea, Liberia, Nepal, Pakistan, Sierra Leone, Sri Lanka, and Turkey, to name a few.

The story of women waging war and peace can be dramatically different. But for this, we must dare to imagine what was previously unimaginable.

As President Mandela states, men, too, need to assume responsibility for altering the narrative of war and violence. We acknowledge the existence of separate male- and female-dominated domains. However, we envision the establishment and viability of a third—a human domain. The stories in this book are more than a glimmer of hope in this direction—we can imagine and work toward actualizing this human domain, where men as well as women are included in the formal and informal political, economic, and social processes in their communities, countries, regions, and around the globe. It is our intent that the stories of hope in this book serve as a launching point for imagining and establishing this new narrative and providing women and men around the world the courage to engage it.

References

Bouta, Tsjeard, George Frerks, and Ian Bannon. 2005. *Gender, Conflict, and Development.* Washington, DC: The International Bank for Reconstruction and Development/The World Bank.

Manchanda, Rita 2010. "Nepali Women Seize the New Political Dawn: Resisting Marginalisation after Ten Years of War." Center for Humanitarian Dialogue., http://peacetalks.hdcentre.org/2010/08/women-in-nepal/comment-page-1/

Manchanda, Rita (ed.). 2001. *Women, War and Peace in South Asia: Beyond Victimhood to Agency.* London: Sage Publications.

Mazurana, Dyan and Khristopher Carlson. 2004. *From Combat to Community: Women and Girls of Sierra Leone.* The Policy Commission, Women Waging Peace, available http://www.peacewomen.org/assets/file/Resources/NGO/PartPPGIssueDisp_CombatToCommunty_WomenWagePeace_2004.pdf.

Schneider, Mary Deutsch. 2008. "About Women, War, and Darfur: The Continued Quest for Gender Violence Justice." *North Dakota Law Review,* 83, 915.

Turshen, Meredith. 1998. "Women's War Stories," in Meredith Turshen and Clotilde Twagiramariya (eds), *What Women Do in Wartime* (pp. 1–26). London and New York: Zed Books Ltd.

United Nations. 2010. Handbook for Legislation on Violence against Women, ASDF, Department of Economic and Social Affairs, Division for the Advancement of Women, http://www.un.org/womenwatch/daw/vaw/handbook/Handbook%20 for%20legislation%20on%20violence%20against%20women.pdf.

Notes

Chapter 3

1 This chapter is dedicated to the memory of Wallace P. Warfield, a great teacher, mentor, and friend whose guidance was invaluable during the conceptualization and drafting of the repositioning framework that resulted in the writing of this chapter. His scholarship and practice lives on through the many lives he touched and the many students he patiently guided.

2 The author benchmarked the year 1983, since women only became involved in the LTTE's combat activities in this year.

Chapter 4

1 The Iraqi embassy in Beirut was totally destroyed in an apparent suicide attack on December 15, 1981. Thirty people were reportedly killed, and 100 were injured.

2 Sana'a Mehaidli was a member of the Syrian Social Nationalist Party. Her car detonated next to an Israeli convoy in Jezzin, South Lebanon, killing two soldiers and injuring two more.

3 Basic human need theory was advanced by John Burton in the field of conflict resolution. It postulates that unmet needs of individuals that go beyond such essentials as food and shelter and include the need for safety, belonging, self-esteem, and identity are the primary root causes of protracted social conflicts.

4 The video footage from some of the widely publicized terrorist attacks and hostage-taking incidents, such as the one in Moscow in October 2002 and in Beslan in September 2004, fueled the image of women dressed in black with explosives strapped to their bodies. Although they are called widows, not all the women were wives of Chechen fighters killed by the Russian forces but rather had some male relative—a brother, father, or son—who died in the conflict. Some of the so-called widows were as young as 15 or 16 years old (Knight and Narozhna 2004).

5 The Moscow theater siege in October 2002: During the performance of the musical, all the people in attendance were taken hostage by 40 terrorists (half of them women). After three days, Russian special forces attempted to release the hostages by pumping paralyzing gas into the building. As a result of the operation and inadequate medical attention, 129 people died, and all the terrorists were killed (Karon 2002; Dolnik and Pilch 2003).In 2003, during a music/rock festival in Tushino, more than a dozen people died in an apparent female suicide terrorist attack (Peuch 2003; RFERL 2004).In 2003–2004 there were a series of terrorist attacks in Moscow metro. More than 60 people died in those attacks (BBC 2010). In April 2010, 38 people were killed and 60 injured in two bombings in the metro during the morning rush hour (BBC 2010; RFERL 2004).Two almost simultaneous explosions brought down two passenger aircraft, killing 90 people aboard in August 2004 (AP 2004; RFERL 2004).On the first day of school on September 1, 2004, terrorists attacked School # 1 in Beslan, North Ossetia, and took more than 1,000 children and their parents hostage. They were held captive for several days. Three hundred eighty-five hostages, a majority of whom were children younger than 12, died, and 783 people were injured during the release operation by the special forces (Giduck 2005; Lynch 2005; RFERL 2004).

Chapter 6

1 The author would like to acknowledge The Institute for Inclusive Security at the Hunt Alternatives Fund, especially Ambassador Swanee Hunt and Miki Jacevic for their generous support during this research. And to Visaka, who has opened up her heart and her home to a practitioner and scholar she hardly knew at the beginning of this project. Thank you from the bottom of my heart—you are an inspiration to us all.

Chapter 7

1 The initiative, run through the UN High Commissioner for Refugees, has since been replicated in Burundi, Kosovo, and Rwanda.

Chapter 8

1 The Ndebele meaning of the word, WOZA coincides with mission of WOZA, which is to encourage women to come forward and let their voices be heard in the socioeconomic and political realms.

2 Founding member, Maria Moyo, died on November 6, 2007, from pneumonia complications, which WOZA says were worsened by her experiences in police custody. She was 57 years old. (http://www.swradioafrica. com/news131107/woza131107.htm.)

3 The Legal Age of Majority Act (LAMA) of 1982 is a piece of legislation that for the first time in Zimbabwe conferred equal adult status on men and women. The act specifies that women 18 years and older could make their own decisions, vote, marry, own and register property, and open and manage a bank account without having to seek male permission. By establishing the principle of equality among men and women, LAMA thus paved the way for further gender reforms in Zimbabwe.

4 The Matrimonial Causes Act of 1987 recognizes women's right to own property independently of their husbands or fathers. The act also provides for equitable distribution of assets between spouses upon divorce.

5 The Equal Pay Regulations, passed in 1980, acknowledged that men and women performing work of equal value would be entitled to earn equal pay.

6 Here, WOZA is apparently borrowing this narrative and imagery from female counterparts in the West. The bread and roses strike is often the name given to the famous strike by women in St. Lawrence, Massachusetts, from January to March 1912. The strike was led by women from the textile industry, and it was over fair wages. The slogan "bread and roses" spoke to the need for fair wages and dignified conditions.

7 Zimbabwe is a soccer-loving nation; hence WOZA employs imagery that citizens are familiar with. In soccer, a yellow card is given by a referee as a warning to a player who has performed a foul. Receipt of a second yellow card is synonymous with being issued a red card, for which the player is dismissed from the match.

8 This phrase is used by the feminist movement to depict how the personal lives of women are intricately connected to the public sphere. The phrase

has been used in feminist writing since the 1960s, including by Carol Hanisch ("The Personal is Political," in *The Red Stockings Collection*, Feminist Revolution, March 1969 (204–5)). Her essay asserts that personal problems are political problems.

9 The entire WOZA People's Charter is available at http://wozazimbabwe. org/?page_id=42 (accessed on August 30, 2008).

Chapter 12

1 In an excellent history of the development of feminist ideas in ICC statutory creation, Janet Halley notes that the feminists involved presented a united front with respect to the substance of their requests, a consensus that insisted on, and sometimes achieved, specific modifications but that, in so doing, covered over longstanding divisions within feminism (Halley 2008).

2 The Rules of Procedure and Evidence that elaborate provisions of the Rome Statute include the following definitions:
   (a) Victims mean natural persons who have suffered harm as a result of the commission of any crime within the jurisdiction of the court;
   (b) Victims may include organizations or institutions that have sustained direct harm to any of their property that is dedicated to religion, education, art, science, or charitable purposes and to their historic monuments, hospitals, and other places and objects for humanitarian purposes. (International Criminal Court) (Rule 85).

3 Katanga was charged with three counts of crimes against humanity and six counts of war crimes involving an attack on a village called Bogoro in the province of Ituri. Hundreds were killed in the assault and many women and girls taken into sexual slavery.

Chapter 13

1 The information about the women's movement and mobilization was collected in Liberia during December 2006—January 2007 through personal interviews conducted as part of research for the thesis "Women Building Peace: The Liberian Women's Peace Movement." The quotes used in this section of the chapter are those of interviewed participants of the women's peace movement in Liberia.

Index